Alfred St. Johnston

A South Sea Lover

A Romance

Alfred St. Johnston

A South Sea Lover
A Romance

ISBN/EAN: 9783744777254

Printed in Europe, USA, Canada, Australia, Japan

Cover: Foto ©ninafisch / pixelio.de

More available books at **www.hansebooks.com**

A SOUTH SEA LOVER

A Romance

BY

ALFRED ST. JOHNSTON

London

MACMILLAN AND CO.

AND NEW YORK

1890

Printed by R. & R. CLARK, *Edinburgh.*

To My Wife

NOTE

THE spelling of the Polynesian words in this work may be different from that usually accepted; but the Omëan dialect has not been reduced to writing, and the Author has had to rely entirely upon his memory of the sound of it.

A SOUTH SEA LOVER

CHAPTER I

THE sun had sunk into the limitless expanse of the South Pacific, and almost before the last glories of his going had vanished, the ripe stars shone out across the silence of the trackless sea. On the soft sand of the shore, in the greater darkness of the palms that fringed it, with eyes that saw nothing but their inner vision, a girl was standing gazing to the south. The water of the calm lagoon flowed in little ripples round her naked feet, gleaming, glancing, flashing starlight where the broken water caught the kiss of heaven. On the reef outside, the never-sleeping surf beat with its unresting song; and the cloud of spray that rose and fell, and rose to fall again, from the coral rocks of the barrier, shone palely like a mystic veil against the low golden warmth of the horizon. The soft breathing of the tropic night, which rustled the slender palm-leaves overhead, was heavy with the odour of the pale, new-opened flowers that, shy of the daylight, unclosed their heavy petals to the night and wafted their love to the stars. The long, level shore was deserted but for her, and everything was very still.

B

'*Ona manu, mbena ra lotu,*' she sang—sang in a voice so soft that the waiting air scarce shook with it. Her lustrous eyes were dark as night, her hair made blackness pale, and her curved lips were so gently parted for her almost soundless song that her white teeth barely gleamed between. Her brown, supple body, naked to the waist, swayed with the force of her passion, and her rounded arms waved in a strange incantation.

> Oh, heats of the north, oh, summer wind!
> Oh, forest fires, consume me, let me die.
> You waves rise up and cover me ;
> Rorutu, take me to the dark :
> She of your worship, Venga, told me false.
> He comes not, and my heart is burnt with love.
> Oh, give me rest, or send some token ;
> He comes not, and I wait.

The darkness of night had now quite come, the last gleam of crimson had died out of the west, and the ripples of the loving water flashed cool fires now as they broke around her feet. With eyes darker than the hour, she seemed to pierce the distance that everywhere stretched level with the sea. A tiny movement shook the air, too faint at first for sound, and then from out the void a pure white tropic bird, *na hiva*, darted to her rounded shoulder, brushing her full slender throat with the warm coolness of its snowy plumage. She raised her little hand and with a happy smile on her lips tried to touch the bird, but it darted from her and was lost in the gloom. But Utamé's prayer was answered, and she knew that he would come.

Far, far below the horizon a great ship with all its white sails spread was heading to the north ; so steady was the cool light breeze that the ship glided along with scarcely any motion, and had it not been for the golden phosphorescence where the bows cut the clear indigo of the sea, and for the dim light of the track behind it, like a faint milky way across the vault of heaven, one might have thought the ship becalmed. For the last ten days since she had caught the Trades the ship had progressed in the same peaceful manner, without so much as furling a sail, until at last the men on board grew to feel almost as though it were a vessel of dream. Without haste but without rest the soft wind silently swept her along, each day becoming hotter and each night more clear and full of stars. At times such as these the hearts of men soon become open books—for very idleness of body the tongue must wag; and though to know a sailor at his best one must see him contending with difficulties and struggling with the storm, yet to learn all the mystery, superstition, and romance of the tender sea-grown heart, days of quiet sailing such as these, with calm sea and tranquil, favourable breezes, are necessary. Warmed by the happy sun, the ice of reserve thaws away, and the sailor, who is often too weary even to think or remember, has time to talk and laugh and air his simple beliefs. That night on board the *Albatross* the crew was talking and singing round the fo'c's'le hatch. Now and then the clear notes of a fiddle rang through the quiet air and died away in sighs of music across the heaving sea; and one and all the men were smoking, as though offering up a sacrifice of incense to the Goddess of Content.

But one man stood apart from the others on the fo'c's'le head, in the very peak of the ship, erect as a dart. With both brown hands upon the rail he gazed straight out to sea, with a strange look of expectancy on his strong face, as though waiting for he knew not what. Seventy years ago, when this man stood facing the sea and eager for his unknown future, the great Southern Ocean was but very little known. Tales of its wonders, of its islands of coral, of its mysterious peoples, of the gigantic denizens of its deep, had been brought home now and then by whalers and exploring ships, but few facts were known. In those days ships were of oak, and smoke and steam had not conspired to defeat the will of God and the pure airs of heaven. The world was a greater secret to man than it is now becoming; and to the man standing lonely there, with youth in his blood and a lust for romance and adventure at his heart, the round great earth was but a field for his exploiting.

A curious volume of romance would the life of Christian North make—the beginning, the middle, and the end alike fantastic and strange, for romance comes to the romantic just as truly as adventures to the adventurous; but it is not his whole life that is being told, only one happy chapter of it, with its mystic prologue. He had at this time already been eleven years at sea since first the strong coursing of some strange Norse blood in his good Saxon veins had urged him, when a lad of fourteen, to ship to sea and forge his own future instead of tamely letting circumstance flow around him and work his destiny, not as he wished, but as it willed. Since then he had grown so to love the sea that the very flow of his blood seemed influenced by its tides. He never stayed in one place long, for God at his birth had dropped into his soul a little of that force which keeps the worlds a-spinning, so that, like them, he could not rest, but was impelled to wander on for ever.

He often thought that the most fortunate chance of his life had been what many people would consider to be its most terrible disgrace and misfortune—his birth. He doubtless missed many things that go far to make the happiness of other men, but never having experienced them, he could not very passionately regret them, and to Christian, in whose veins the blood of Ishmael pulsed strong and ungoverned, they were much more than compensated for by the freedom from restraint and the control of his own actions that were thus gained. There is, too, in being a love-child something that other men often lack—he feels in the flow of his blood, the strength of his passions, and in the very vigour and manhood of his limbs and muscles, that at any rate love was present at the beginning of things. From the warm-hearted, large-souled nature that they had endowed him with, Christian had a strange tenderness for his unknown father and mother, and bore them no grudge, poor young things, because that and his noble strength and health were their only gifts.

Running along with the vigorous, active side of his character was a strain of reflection and reverie which, at times, mingled with the warm and passionate nature of the big, gentle, lovable fellow, and which under other circumstances might have made a poet of him. But, as it was, Christian was only one of those silent poets to whom the world is a vast inheritance of beauty, and for whom the soft dreamy veil that imagination casts upon the commonplace tinges all life with romance.

Without noticing the flight of time or the gradual oncoming of night, he stood there thinking of the strange incidents that had brought him on board that vessel, and of the still stranger prophecy or second sight of which he was told he was the object, and which his very presence on board seemed to corroborate. Little puffs of warm wind blew his curly hair about, and the clear water, creaming to a golden flush where the bows of the ship cut the sea, sang a little low song as it rippled and fell from the copper sides of the hull; but he neither felt the one nor heard the other. His mind was looking back.

Eight or nine weeks before that summer night Christian had been stranded without a penny in his pocket, or a care on his shoulders, in the little settlement of a few timber huts and houses which then was Sydney. He had been having a spell on shore, and had managed to get through in a very short time, and not too wisely, the hard-earned pay of the last six months at sea. Christian was no saint, but a very human mortal; he had had a good time and enjoyed it, and he did not look back with a single regret on the money he had spent to attain it. He was generous, even prodigal, with his money while it lasted, but was quite happy when it was gone. What cared he, more than any other young sailor, about 'making a provision for his old age'! old age was a long way off yet, and he might never reach it. Others might call him a prodigal, but again, what cared he! at least he enjoyed with all his strength every day of his youth-time, the most precious of all our possessions. He got full value out of every hour, and instead of squandering the greatest of all God's gifts in the toil and moil for gold, he spent it wisely in the sunshine of far-off wider skies, and in the pure air of the fresh salt-breathing sea.

He knew that he must ship again, but that he regarded as being so perfectly natural that he gave no thought to any alternative, indeed he always felt that his broad chest expanded and that he breathed more freely when once his face was turned seaward again.   Desertions from the ships to the then young colony were so frequent that he knew he would have no difficulty in getting a berth, so that it was with a calmness untinged with anxiety that he walked in the early morning to the wooden wharf.   For fully an hour he sat in the glorious sunshine of an Australian spring, enjoying the clean, pungent smell of the seaweed on the piles that the tide had not yet covered, which mingled with the flavour of his pipe.   At times of complete physical content such as this, with the calmness and even flow of the blood that is experienced at the end of a time of dissipation, the robuster side of Christian's character lay dormant.   He did not think at all; he knew that the blue sea lay before him, and that his whole body was bathed in the warm gold of sunshine.   Images and pictures passed through his brain, and he saw them; but they came and went without effort on his part, and he neither called for them nor marshalled them when there.

It was in this quiet, dreamy state that Christian was sitting, watching the white flight of the gulls that swooped about the end of the little wharf, with the hoarse, strident cry that is the same all the world over, when from the other side of a large barque out in the bay a small boat with four men in it swept into view. It was just the thing for an idle man to watch, for the labour of others always gives emphasis to our own leisure ; and to see the little boat come slowly dancing to the shore from the place where the ship lay so gracefully on the water as she rode at anchor was a pleasant sight. Christian watched it with an indifference that was strange when he came to look back upon it in the light of after events.

It took the boat some time to get to land, though the two men pulled well, for the barque lay fully half a mile from shore. It struck Christian that they seemed to be in a hurry, and in a drowsy way he speculated upon the reason for their haste. They were evidently making for the landing stairs close to him, on which the bright green water lapped with a gentle sound, just stirring the filaments of mossy weed on the last step that the rising tide had reached. As the boat neared the wharf Christian saw that the man in the bows was a superb Polynesian, tall, brown, and magnificently made, and with no covering on his head but his jet-black wavy hair; he wore nothing but a pair of old duck trousers, and his strong arms and muscular breast shone in the morning sunshine. To his surprise Christian saw this man speak to the skipper, who was steering, and lift up his arm and point him out.

'Ship your oars!' sang out the man in the stern. The order was obeyed almost as deftly as though they were man-of-war's men. The man in the bows turned round, and with his outstretched hand just stopped the boat from bumping her nose into the timbers of the wharf; and swilling the green slime from his hand, he held her side in to the steps for the others to land. Stepping briskly from the gunwale of the boat, the skipper and the two men sprang up the steps, and giving one or two sharp glances down the wharf, they bore straight down on Christian. As they approached him North heard the skipper say with a tone of the utmost astonishment, ' By the Lord! the Kanaka was right.'

Christian looked him clearly in the eyes as he came up, thinking that he was going to make an inquiry of some sort.

' Are you out of a berth?' was his remark.

' Yes,' replied Christian.

' Will you sign with me?'

' When do you sail, and where are you bound?'

' Five minutes after we're back aboard, and where we're bound is no matter.'

' That won't suit me.'

' Then it will have to suit you.'

' My chest and my kit are up in the township.'

' Then you'll come without them.'

' I'm damned if I do,' said Christian, springing up.

' We'll see about that. You've deserted and I'm short-handed, so I'll just press you. Fling him into the boat, you two.'

Whereupon, without more ado, the two men rushed upon him; but Christian's blood was up, and with one blow of his fist, that came straight from the shoulder like the stroke of a sledge-hammer, he felled one man. But before he could turn, the skipper and the second man had rushed upon him; and the first man, staggering to his feet, came to their assistance, and in less time than it takes to tell of it they had pushed and tumbled Christian down the few steps and flung him, bruised and bleeding, into the bottom of the stout whale boat. Had it not been for the Polynesian, who caught him by the shoulders as he fell, Christian must have been seriously hurt; but, thanks to this fellow's quick eyes and strong arms, he was not injured.

Seeing the uselessness of resisting further, Christian

resigned himself with philosophy to his fate. He knew that in the lawless and unsettled state of the new settlement he could gain no redress even had he been able to get ashore, which was rendered impossible by the number of his opponents, and by the fact that he was prevented from rising by the great leg of the islander being stretched across his body. To Christian's intense surprise he noticed that this fellow was regarding him with eyes full of the deepest tenderness; he stooped over him once with a happy smile on his face, and laying his hand gently on Christian's shoulder, said in a low voice and in broken English—

'Lie still; you won't be hurt. A long time I have been looking for you. To-night I will tell you.'

Seeing that this fellow would say no more at that time, and recognising by every look that he was his friend, Christian lay quite quietly in the bottom of the boat with the warm weight pressing upon his chest, listening to the slow, regular rumble of the oars in the rowlocks until they reached the side of the *Albatross*, as he found the barque was named. The skipper watched him narrowly as he scrambled up the ship's side, and said, not unpleasantly, as he joined him on the deck—

'You are a sailor, I can see with half an eye. That's what I want. We begun rough but may get on smoother if you are no skulker. All hands to the capstan,' he bellowed, as soon as the boat was hoisted to the davits. 'You turn to, as well,' said he to Christian, 'and then go forrad and get your breakfast.'

The anchor was weighed, sail was set, and before noon the heads were cleared, and the *Albatross* was sailing before a flowing breeze for the great South Sea.

That same night at about four bells Christian was

alone on the fo'c's'le head thinking of the strange
chances of the day, which had excited him too much
for sleep to visit him at present. The night was so
warm and clear that he could not force himself to
stay in the hot and crowded forecastle, at the far end
of which was the narrow bunk that had been pointed
out to him as his. He had dragged a sail that was
in process of mending, and which had been folded up
and left there when night fell, and placed it on a
great coil of cable, and leaning his back against the capstan he tried to solve the strange words of Soma, the
Polynesian. He had not been there very long when
the solution presented itself, for it happened that both
were in the starboard watch; Christian heard the soft
thump, thump of naked feet on the deck behind him,
and looking round he saw by the dim light of the
starlit sky the handsome face and beautiful antique
form of the islander. As he stood there motionless before Christian he looked like an ancient
statue in rich bronze of some hero or great warrior;
the lines of his half-nude figure were so grand,
and the great muscular development of his chest,
arms, and shoulders so strong, yet so reposeful. Christian looked at him admiringly, for he was fine
enough man himself to be able to admire another
man's beauty and strength without reservation or
detraction as without envy. Then moving a little to
one side he patted the sail he was sitting on and said
in his pleasant, mellow voice, that Soma had, as yet,
only heard angry and excited in the brief altercation of
the morning—

'Sit down and tell me what you meant when you
said that you would tell me all to-night. I came
here on purpose.'

But Soma preferred sitting in a way more natural to him, and chose the bare deck in front of Christian, and crossing his legs in island fashion, and resting his hands on his bare feet, he began.

His speech was hesitating and slow, and he spoke in broken English, lapsing every now and then into some Polynesian tongue of which North was, of course, ignorant; but he was perfectly intelligible and sometimes even poetic, when he dropped into the semi-allegoric manner that is natural with those people.

'Many months ago,' he began, 'when I was at home in Omëo, my island where I live, I first heard of you my brother, and over all the lands and great seas,' with a wave of his hand as though he comprehended the whole earth, 'since then have I sought you. Moons came and moons went, and you did not come, but I knew I should find you, for Venga had said it.'

The earnestness of the fellow and the perfect confidence that he evidently had in his mission, whatever it might be, and the entire and childlike faith that he had in Venga's prophecy and in Christian's acceptance of it, were so many mysteries to North. He listened with such a puzzled expression on his face that Soma, even in that faint light, could not fail to see it.

'Are you not glad?' said he, with a tone of such mingled surprise and dejection in his voice that Christian had to smile as he answered—

'Yes, I am glad, very glad, if it means that you and I are to be friends. But who is Venga? and why did you seek me? and how do you know I am the man you were to look for?'

As he spoke he laid his hand on Soma's warm,

breeze-freshened shoulder, and made him look up. The Polynesian smiled a quick smile at the touch, as though he instantly detected the sympathy in it.

'Venga? not know Venga?' he said with an incredulous air. 'She is the old witch who watches on Monoriro, the fire mountain where Rorutu lives, and who knows everything, even things not born. She told me that I must sail away many days' journey in my canoe to Wakauau, the big island, where I should find a large ship with white wings, into which I must go and travel to the land of the white people at the place where those stars sink into the sea.' He pointed as he spoke to one of the bright constellations of the southern sky that sets in the horizon in the south-west, which would roughly indicate the position of Australia from the tropical islands of the Eastern Pacific.

Christian was each moment becoming more and more interested in the wild and improbable story that Soma was relating with as simple and straightforward an air as though the whole were an ordinary occurrence; he turned to him and said, 'But why did you wish to find me?'

The whole circumstance was so plain to Soma, and he had looked forward for so long and with such certainty to the end of his pilgrimage, that he seemed to think that Christian must understand it at once, and be ready to act the part that was so definitely laid out for him. He looked a little astonished at the question, as though Christian ought to understand his motives without explanation.

'Why did I seek you?' said Soma, leaning forward till Christian felt his breath on his cheek. 'Because you were my friend. Ever since I was first a man as tall as now, I have had in Omëo one friend only, Maraki, who was just the same along o' me. He dug in my garden, together we fished for sharks, and always together we went to Olasangu, where we at night made songs to the girls and the music of the *fango*. We made our spears of the same tree, and carved our war clubs with the same patterns; and when Tangaru made war on Ito, Maraki and I fought side by side at the taking of the town. Ito was beaten and eight of his fighting men lay dead, when Ito himself and many of his chiefs ran out from behind the fence of the town and tried to drive us back to the canoes. Then it was that Esoku, the tall chief of Pangu, picked out Maraki, and ran upon him and beat down his club and killed him then. I, Soma, was close by and saw Maraki fall, and I left my man who was fighting me and ran to where Esoku stood, for I felt that I was burning as with a fire when Maraki was killed. I had in my hand my great club, which is called *Paku-nu*, and I lifted it in the air as I ran upon Esoku. He ran back towards the fence when he saw me coming, but I had seen him slay Maraki, and I was swifter, and I jumped in the air, for he is very tall, and put out all my strength, and *Paku-nu* killed him and drank of his brains.'

Soma told this long story with the utmost passion, evidently seeing everything in his mind's eye exactly as it occurred, and his breathing became quick and his great chest heaved just as though he had even now undergone the physical exertion of the fight. But for all this, and interested as he was in the history, Christian felt that it threw very little light upon the matter in hand. He had heard stories from South Sea whalers who had been landed on the islands of the

Pacific, of the strange heroic friendships that sometimes exist among the Polynesians, lasting lifelong friendships, which time does not weaken and love does not destroy, but he had never come face to face with one of them before. The intense earnestness of Soma's voice, and the moisture with which sorrow and anger had deepened the night of his eyes, convinced him that he was in the presence of real passion, and to feel this strange mingling of unphysical, almost spiritual love, with the very physical courage, revenge, and fidelity of which this friendship consisted, was like a breath from an older world. He felt his heart strangely drawn to this islander, this Kanaka, as the crew contemptuously called him, in whose half-savage breast such depths of tenderness were to be found, and it was with a voice in which his sympathy sounded that Christian next spoke.

'But this does not tell me why you came to our land, or what I, a white man, could do for you.'

Soma listened, with his head leaning to one side, that he might lose no single word of what Christian said, for he not only spoke but understood slowly. He kept his eyes intently fixed on Christian's even in that half light, that their expression might help out his meaning.

'I will tell you. When Maraki was dead nothing was beautiful, all was dark and the sun was cold. I went to the mountains and all the parts of the island, but though the flowers bloomed and the rivers fell from the rocks, and the people were glad when I came, nowhere could I find joy. War was ended with Ito, for he was killed, and much *tappa* and many mats were taken, or I would always have been in battle. I was alone, and I walked many days and many nights alone, and I could not eat, though many pigs were killed, and they caught *toëmana* on the reef. I wept and I could not eat, and once at night outside the house, in the dark beyond the canoe shed, Maraki called me and then the wind blew it away. Then they said, "He is called; they want him in Bolutu. He will die." But in the morning Utamè, Ngawa's daughter, took me by the hand and said, "You will not die. Let us go to Venga, on the mountain Monoriro; she is wise and knows what you must do." So all day long we travelled to the mountain, and at night, when Rorutu's breath was red, we came to the house which Rorutu has built for Venga. At first she would not speak to us, but Utamè said, "It is Motuiti's son." Then she turned, for my father is a great chief, and she said—

'"Because of Maraki's death you have no peace."

'I was going to answer, but she lifted up her hand and I was silent, and she went on—

'"I know all. It is right to mourn for a friend, but you have one other. It was not you that Maraki called, but Oboku, your father's sister's son. You must sail in your canoe, *Te-huona*, to Wakauau. There is a great ship there with white wings, and you must go to the land of the Papalangi, which lies where those sky flowers" (*i.e.* stars) "sink into the sea. There in that white land your friend will be waiting for you. He will not know Soma, but Soma will know him, for he is tall—tall as E-koe; his eyes are like the sea at noon and his hair is like the colour of the *kamari* flower. When many moons are past and Soma's face is turned towards Omëo, then will he find the friend who will do the blood oath with him."

'And when I was home I knew that what Venga

saw would be born, for I told them what she had said, and in three days Oboku died. He heard Maraki call him and he died.

'Then I took much food and water and put them in *Te-huona*, and when the wind came from Monoriro I sailed to Wakanau with six men and left them there; but I came on the *Albatross*, and looked for you many months in all places where we come. I have not seen you once, but this morning when the skipper said there was not enough men, but he must go that day, I saw you on the land, and Soma said, "There is one sailor on the land;" and we came, and I knew that it was you.'

CHAPTER II

THESE were the reminiscences of Christian as he stood that summer night in the peak of the ship. Many times since he had had that first talk with Soma had he thought over what had been told him, and tried to account for all the Polynesian's story by calling it superstition, or by saying to himself that it was a mere coincidence. But all the mysticism of his character inclined him to accept it as true, and Soma's absolute belief in the truth of Venga's promise gradually began to have its effect upon him, as the absolute and confident faith of one person always influences another who is half willing to accept it. Added to which was the daily growing affection and friendship which he felt for Soma, whose dog-like fidelity, cheerful unselfishness, and the quiet and contented happiness which he always showed when with him, bound him more and more to the great joyous childlike fellow. It almost seemed that the spirit of the dead Maraki had found a new home in Christian's body. He seemed to understand the nature of the Polynesian so well that he almost felt that singular race brotherhood that binds nationalities so strongly together. He had even learned in the nine weeks of the voyage to understand the language of Omëo fairly well, so that difference of tongue no longer formed a barrier between him and his friend.

In that unknown limbo where the souls of unborn men drift and wait for their birth call, there must be, I think, tempests and cyclones which at times tear away an odd soul or two from the company of their fellows, and fling them, poor little breaths of alien air, into a throng of those who, when born, will be absolutely different from them.   Christian North was one of those tossed and tempest-torn spirits, or how else account for him?   His body was white and fair, his eyes the colour of the open sea, and though his eyebrows and lashes were dark and strongly marked, his hair was light, yet at heart he was as true a Polynesian as though he had been born brown-skinned and black-haired on a coral atoll in the shade of a grove of palms.   When first he landed on an island of the South Pacific and breathed its air and heard the mellow voices of his peers, his spirit stirred within him, and he knew his people and recognised his home. Those men, though brown and naked and talking in a tongue he could understand but could not speak, were his true brothers; their land was his land and their blue sea his own.

Since he had been aboard the vessel Christian had easily gained from the crew the information that the skipper had refused to give him the day that he was so unceremoniously pressed.   The *Albatross* was a whaler, as, of course, he had detected the instant his foot was on the deck, and she had left Sydney on a cruise in Southern waters of probably three years' duration.   This last information was not at all satisfactory to Christian, who could not tolerate the years' long monotony of a slow whaling cruise, and the fact of his having been kidnapped and forced to this service against his will made the compulsory voyage ten times

more distasteful than it otherwise would have been.
He determined to desert upon the first occasion that
presented itself and to throw in his lot with Soma,
who was always urging upon him the desirability and
possibility of a return to Omëo.

The passion of devotion which Soma showed for
him might have seemed strange and unaccountable to
many a young European unaccustomed to the heights
of such heroic sentiment, but to Christian's romantic
nature it seemed natural enough, and he welcomed this
new love to his heart with a readiness and simplicity
that were characteristic of his large-souled nature.   It
almost seemed to him that what Soma said must be
true, for the fellow seemed to supply a want and fill an
emptiness in his life of which he had only been dimly
conscious before ; and all the strength of love that had
been bound up in him before went out to this brown
friend of his.   Other men had families and relations,
Christian had none ; other men had lifelong friendships, this too had been denied to North ; so that
it was a quite undivided love and a perfectly entire
and rivalless friendship that Soma received from him.
There was nothing weak or puny about either man,
and as their lives and deeds were strong so was the
love that united them.   There was no touch of sentimentality about them, for in that respect, as in others
where civilisation has tended to weaken emotion,
Christian was as great a savage as Soma.   His friendship, his loves, and his hates were alike cast in classic
mould, and assumed grandeur from their very strength
and proportions.

Both men were almost equally anxious to leave the
ship, which Christian had no compunction about doing,
and Soma, who understood nothing about articles or

written agreements, thought that he had a perfect right to go away as soon as he wanted to stay no longer. He had never been accustomed to the restraints, restrictions, and legalities of civilised life, and he considered that, having done his duty during the whole time of the voyage, he could end the connection when he chose. It almost seemed that the stars in their courses fought for them, for two of the crew, who had been ill and suffering ever since they sailed from Sydney, had succumbed to the weakness which want of all care and medicines had daily augmented. Although thinking little about death, from its constant nearness to them, sailors hate and dread its presence aboard, so that when a death occurs the body receives scant ceremony, and is hastily hustled out of the ship. These two men—Perritt and a cheerful little fat man who went by the name of Barrel Dick—died within a few hours of each other, curiously enough, and that same evening towards sunset—last sunset—they two joined that mighty brotherhood of the dead that arm in arm encircles all the world.

Christian had helped to sew them in their rough shrouds of sailcloth, and had seen the weights tied to their still shod feet. He had watched them as they made the sullen and dull-sounding plunge into the calm water, and saw the air that they had carried down rise in two lines of little bubbles, symbolic little bubbles that rose and burst and vanished as the lives of those two men had come and gone; and, as fleeting in effect as these little spheres of sea-girt air, their bodies disappeared from sight and their very names were forgotten in a week. The soul of Christian never slept, but it was dreaming always, and as those still bales of dead humanity and old canvas dived expressionless into the eternal rest of the sea, he could not help but follow them in their swift downgoing into those unknown crystal depths erect on their weighted feet, with the sharks and strange unnamed fishes starting affrighted from these odd visitants ; descending more and more slowly with the wan daylight growing dim, and the green and sapphire waters becoming each moment richer and more full of gloom, until at last these two silent companions—maybe in ten thousand fathoms of clear sea—would come to rest with still beneath them ten thousand fathoms more of solid, lifeless water.

The loss of these two men from a crew that was already too small for the proper working of the ship, and for the constant look-out that was maintained for the blowing of their sea-prey, determined the skipper to put in to one of the many islands that dot that part of the Pacific, to try to recruit a few men to bring the number of his crew up to an efficient working strength. The *Albatross* was then about in 7·20 S. and 162·37 W., as Christian had found out from the second mate, who had from the first shown a rough sort of good-fellowship towards him, and on consulting an old, worn, thumb-marked Admiralty chart that Grey-poll, the veteran of the crew, had in his chest, and which was scored, pricked, and lined in every direction, he learned that they were within ninety or a hundred miles of the island of Wakauau, to which Soma had first sailed in his canoe from his own island Omëo ; which latter island was not even indicated on the chart. It had caused Christian no surprise in the early afternoon when the skipper, having worked out his latitude, had ordered the man at the wheel to keep her off two or three points, as he had thought it very probable that he would head direct for the island. As yet he had

not been able to give this news to Soma, but now that
night was come, he expected his friend to join him
where he stood in the peak of the ship, watching the
golden flush of the parted water and listening to the
low music that the ship made as the little waves
tinkled and rustled against her sides.

Christian had been standing there when the sun
had sunk in regal crimson, and had watched the burning gold of the long sunset islands fade to an ethereal
green, and gradually die out in the quickly falling tropic
night. And now the majestic march of the stars
overhead had begun, that nightly, through the long,
warm-breathing hours, stirred the spiritual mysticism
of the man, and awed him to a happy reverence by
this infinite scroll of a universe thus unrolled before
him.   He had heard no sound of footsteps behind him,
for Soma's bare feet made no sound on the deck, but
when he felt a warm hand laid firmly on each of his
as they grasped the rail, he knew well enough who it
was.   Without turning round he said—

'Why aren't you sleeping; what brings you here?'

'I knew you were up here, and I could not sleep.
Did you think I could sleep whilst you were watching
all alone? You know that great white *hina-manu*
(albatross) that all day and all night, too, has been
flying round the ship. That is like what you and I
are. You are the boat and I am the bird. My
thoughts fly round you always.'

'I thought you would come,' said Christian, turning round and seating himself on the slender rail,
where he kept himself from falling by twisting one
bare foot round the iron stanchion.

'I have news for you to-day. If you were in
Wakanau, could you get back to Omëo?'

'Yes,' answered Soma.

'How many days did it take you to sail in your canoe to Wakauau?'

'Four days,' said Soma, 'but to sail to Omëo would take longer, for the wind often blows towards the setting sun, and from Wakauau Omëo lies in the sea where he rises. But why do you ask?'

'Because to-morrow—the breeze is freshening, see!—we shall put in to Wakauau to recruit a few men. Tall Ted' (the second mate) 'told me our position at noon to-day, and that is what the skipper means to do. We are heading straight for the land now.'

Soma breathed thick at this good and surprising news, and then leaning forward he whispered in so low a voice that Christian could not help smiling, for there was no one who could possibly overhear them, and with a tone in it almost of awe at what to him was the apparent fulfilment of a prophecy—

'That is our chance; I knew it would come. We must leave the ship; we can hide on shore till she sails again. I know.'

'Hush,' whispered Christian hurriedly, 'there's the mate coming on to the fo'c's'le. Don't let him see us together.'

Noiseless as a shadow himself, Soma glided into the sharply-defined shadow of the foremast, and as the mate lounged up to where Christian was sitting, he slipped down the steps to the main deck.

'Breeze is freshening a bit,' said the mate.

'Yes,' answered North, looking over the side, 'she's moving along now.'

CHAPTER III

LONG before daybreak next morning Christian was on deck, and found that Soma had already preceded him. Such was the anxiety of both to see whether their hopes were to be realised or not that they had turned out from their bunks into the refreshing, almost keen air of the morning whilst still night lay upon the sea, and the stars still shone undimmed in the sky. What an infinite hush seems spread upon the world in that mysterious gray hour before the spreading of the dawn! At sea, out on that profound Pacific, the wonder and the awe of it, as of all else, are intensified by the very magnitude of everything; the vastness of the sea, the clear profundity of that high arched heaven, the very silence of that Pacific calm all tend to this end. This is one of those strange influences that the great Southern Ocean has upon all reflective minds; whilst the broad Atlantic seems a wakeful sea of life, active movement, and stirring adventure, the brooding Pacific is the ocean of thought and reverie, of contemplation and philosophic calm. Its slow heaving seems to be the deep breathing of a power that thinks and dreams but does not sleep.

The two men stood together on the deck and watched the slow melting of the darkness to what at first was more a warmth than light, as though the sleeping night were smiling to a waking. Slowly and slowly the warmth spread upwards, and a pale pink tint flushed the sky above the eastern horizon. One by one the cold stars overhead paled and died out, till at last, as the glories of crimson and gold replaced their heralds of faint daffodil and primrose, only the glowing orbs of the planets and the greatest stars still shone in the sky of delicate blue. Then, like a star himself at first, the regal sun peeped above the sea line, and all the waves and every broken bit of water flashed into golden glory in honour of his advent.

A light pearly haze still hung about the surface of the sea, but it lifted at last, and Soma's quick vision detected the outline of a long hilly island on the horizon that must then have been about eight miles away. He grasped Christian quickly by the elbow and whispered—

'Wakauau!'

North gave one glance in the direction indicated by Soma's great outstretched arm, and then quickly pulling it down, he said—

'Don't take any notice or say anything. It will be seen soon enough, and it won't do for us to seem anxious about the land. Come, let's get down to the main deck. We can make no plans about our escape, for it all depends upon chance; but we must manage to keep as near each other as possible all day, so that we shall not lose the opportunity if it occurs.'

Soma nodded a quick assent, and Christian turned and left him hurriedly; for at that moment a voice rang out, 'Land-ho, Land-ho!' and directly the whole ship was astir. The skipper ran out of his cabin as he was at the first cry, and seeing the position of the land, altered the ship's course a point or two, which reduced her rate of sailing; but the morning was still young when they were within a mile or two of the land. Soon after sunrise the wind veered round and blew off the shore, carrying strange, wild, spicy perfumes to the ship from the flowers and scented bushes of the island, which seemed strangely to excite all the men on board. A craving for the flowery land seemed to possess them one and all, as the intoxicating fragrance came in warm puffs from the shore and flooded all the ship. As for Soma, he was a different man; every breath that he drew seemed a message from his home, from his own land, that stirred thoughts of happiness, and love and liberty with the friend that he had sought and sacrificed so much to win. An eager passion was added to the tenderness of his dark eyes; his nostrils were dilated to breathe in this wild, free native air; a flush had mounted to his cheeks, which glowed darkly through the golden brown of his skin; and his high breast seemed scarce large enough for the great heart that beat within. He seemed to move to unheard music, and as he passed his friend he would break into a laugh so full of happiness that it might have been the voice of Joy personified; he looked at Christian with eyes so full of meaning that North, who knew their secret, almost feared that all the ship must read it there.

But the constant tacking of the vessel that was necessary to draw near the shore kept officers and crew alike from noticing anything strange in the behaviour of the islander. Christian was wise in cautioning Soma against giving any cause for suspicion, for the skipper was already distrustful enough of his crew. He well knew how often men engaged for a long whaling cruise repented them of their bargains when only the first few months of the voyage were over, and that desertion was a common enough thing to any island where their ships might call for water or fresh provisions. To prevent this he determined to lie off about a mile from shore, and to keep the ship on and off whilst he landed in his gig and tried to engage some men. There was no anchorage outside the reef; and seventy years ago the islands of the Pacific were still unsurveyed, and the charts rarely did more than give their position, so that the skipper would not run the risk of passing through the opening to the lagoon, which showed as a patch of dark blue in the midst of the line of surf-broken water.

Christian was not one of those who were called to man the captain's gig, but Soma was taken, not only because he could pull a good oar, but that he might act as interpreter, and make the necessary bargain between the skipper and the chief of the bay. It seemed that his services were successful, for early in the afternoon the gig came back with three strapping young Kanakas, who came swaggering up the side with an assumed unconcern that very ill concealed their nervousness.

The first moment that he could find to speak to Christian after his return, Soma told him that the captain had made arrangements with Rape-hia, the local chief, to take a lot of pigs and fowls and vegetables from him the next morning, and that they were to be brought alongside at sunrise, when the payment would be made. This gave great relief to Christian, who feared that the captain, having succeeded in his recruiting, might set sail at once before night had given them the opportunity to escape.

All that long burning afternoon the *Albatross* was surrounded by a little fleet of outrigged canoes manned by two or more men, or sometimes women, who brought all sorts of island produce, which they were only too eager to exchange for a nail, a bit of hoop iron, or a few rags of European clothing. Some few of the men were from time to time allowed on board, but never many together, as the skipper remembered the common custom among many of the Polynesian islands of getting a large number of their men on board unsuspecting ships, and then suddenly producing hidden weapons, killing the crew and seizing the vessel.

No chance offered itself all day to Christian of slipping with Soma into one of the canoes and getting the occupants to paddle them ashore, for the captain and officers kept a very keen eye upon the movements of this dancing, darting, fruit-laden little *flotilla* ; besides, he knew the probability of recapture would have been too great. He possessed his soul with what patience he could, and waited for the coming of night. He was unusually merry, even for him, and was singing snatches of old songs, and laughing and joking with the rest of the crew all day, for the thought of escape to one of these beautiful green, sea-beat islands, with this true friend of his for companion, and a life of strange adventure to look forward to, set all the blood a-coursing so merrily through his veins that he could not for his life be still. He had told Soma his plan of cutting the boat adrift, which was rocking and tugging at the stern, and of pulling ashore in her and hiding inland, and he set him to gain all the information that he thought would be useful from the three shy new members of the crew.

At last night fell, and the full moon rose in mellow splendour as the crimson fires of the burning west died out; the great stars glowed again in the warm blue of the sky, which seemed all tremulous with the still unfallen dew. One by one the sounds on board died out; the men had got their supper from the galley, the smokers, who had lain upon the fo'c's'le with their eyes turned landwards, had finished their pipes and their grumblings at being on board when such a land was in sight, and had gone to their bunks. Four bells had struck, and Christian and Soma were the only men in the peak, where they lay in the strong blue shadows cast by the mounting moon. They both were perfectly silent, partly from caution, and partly because their hearts were beating in their throats as the time drew near for their attempt. Every now and then one of them would stoop across and whisper something hotly in the other's ear, and then lean quickly back again, as though their very whispers might vibrate through the ship.

They were only waiting for the moment when the skipper should leave the deck and go to his own cabin; but the beauty of the night was such, and its coolness so grateful, that he seemed in no hurry to do this. At last he got up, straightened his back, stretched his arms, and moved towards the companion. Without turning his head Christian, whose gaze was fixed on the movements of the captain, touched Soma to call his attention, and at the same time held up a warning hand to caution him to silence. Suddenly Soma felt Christian's grasp tighten fiercely on his knee, and leaning forward to see what had occasioned it, he saw the skipper stop and walk to the side and

look over.   The next moment they heard him sing
out—

'Mr. Solly, why hasn't that boat been taken in ?
Do you think our friends on shore are likely to miss
such a chance as that ?   You'd find the painter neatly
cut and the boat vanished in the morning.'

No sooner said than done.   The watch was called,
and in a few minutes the boat was hauled aboard, the
sleepy men had stumbled back to their berths and
hammocks, and the moon once more shone down upon
the deserted deck.

This was a crushing blow to North, who thus saw
their only chance of escape snatched from them ; he
turned to Soma and said in his natural voice—he
thought it was no use whispering any more—

'Well, boy, that being done, we may as well turn
in.   What do you———'

He did not finish his sentence, for he felt Soma's
hand tightly pressed over his lips.

'Don't speak.   Lie down,' said Soma, putting his
arm round Christian's neck and pulling him into the
shadow.   'The watch is looking round.'

'What's it matter ?' whispered Christian.

'We can swim,' answered Soma in the most natural
voice. So accustomed was Soma—as indeed are all
Polynesians—to life in the water that it never for one
moment occurred to him that North could not swim
as well as he, to whom it was as natural as walking,
and perhaps, of the two, the easier.

'I can swim, and swim fairly well,' said Christian,
'but the shore is a devil of a way off.'

'If you are tired I can carry you,' said Soma with
confidence, and as though the thought pleased him.
'Can you trust me ?'

'Why, yes, of course, man, if you say so,' answered Christian, smiling at the idea of his being carried by any one.

'Let us go, then,' said Soma, standing up and shaking himself free of his clothes in a few seconds.

'Wait a moment; they must not hear us plunge into the water. I'll hitch something round a pin and heave it over the side, and then we can slip down it into the water without making a sound.'

Moving to the side of the ship that lay in shadow, Christian fastened a rope securely, and then lowered the end over the side.

'Hush! Is all quiet?' he said to Soma, as he put his hand to the rail to climb over.

'Take off all your clothes; you cannot swim like that,' said Soma hurriedly, and pulling him back as he spoke.

It was not a very long business for Christian to undress, as he only wore two garments, and with two quick rips they were loose and lying at his feet. With a quick glance along the deck to see whether the watch was looking that way, he stepped to the side where the shadow lay thickest, and silently sprang on to the bulwarks. For one brief moment the moonlight shone full upon him, and gleamed so brightly on his white skin that had the watch or the man at the wheel been looking that way they must have seen him; fortunately it was a thing of but a second, and he vanished over the side without being noticed. Soma followed more cautiously, and the quickest-sighted person could hardly have seen his dusky form as he crept along in the shadow and let himself down, hand over hand, to where Christian was awaiting him below.

Without a word they swam silently round the black hull, and then facing the land struck out boldly for the opening in the reef, the position of which they had carefully noted from the ship. Although he was a strong, even a fine swimmer, Christian could see that his powers were nothing to those of Soma. He was accustomed to every manly exercise; constant work and a temperate life, and salt water and cold sea winds, had turned his muscles to steel, but all these could not make him the equal of the islander; swimming, after all, was something of an effort to him, whereas to Soma it was perfectly natural. Long before their sturdy little brown legs can support them on land, Polynesian children are taken by their mothers to the shore, where they place them among the quiet ripples of the calm and sun-warmed lagoon, and almost growing up in the water as they do, these islanders are as much at home in one element as on the other.

This inequality did not at first cause Christian the least uneasiness, as he knew that he could hold on almost indefinitely at their present leisurely pace, but, to his horror, when they were only about three hundred yards on their journey, he heard a loud cry ring out from the ship, and he knew that their desertion was discovered.

'We must make haste,' said Soma.

Christian responded to the call and struck out bravely, but he quickly began to feel the effects of the effort at greatly increased speed. A few moments after, across the still water, they could hear the command given—

'Lower away!'

And then almost immediately the loud smack, made

as the boat struck the water, sounded in their ears. Although they knew that they were being pursued, they hoped at first that the direction they had taken was not known, but in a few moments this hope was destroyed. The man who was steering the boat evidently had not seen them at first, for shortly after the regular rumbling sound of the heavy oars in the rowlocks told the swimmers that the boat was fairly under way, they heard a loud voice, apparently from the masthead, where the day-long watch was kept, cry out—

'There they are, there they are, more to the left, more still. I see both their heads.'

This cry was like a spur in the side to Christian, who had been swimming with the strong slow movement of a good swimmer; he now turned on his side and began a quicker stroke. But this, he soon felt, he could not keep up, and every moment he could hear the sound of the oars gaining on them. His breath was becoming short, and the laboured beating of his strong heart warned him that he must slacken his speed. He felt that before many minutes had passed he must be caught, so he touched Soma, who was close to him, and said—

'Swim on, go quicker, you are stronger than I in the water. I can't keep this pace up, and you could get safe off if it were not for me.'

'Pull away, men,' rang out a voice from the boat, 'they're slackening. Pull away, y' devils. I see 'em.'

Christian was not the sort that ever gives up; he knew that he must be captured, but he swam on, as grimly determined as though he felt escape were possible, but this did not make him forget that Soma was as eager for his freedom as he, so he turned and again urged him to swim on, adding—

'I will go slowly, and then as the boat follows I'll turn off in another direction, and it will give you time to get well through the opening of the reef.'

For answer Soma stretched out his strong arm and quickly clasped Christian across the back and under the shoulder, and suddenly drew him close to his smooth side. Christian felt the strange water-given polish of his skin as he touched him.

'Now,' said Soma, with a calm tone of command, 'we go together; we both are taken or we both are free. Strike out slowly, at the same time along o' me, and get your breath, and then one more try.'

'Yes,' said Christian, who, with all the magnanimity of a brave man, could accept brave help, and was not ashamed to own himself the weaker. He felt that it was useless to urge his friend to leave him and save himself, for he judged him by the light of his own character. There was, too, something that, despite the danger of capture, made him happy to accept the strength and help of this fellow, it was so novel for him not to be the one to render them.

For some few minutes they continued thus, until Christian's even breathing showed that he was rested and was ready for a further effort. By this time the pursuers were within a few boat-lengths of them, and they could hear everything that was said by the men in the boat almost as distinctly as though they were in her. It almost seemed as if the sympathy of the two men at the oars was with the deserters, for the boat did not make the progress that she would have done under other circumstances. The mate saw this too, for he was swearing at the men and urging them to 'put their backs to it,' though without betraying much anxiety as to the result of the chase. Every now and then he shouted out—

'Now, you two —— fools, what's the use of going on with this? You may just as well spare yourselves the trouble, for I've got you, and be damned to you.'

It seemed that what he said was true, for they were close upon them, but Christian swam on. Then it was, when only a distance of about twenty yards divided them from the boat, that Soma was inspired with an idea. He was close to Christian, and spoke so low that the men in the boat could not possibly overhear.

'Swim on—make haste, make haste, straight for the reef, not for the opening. I will join you in one minute. Don't look back; that loses time. Swim, quick, *quick!*'

So saying he slackened his pace for a moment, and then breathing deeply two or three times in rapid succession, he dived noiselessly beneath the surface, and exerting all his great strength, he swam under the pursuing boat and came up on the other side of her. The mate saw him make this plunge, and was quite at a loss to understand it, and uttered a cry of astonishment. Hearing this the men at the oars turned their heads, and whilst still pulling after Christian, who was a few yards ahead, they kept their eyes fixed upon the place where Soma had disappeared. This gave the plucky fellow the opportunity he wanted. He was so close to the boat that he could have put his hand upon the gunwale; but that was not his intention. He suddenly lifted his brown and gleaming arms out of the water, and seizing hold of the oar, he gave it so strong and unexpected a jerk that it was snatched out of the grasp of the astonished man who held it. With a wild cry, as the end of the oar struck him under the chin, the sailor fell backwards, and before the mate or the other man could understand what had happened, Soma had swum away with the oar to some distance.

The islander's intention was to stop the boat and to give Christian time to make his escape, so he naturally swam with the oar back towards the *Albatross*, and when he had carried it to some distance he took it by the blade and jerked it, quivering along the surface, still farther from the arrested boat. He then turned once more and swam after his companion at his utmost speed. The surprise and wrath of the mate were almost comical to see, so enraged was he by the trick that had been played upon him; and even the men, who had been friendly until now, were annoyed at being thus made the laughing-stock of the crew. It did not need the oaths and swearing of the mate to urge them to hurry to pick up the stolen oar. They made what haste they could by using the remaining oar as a scull in the stern of the gig; but by the time they were once more fairly in chase Soma had rejoined his companion, and they were again some way ahead. Now the race began in earnest, for the mate was half mad with anger and the men were burning to revenge themselves for the trick that had been played upon them.

By the time that the two men in the water—who naturally travelled more slowly than the pursuing boat —had drawn near to the reef that encircled the island at about the distance of a quarter of a mile from the shore, the gig was again close upon them, and it was evident that they would be unable to reach the opening in the reef before they were overtaken. Soma had foreseen this when he told Christian to swim straight to the reef and not to attempt to make the opening. He had his reasons for this. The boat was now but a very few yards behind them, and Soma had again encircled Christian with his arm that he might enable him to keep up with him, and also that they might be together when they made the bold stroke for their liberty that he intended. The reef was now but a yard or two in front of them, and the great ocean swell, rolling majestically in from the open Pacific, beating upon it with a low deep roar, caused a terrifying wall of foaming water and gleaming spray to rise and fall with each great throb of the ocean heart.

Christian was ignorant of Soma's intention, for there had been no time for explanations; but he trusted so entirely to him that he swam on as he was bidden. He felt the islander's arm clutch him tighter as a voice rang out from the boat—

'Stop! or I'll fire.'

At the same moment he clearly heard Soma's eager voice, for all the mighty rush and roar of the thundering water, for he was shouting quite close to his ear—

'Take a big breath, and then rise on this great wave that is coming.'

He had scarcely done as he was told before he felt himself uplifted, as though by some gigantic and superhuman hand, and then carried resistlessly along straight into the mad whirl of the boiling waters, where they rose in a cloud of spray thirty feet into the air. For one breathless moment he neither saw, heard, nor felt anything, and was only conscious of some mighty force let loose in noise and darkness; and then the next, dazed, bruised, and breathless, he found himself wildly gripping his friend in both his arms, and as tightly enfolded in his, in the calm water of the lagoon. They were both gasping for breath and blinded by the spray, bruised by the water, and cut in many places by the sharp points of the jagged coral rock ; but, as they loosed their close grip and slowly struck out for the shore, they turned to one another and smiled, for they felt that they were free.

CHAPTER IV

By the time that they reached the land Christian was entirely exhausted, and it was only with Soma's sturdy assistance that he staggered through the shallow water to the shore. There he flung himself down on the sand and lay for some minutes quite speechless, whilst the islander was kneeling by his side in a state of the utmost alarm. The ludicrousness of the situation was the first emotion that North experienced, and as soon as he had breath enough he burst into a great laugh at the thought of his beginning his new life and making his appearance in a fresh world in his present stripped and destitute condition. This great roar of boyish laughter relieved Soma's mind, and though he was ignorant of its cause, he laughed from sympathy.

They had been lying thus upon the sand for some little time, gradually recovering their breath and regaining the strength which their great exertions and the wild buffeting they had received at the reef had exhausted, when, beyond the great bushes of hibiscus that fringed the shore beneath the palms, they heard a low sweet sound of music. It was quite unlike any music that Christian had ever heard, for it was not one continuous strain, but just short snatches of sad melody, that began and ended in a breath, as though some lover's sighs were tuned to harmony.

' What's that ? ' whispered Christian, for the sound was so sad and sweet, and harmonised so well with the moonlit night, the gentle lapping of the sea as it broke in tiny waves upon the beach, and the sighing of the slender palm-trees overhead, that he would not speak aloud for fear of marring its sweet influence.

' That is some one playing on the *fango*,' said Soma instantly ; ' all the young men make music for the girls. Maraki and I used always to go together to Olasangu to play the *fango*.'

' Well, it shows that there is some one about, and that we cannot be very far from a house ; you had better go and speak to him ; as he is in love,' said Christian with a smile, ' perhaps he will be more inclined to be amiable than he otherwise might be.'

Soma rose at once, but before he went off on his search he collected an armful or two of the convolvulus-like creeper that grew about the bushes just above high-water mark and deftly wove a sort of girdle and fringe from their thickly leaved shoots, that did very well as a covering for himself and North. Polynesians, as a race, although wanton in conversation and voluptuous to lasciviousness in their customs, preserve through it all queer but very strong ideas upon modesty,—so much so that one of the greatest indignities that could be offered to a conquered foe was to expose him in a state of complete nakedness to the gaze of his jeering victors.

The two fellows had scarcely put on their cool leafy girdles before the bushes above the strip of yellow sand were parted and a young man, laughing to himself as though at some success, leaped lightly to the shore. His mirth ended in utter astonishment when he saw Christian and Soma standing silently there, and he turned to run back to the shelter of the shrubs, for a Polynesian is always expecting ambushes and surprises, and his first thought, if alone, is flight. Soma called to him in his own language, and this seemed to give him confidence, for he stopped, and, upon hearing his explanation of their sudden appearance upon the island, turned with the readiest welcome and bade them come to his house, which lay some short distance back in the bush.

Then began for Christian that wonderful first experience of a tropic night upon a coral island; he thought nothing of dangers past or danger to come, his soul was so full of this mysterious new beauty all around him, half veiled by the night and half revealed by the glory of the mounting moon, that he had no time or will for any such purely personal feeling. After leaving the shore they passed through a narrow strip of bushes which were covered with large pale yellow flowers that looked almost white in the moonlight, and round which great ghostly moths were fluttering. Beyond this lay a wide belt of palms growing thickly together, their slender stems leaning this way and that, and not all erect and straight, so that they cast a black network of shadow on the coarse harsh grass with which the ground was covered. The beauty of this silent glade was a revelation to Christian, the slenderness of the slight stems was so graceful and the height to which they lifted their crowns of feathery branches so great. All the still air within this place of shadowy calm was filled with a low soothing sound, which he thought at first was the sighing of the sea as it softly kissed the shore, but he soon detected that it was far overhead, a hundred feet higher in the moonlit air, and then he knew that it was the low rustling of a myriad palm leaves as the cool sea air flowed through them to the hills.

After passing for some little distance through this semi-open space their guide turned aside into a narrow path, where the night lay darker as the thick forest, that covered the island beyond the girdle of palms, seemed to cover everything with a dense black mantle of shade. Here the palms were not so numerous, though their ringed columns still rose amongst the noble trees, making the great strength and massiveness of the forest giants more striking by the very lightness and grace of their own growth. It almost seemed to Christian— with his northern coldness of imagination—that Nature was too lavish of her gifts. Everywhere were leaves and flowers and ferns and tendrils; the sky was darkened by them, the ground was covered with them, the very tree-trunks and the great gnarled boughs were wreathed and draped with a wild growth of tangled vines and strange luxuriant creepers. The forest air was perfumed by ten thousand flowers, great bushes of the starlike single gardenia were covered with white blossom, so that every moving breeze that breathed about them enriched still further the perfumed air. Then upon Christian began to fall that mysterious intoxication of the tropic night that one must have felt to understand; warmth was added to his blood and he breathed deeply, his eyes grew tender, and a gentle languor, that did not affect him physically, flowed into his mind. He scarcely thought, he only felt and allowed this beauty to flow into his heart, and in perfect silence he followed the two Polynesians, who were walking ahead talking fast in their soft rich voices, without noting whither they were leading him.

The path for some short distance led them deeper

into the rich shadow of the forest, the sound of the sea was almost lost, and though the roar of the surf still sounded its quiet bass, the music of it was so constant that it was hardly noticeable. The rustle overhead had ceased and silence reigned. It seemed to Christian that he had stepped into an enchanted land where beauty lay entranced to silence, and over which Sleep had cast his purple mantle so closely that all below had succumbed to his dear influence. He himself forgot his friend, and even his own position, and that strange loss of identity which he experienced now and again slowly crept upon him. His pace lessened, though he still walked mechanically along, but he no longer saw the shadowy beauties of that land of clear-obscure—his soul was wandering in the brighter world of the poet's vision. From what brief immeasurable dreams was he at last aroused by the warm clasp of Soma's hand upon his shoulder, and the little loving shake he gave him to rouse him to himself!

'I called to you three times,' he said, 'and could not make you hear. I thought you were asleep.'

'Perhaps I was,' answered Christian with a smile.

He was a strange mass of contradictions and incongruities, living a life that lay upon that narrow line that divides the mystic and dreamer of dreams from his this-world mates; at times so full of life, energy, and passion, and at others so unsubstantial and in the clouds. It almost seemed that at moments unseen hands were laid upon his soul that led him unresisting, even willing, across the dark borderland into that misty region where dreams live and visions are the only truth. He had been wandering there to-night, and for a time had lost his way.

He found that he was standing at the edge of a

little open space in which two or three brown houses stood by the side of a plantation of bananas and yams. The friendly young native, whom Soma had so opportunely enlisted in their cause, had entered the largest house to announce the arrival of two strangers, and Christian and Soma stood on the edge of the shadow cast by the great forest trees and watched in silence the moonlight play upon the great broad leaves of the bananas, which caught the light air that was stirring and slowly fanned the masses of green or golden fruit that hung down from their midst.

They had not waited more than a moment or two before Ebinibi, for such he had told Soma was his name, returned with an oldish man, who was evidently still half dazed with sleep, but who offered them the shelter of his home with all the usual Polynesian hospitality. On their way to the house Soma informed him who he was, and Christian noticed for the first time a slight tone of haughtiness in his voice that he did not think unbecoming; indeed, over the whole man there seemed to have crept some almost imperceptible change. It seemed that away from the ship, where he was treated as an inferior, he felt his chiefdom once more ; now that he was again amongst his own people, as it were, his old habit of command had returned to him, and he held his head higher, and walked with a freer mien. This island was not his native one, but Oméo was not far off, and Motuiti's son was treated with all the respect that was due to his father.

Stooping their heads, for the eaves of the roof were not more than four feet from the ground, Ebinibi led them by the hand into the house, for it was quite dark inside, and then pulling down a clean mat from the rafters, he spread it on the floor and invited them to sit down whilst he got a light. There was no fireplace in the house itself, and he had to run to the little cooking hut at the back of it to gain one from the still glowing embers of the logs that smouldered there. By the poor glimmer shed by the rough candle, formed of a dozen oil-nuts pierced by a thin wick of light wood, they could see the size of the house, which consisted of one room, and the great hive-shaped roof, which was filled with shadows that the feeble light only rendered darker.

There were several men in the house, whom the noise of their entrance had disturbed from sleep, and Christian, when he first looked round, saw them all sitting up, with their light coverings of thin *tappa* still folded about their stalwart forms, gazing at him with their black eyes full of wonder. The old man, who was evidently the master of the house, soon roused them with a few quick words and sent them flying in search of the food which is the first idea of a Polynesian to offer to guests—expected or otherwise. In a very short time food that was already cooked was brought to them, but Christian was not in a mood to eat—the events of the last few hours had been too exciting to leave him much appetite. He told Soma, who was eating his meal with all the relish of one who has not tasted his native food for many months, that he only wanted to drink and to sleep. On North's wish being translated one of the young men was sent out of the house, and a moment after he heard the sound of a great nut coming crashing down from one of the lofty palms outside.

Then they spread a sweet, fresh, woven mat for him, and loosening his rustling girdle he flung himself down full length. The old chief raised his hand, and the house was silent save for the softened breathing of the men. Soon the little light grew dim, and as the last nut flickered out darkness grew quietly upon the place. Christian was not quite asleep when his mat moved under the bare foot placed upon it, and a thin covering of *tappa* was placed upon him, and he felt some one lie down by his side. By the warm, firm hand that grasped his arm he knew that it was Soma; without speaking, and smiling in the dark, he made a little sign to show him that he knew who was there; and, with the happy confidence of a child who knows that even in its sleep it is cared for, he closed his eyes and drifted out into the great unknown sea of sleep.

The perfumed night grew stiller; no leaf moved, and no bird stirred nor any living thing; it almost seemed, so silent was the hour, that Nature herself slept, and all the earth was fearful of awaking her. Night drew her solemn curtain closer in folds about her, and the very voice of the unresting sea breathed low.

CHAPTER V

When Christian awoke next morning the light of the dawn was still so faint that he could no more than distinguish the outline of the eaves and the black uprights of the house-posts against the gray of the outer day; but the night had restored to him all his vigour, and he felt his life pulsing and rising so strongly within him that he sprang up at once, and, without disturbing any one, left the house. It was still almost night, though in the sky there was a promise of day. The greater stars were burning yet, and even in the pale faint glow in the east, the first outpost of the sun, the great golden globe of Venus, glowed un-dimmed. As he passed out of the house and brushed through the thick vegetation that grew close to it, the heavy dew that lay upon everything refreshed his warm body, and he stooped his curly head to a little bush on which the white flowers shone dimly in the faint light and bathed his face with the fragrant dew. There was a narrow foot-track that ran through the garden, and this Christian followed for some short distance, when it began to mount a little craggy hill, which he found was bare of trees, and from which he thought that he could see, when daylight had come, whether the *Albatross* was still in sight.

There was a cool breeze blowing from the sea, which

often in those latitudes heralds the break of day; and enjoying its freshness, Christian sat down with his usual light-hearted philosophy to wait for daylight. He had not been sitting there very long before he was joined by Soma, who, having missed him from his side, had hurried out to find him.

'I wanted to see whether the ship has sailed,' said North.

'That does not matter. She will to-morrow, if not to-day.'

'Yes, and in the meantime the skipper will have a search party out after us.'

'He would not find us.'

'No, but he would bribe the chief of the bay, over yonder, with the promise of a musket or two, and we should soon be found.'

'I have friends, many friends.'

'I don't doubt it; but I hope we shan't be put to that.'

This time Christian's hopes were not doomed to be blighted, for now daylight began swiftly to flow upon the world, and the mist that hung upon the sea slowly lifted and melted away, and there, already a mile or so from land, was the *Albatross* with all her canvas set, heading away from land, and the little fleet of canoes which had taken out the fresh provisions was already putting back to the beach. Christian sprang to his feet and waved a farewell after the vessel, which as she went took along with her his last shade of care.

Anxieties and troubles are nearly always for other people and not for ourselves, and as Christian was alone in the world he had fewer than most men; but even had he had many he would not have let them weigh him down. There are some joyous souls in the world who are so happy and careless, who so persistently make the best of everything, that they even turn the skeletons in their closets into clowns for their amusement; and Christian was of that bright class.

'There she goes,' said North. 'I don't think, after last night's experience, that I have much of the *Albatross's* dust left upon my feet. All the same, let us run down and have a dip in the sea, and I'll wash off—in the absence of a shake—any that may be left.'

Soma, of course, could not understand what he meant, but he saw that he wanted a swim, and was gravely saying 'Yes, wash off,' when Christian turned, and seizing him by the waist, ran him full tilt down to the beach, which he could see shining through the palms below them.

That day Soma began to make arrangements for their return to Omëo; he left North in the care of Ebinibi and set off to have an interview with the chief, with the result that he obtained a large canoe and the loan of a crew to work it across to the island.

When one has nothing to pack up and no farewells to make it does not take very long to prepare for a voyage, so that when Soma announced that evening that everything was ready for a start next morning, there was none of the hurry and confusion that generally reign upon these occasions.

The next day dawned bright and fair, and food had been eaten and good-byes said almost before the sun was above the horizon. Ebinibi had given his friends two small pieces of *tappa* the day before, and had taught Christian how to fold the narrow strip of cloth round his loins, and fasten it at the side by thrusting a crumpled lump of the material down inside the first tight fold, so that they no longer wore their impromptu dresses of leaves. The canoe that the chief of the bay had lent to Soma was lying at the little town some mile or two down the coast, to which he had gone the morning before, and to this these two strangely-assorted companions, accompanied by Ebinibi and two or three of the young men from the house, walked in the dewy morning, whilst the day was still tempered by the freshness of the vanished night.

The little town consisted of a scattered line of brown hive-shaped houses dotted along the beach beneath the palms that here, as elsewhere, fringed it. There was no plan exhibited in the arrangement of the houses, which were placed anyhow, according to the taste of the builder. The only street was the beaten path that ran along the narrow space of level ground above high-water mark, from which many little paths diverged to the forest and to the houses.

The appearance of the white man was expected, as Soma had said that they would sail that morning, so that the people had not set about their usual occupations, but with characteristic Polynesian disregard for the value of time, were amusing themselves or lying about in shady corners until the expected visitor arrived.

As soon as they had passed the little rocky headland that bounded the bay on one side and began to approach the town, Christian could see that he was the chief object of interest to the assembled people, for two lads, who had been stationed there as outposts, started off at a run to the town to give notice of his coming directly they saw that he was of the little party. He was in wild spirits that morning, and all the boyish folly that was in him was on the surface, and inspired him with the idea of surprising them and gratifying their very natural curiosity. As soon as he was in the town he began the most extraordinary series of antics and capers, bowing, leaping, running, and waving his arms, with the most engaging smile upon his face all the time. He proceeded for some little distance in this ridiculous fashion, increasing the wildness of his vagaries, when he saw a tall man with a carved staff, who was evidently the chief of the bay, followed at a little distance by a band of handsome, stalwart warriors. The wind was completely taken out of his sails by the method of his reception, for the chief, instead of expressing the least astonishment or surprise, evidently accepted this extraordinary proceeding as a white man's custom; and addressing a word or two to his companions, who instantly followed his example, he proceeded to imitate, to the very best of his powers, the leaps and gyrations of Christian.

In those happy times of seventy years ago, before the blighting breath of European civilisation, which since then has done so much to ruin the islands of the South Pacific, had blown upon them, all white men were considered by the unsophisticated people to be peers. They were regarded almost as heaven-descended guests, and a shipwrecked sailor was looked upon as the equal of a king. It is true that occasionally this assumed divinity was the cause of some awkward and not altogether pleasing results, as they have been known, whilst honouring the god, to ceremoniously eat the man, in the hope of thus securing a meal without injuring the being whom they deemed immortal. Such honours, whilst perhaps satisfactory to the ambition of some men, would probably by the majority be regarded as illusory and barren. In

Christian's case, however, this mistaken notion had more agreeable results, for he was garlanded with fragrant *sessis*, as they call the wreaths of perfumed flowers with which they adorn themselves, and led to the beach of coral sand, where already the large canoe was launched which was to bear him and his friend to Omëo.

Knowing the distance that he had to travel, Soma had borrowed one of the largest canoes that Ruanui possessed, and this had been provisioned for a five or six days' cruise. The canoe was a beautiful example of the shipbuilder's art, for it was not merely a tree-trunk hollowed out—it was built of solid timbers that had, with infinite patience, been shaped by rude stone adzes. These planks were then strongly sewn together with cords passed through little projecting notches that were left for the purpose, and the crevices, where there were any, were filled in with a resinous varnish. The one that Christian was examining with a sailor's critical eye was of the double kind, which, in those parts of the South Pacific, where navigation is best understood, is always used for canoes intended for long journeys. The two canoes are connected by a kind of deck of planks laid across from one to the other, and on this there is often built a sort of little cabin. There was only one mast which supported the yard, upon which was hung the large brown sail of matting.

Very soon after they were aboard this great sail was spread, and the canoe began slowly to float out to the reef, the men which Ruanui had lent them to work the canoe chanting a wild rhythmical song as they plied their dark wood paddles. When they were close to the reef the chief and some of his friends who had accompanied them said their *ofas*, and leaping lightly over the side, began to swim to land, often turning in the water to shout or wave a last farewell to those on board.

The opening in the reef was safely passed, towards which so short a time ago Christian and his friend had at first directed their flight, and the open water being reached the canoe began to dance along. It was a queer sort of craft, Christian thought, to undertake a long sea voyage in, and at another time he might have doubted her sea-going and sea-worthy qualities; but now so keen was his delight in the sense of freedom which he enjoyed, and the feeling of adventure well begun, that he felt the greatest confidence in all the good qualities of the canoe. He looked up at the swelling sail above him and thought that it was like the great wing of some bird that was bearing him through the blue, from the known to the unknown, from servitude to freedom.

Towards evening, when the day-long furnace of the sun was cooled but unextinguished, the last height of the island they had left had sunk below the horizon, and alone in the immensity of the unknown and boundless Pacific, the canoe, a tiny brown spot lost in all that infinity of sea and blue clear air, slowly rose and fell with every beat of the great ocean heart. The sun sank royally, lavishly squandering his splendours on the barren ocean out of mere youthful prodigality——for the million-year-old sun is youthful yet ——and the mitigated darkness of a tropic night at sea came on with a swiftness that to a Northerner never altogether loses its first surprise.

As the noble stars came out, not one by one but in troops together, like soldiers from the fortress of the dark, Soma altered slightly the course of the canoe, for it was by the points of that eternal compass that he steered, and until now he had judged his course merely by the flow of the wind, which at that time of the year blows steadily to the east.

After the evening meal most of the men who formed the crew, worn out by their long day's work, lay down in different corners of the canoe, leaving Soma, who best knew the course, to steer with the long paddle, which he managed in the stern. The breeze was light, but so steady as to necessitate very little working of the craft.

Christian could not sleep for very beauty of the night. He lay on the little mat-covered deck watching the eternal fires of the stars grow brighter as that darkness set in, which, like death, shuts out the earth but opens all heaven's glories to us. It was so very still that the little lapping sound made by the ripples against the canoe seemed to fill the air. The waves did not break but rose and fell quite rhythmically, and as calm and strong as Samson's heaving breast when, deep in sleep he lay, the night Delilah gave him to his enemies.

The masculine great sea was so close to him that night, and was so beautiful in the might of its deep calm, that Christian, with that strange melancholy that when one is young makes us 'half in love with death,' for one brief moment thought how sweet it would be to make his happiness eternal by diving silently into that heaving infinity around him and merging his youth and individuality in its everlasting impersonality. But the next moment he felt that his time was not yet come, he had not lived enough; life surged too strongly in him for any such emotion—it was not thought—to be more than momentary. He felt his incompleteness.

Death is so common in the world, and wounds the living so deftly with his scythe, that it almost seems to many of us more a place to die in than to live in. But not so to Christian; all the earth's life seemed to flow through him, so that every moment was an experience.

He could not sleep, or did not wish to do so, so going to Soma and learning their direction from him, he took his place at the stern and made his friend lie down. At first Soma objected, saying truly that he was not tired, but as usual Christian had his way, and soon he was the only waking soul on all the little ship. Silently and sleeplessly all through the long night, with his eyes fixed on the stars that guided him, he steered the canoe towards that unknown land in the east, the charm and attraction of which lay perhaps, as in so many things, in its very mystery and remoteness.

For five days and nights they sailed, and plied their paddles when the breeze fell dead, upon the same course, but the sun rose and set and showed them nothing but the unchanging circle of the horizon, with themselves an unmoved centre. Slowly rising, slowly sinking over the broad swells of that great sea, the tranced craft steadily held its course between the two oceans of the water and the air—which was the bluer Christian could not say; and sometimes, when the heat had melted away all the line of the horizon, and sea and sky were merged together, it seemed to him as though he were enclosed, as flies in amber sometimes are, in one great sphere of sapphire. The great globe of the sun itself, the blinding apex of the day, when for one brief moment he looked into its glory, shone blue also.

As the days passed, and the provisions began to

grow scant, and still no land appeared, Christian had many an anxious talk with Soma and one of the men who before this had made the voyage to Omëo. He thought that they must have steered a point or two wrong in their course, and thus have passed the island to the north or south, but both men reassured him. Soma reminded him of what he had said on board the *Albatross,* that it had taken him four days to make the voyage to Wakauau, and that it would take one or two more days in going back. The fact proved that they were right, for on the evening of the sixth day Christian, who was sitting in the bottom of the canoe with his face almost on a level with the water, that he might watch the beautiful shapes and colours of the unknown creatures that floated past him, like seconds in eternity, seen for one moment then lost for ever, saw Soma leave the stern and come towards him. A great joy lit up his face, and his dark eyes that were always tender to Christian had a happiness in them that told his story before he spoke.

'Come, come,' he said, and seizing Christian by the wrist he pulled him to his feet; 'Soma did not lie.'

He hurried North across the paddlers' seats right into the peak of the canoe, and standing there with one great arm outstretched—a grand heroic figure against the evening sky—he pointed to a low dim something on the sea-line. Shading his dazzled eyes with his hand Christian followed the direction of the pointing arm and saw—was it a cloud? he thought so at first—a shadowy outline of what perhaps were mountains staining the sunset colours.

'Omëo! *Omëo!*' was Soma's cry; 'there is my land. I knew we should find it. Did I not promise you? My friend, my friend, there is *our* land.'

Though he smiled his lip quivered and his eyes were full of tears, and there was such rapture in his gaze and such love in his voice that Christian, as he turned and grasped the arm of the dear fellow, felt his eyes grow dim in sympathy, and his heart beat fast at recognising once again the great love that he bore for him.

CHAPTER VI

THERE is an island of that far under-world so wrapped about with the silence of thousands of leagues of blue slow-breathing ocean and the blue stillness of the soft Pacific sky that it almost seems a land of dreams lost in a sea of sleep—a secret place that Nature loves, and that she has chosen for its remoteness that she may there keep hid all her choicest treasures for herself and her true children whom she has placed there. The love I bear for it is more like the love that women claim from men; there is something of the same ardour in it and the same infinite tenderness. It is almost as though that dear island were a sentient thing that had cast a spell upon me, for my thoughts turn to it when my hours are happiest, and even much more quickly when my heart is sad. It was thither that Christian came.

Directly that Soma had seen the island the canoe had been steered straight to it, and, as during the first part of the night the breeze was very fresh and favourable, they made such good headway that Omëo was looming close upon them before the day gave any sign of breaking. All the crew were awake and stirring, for the loud booming of the surf as it thundered on the barrier reef gave warning of the danger that lay ahead. The sail was brought down at a run, and for some little time the canoe was kept on and off by the exertions of the stalwart paddlers until there was light enough to make the opening in the reef that was the only entrance on that side of the island to the sheltered lagoon beyond it.

At first all that Christian could see of the island was that it consisted of a mass of great hills and mountains towering high in pinnacled crags thousands of feet above the sea. From one of which, far inland, there rose a fluctuating line of dull-coloured smoke. This was Monoriro, Soma said, the mountain of fires, where the god Rorutu lived. But at last daybreak came—never day dawned so slowly, Chris thought— and as the eastern sky glowed and blushed at the sun's coming he could see the mass of its forest-covered hills and its lofty mountain summits, all wreathed and draped in floating mist, standing in the very heart of the sunrise. Swiftly the sun upsprang, gilding the topmost spires of the mountains with an outline of fire, and, as it rose, melting away the pale white mists that hung about the hills. As one by one these gauzy veils were drawn away, Christian could see more and more plainly this land of his hopes. Its glories increased as it slowly revealed itself, until the moment when the mounting sun had overleaped the brow of a forest-covered hill, and was pouring all the gold of his sunshine on the mountains and into the valleys, Omëo shone before him in all the splendour of her beauty. Like a queen of the ocean, she rode upon the blue waters of the calm lagoon, where the very waves, awed by her loveliness, broke in little humble kisses at her feet.

Whilst he was gazing at the land the canoe had approached the opening in the reef, which, at a distance

of about half a mile, surrounded all the island, and he
was recalled to himself by the voice of Soma, who
shouted to him to help them hoist the sail.   Ashamed
of appearing to shrink from his share of the work, he
came amidship and worked with a will.   The opening
in the reef was just before them, and the water of the
passage showed dark and blue against the lighter green
colour of the shallows.   On either side, a bent, uneven
line, the coral reef extended, and on this wonderful
barrier the great long swells of the open ocean rolled,
curving into breakers, which shone with all the glories
of emerald and sapphire as the light shone through
them, breaking with the crash and roar of a cataract,
and rising in a fluctuating white wall of water, which
shone with every hue of the rainbow in the sunlight.
The noise of the beating surf is the most characteristic
sound of the coral islands; it never ceases; in calm or
storm it still roars on, with angrier voice or gentler
song, but never ending.

Once having passed the dangerous reef—which is
at the same time the great safeguard of these islands,
acting as it does as a natural breakwater—the whole
sea-scene is changed, the blue transparent water lying
as calm and clear as though a spell were cast upon it.
Although many fathoms deep in places, the water is
of so wondrous and crystal-like a quality that every
object at the bottom can be seen as plainly as though
it were only air that came between.   It was like an
enchanted garden of flowers through which no breeze
blew and where every leaf was still, for the whole
sea bottom was a glow of living colour.   Corals, white
and red, and branched with azure tops, and strange
zoophytes of every hue, grew upon the rocks; and
masses of delicate, filmy sea-weeds, of deep crimson

and every shade of green and golden brown, filled each chink and cranny. Fish of the wildest colouring and strangest forms darted in and out of this mimic forest, like gorgeous birds in tropic woods, and sprang away alarmed as the shadow of the silent canoe fell on them through all that depth of sea.

But Christian's interest was so centred on the land that he hardly gave more than a glance at all these marvels; his future home was before him, and every moment Soma was calling his attention to something on the shore. The town of Otorangi, although quite close, was not opposite to the opening in the reef; it was situated in a bay beyond a bold and rocky cliff, which formed a sort of little promontory, so that at first it could not be seen from the canoe. Soma was in a state of feverish excitement, though he endeavoured to preserve a chief-like calm; he looked at the sail, and shouted directions to the man who was steering, and urged the paddlers to greater exertions. Very soon the wave-worn point was passed, and Otorangi was in sight.

The town of brown houses, thatched with leaves and grasses that were bleached almost white by the fierce glare of the sun, was larger than the one they had sailed from on Wakanau, and to Christian appeared to be neater and better in every respect. The bay, which stretched in a beautiful even curve, as though the land were opening wide its arms to embrace the sea, was lined by a beach of white and dazzling sand, which ended, above high-water mark, in a low bank all a tangle of bushes and flowering creepers. Beyond this was a level space that was almost cleared of trees, though clumps of slender palms and here and there a dark green bread - fruit dotted its grassy surface.

Beyond this was the town, which was built upon no particular plan, the houses facing this way or that at the builder's will, and all of them shaded and partly surrounded with palms and great bushes of scarlet hibiscus, which then were in full bloom. At the back of the town, which extended some little distance inland, though it followed the curve of the bay, lay the bright green gardens of bananas and *talo*, and the mass of the dark forest, in which every shade of green from olive to light emerald was displayed by the nobly growing trees, through which, lifting high their feathery crowns, the palms had thrust themselves in their search for sun and air.

This dense forest covered all the gently swelling hills that lay between Otorangi and the great mountains of the interior, which rose in spires and minarets of broken gray rock high into the air, and round which thin wisps of morning mist still floated. In places, marked by shadow, deep valleys ran back from the shore to the central mountains, and down most of these clear streams of water ran to the lagoon. High up in the hills a narrow band of silver, that shone brightly in the sun, showed where one wild mountain brook dashed over a bare crag in its haste to the singing sea, whose voice could be heard at times even so far back in the trackless woods. One large stream flowed out just opposite the opening in the reef.

Every moment now Soma kept crying out—

'The *pure*' (house) 'of Lomangatini is moved. There is a new one next to Ilo's. Look where the Wai-malo falls.'

And then at last he shouted, as two or three figures in the greatest excitement came running across the *bara*—

'They see us, they see us; they come to the beach.'

It was evident that at last the canoe was seen, for in another moment a loud drumming noise was heard in the town, and the brown people came swarming from their houses and ran to the shore. It appeared that at first they did not understand the object of this visit—for they could see at a glance that the canoe was not one of theirs—as many of the men appeared with their clubs and spears in their hands. A Polynesian town will never, if it can help it, let itself be taken unawares, and though there was only one canoe with ten men on it in sight, who could tell that there were not many more round the point.

'Do they think we are coming to fight?' asked Christian; 'and what is that awful noise?'

'Oh, that is *Tai-moana*' ('the sound of the seas'), 'the great drum that is outside Ilo's house. They beat it to call the town together.'

'What are they afraid of?' said Christian, laughing.

'Perhaps they think we are Pangu men come to make war; but this is not a war canoe, and the Pangu men are not fools to come thus in the daytime. They will see me soon and know me.'

Soma rose up in the prow as he spoke, and rested one hand on the hideously carved figure-head of the canoe, which stood about five feet above the water, and was sculptured in the grotesque resemblance of a human being with arms akimbo, and eyes of white shell. Whilst one hand rested on the mass of dark feathers which represented its hair, with the other he waved aloft his *mahi* of white native cloth, which for a moment he tore from his waist. When at last they were about a quarter of a mile from the beach a loud cry went up of '*Soma, e Soma Motuiti oë*,' and the same moment two or three small canoes were pushed down the incline of the bank into the water. Six or eight men sprang into these, and began paddling out to the canoe with the utmost haste, whilst others at the first cry had rushed into the sea, and were already swimming out to meet her.

Directly he saw that he was recognised, and that his friends were putting off from shore, Soma turned to Christian and said—

'They have never seen a white man before, and they may fear you, and in their fear may harm you. Lie down in the canoe until I tell my people that I bring a friend, and that it is you.'

'No,' said Christian, 'I am not afraid. I will stand by your side, and they will see me with you. They would know me for a coward if I hid.'

So they stood side by side, and in a moment or two the canoes had met. The occupants of the small ones drew away for a moment when first they saw North, but Soma shouted to them to come along, and explained who he was. The meeting was a tumultuous one and grew noisier every moment, for the swimmers came alongside and were hauled into the canoe, and all embraced and rubbed noses, and shouted and talked at the same time. But this first meeting was quietness to the uproar that greeted them when the canoe touched land. A hundred men were in the water to haul her high and dry upon the beach, and by this time every man, woman, and child in the town had assembled to welcome Soma home. His father Motuiti was there, and vainly tried to control himself, the tears pouring down his old face as again and again he clasped his son in his arms and pressed his nose and lips to Soma's.

'Where had he been?' they said. They had

thought him dead, it was so many moons since he had gone.

Then with the quick change of emotion—in which children and savages are so much alike—all their interest was centred in this wonderful white-skinned, yellow-haired, and blue-eyed stranger. What was he? whence had he come? The men stood in awe of him, and the women and children fled, notwithstanding his smile, whenever he looked their way.

But this fear was not for long; it lasted only for a day or two, for Christian was one of those rare beings who are at home anywhere, and who seem to carry sunshine in their very presence; a sort of happy atmosphere surrounds them which radiates upon all who come within it. There was a contagion of mirth in his laugh, as of love in his eyes, and his glad enjoyment of life and youth was so frank and debonair that man and woman, old and young alike, bowed themselves willing victims to its charm. This had been true of him in his old life—which he looked upon as ended—and now was much more so with this people of his adoption, who judge almost entirely by externals, and are almost Greek in their love of personal beauty. Thus the Omëans' shyness of him wore off very quickly, which result was greatly helped by the fact that he could talk to them fairly well in their own language from the first, and rapidly improved in it. His voice, too, aided him, for as he sang or spoke it rang with the blitheness of youth and carelessness.

All those first few days he seemed to be in a dream; all his preconceived notions of the order of things received every moment such rude shocks that he could hardly assure himself of the reality of his existence until he had reconstructed his ideas upon the basis of Omëan life and customs. His mind received at this time so many novel pictures that he had only time for observation and none for reflection.

Naturally enough, the people themselves were the chief object of curiosity during those early days, and the interest he began to feel for them was of no ephemeral kind, for it increased as he knew them better, and the only change that occurred in it was that what at first was interest only became later on a very sincere affection. They were primarily a lovable people, of a hospitable, generous, affectionate nature, and unless stirred by one of their many strong passions, of a gentle and easy-going character. It surprised Christian to discover in a nation which he expected to find mere savages such fine sentiment as some of them possessed, and such good manners as were pretty general among them. In civilised countries people shroud the real man by their good manners; among the Omëans the manners were but the means of showing the true feelings of the man. Of course by this is not meant that these Polynesian savages had the customs of European gentlemen; they had many barbarous habits, and very many cruel and awful usages; but they had made many and long strides along the road towards a civilisation of their own.

First and foremost among these was their treatment of their women, which was very different from that employed by the lords of creation towards the weaker sex in the islands of the Western Pacific. In Omëo the women were not merely the drudges and hard-working, ill-treated slaves of the Western Islands; they had somehow emancipated themselves from this; and beyond their household duties and the lighter forms of labour for which they were suited, their chief employment was in gathering flowers and weaving them into wreaths and garlands, in practising dances—in which art they were proficient—and in the lengthy but pleasant work of beautifying themselves. They were the makers of the native cloth and the weavers of the fine mats, in which an Omöan's wealth chiefly consisted; but these duties, performed by bands of girls and young women, were far from laborious.

As for the people themselves, Christian was struck from the first with their great physical beauty. The women—who were of course first in his estimation, for Christian was a true sailor—whilst still young, were the perfection of feminine beauty; not very tall, indeed rather small when compared with the immensely stalwart men, but of a form that was grace personified; of a clear light olive tint, faces of the purest oval, laughing lips and white teeth, and with deep mysterious eyes that often retained a strange dreamy look of melancholy even when the lips were smiling. Their silky hair fell in waves and curls about their shoulders, and was of the darkest, shiniest brown or the most lustrous black, and long eyelashes fringed their eyes with shadow. And of all the arts that render women fascinating to the other sex, they were past mistresses; apparently it was their chief, if not their only study.

The men were the most magnificent fellows that Christian had ever seen, although few of them had such handsome features as Soma. Almost all of them were tall and superbly proportioned, erect as darts and strong as bulls, with great chests whose broad muscular expanse showed their immense power, and with arms and backs ridged with muscles; almost any one of them might have been taken as a sculptor's model, and the handsomest of them, with their grace of movement and the dignity of pose that is gained by freedom from all artificial restraint, and the constant athletic exercise of all kinds which is their principal employment, might have satisfied the ideals of those who in ancient times sought to express in manly perfection the attributes of their gods. Their dress, which consisted only of a narrow girdle of *tappa*, which was tied around the waist and passed between the legs (except upon ceremonious occasions, when it was very elaborate), showed to the greatest advantage all their physical excellence, and at the same time hid none of the intricate and marvellous patterns of the tattooing with which the chiefs amongst them were almost covered. They were darker in tint than the women, and unlike them inasmuch as they, as a rule, cut their wavy hair quite short, though some of the greater dandies among them elaborated theirs into wonderful and, in Christian's opinion, hideous erections. All the men, except the very old ones, shaved the beard and whiskers, generally leaving the moustache, and for this purpose they used two shells, rubbing the serrated edges together, and afterwards smoothing the cheek with pumice-stone, which floated in quantities to their shores after an eruption of Mouoriro.

But it was the little children who first of all made their way straight to Christian's kindly heart. They were the gayest, brightest, merriest, and most impudent crew that he had ever come across, and the very difficulties that he experienced in overcoming their shyness, and the natural fear they felt for this strange being, was but another reason for loving them the more when once their confidence was gained. After the first few days they were his constant companions, and it was in talking with them that he so quickly gained fluency in the Omëan language. They played about all day on the beach, and in the little river or the sea, absolutely naked, and without seeming to feel the intense heat of the sun; even the natural protection that the hair affords was taken away, for their little heads were shaved as bare as the palm of your hand.

It was a sight to see them in the morning running up to Christian as he came up from the sea all freshened by his swim. There they came in little naked shoals across the *bara* to the beach, boys carrying babies, little ones hand-in-hand together toddling unsteadily over the uneven ground, some of them with dewy flowers fresh picked at the edge of the forest, and others with ripe fruit or a piece of cold cooked *talo*, which they ate as they hurried along. No sooner was Christian on the warm sand than they were all about him, round his neck and in his arms, and swarming up his legs till he had to lie down and let them play and crawl about him as they wished; their little warm fat bodies tumbling about his naked limbs making him look, by contrast, almost fair again for all the sunburnt brown with which the last few weeks had painted him. They would offer him the fruit, and little baby girls would stick their flowers in his hair, till Soma, who was generally with him, would laugh and say he was like an Olasangu girl dressed ready for the dance.

CHAPTER VII

ONE chief reason why North was accepted so readily into their midst by the Omëans, who beneath their genial exterior had much of the distrust that is so characteristic of savage peoples, was that on the day of their arrival at the island, Soma, in full conclave of the chiefs and people, who were assembled at the first news of his return, had announced that Christian had been adopted by his father into his own particular clan or family, and had thus acquired the right of admission into the tribe. This statement requires some little explanation; Christian himself did not at first fully understand its meaning. At that time in some of the remote islands of the Eastern Pacific there existed—and still may exist in its primitive form in some places—a curious custom of adoption by which a stranger (by which, in those times, was meant the native of another island or district) could be received into a family other than his own. This adoption not only gained for him all the rights that would have been his had he been born a member of the family which received him, but also full tribal rights of the community. To do this the consent of the chief was necessary. This power Soma possessed in his own person, but knowing instinctively the strong conservative feeling of his people and their objection to all innovation, Soma had thought it advisable to induce his father Motuiti to be the nominal adopter, and to place his *tabu* on his friend as a stronger protection than his own might have been.

To complete and render stronger this strange tie there was still a further ceremony to be undergone. This consisted of the rite of 'blood brotherhood,' of which Soma had many times spoken to Christian. One of the old hands on board the *Albatross* had spoken to North of this same ceremony, which obtains on some of the islands in the Western Pacific as well as in Omëo, and from him, as also from Soma, he learned that this oath was one that never was broken, and was only ended by death. It is a vow taken by Polynesians when inspired—as it is well known they sometimes are—by that heroic, old-time sentiment of friendship in which entire self-abnegation is no virtue but normal and expected, and sacrifice of time, tastes, passion, wealth, and even life is not unusual. The full import of what is undertaken by this oath being known, it is never entered upon rashly ; for the deepest term of reproach that can be used by one Polynesian of another is that he has broken his 'blood brotherhood' (*è ofa-namu*), or betrayed his 'blood brother.' Many of their mythical stories and half-poetic tales, which are so numerous, and which they so frequently narrate without the changing of a single word in the relation, turn upon this custom.

Soma was most anxious to swear this with North ; and he for his part bore so strong a love for his friend that he was not only willing but desirous of giving an expression of all the gratitude and affection that he felt. There was, too, something in the nature of the bond that was pleasing to his imaginative mind ; it was like a page from the book of 'old romance,' and the very wildness of the rite itself appealed strongly to the savagery that was latent in him, both for love and hate; for Christian could hate fiercely as well as love strongly. All men who can love have at least the power for the other in their hearts. There are some people of so ambiguous a character that they are not sure of even their likes or dislikes; but Christian was not of this vague crew—he was sure of his loves and hates without any tapping of his mental barometer.

So that when one day, after Christian had been a few weeks in Omëo, Soma told him that all was prepared for the ceremony, he said he was quite ready. Almost every afternoon of the Omëan day the people indulge in *siesta* (*mote a'ho*, 'mid-day sleep'), and it is then that much of the talking is done, for although they lie down on the mats they do not sleep much. It was at this time that Soma told North of the plans.

But perhaps before this subject is entered upon it would be as well to describe in a little further detail the houses and the town that were North's home for so long. It is difficult for one who has lived so long and so full a life in precisely similar Polynesian scenes to remember how entirely dissimilar the life is from that to which we are accustomed, not from any forgetfulness, but from exactly the opposite reason. All the scenes and all the surroundings are so fresh and vivid in his mind that he is apt to accept them as facts common to the memory of us all, and in consequence to pass them over in silence that he may go on to speak of actions and people which seem to be of more interest and importance.

The town of Otorangi was built on both sides of a small rapid stream that flowed down the valley from the mountains of the interior. In the first part of its course, in its higher reaches, the little river rushed impetuously enough through the narrow valley, but when the land became more level, as the valley opened out to the sea, it flowed in quieter sweeps till it reached the ocean. In places, some way back of the town, the land was almost marshy, and there the people had made their gardens of the moisture-loving *talo*. In most Omëan towns the houses are built about an open public square, but at Otorangi the level ground above the beach had been taken for a *bara*, and the houses, roughly speaking, formed three sides of a square, with its fourth side open and facing the sea.

The houses of rich and poor were alike in design, though they differed much in size and in material of construction. Motuiti's house, which Christian now occupied by right, was a typical one of the better sort. It was built on a platform, slightly raised above the level of the surrounding ground, which was faced and paved with slabs of coral rock. This paved space extended for some little way beyond the house, making, as it were, a small court about it. The house itself was about fifty feet long, and was a marvel of neatness and finish in its construction. Two polished posts of great thickness and about twenty feet in height supported the roof pole of dark red *koa* wood, and from this long and stout bamboos descended on both sides to the eaves, which projected a foot or more beyond the short posts which formed the open walls of the house. The roof was rounded at both ends, and was covered with a thick rain-proof thatch of great dried leaves, which had become almost white in the bleaching heat of the sun. In most of these houses the walls were left quite open, to admit every breath of air that stirred, but the inhabitants had a sort of stiff reed matting with which they closed up the openings on the side from which wind or rain came.

Of furniture, strictly speaking, there was none. The floor was covered with two or three thicknesses of mats, and a sort of divan was made at one end of the house by laying a log of timber all across the floor and filling up the space thus formed with dried aromatic fern and covering it with finely woven mats. Here the men took their *siesta* and slept at night, the women of the tribe being forbidden, under *tabu*, to enter the men's house. A few wooden pillows, some coco-nut-shell cups and wooden utensils, conspicuous amongst which, by its size and polish, was the great *ava* bowl, and some beautifully decorated curtains of *tappa*, were almost all the house contained, with the exception of the arms and spears and tools which were grouped about the central posts. All their dresses and finery, and stores of cloth and fine mats, were rolled up into bales, which were hung from the rafters. The house was built on the bank of the little river, and was made beautiful by the group of tall coco palms which rose behind it, and by the great bushes of white gardenia, scarlet hibiscus, and brilliantly coloured foliage plants which had been planted about it. For the love of flowers and gay colours is so general in Oméa that every house has beautiful bushes planted near it.

The most populous part of the town was on either side the stream, and it was here that the great *pure atua* (house of the gods) stood. No bridge spanned the stream, nor was it necessary, for it was but shallow, and as the people wore no clothes to speak of, it could not very well wet them. But a little way beyond Motuiti's house was a row of great stepping-stones, two or three feet above the usual level of the little river, and these were used in times of flood, when the swollen stream poured a great volume of water through the valley.

One end of Motuiti's house looked on to this clear flowing water, whilst the front of the house faced the sea, so that the place was usually flooded with cool sea air, which, as it blew across the open space, perfumed itself with the odours of the *uru* flowers and the *pandanus* trees. It was in this cool, breeze-swept house, which was always filled with the rippling sound of the flowing water and the subdued far-away rustle of the palm leaves overhead, that North and Soma were talking. It is difficult at first to follow the meaning of any Polynesian; he speaks in a fragmentary manner, which is very characteristic of the broken sequence of his ideas, and he often uses metaphor in place of direct expression; so that when Christian said that he was ready then and there to take the oath that Soma so much wished, he answered, 'One does not approach the temple' (*pure atua*) 'from the *talo*-field'—meaning that one must not visit the house of the gods unceremoniously, clad in work-a-day undress.

'But why need we go to the *pure atua* at all? Cannot we swear friendship here in this house as well as in another?'

'It always has been done before Tamagoru at the *marae* on the mountain,' said Soma simply, with that reliance on precedent that is so customary with them.

Now North had not begun any violent proselytising —he was sensible man enough not to try to force an elaborate system of philosophy down the throat of an uneducated savage all at once, particularly as it seemed to him their own system worked so well and produced such good results; but he was anxious, if possible, to take away the load of shadowy fears that weighs so heavily on the souls of so many savage races, and with this result in view had had many talks with Soma.

'It has always been done before the *atuas*, you say; but, Soma, you know they are dead, and nothing but wood and stone.'

'Yes, Klis, you say they are dead; but perhaps some of them have escaped. Come, it is easy to go to the *pure*. The *marete*' (priest) 'will be ready for us. Why risk offending the *atuas*?'

So North agreed to go, knowing how important to the childish mind of an Omëan the mere ritual or outward part of any ceremony was. The strictest etiquette prevailed in all the important affairs of life, and it was even considered most derogatory to the dignity of a chief to die—unless killed in battle—in any other manner than that prescribed by custom. So Christian was not surprised when Soma said that they must begin to get ready for the ceremony, which he said could only take place after dark. He called a young man into the house, and sent him off to the *marete* to say that they would be at the *pure atua* after sunset, and that he was to hold himself in readiness for their coming; and then turning to Christian he said, 'Only the pure are acceptable; we must go down and wash.'

For this North was always ready, and he sprang up to leave the house, when they were stopped by Motuiti, who asked whither they were bound. On Soma telling him, he asked, 'Have you the oil for anointment?' and gave his son a little calabash cruse of oil, perfumed with *pandanus*, which he took down from where it hung in the roof. Soma, before leaving, let down one of the bales of *tappa* that were also hung from the rafters, and unwrapping it, took out two pieces of beautifully fine decorated *tappa* of many yards in length, and some of their choicest personal adornments. Taking these they walked the little distance to the beach, and in a few moments were swimming in the warm lagoon ; diving down like otters to the brilliant gardens of the sea, and startling little fishes from their shelter in the slow-waving masses of floating translucent seaweed.

There was always something invigorating to Christian in these long swims ; they were no mere dippings, for the temperature of the water was such that one could stay in it indefinitely, but real athletic exercises, in which strength and speed and endurance called all his glowing vitality into play. He and Soma and a young man named Okotai, who often joined them, swam every day, and sometimes twice, so that he soon became as amphibious as a true Polynesian, though he never acquired all the water tricks and accomplishments that they possessed.

At length Soma said they must return, and they swam to the land. As North came out from the sea, all shining with water and glorious with health, he lifted up his face and filled his great chest, and stretched out his brawny arms with the delight of being a man. Every muscle of him was hard as steel, every joint supple, and every sinew and fibre elastic and strong, his wholesome skin glowed with health, and his soul was filled with the joy of masculinity and strength in which we all glory in wellbeing.

The two friends made a strongly contrasted but

magnificent pair of specimens of manly beauty as they turned to re-enter the town; even the strange dress in which Soma had instructed North to array himself, and which he too wore, added to the effect. The whole upper part of the body was entirely bare, but round the waist they wore a deep sort of girdle, which consisted of a black fringe made of a wiry, fibrous grass. This parted at every step, and allowed all the elaborate pattern of the tattooed thigh to be seen. Above this was a very long strip of fine white *tappa*, decorated with a rich design in brown; this was folded into a very narrow band around the waist, and opened behind in voluminous soft folds that trailed upon the ground. Around the great neck of each man was tied a necklace of a beautiful bluish-purple pearl shell, and upon their heads Soma deftly tied and twisted a soft piece of gauzy, smoke-coloured *tappa* into a turban of the shape and size of a Phrygian cap.

Thus attired, they returned to the town, where their appearance attracted much attention from both sexes, but as every one knew the importance of the affair they were engaged upon no one directly addressed them, though Christian overheard many soft laughs from the girls, and one or two flattering remarks upon the looks of both of them. It was now long after sunset, and only stopping at Motuiti's house long enough for Soma to find and put in his girdle two small stone implements set like knives in handles of *koa* wood, they followed the trodden pathway that lay along the bank of the stream until they came to a dark opening that seemed to lead to the heart of the forest. Here darkness fell upon them, for although the fleeting twilight of a tropic night had not quite vanished from the sky, in the shade of the almost impenetrable forest that they now entered—where even daylight at noon is dimmed and subdued—the blackness of midnight lay amongst the close-growing trunks of the trees.

The little-used track was narrow and broken with the slippery roots of many a forest giant, but Soma knew the road and marched boldly along, the light colour of the *tappa* that he wore about his waist gleaming dimly and serving as a sort of guide to North, who followed closely on his footsteps. After a short distance the track became very steep, and Christian knew that they must be mounting one of the hills that rose abruptly at the back of the town. They must have been walking for an hour in almost unbroken silence, for although at first Christian spoke several times, Soma answered him in such a preoccupied manner that he knew he was moved by the solemnity of his thoughts and of the coming rite, so he desisted.

Slowly the darkness, the forest stillness, and the unusual and impressive quiet of his companion wrought a feeling of awe in Christian, that he felt, in an unthinking way, was fitting for the occasion, and he followed Soma in absolute silence. Seeing nothing, hearing nothing, and only conscious in a dim sort of way of his friend's presence, there crept upon him again that dreamy feeling of the unreality of things which, after a time, attacks even one's own identity. Was it really he, Christian North, who was passing on so strange an errand through that enchanted wood? It grew even darker as the young moon sank, and Christian could no longer see Soma, though he was aware of his presence by the strange, haunting, memory-stirring perfume of the oil which he had asked Christian to rub into his skin after their sea-bath.

At last North was aroused from his reverie by the voice of Soma, which was hushed with the awe of that midnight quiet, calling him by name.

'Here I am. What is it?' he asked.

'It is nothing, now,' he said as he stopped and took hold of Christian's friendly hand. 'But we are near the *pure* of Tamagoru, *and I saw the darkness moving.*'

There was something so impressive in the soundless calm of the forest on the black and windless night that Christian, into whose mystic and emotional nature many a weird sea superstition had entered deeply, almost felt with Soma that some strange unseen influences were about, wafting sudden chills upon them and waving, as a curtain, the dense blackness of the night. So, hand-in-hand like two children, they trod the last upward stretch of the path, until before them, still far off it seemed, there gleamed a sudden flash of firelight between the intervening trunks. Soma nipped North's hand quickly and whispered—

'He awaits us.'

Almost directly afterwards the path ended, and they saw above them an open space of sky and the stars shining quietly. Here the forest had been cleared, and with immense labour a huge platform of roughly squared blocks of limestone had been built. It was about five feet above the level of the ground, and extended about thirty yards each way, and on one side a flight of steps led up to it. In the middle was erected a trilithon of such huge stones as to astonish Christian, who was quite ignorant of the stupendous monuments that exist in many parts of Eastern Poly-nesia, which are all that is left of a race long since passed away into the limbo of lost nation-alities. A race of giants built them, the Omëans said, when the gods first haled the islands up from the bottom of the sea. A large fire burned brightly beneath the rude arch formed by the stones, which cast a ruddy glare upon the scene, and fitfully lit up the un-wieldy and hideous figure of the god and the dark masses of the forest trees all round. Before this fire in times of old, Soma whispered to North, a human sacrifice was always offered up to Tamagoru, and into it the body of the still quivering victim was cast to appease the god; but now the old religion was fading, and a less fearful oblation was made in its place, which was emblematic of the more ancient rite.

By the red blaze of the fire, which every now and then he stooped to replenish, the wild figure of the *marete* could be seen as he paced upon the platform. His costume was a strange one, and was meant to be awe-inspiring. It consisted of the usual T band, that was worn by all the men, and in addition festoons and loops of human hair were tied in bunches to his ankles, knees, wrists, and elbows, and a heavy girdle of it was round his waist. His face was painted with some bright red volcanic earth, and his own hair was frizzed and tortured into a wild sort of halo which stood out all round his head. At first he pretended not to see them, and continued to walk about and gesticulate as though he were possessed; he was successful in producing this impression, for Soma said in an awe-struck voice—

' See, Tamagoru is with him.'

After a few moments Soma, who had cautioned North to stand quite still lest some mysterious harm might befall him, ventured to call to the *marete* that they were here; and with a few preliminary shivers, which seemed to convulse his whole frame, the priest

came sufficiently to himself—'the god had left him'—
to notice them.   He beckoned to the two votaries to
come up the steps to the *malae,* and at the same time
advanced to meet them.   He took Soma aside for a
moment and spoke rapidly with him, and on Soma
nodding an assent, he led them to the fire and the
great trilithon, and placing them before him, he
addressed them for a short time in a language which
neither Soma nor North understood, and of the meaning of which he himself was probably ignorant, for
it was the sacred priest's language, which was an old
and obsolete form of Omëan.   At the end of this
he stood for a few seconds perfectly silent as
though listening intently, then the same strange con-
vulsive shiver passed over him, and he said in a high,
thin, whistling voice, which was supposed to be that of
the god, who again possessed him—

   '*Io, liki hi tappa.*'   (Yes, throw in the *tappa*.)

At this Soma stepped towards the fire, and telling
North to do exactly as he did, he untied the great
knot of his dress of state, which fell in soft folds at his
feet.   Gathering all this up in his arms, he threw it
on the fire.   Christian did as he was bid, and for a
moment the light of the flames was dimmed by the
mass that lay upon it, but the next it sprang up with
renewed vigour, and rose in long tongues of quivering
flame that licked and curled about the great stones of
the trilithon above it.   The heat upon their naked
bodies, for now they wore nothing but the *mahi*, was
so great that for a time they had to step back, but
the voice of the priest, still speaking in the shrill tones
of Tamagoru, called them back.

   '*Bemo hi tauto*' (now the blood also), he cried.

At these words Soma looked at Christian to see

whether he could discover any signs of a wish to retreat, but he only answered this glance with a smile. Of the two men the Polynesian was the more moved, for an inherited reverence and a lifelong fear of the god before whom he was acting possessed his soul. It was not that Christian was unmoved, the whole surroundings were too solemn and impressive not to appeal to his emotional nature; but he, of course, had no fear of the deity, and only felt a strange thrill of delight as the moment arrived for the ceremony which was at once so barbaric and so savagely poetic.

The two men faced each other before the trilithon, through which gleamed the hideous carved face and shapeless trunk of the idol, and the firelight shone full upon them, throwing into startling relief the prominences of their swelling muscles, and marking with a vivid contrast the colouring of the men. Soma had evidently been well instructed as to the ritual of the ceremony, for he never had to appeal to the watching *marete*, and Christian, who was quick enough of perception, had only to act exactly as his friend did. Soma lifted North's left hand and placed it open-palmed upon his breast, and then giving him one of the small stone knives, he put his own hand upon Christian, lifting the right, grasping his knife, high in the air. Then looking deeply in his friend's eyes, which were level with his own dark ones, he said—

'Strike into my arm till the blood flows down.'

As he spoke both he and Christian struck simultaneously, and the blood poured swiftly down the smooth skin of the upper arm, gleaming rich and ruddy in the leaping firelight.

'Now drink my life as I drink yours.'

It was a moment of strange savage exhilaration, and neither man felt the pain of the wound as each bowed his head for a second to the arm that rested on his breast.

'And now give drink to the god,' said Soma in a husky voice, and grasping Christian, who moved like a man in a dream, by the hand, he led him to the fire which burned before the deity, and each shook off into the flames an offering of the life-blood which pulsed strong and warm from their true hearts.

They only stayed a few moments after this at the *malae*; the priest bound up their arms to stanch the bleeding, then they turned and retraced their steps to the town.   They walked, as they had come, in almost absolute silence.   Perhaps both had much to think of; it seemed, at any rate, to Christian that those few drops of alien blood in his veins were already acting as a ferment, and producing a strange, subtle, savage change in him; and, without thinking about it, he felt, with an absolute conviction, that a new mysterious tie had been created between them that was irrevocably binding.

CHAPTER VIII

IT is sad how soon we forget the dreams we dreamed in childhood—the waking dreams I mean—for they would suffice to gild much of after-life for us. Christian had not forgotten all of his, and perhaps it was this very thing that tinged his waking thoughts with poetry, and kept the clear, frank look of childhood in his eyes, for all he had seen and experienced and done. For without being particularly inclined to wrongdoing, there was still enough of the old Adam in him to let him often go astray; but what he may have done had left no marks upon his character, for none of his sins were sins of meanness or deceit. It is the knowledge of our guilt that stains us, and he had sinned in innocence.

The next morning, after the visit to the *marae* on the mountain, it almost seemed to Christian that he was living in one of those early, glowing visions, the world was so very fair. The sun had not yet risen, although the day was light. He looked across the house to where Soma lay, and saw that he still slept soundly, so he sprang up quietly and left the place without disturbing any of the men. A soft mist filled the valley and hid the sprouting of the grass and the budding of the leaves, as though Nature were coy and desirous of hiding her spring mysteries from the prying eyes of men.   Christian stepped out into this sweet, soft sea which drifted round him in cool white clouds. Above him he could see the gray palm crowns waving slowly in the clear upper air, and near at hand the great green banana leaves glistening with the dew.

He looked about him with all the gladness of the morning in his soul, and felt with rapture that he was alive, *alive*; and as he walked across the *bara* towards the forest he burst out singing from sheer happiness and fulness of life, as birds do at the coming of another day.   He thanked God daily—that great God of whom, poor mortal, he knew nothing and whom he could not understand—by the happy psalm of living, better than he ever could with hymns and praise.   Most of us are thankless wretches who go grumbling through life at the powers that be, forgetting all the time that we have life, the greatest gift of all.   It is our own fault if we fail to make the most of it.   Here was this poor castaway, with not one of the things that people think are conducive, and even necessary, to happiness; he had neither house nor home of his own, no family, no wealth, but he had youth and health and strength and freedom—and he sang.   He had life to enjoy, and time to enjoy it in.

At times when he thought of the boundless lands that were his to travel in—when he felt the wild wind of heaven blow upon him and remembered that all the great blue sea of air was his—when he heard the dear voice of the ocean, and saw it racing beneath him as it bore him along, he felt that his heart was too great for him, and, drinking in a draught of freedom, he would shout for very happiness.   One thing only is necessary to him who would know what life has of living and what the world has for bestowal—freedom.   Not freedom alone of time and command of one's own body, but freedom from wants. He whose happiness depends upon mere luxuries of living is a slave. Food and drink we all can gain, thank Heaven, with little labour, if simplicity will satisfy us—if not, we are bondsmen till death frees us.

How comically strange it is that men should labour, as they do, through all the best hours of the day, through all the best years of their life, to gain things which not only are not necessary but which they would be better without. We are slaves to a mere idea, and we toil the long years through for it. Mankind is always struggling for something it wants, but which it does not need in the least.

Christian was evidently intent upon some purpose, for as he left the still sleeping town he closely examined every flowering plant and bush that he passed, and sometimes, when he thought he recognised a resemblance to what he sought, he would stop and look more closely, and compare the blossoms with a little bunch of still unfaded flowers he carried in his hand, which, even in dying, exhaled an exquisite and delicate perfume that had a peculiar, penetrating fragrance unlike that of any other flower he had ever smelled. They were fragile and white, of a dazzling untransparent whiteness, their centres were of a curious green colour dusted with a heavy pollen, and the small bright leaves themselves had a healthy, delicious, aromatic odour, as though the sweetness of the plant ran riot through it, and was not to be confined alone to the moment of its blossoming.

Although he had now been in the island some time he had never found it growing, though, as a rule, nothing escaped his observing eye; yet this morning was not the first by many times that he had seen the flower. He had determined to find it growing, and to try thus to discover the mystery that hung about it, for its strange perfume haunted him; it seemed to linger all day long in some deep recess of his brain, and then at unexpected moments the unforgotten fragrance would pour itself upon his soul. It was thus he had found it.

One morning, some days back, when Christian awoke from his dreamless, youthful sleep, he found lying by his wooden pillow a bunch of these fragile forest flowers, still cool with the night's unvanished dew. He was naturally surprised, and asked Soma whether he had put them there or knew anything of them. This his friend denied. Night after night the same mysterious visitor placed these flowers near him, but never till he slept, so that North had never seen the girl who he knew must have made the maidenly gift. It seemed to him that it was the flowers that awoke him; he was half conscious of them in his sleep, and awoke to find them there. This went on for many days without any token being given of the hand that placed them there, until gradually a sweet dream-maiden formed herself in Christian's fancy to suit the fresh virginal perfume and the dainty charm of the flower, and a strange anxiety possessed him to find this girl who was so coy and yet so simply frank. He laughed at himself sometimes when he thought how dear this shadowy image was becoming to him, and half feared to destroy his ideal by meeting the real maiden. She was his constant companion when otherwise alone, and at times when, faithless to his high ideal, he was passing an hour with girls less demure than the damsel of the *somala*—as he learned the flower was called—he would suddenly think of her, and the warm flesh-and-blood maidens around him would become commonplace and lose their charm.

Christian's expedition that morning was useless; he could find none of the flowers, and after an hour so spent in the edge of the awakening forest, he came back to the town, to find Soma looking for him in all their usual haunts. Although he had told Soma of these nightly visits, he was unable to explain to him the poetic vision he had created for himself, and the great Omëan had laughed and said that Christian was in love with a shadow, and that he had much better console himself again, as he did, with all the pretty girls of the bay to whom he could make himself agreeable. Christian laughed and blushed, and said that this was quite another thing. He had a queer, charming way of blushing without being ashamed or confused, looking one in the face all the time, with his gray eyes undimmed, as though quite unconscious of it himself. It was this perhaps, as much as the fairness of his colour and the red that was so bright in his cheeks and lips, that had gained for him from the first the name of 'Papalangi tëa,' which Soma told him meant bright or rosy-faced stranger. By this title he was always spoken of, but his friends, as a rule, called him 'Kliss,' being the nearest that the genius of their language would allow them to approach to Chris.

That day Soma and North spent in their usual manner. There was always something to be done. Being a chief, Soma was not compelled to work in the *talo* or yam patches; his father's people did this, though he and Motuiti often joined in the labour if they had gone out to oversee them. The system of Omëo in that respect was feudal, or, more correctly, patriarchal; each chief was not only head but father of his own little clan, and had to see to the feeding and housing of his people, and they in return worked for him in times of peace and followed him in times of war. Very little work was exacted of them, for the ground was so rich and the climate so genial that small labour in Omëo had large results. That day Soma suggested, after they had worked some time upon the great canoe that Motuiti was building, that it was the best season for catching the land crabs, which not only do much damage to the crop of coco-nuts, but are also most excellent to eat. These crabs, besides being very large, are very brave and fierce, and give an exceedingly painful and even sometimes dangerous wound to their naked aggressors, for if they once get a firm hold of the flesh nothing will make them loose; and as they are very tenacious of life, it is often a long time before their clutch is relaxed. This element of risk adds great zest to the sport, and at certain seasons of the year—particularly when the young nuts are just ripening—it is frequently indulged in.

This expedition having been decided upon, Soma went to find Okotai, the young man who frequently joined in their sports, and having consulted with him as to which part of the coast they should go to, they started out for a place some distance round the western point of the bay. It took them an hour to reach this spot, which was favourable on account of the great number of coco palms that grew there on the beach, almost within reach of the wind-blown spray from the reef, which at that part of the island was close in-shore. The day was hot, so that it was with a feeling of relief that North flung himself down in the shade of a closely-growing hibiscus, for he had not as yet become quite acclimatised. Okotai and Soma appeared to be perfectly insensible to the direct heat of the sun, though their polished skins felt glowing to Christian when he touched them as he questioned them about it.

Okotai saw that North was parched with thirst, and offered to get him one of the great nuts that he might drink, but Soma stopped him with a word.

'Stay where you are. It is not you who have sworn *e ofa-namu* with Papalangi tëa.'

With this Soma singled out one of the tallest of the great palms that lifted its waving crest a hundred feet and more above the sand, as though in his willing service the greater the difficulty the greater the pleasure. It always gave Christian the greatest delight to see one of these fine Omëans climb a palm; they did it with such easy disdain of the really athletic feat. He never could accomplish it himself, though he often tried; it seems as though the necessary training and practice can only be gained in childhood. The way Soma climbed the smooth branchless trunk was this: clasping the stem with his hands as high above his head as he could reach, he placed the soles of his bare feet on the sides of the tree, and throwing his body back till his arms were straight, he moved first a hand and then a foot, as though he were walking up the tree on all fours. It was a splendid sight to see the easy play of his great muscles beneath his polished skin; and as he neared the top of the palm, where the slender stem grew slenderer still, it bent and swayed about beneath his weight at every movement he made. He stopped for a moment and laughed, and called down to Christian to come and join him, saying that it was like being at sea. When he had reached the top, where the great leaves sprang in noble curves, he passed an arm over one of the stout central ribs, and choosing two of the finest nuts from the number that were clustered thickly together where the leaves began to grow, he twisted the great green shining fruit from the tree and flung them crashing down. He descended the tree quickly, and tearing away the tough green husk and carefully knocking off the top of the thin white shell, he handed it to North—a large ivory cup filled with the coolest and clearest of liquids.

They sat after this very quietly in the shade of the bush where Christian was lying, that they might not frighten away their intended prey, and after a short time they were rewarded by hearing a tiny, tinkling, rustling sound on the stones and sand of the beach, which announced the approach of one of the large crabs. Okotai, who was nearest, held up a cautioning hand, and peering through the leaves he saw a superb crab approaching a palm. This it quickly began to ascend. When it had almost reached the top the men ran out and gathered a great bundle of the coarse grass that grew on the shore just above high-water mark; this they tied round the stem of the palm at about a height of seven feet from the ground. North watched this proceeding with the greatest interest, for he quite failed to understand for what purpose this was done. He soon learned.

As soon as the grass was securely tied Okotai struck the palm sharply with a heavy stone several times to alarm the crab, which immediately began to climb down to escape to the sea. When it reached the little ledge of grass it thought it had arrived at the bottom, and loosing its hold it prepared to hurry off; instead of which it was dashed to the ground, and whilst it was stunned Okotai securely tied the one great claw together, which it uses to open the nut and to attack its enemies, and then made it captive to the end of a pole, by which means he meant to carry it back home. The sport went on for some little time, several large crabs being caught, and then after a long swim in the sea, they returned with the fruits of their labour to the town.

The evening of the same day, whilst the *ava* drinking was going on in Motuiti's house, Christian slipped out into the deserted *bara*, and made his way unobserved to the beach. It was one of the occasions when he wished to be alone, from no feeling of moroseness or melancholy, but simply with the desire of being by himself and enjoying the thoughts which no one could enter into, for the reason that they were not defined enough for himself to express. They were more moods of feeling or states of experience than formulated ideas.

It was one of those tender, odorous nights that are unknown in our cold northern world, with the sweet warm air all murmurous with the sleepy sound of the surf slowly beating on the reef—a sound that seemed rather to *fill* the silence than to break it. The wide-eyed stars burned steadily in the great purple arch of the sky, and the moon, as it slowly sank amidst the sleeping hills, fringed the long line of the shore palms with silver light. It was the sort of night when God seems young again, and to smile on this old earth of ours with His earlier smile. All Nature then seems large and sympathetic, and to love is as easy as to breathe—and almost as necessary. Love is then not outside of us, but part of us.

As Christian crossed the *bara* several of the young

men, with their evening wraps of white *tappa* floating behind them, hurried past him without a word; he knew what their errand was, and shortly from the groves of *dakuru* and the bread-fruit there rose their lovers' music.   Hush! for a moment, and then from beyond the valley of bananas came an answering song.   Often, after sleep had fallen on forest and town, on mountain and dusky valley, this serenaders' music rose, and frequently the midnight moon was high before the sweet sounds ceased to echo amidst the shadowy hills.

The shore was quite deserted when Christian reached it, and he turned and walked past the great canoe-shed, the shadow of which, sharply defined on the white sand, stretched out to where the little lagoon waves broke rippling on the beach.   He walked past this towards a certain little bay, where rocky walls enclosed the beach of smooth white sand, and, as though to screen it further from sight of the town, tall bushes, and here and there a palm, grew thickly in their crevices, almost within reach of the spray.   Down the gray moss-grown rocks heavy festoons of night-blooming creepers grew, that in places wove between the tree-trunks a dense and almost impenetrable veil of foliage and flowers.   This little cove was one of Christian's favourite haunts, and that night its silence and remoteness seemed to call to him to come.

He scrambled through a narrow opening in the mass of weathered rocks, brushing aside the sweeping fronds of the ferns that grew there, to get to the beach. Here, at the foot of a gnarled hibiscus, he threw himself down, and leaning against the trunk, looked out to sea, following the broad shimmering pathway that the moon made on the water till it ended in the white

fluctuating veil of the surf.   Nothing moved save now
and then a bird in the bushes near him, or some of the
great winged bats would skim before him without a
sound, like a drifting shadow between him and the
moon.   The softened music of the lovers' *fangos* still
went on, but that seemed as much a part of the tropic
night as the perfume of the *udu* and the wild jasmine
flowers.   North sat there—at least it seemed so to
him afterwards—in a curious state of expectancy, but
expectancy of what he knew not.

How long he had lain there he knew not when a
slight sound of rustling leaves on the rocks above him
made him turn his head just in time to see a young
and slender girl part the branches and come springing
lightly from one rock to another till she reached the
sand.   She never looked towards where Christian was,
and had she done so she would have failed to see him,
so darkly he lay in the shadow.   For a moment she
stood irresolute, as though trying to be afraid, as girls
will all the wide world over, and Christian could see
by the clear bright moonlight that not only was she as
exquisitely formed and as graceful as a wood nymph,
but her face, round which her soft hair fell in masses
of long waves and curls, was as lovely as a dream.

She stood thus for a moment, and then seeing how
bright and clear the moonlight fell upon the sand, she
turned her face towards the water, and casting aside
the light covering she wore round her shoulders, she
raised her shapely young arms above her head, and
waving them gracefully as she moved she broke into
a strange little surging song and danced downwards
to the sea.

Now all the young men and maidens in Omëo dance
as no other people in the world can do; with such

exquisite grace in the restrained freedom of the measure, with such litheness and buoyancy and such unerring precision, but never had Christian seen dancing like this. The girl danced for sheer happiness and fulness of life, with delight in the poetry of her movement and the maidenly passion of her *abandon.* It seemed to North as though she were the very spirit of young and happy girlhood, whilst still the untouched heart of a child beats in the breast of the perfected woman.

As the little waves crept up the shore, broke with a silver murmur and then rolled back, she advanced and receded too, with a pretty mockery of them that was inexpressibly poetic. It almost seemed that her dance was copied from the movement of the water. At length she followed with her dancing step a wave as it ran back to the sea, stooping and moving her arms as though she drove it before her, and then stood still dabbling her pretty arched feet in the little foaming shallows. She swayed from side to side—as though the spirit of the measure still were in her— like a graceful young palm in a breeze, watching her dark shadow on the level sand. Suddenly the idea seized the wilful young creature to dance a wild dance with her own silhouette for a companion, and Christian could hear, where he stood, the laughter of the girl at her own distorted image.

It was now that for the first time Christian noticed that her dark hair was surmounted with a coronal of starry white blossoms, and that round her neck and resting on her bosom was a little wreath of the same pale flowers. The conviction flashed upon him suddenly that this beautiful young thing was the secret giver of the *somala,* and his heart gave one great throb in his throat as he thought it. All the dreams he had been dreaming for the last hour in that moon-haunted place vanished away then; life was beautiful enough from that moment without the aid of visions.

He dare not speak or call to her, for he knew that if he startled her she would spring away and be lost to him, perhaps for ever, and for a little time he stood there—for he had risen to his feet before her beauty as a knight before his lady—thinking how he might let her know who it was that was there without frightening her away at the first sound. Then it occurred to him that she might have heard him sing, as he often did all about the town, so in a voice so low as scarcely to be above a whisper, he began very quietly to sing.

The girl heard him at once and stood quite still, with her arms raised in the air in the startled position she took at the first note, and with her face turned towards the sound. She must have known Christian from the first, for it was one of his favourite songs, and his voice and the music were both so unlike anything Omëan. She slowly let her arms fall to her sides, but otherwise she did not move as Christian, still singing, softly came out of the shadow on to the sand.

He held out his open hands to her, entreating her not to go, and she stood still as though enchanted, though her heart, poor child, beat thick and fast. As Christian drew near to her he ended his song suddenly, for by the odour of the flowers she wore he was sure it was his nightly visitant. How beautiful she was,—how clear and deep her wondrous eyes! He felt in that moment that the real and the ideal girl were one,—that here at last was the woman he could love. He was sure of it, for such a flood of love surged from his beating heart that in that one moment all the world was

changed. He did not stop to think what he should say,
in moments of such high passion words somehow find
themselves; but speak he did, and in a voice so low and
sweet that he could not recognise it for his own.

'*Mo gua somala a'cu; O'ia fe gua te ofa.*' (You are
my somala flower; oh, how I love you.)

'*Io, te i he cacala.*' (Yes, it is I who put the flowers.)

Life runs in simple lines in Polynesia; thank Heaven,
it is an Eden yet, where Eve still keeps her simplicity
and Adam his directness; so that this was introduction
enough for these two very human beings. North's
arms were no longer empty, for Utamè had run to their
embracing shelter, hiding her face on his breast.

CHAPTER IX

THE next few months were for Christian perhaps the happiest in his life; something new and beautiful had entered it, which seemed to change him in some mysterious manner without altering the outer man. His character was deepened and ripened by a love that he felt from the first was different from anything that he had before experienced. His emotions and affections became concentrated as though the expansiveness of his bright nature being confined within narrower limits flowed fuller and deeper. It was not that the broad generousness of his character was lessened by this new great love, but it was as though a strong river had forced a passage through some wide lake, which left its surface unchanged but had within it a hidden passage where all the deeper currents flowed.

He felt this change himself in many ways, but particularly in the curious alteration in his feelings for other women. All men, as males, love all women—unless old and ugly—but there comes a time, or should do, when each man loves one woman only, and with *all* his heart. There should be another word for this love, which may be of the same great genus as the first, but is most certainly of another species altogether. Then other women fade, as such, and have no power of feminine attraction for that one man. It was this change that had befallen Christian.

Since that first night when he had found Utamè dancing in the moonlight, many complications had entered his life ; the simple strand of it had become entangled into a more intricate web. He had now gained a perfect mastery of the not difficult language, and with it a knowledge of their beliefs and customs without which the force of the intricacies would not have been comprehensible. It was from Soma and Utamè herself that he first learned the difficulties that lay in his path. She had warned him from the first hour that their love and their meetings must be secret, and had tried to explain to him the reason, but it was from Soma that he had learned the validity of her statement.

In Omëo, as in all Polynesia at that time, the strictest system of *tabu* existed, as it had always done from time immemorial. The power of *tabu* was absolutely in the hands of the chiefs, who claimed descent from the *atuas* (the divinities and divine heroes of the people), and by them was rigidly enforced as their chief means of control of the populace. By *tabu* all the rights of the chiefs were protected, their property was respected, and by it they could not only veto anything that their inferiors thought of doing, but they could claim almost anything that they possessed. By tabuing a grove of coco palms, or a crop of *talo* or yam, these were better protected than they would have been by any actual guard, for the direst consequences—disease and death—followed any infringement of this unwritten law.

So that when Utamè, soon after she and Christian first met, told her lover that from her birth she had been tabued to the son of Faäori, the great chief of the eastern district of the island, he knew the consequences of the risk they ran in putting themselves in opposition, not only to the chief Faäori himself but to the whole system of *tabu* which they were breaking. Christian naturally had no fear of any but natural physical results, but Utamè shared the general opinion of the dangers of thus opposing the gods; but the natural bravery which seems to be instinctive in women when they love or when any danger threatens the object of their affection, made the girl forgetful or careless of the issues. She loved and she abandoned herself to that, and happy in the knowledge that Christian loved her as ardently as she loved him, she closed her eyes to the future.

Nor was this the only difficulty that lay before them : another and a darker thread wove itself into the warp that crossed the bright woof of their life. Utamè had told North of this very soon after they had first met, not only as a warning for himself but to ask his assistance to protect her from, and possibly revenge herself upon, a certain Tama-iru who had for some months, regardless of the *tabu* under which Utamè was placed, been making a savage courtship to her.

Just as in other countries a love that is not returned becomes, if too sedulously forced upon a woman, at first distasteful, then annoying, and finally hateful, so it was in Omëo, and Utamè, who at the beginning may not have disliked this man Tama-iru, grew to hate him when he would take no refusal. Christian, who had had some experience, found that European women were after all not very different at heart from their Omëan sisters—for woman never civilises. It is she who keeps alive the elemental passions ; love, hate, and jealousy all are hers, and ten times stronger than in civilised man.

Christian had made allowances for feminine exaggeration in Utamè's statement, but one night some time after he had first heard Tama-iru's name, he received from Soma corroborative evidence as to the man's character. North had had a tiring day, fishing on the reef beyond Raiëtea with a band of joyous comrades, and he had lain down to sleep before the rest of the household. He was just entering that first great field of sleep, where on one hand dreams lie and on the other facts, so that the wanderer therein scarce knows truth from fantasy, when he felt some one leaning over him. It was Soma, who had come in and thought his friend was sleeping.

Perhaps North was tired, or the flickering light of the burning *dakua* gum cast some sad shadow on his face, for as he lay half asleep his expression was melancholy. Sleeping faces are often sad, as though the body mourned its absent intelligence, or because the soul remembers then some earlier joy that our waking moments forget. In Christian this was the more marked as his expression was usually so happy a one, and now all the daytime smiles were gone. He did not open his eyes, for he was only in that state of half asleep which makes everything seem dreamlike that goes on though the faculties are awake, and he knew who it was above him. He heard Soma sigh and then say—

'Does he wish he were back in his own country? Is he tired (*fuka bibiko ange*) of us Omëans? Perhaps he wants the white folk again. He does not know that his friends and his *ofa-namu* love him more than they.'

'Yes, he does,' said Christian suddenly, and lifting his arms he clipped the dear fellow round his warm brown neck. 'He does know it, and Soma *he loto-ua* (the double-minded) knows it quite as well. But I am in trouble. Utamè says she is in danger, and thinks that I am, from Tama-iru, and I do not know him or where he lives.'

'I know Tama-iru,' Soma said; 'he is strong, he has many men in his following (*kau takanga*), and he is false and very cunning. You must fear him, for he is one that strikes without calling. He is Faäori's sister's son, and is a chief in Oneroa (the eastern part of the island), but he is also *tabu* here in Otorangi.'

'But Utamè is *tabu* to Faäori's son; he cannot marry her any more than I.'

'No, but Tama-iru is strong, and he may make Faäori and our chief Ilo take off the *tabu*. But your heart is sick, my *ofa-namu*, for love of a woman. The dances no more please you and the *ava* is tasteless. You shall take her away. This thing shall be done.'

Christian had sat up when he began to speak, and at Soma's last words he nipped his friend's hand with so sudden and almost fierce a grip that he left little doubt of his wishes.

'How, when?' he said, with his voice a little raised, perhaps, above a tone of caution.

'To-morrow; just before the sun is up the fishes bite the best,' answered Soma, in a clear conversational tone, and unexpectedly extinguishing the flaming gum with a sudden movement of his foot. 'Hush! there is some one there. I saw his face by that post.'

The other men began to come straggling in, so that no more could be said just then, and Christian had to possess his soul in patience with the little hope that Soma's words had given as a comfort to his heart.

Some months went on after this, and in that time, although North had made many plans for taking Utamè off to another part of the island where neither Faäori's nor Ilo's *tabu* would be of consequence, he had been unable to carry any of them into execution. But it was not likely that he and Utamè had not often met in the interval, for when two lovers are determined to meet they are more than a match for the rest of the world, if only they are not suspected, and so far their secret had been kept. It was a rare occurrence if they did not see each other some time in each twenty-four hours; and the love that they bore for one another had grown steadily in their hearts.

They had turned to their advantage the one great difficulty that lay between them—the *tabu*, for the place where they most often met was the little river that flowed out into the lagoon, a mile or two from Otorangi, and opposite to which was the opening in the reef through which Soma and Christian had passed in their canoe. This stream had always been *tabu* to the god Rorutu, from the foot of whose mountain, Monoriro, it flowed down. The name of the river accounted for its sacredness, for it was called Mimi-Rorutu. This stream was accounted so holy that none but the chiefs, and they very rarely, visited it, and for this reason Christian had taken a small canoe to it, that Soma had given him, and had hidden it some little distance up the stream under the close-growing bushes that overhung it in one place. In this canoe he and Utamè had spent many a long hot day, and sometimes Soma would be with them, sinking the frail craft with his weight to within an inch or two of the gunwale.

They were a joyous crew, laughing and singing like children, and, landing sometimes on one bank and sometimes on another, far back in the heart of the forest, they would picnic through the heat of the day, and come gliding down with the current as evening fell. But oftenest Christian and Utamè were alone.

It was a constant surprise to him to find such depths of feeling in the heart of this young girl, for notwithstanding her simplicity and innocence, or perhaps because of them, there were profundities of passion within her which found expression sometimes in most poetic language. Nothing to her was quite the simple fact that it would appear to others—things had inner meanings : flowers, birds, winds and mountains, sky and streams were so connected with gods and spirits and dead-and-gone heroes as to acquire a sort of second signification. All these things Christian loved to hear, and to watch Utamè's beautiful face and grave mysterious eyes as she told him of them was a joy that never ended. The very earnestness of their recital, and the simple, straightforward language in which she clothed her ideas, bore with them a sort of conviction, to the charm of which Christian was willing enough to lend himself. He could not bear to destroy their beautiful ideas too roughly, though gradually he taught her some of the nobler truths that he himself accepted.

He had another reason for not contradicting, both to Utamè and to others, all the facts of their religion : he knew that the religion of any people was according to their spiritual wants and requirements, and he saw with the keenest interest that with the civilisation that the Omüans were developing from their savagery, their religion was advancing with equal steps. This subject had always been of special interest to Christian's inquiring mind, for although poor he was not uneducated, and to watch, as it were, the gradual birth of a new religion which was taking place before his very eyes was an occupation exactly suited to the quiet, contemplative side of his character.

It was evident that over the old religion of Omëo—a religion of cruelty, blood, and threat—a strange sea-change was flowing; new ideas of beauty, tenderness, and grace were in the air, and with the instinct that is present in all human souls, these ideas were attaching themselves to personalities, and were weaving themselves slowly into the beliefs of the people from the very tenderness of memory with which they were recalled. New gods were being born—gods more beauteous, blithe, and human than those awful blighting powers of pain and pestilence, terror and death from which they sprang. A people who were joyous, happy, and glad in their very nature yearned for other gods than those which horror and hideousness expressed, those gods of which the frightful images in wood and rudely sculptured stone only too truly expressed the attributes. Beautiful themselves, they longed for deities they could love instead of those before whom they humbled themselves in terror.

This new, ideal movement was in the air, and the heroes of a recent past were quickly mounting to be the gods of the near future. People spoke with happy reverence of Iro Vearu, the beautiful young warrior whom the great-grandfathers of those then living as old men had known and fought with. He, they said, had never died and never grown old; he was the son of Tangaloa and a woman of Omëo; he had killed the last of the *hotua-pau*—the demons who had scourged the island; he had taught a new way of planting the *talo*; and the delight and ardour of the semi-worship offered to the son dimmed all the glory of that given to his dread father.

Whenever they passed it men cast flowers on the rock where the wondrous Teoroa first landed from her canoe on the island from that strange solitary, voyage she had made from the unknown to their known world. It brought them luck, they said, in love. To her the women prayed for help to win the men they loved, and for male children when they had won them. Here was a new Aphrodite.

To Lomangatini, who had crushed rocks and torn up trees for weapons in his warfare with the older gods who sought his destruction, all tales of heroism and strength were traced. He was the crystallised idea of all male force and valour; he was of larger growth than mortal men, and strength and courage were his gifts. He, too, was strong in love, and men laughed and flushed and prayed his aid sometimes when no danger was awaiting.

It was like being present at the birth of a new mythology, and Christian watched with the greatest delight the meeting of new thought with the old ideal, for the mass of the people still followed the older worship, so that the mountains and the fastnesses of the hills were ghost-haunted and made terrible by a superstition that was very living and which the new feeling had failed as yet to touch. Priests of the old worship were to be found all over the island, and in most of their groves and high places the altar-stones still ran with blood, for the Omëan gods hungered for human sacrifices, and nothing else than these noblest of victims would appease them when insulted or pro-

pitiate when their help was called. It was not only
the bulk of the population that bowed in terror of the
old worship, for the chiefs were the stanchest allies of
the priests, whose prayers and incantations, mysteries
and poisonings, were always at their service in return for
the protection that they gave.

Ideas of right and wrong were of course existing in
the old religion from the very fact of the partial civilisation of the people—that is to say, if the highest
ethical meaning of right and wrong did not exist, at
least it was decided by the unwritten laws, which lie
at the base of the simplest societies, what acts were
permissible and what punishable. But for all this
morals—according to our code—were wanting, and
the new religion that was forming, but not formulated
as yet, was little purer but much kinder than the old.

But amongst all the horrors and the incongruities
of the old Omëan faith one fact struck Christian as
being most strange, and that was that the theory of
atonement was thoroughly understood; a propitiation
of the gods was recognised by the means of the sub-
stitution of a self-sacrifice, or at times an enforced
sacrifice was sufficient, which was theoretically volun-
tary. It was this idea that lay at the root of all their
human offerings. Instances had been known of young
men immolating themselves to save the life of a well-
beloved chief, and women had destroyed their lives to
win their lovers back from disease or death, which
they believed were imposed directly by offended deities.
These heroic figures were the themes of many of their
songs, for all their history and their poems were sung
to music.

There was much that was beautiful in their simple
worship of the personification of the natural forces,

though in practice it was often terrible enough, and Christian grew to have a sort of affection for this old and superstitious faith in which he had not the least belief. There was a kind of half-tender, half-sorrowful feeling of veneration and romance about it which was greatly strengthened by the sincere and ardent love that he felt for a follower of it. He always wore a sacred charm of whale ivory about his neck that Utamè had given him, just as a Protestant lover might have worn a medal or a crucifix given by his Catholic mistress.

CHAPTER X

So the days passed, and weeks glided imperceptibly into mouths, until Christian had been a year on the island. Still no opportunity had occurred for the carrying out of Soma's plan; indeed the necessity for it had not arisen, as Faäori had not sent to claim Utamè for his son, and the girl had managed to keep secret her constant meetings with North. During this time Christian had not been idle; he had taught the people much, and by diverting a little stream along a hill-side he had begun a simple method of irrigation which greatly increased the quantity of land that was suitable for the growing of the *talo*—the root which was the staple of their food. By this and many a little contrivance that would have been considered simple and clumsy enough in Europe, he had gained a high place in the esteem of Ilo, the head chief of all the district, and in that of Motuiti and many of the lesser chiefs.

One great difficulty he had to contend with in the production of the articles he required for his improvements was the absence of all tools to which he was accustomed, for Omëo was in the stone age still, and everything that he wanted had to be fashioned with the utmost labour by means of the beautifully polished stone axes, adzes, and drills that the people themselves were in the habit of using. Fortunately the intelligence of the Omëans was of a high order, so that his workmen usually could carry out his intentions fairly well after he had given careful and reiterated instructions.

But notwithstanding all that he had done, and the constant goodwill that he evinced towards the chiefs and the people, he often found his plans obstructed, and that evil constructions were put upon his simplest actions, so that he was frequently hampered in the execution of his designs. This puzzled him at first, for he was unwilling to think that improvements could be objected to simply because they were innovations, though it was to that reason that he laid the difficulties placed in his path; but after some time he was able to trace all this ill-feeling to its source. It was Tama-iru, who by some strange instinct had discovered that it was North who came between him and Utamè, who, not daring to mention his own love for the girl, vented his jealousy by poisoning the ears of Ilo and the other chiefs with doubts and suspicions of North. All these reports having been proved by events to be groundless, North suffered really very little diminution of esteem.

Although Christian's temper was a sweet one and usually equable enough, it was not altogether angelic, and this constant backbiting and interference roused it to fever heat at last; so that one night when having gone to the canoe-shed, where he was building a boat for Ilo on a European model, for something he had left there, he found Tama-iru attempting to spoil the result of many weeks' work, he took the law into his own hands and punished him. As wrestling and boxing are two of the principal amusements of the Omëans,

Tama-iru was quite prepared to fight on equal terms with North, who fortunately had often boxed with Soma, Okotai, and other men, so that he knew the Omëan method and was acquainted with their tricks. On seeing who it was that was interfering with his work, North rushed up, and with the concentrated anger of many months of self-repression, he struck Tama-iru a blow on the side of the head that sent him reeling out of the shed. Then, thinking it unfair to take advantage of this first sudden attack—like the chivalrous fool that he was—even in dealing with so underhand an opponent as Tama-iru, he followed him out to the beach and waited a moment for the islander to recover.

Both men were eager to fight, and they rushed at one another like bulls when, pouring out a string of wild oaths upon his enemy, Tama-iru said he was ready. Christian soon found that his work would not be easy, for Tama-iru was not only very wiry and strong, but was an accomplished and practised boxer; but he had not Christian's dogged pluck. For some time they fought in perfect silence—their heavy breathing and the scattering of the dry sand as they madly turned and struggled being the only sounds— without either man gaining much advantage; but at last, as Christian landed a furious blow straight in Tama-iru's mouth, knocking out two of his strong white teeth, he overbalanced himself and fell full length on the sand.

According to Omëan rules of fairplay, Tama-iru should have waited till Christian had risen to his feet, but, maddened as he was by the pain of North's last blow, he rushed at him and, kneeling on his chest, attempted to strangle him as he lay beneath him. And here would have abruptly ended the history of Christian North had not the extraordinary strength of the muscles of his loins and back come to his assistance, for Tama-iru nipping his chest, with his knees on either side, as in a vice, would have kept him helpless beneath him till he was dead. But Christian did not mean to die, and digging his heels into the firm sand, and suddenly loosing his hold of his opponent's wrists, he seized him round the waist, and making a stupendous effort with his thighs and back, managed to roll over. Tama-iru's grasp relaxed a little as he tried to save himself from falling, and Christian sprang to his feet; and before Tama-iru had time to rise North turned, and seizing him at the back by the narrow *mahi* that was firmly tied about his waist, he grated his teeth together for the supreme effort, and with legs apart and the muscles of his shoulders and arms almost bursting through the skin, he lifted his wildly struggling enemy in the air, and, hoisting him to his breast with an effort that was worthy of Lomangatini himself, threw him clear over his head.

Tama-iru gave one despairing shriek as North threw him, and he fell head first upon the sand with a sickening thud. He lay there perfectly motionless, and Christian thought for a moment that he was dead, and in his then condition of hatred, heated by the violence of the life - and - death struggle only now finished, he little cared if he were. Stooping over the man, who lay in a heap just as he had fallen, he found that he was breathing, although completely stunned, and taking hold of him by the shoulders he moved him, with the utmost difficulty, for his own limbs were quivering with the intense exertion he had just undergone, to a more comfortable position. And now for a moment or two North was quite exhausted, and seated himself upon the sand by his senseless enemy. In a short time, seeing signs of returning consciousness in Tama-iru, he got up and went home, where, after telling Soma of the events of the night, he flung himself down on the mat-spread bed of fern and slept the sleep of the just.

This had occurred a couple of months ago now, and receiving no further challenge from Tama-iru, and hearing nothing said of the affair, about which Tama-iru had kept his own counsel, Christian was beginning to forget all about it; but Soma, who knew the nature of his countryman better than North could, cautioned him not to become careless. As nothing happened, however, Christian believed that Tama-iru had taken his punishment as a wise man, and meant to say and do no more in the matter.

The boat that he was building was now almost finished, and Christian began to feel that longing to have his work ended that all artists experience; he endured the anxiety as to its qualities, mingled with the delightful sensation of hope, that men feel towards the termination of a work into which they have thrown their whole heart. He had not seen Utamè for the last three days, which had been unusually stormy and wild; so high had been the wind for these three days and nights of tempest, that the huge waves of the open ocean rushed upon the shores of the island in such gigantic rollers that they leaped the barrier of the reef and came crashing on the beach. But that day had dawned fair, and by noon the tranquil-hearted sun, never doubting the boon of his charity, shone out royally and genially, and flooded the earth with gold more precious than Ophir's, for his gold is a universal happiness.

Christian had not seen Soma since their morning meal; he was much occupied just then in paying his court to a very beautiful and well-born girl of Olasangu, whither he and his dead friend Maraki used to go, but at mid-day he came rushing into the shady canoe-shed where North was at work with his men. It always astonished him to find Christian steadily going on with his boat-building, for a Polynesian, although he can work hard by fits and starts, cannot understand a long-continued effort.

'Ilo has sent me for you,' he said. 'Leave your work. All of us are going to the shore with our *gualu lo-papa* (surf-boards). The wind is on shore, and the breakers pass over the reef.'

Several times since Christian had been in Omëo he had witnessed, and endeavoured to take part in, that noblest of all sports—surf-riding, and he was glad enough to join in it to-day. He left his work, and, like two boys let out of school, he and Soma ran back to the house to get the great polished surf-board. When they got back to the part of the beach where the greatest of the great rollers came swiftly but solemnly rushing on the shore, it was already trampled by the little crowd that had collected there. The place chosen was opposite the opening in the reef, for there the huge waves, unbroken by the coral barrier, came rolling into the land almost mountain high.

Surf-riding, besides being the most madly exhilarating of all manly and athletic sports, is one of the most beautiful and exciting to witness; for the players in it, who trust themselves in the midst of such gigantic force, seem so feeble and puny when compared with the strength of the elements they combat with and conquer. Already there were many men and women

in the water ; some far out at sea, and others close in
shore in the midst of foam and spray, being borne
lightly and swiftly along by the racing water beneath
them. The swimmers, carrying their light surf-boards
with them, enter the foaming water just as a huge
roller is about to break, and, diving through the dark
green mass of the moving water, they come to the
surface for a moment, and swim to meet the next great
wave, through which they plunge in the same manner.
They have to dive and swim through the roller, for if
they were caught on its moving crest they would be
carried back resistlessly and dashed upon the beach.

They swim in this manner steadily out to sea,
sometimes as far as a mile from land, pushing their
light boards before them ; then, having reached the
comparatively smooth water beyond the reef, they
wait a moment to choose some great splendid roller
on which to launch themselves. Getting on to the
very crest of this they throw themselves upon their
board, and taking the utmost care to keep the plank
at the right angle with the ridge of the wave, they are
carried along madly to the shore. It is a sort of wild
bird's flight between sea and heaven ; the strong wind
hurrying them along, and blowing out their wet and
tangled hair.

'I must go,' said Soma, his dark eyes flashing with
excitement; 'I cannot stay. The wind says to me,
"Come out to sea and fly back like a bird." Will you
come? I should love to be out there with my *ofa-
namu.*'

'I would come, I long to come; but you know,
Soma-gita, that the Papalangi cannot work the board.'

'Mine is large enough for two. If we can get out
I can bring you back. We must keep together.'

Without more ado the two men put on *mahis* of sea-weed—as is always done—and, only waiting for the oncoming of a gigantic billow, they plunged into the dark-rushing water. Soma felt Christian close to him in the water, and when they came to the surface they were shoulder to shoulder. Although Christian had many doubts as to his powers as a surf-rider, in which art he was absolutely a novice, it gave him a keen thrill of pleasure to be once more risking dangers with his companion in former perils, and it reminded him very vividly of that night, now long ago, when side by side they two escaped from the ship. There is always a strange sharp feeling of pleasure in knowing that the life one holds so dear is in jeopardy—it accentuates the sensation of living to feel that perhaps one may not enjoy it long; and although the danger that Christian ran was perhaps not very great, as he was with so tried and expert a swimmer as Soma, still it was present enough to his thoughts to add that wild thrill to his heart which he who bears aloft his life in his own hand feels.

So they swam out to sea, passing, as they went, many friends who were being borne back racing to the land; some of these were kneeling on their boards, some lying down, and others standing upright with feet apart, and with their sea-weed girdles and long hair blowing in the wind, which drowned their voices as they gaily shouted some short message to the outward bound. At last they passed through the great gates of the reef, and were out on the open breast of the heaving ocean, with its waves careering in unbroken force and the strength of the wind unchecked. They swam on until they passed the farthest man, and then they turned and waited for one of the

greatest waves which they could trust would roll on
with increasing swiftness to the land without a fall or
break. It was strange to be so near the land and yet
have no glimpse of it; but so it was, for the water ran
so high between them and the shore that they could
only have seen it from the crest of the waves, and
these they had had to dive through.

'*Gua mo teü ?*' (are you ready?) asked Soma. 'That
is the wave. You must lie down. I must stand up.'

Almost as he spoke they rose on the wave, and
Christian flung himself chest down on the broad
smooth plank, whilst Soma, who had not let go of the
board, flung himself on the top of him, and gradually
and steadily pulled himself up till he had a foot on
each side of North, and stood up to his full height.
They were safely launched, and the roller carried them
swiftly along with a perfectly steady motion that increased in speed as they neared the land.

It was a glorious time, worth all the labour and
effort necessary to gain it, and the delight of the
repose and the swift airy flight was rendered doubly
intense by the strength of the full fresh gale of wind
and the awfulness of the sea's great roaring as it broke
on the reef and again on the shore. North turned and
looked up at Soma as he stood above him in all the
magnificence of his manly beauty, like Neptune con-
trolling whilst delighting in his subject elements, and
his face glowed with a sort of inspiration.

All sense of danger was lost to Christian, and there
was nothing left but the delight in the wild beauty of
the moment and the strange rapture of abandoning himself to the great forces around, which bore him along like
a feather in the wind. It seemed to him for the time
that he and his friend were alone in the universe

amidst all God's elements let loose about them, of which they seemed—so impersonal was the moment—an undivided part.   He forgot Utamè, he forgot his great love for her, and Soma was as oblivious of all that he held dear.   It was one of those times when Christian's sight was as a veil through which facts passed to the vision within and strangely mingled truth with fantasy.

As the sea grew shallow the great waves rose higher yet as they rolled upon the land, and it is then that the real danger of surf-swimming begins, for if the swimmers fail to guide their frail barks to a safe, sandy part of the beach, they have to turn and strike out again to sea to avoid being dashed upon the rocks. This decisive moment had now come for Soma and Christian; from the crest of their great roller, which was beginning to curve for its breaking, Soma could see the crowded beach, and he saw, too, that they were being carried upon a low and jagged reef of limestone that in one place jutted up through the sand.

'*Hugu koi ma kakau!*' (dive and swim back), he shouted to Christian; but he either failed to understand him, or the crashing of the breakers drowned his voice, for Christian did not dive until a moment too late, and he and Soma were torn from the board and swept along like straws in a mill-dam. Blinded in the whirl of waters Christian seemed to lose consciousness, though he turned and tried vainly to swim back; then he felt himself seized by two strong arms, and he was pulled down under the great dim wall of water.   The next moment Soma was flung upon the sand, and, with Christian in his arms, staggered out of the back rush of the water.   He had managed to dive as they were being cast upon the rocks, and the swimmers making a few superhuman strokes the following wave threw them on the beach. Breast to breast, and with his great heart beating against Christian's, he dragged him back from the very jaws of Death, whose breath had chilled their souls.

CHAPTER XI

THE old priest Paori was about to die. When Christian had first come to the island this old man, who was a chief as well as priest, had shown much more reserve in accepting him than the rest of the people had done; but after some time, when he saw that North meant them no ill, and he had had time to study his character, this reserve had melted, and Christian had constantly visited him at the *pure atua* as well as at his own house. Slowly quite an affectionate relationship grew up between the old and the young man, for, savage as the one was and civilised as was the other, they were both thoughtful men, and they met on common ground in some cases. If Paori learned much from Christian, he on his side gained a great deal from the Omëan, for they frequently met, and their talks often extended far into the night.

Christian could not help admiring the bold determination of the dying priest to retain his old faiths in all their crudeness, for nothing North could say and none of the arguments he could produce had any effect on the belief of the staunch old heathen.

'*Mea tu ke*' (these be strange things), he would say sometimes to Christian; 'but I know they are not true. You cannot prove them, Papalangi tëa. And Paori has his gods and has seen their works.'

And now it was his time to die. He sent for
Christian early one evening, feeling that his end
was not far off, and the Englishman went to his
house, but the young men there said that Paori
was not there; he had been carried to the *pure atua*,
where he was having talk with the gods. Thither
across the *bara* North followed him, and, passing
through the palisade that surrounded it, he entered the
high-roofed temple. It was growing dusk outside, the
fleeting glory of the tropic sunset had faded, and in
the great house of the gods it was almost dark; still,
Christian could see his way across the house to where
Paori lay. But another darkness was falling upon
the old man, and though he recognised the step he
could not see his visitor.

'*Gua aku faho?*' (is it you, my son?) he asked.
He often in these last days had called Christian so,
for the dying priest was childless.

'I have been talking with the gods this night,' he
went on. 'Paori is going away. You must not seek
me, for I cannot be found.'

'Do you suffer much to-night?' asked North,
sitting down upon the mats where the old man
lay.

'No, nothing,' he answered stoically, though Christian could see that he was in pain. He had always,
without exception, given the same answer to North
when he had asked him similar questions, though it
was apparent that it was not as well with him as he
said. The break-up of a strong constitution, though
it was old age alone that Paori suffered from, must
necessarily be painful in some degree.

'Before I go away I want to give you something.
It is the *kahua* (neck ornament) that the god Tane

gave to his first *marete*. Keep it hidden in the folds of your *mahi*. It will bring you luck.'

As he spoke he pulled with difficulty out of his own waist-cloth a small and very rudely-carved flat figure in dull gray stone, and handed it to North by the worn piece of sinnet from which it hung. Christian had never seen the like of it in the island, for it was quite dissimilar to any of the carved wooden figures that he had seen in the temples or on the house-posts. Whether it represented a male or female he could not say, as it was of so venerable an age that, although the stone was of the hardest quality, the features had all been rubbed smooth.

'Show that to any *marete* on the island in times of danger,' Paori went on, 'and he will aid you.'

'But why give it me to-night?'

'To-morrow I shall be gone.'

He spoke quite calmly, and evidently had not the slightest fear of death; he had lived his life and was weary now, and was quite content to sleep at the end of it. He had sent all the men out of the temple when Christian came, and they were quite alone together. To his surprise, North felt no uneasiness or fear at being thus alone with the dying man, for Paori accepted the fact so simply, and had so little fear of an event that appeared to him so natural, that Christian was quite calm, and talked quietly with him of those great questions which were uppermost in his mind.

It had grown quite dark whilst they were talking, and suddenly from the *bara* came the happy sound of girls laughing and the shouting of the young men. Soon a little wavering, flickering light came in at the open door of the *pure*, as they lighted their torches and the great fires of dry coco-nut husks for a night dance that had long been spoken of.   Then shortly the sound of the singing and the regular beating of the music, and the low 'thud, thud' and soft rustling noise of the naked feet as they fell in measured time upon the hard dry surface of the flattened ground, rose up in the silent night.

'Do you hear the young girls and the men dancing?' said Paori.   'That is right; they are young, and I, I have seen their grandfathers and their fathers die. I will sit up that I can see them in the doorway,' and with a surprising energy he raised himself on the mats and sat there cross-legged.

'Tell me,' said Christian presently, for he was anxious to know the real thoughts of the old savage, 'when you go shall you see again those fathers and grandfathers that you saw die?   Tell me, for you are old, I am young.'

'All chiefs, all those descended from the gods, can never die.   They live again somewhere and are chiefs again.   This will die, and this,' said the old man, laying a hand on Christian's leg and next upon his hand; and then, as he touched him on the breast, he added, 'but there is something here that will not die.'

He could not explain his meaning when Christian questioned him.   'It is true,' he said.   And then, as though to dismiss the subject, he said, 'Go, call in all the chiefs; I want the *ava*.'

This drinking of the *ava*, which has not been spoken of before, was one of the most important and ceremonious customs of the Omëans, besides being one of their chief pleasures.   The practice of it was confined almost entirely to the upper class, and was in a manner connected with their religion, so that although it was most frequently indulged in, it never quite lost its sacred significance. All feasts ended with it, and all important questions were discussed over it, and *ava* was drunk upon all serious occasions, so that Christian was not surprised that Paori called for it now that he was about to take his farewell of his tribe.

Christian went out and left the old man in the great dark house, sitting up alone before the rude images of his gods, facing Death, in whose presence he felt himself, with a dignity that nothing could disturb. Christian walked to the *nufa*, the great wooden drum that stood on the raised platform on which the *pure* was built, and beat loudly upon it to call together all the chiefs in the town, and sent a young man, whom he found sitting at the opening in the palisade, to inform Ilo of Paori's wish. The dancing on the *bara* ceased at the first stroke, and the men came running up to know the reason for the summons.

In a short time the chiefs had assembled at the *pure*, a torch was lighted, and the preparations were begun. The men seated themselves cross-legged round three sides of the house, whilst the fourth was occupied by a little crowd of singers and dancers, who performed during the whole time of the preparation of the *ava*. Before one young man the great, beautifully-polished *ava* bowl, which was taken down from its place in the roof of the temple, was placed, and then Ilo, being the greatest chief present, broke up and distributed the dry root of the plant, from which the drink is made, to ten or twelve of the finest and youngest men of the party. These pieces were presented and received with motions all made according to a strict etiquette, and then with great propriety and decorum the lads began to chew the root to a soft paste, with their strong and gleaming white teeth. This was a process of some little time, for the root is hard and tough, but none of the men in the house moved or talked during the whole of it, with the exception of the seated dancers, who performed a beautiful series of uniform movements in exact time to the singing of the chorus. It almost seemed that appropriate music had been chosen, for the air was slow and dignified and sad, and the *hiba*, as this species of dance is called, was of the same character.

When all the *ava* root was reduced by this primitive method to a paste it was collected in the great three-legged bowl, which was pulled close up between the thighs of the drink-maker, and water being added, he manipulated it for some time and strained it often with a rough sieve. When all was ready he cried—

'*Gua ochi he ava, chii.*' (The *ava* is made, O chiefs.)

Then Ilo from his place cried out the name of Paori, and a young man stepping forward, received a cup of the drink, and walking across to where the old man sat, partly propped up by North's shoulder, he handed it to him, saying simply—

'*Inu koi*' (drink).

The old man took the cup, and resting it on one knee, for he was too feeble now to hold it up, he began to speak. His voice at first was very weak—though such was the breathless silence in the house that every word was plainly heard—but it grew in power as he went on.

'Chiefs,' he said, 'I am about to die. Paori drinks his last *ava*. To-night he will leave you. To-day the gods have been with me, and they have said that I should go this night. But, chiefs, the gods are jealous (*loto maharo*). All your hearts are not theirs as beforetimes. Evil will fall on Omëo. Who is Lomangatini that you worship him, and who Iro Vearu ? To show you for a sign that Tane still is Tane, and that Rorutu still is over all, to-morrow when you seek me I shall not be here. The gods have called Paori and they will take him away. Farewell, chiefs. Now go, leave me alone ; but you, Soma, son of Motuiti, stay with me.'

Then all those in the house rose and went out, one by one, each man pausing before Paori, saying, ' Farewell ! ' North had stayed to the last, as the old man was leaning heavily upon his shoulder, but he went too, as Paori said to him—

' You also, my son. I must speak with Soma alone. *Toëfua*, farewell ! '

As Christian gently moved the old priest to get up, Paori pulled his face to his and gave him the *uma*, which is the greatest sign of affection in Omëo, by pressing his nose to the forehead of the young man. North returned this salute and went out, followed to the last by the eyes of his old friend.

No sooner was he gone than Paori called to Soma, and, with a force that was surprising in a dying man, began to talk.

' Soma e Motuiti,' he said, ' this day the gods have called me and have said that you are chosen to help me in my going away. But you must swear an oath to keep secret from every one what the gods have told you to do. Swear.'

' I must tell the Papalangi tëa ; he is my *ofa-namu.*'

' There are no secrets between *ofa-namu* ; they are one man.'

Then Christian took the oath, the *fua ara*, on the *ava* they had just shared; and the old man said—

'You must go to the beach at Koiti-iti' (the place opposite to the opening in the reef), 'and there prepare a small canoe, putting in the paddle but no food or water. Then when the town is asleep return to me. Tell no one whither you go.'

Without hesitation or pause to inquire into the reasons of Paori's request Soma went out to do as he was bidden, leaving the old man facing his idols, which he could still see gazing at him with their sightless eyes of pearl shell and grinning with their teeth of cowries; then the last flicker of the dying torch went out and left him in the darkness and stillness of the house. What strange thoughts of a future or what brightened dreams of a long dim past filled the last hours of the solitary man! One grim determination was there that was unshaken by the icy hand of Death, which was stealing closer and closer upon him. He knew what that coldness meant, and all he hoped of Time was that he would leave him moments enough to execute his intention. The gods, these gods of his worship, had suffered slight, and his one hope was by his last hour to vindicate their strength. Was it a wilful, priestly trick, or did he deceive himself into believing his own message?

When Soma came back the whole *bara* was deserted; feeling that something mysterious was taking place that night, the people had all gone to their own homes. He entered the dark house where Paori, exhausted by the trying hour he had passed through in making his farewells to the chief, was lying on his mat breathing heavily. At first he thought that Paori slept, but the voice of the old man calling him by name brought him with less stealthy tread to where he lay.

'Is all ready?' he said. 'Have you the canoe prepared?'

'All is ready, *marete*,' answered Soma; 'but how will you get to the place? Koiti-iti is not near, and you have no strength.'

'I have strength but I must save it. Who knows what the gods may want of me this night. You must carry me, Soma-eki; your back is strong. It is for the gods.'

Soma said that he was ready if the old man would wait until he got a light from one of the cooking sheds near, as he wanted a piece of cloth to tie round his waist to better support his heavy burden. He came back in a moment with a burning stick and, Paori telling him where he would find a candle-nut torch, quickly got a light and took down one of the bales of cloth from the roof. From this he unrolled a piece of cloth long enough for his purpose, and tying it tightly round his waist, said he was ready.

Kneeling down before the mat and putting Paori's arms round his neck, he managed to get him on to his back, and stooping down at the low door of the temple he passed out, and descending the little steps of the platform on which the *pure atua* was built, started on his journey. The dying priest, though old and wasted, was a tall and strongly built man, so that the weight Soma carried was great, but he did not pause to rest until the whole length of the *bara* was crossed. It was fortunately quite deserted, and no one could have seen them from the houses, the night was so dark. It took them a long time to reach the beach at Koiti-iti, for it was some distance from the temple, but it was reached at last. No word had been said on that strange journey save once, when Soma heard Paori groan softly and asked if he were in pain and if he should stop, but the determined old fellow said—

'It is nothing; go on.'

It was nearly midnight when Soma lowered his burden gently to the sand, and the sky was so overcast that at first he could see nothing but the dim shimmer of the water where it broke with a dull phosphorescence on the beach, but he soon found the canoe where he had left it floating tied to one of the posts driven into the sand there for that purpose. When he had rested for a short time, he lifted the old man up in his arms, and wading out the short distance to the canoe, placed Paori in it.

'Get in also,' said the priest, 'and paddle me out to the reef.'

This Soma did, and guided by the patch of darkness between the white water of the thundering surf, he found the opening and passed out to sea. Then the old man, who had been crouching in the bottom of the little skiff, rose stiffly and with difficulty into a sitting position and said—

'That is enough. Your work is done and the will of the gods begins. Remember, Soma-eki, your oath. Tell no man, or the gods will strike you dead.'

'Have I not sworn the *fua ara*?' said Soma, awed by the darkness and the inherited fear of the gods' vengeance.

'Now swim back to land and forget what you have done to-night. Give me the paddle.'

'Must I leave you alone?' asked Soma.

'I am not alone,' said the old priest, with a thrilling

tone of mystery and undoubted belief in his voice;
'they are close around me now.'

'You are cold, *marete*,' said Soma, pitying the dying
man, but awed by his determination. As Paori made
no answer, but began to paddle out to sea with stronger
strokes than Soma thought possible for a man in his
condition, he unwound the *tappa* from his waist and
put it about the bony shoulders of the resolute old
man.

'Farewell, Paori e Tane,' said Soma; and between
the rattle of his gasping breathing, almost as though he did
not hear him, the stern, determined priest whispered—

'Farewell! Be it well with Soma e Motuiti.'

Before he plunged into the black water Soma took
one last glance at his self-doomed companion, and saw
that, with head slightly raised and looking straight
before him, as though he had already forgotten the
presence of Soma in the canoe, he was still feverishly
paddling straight out to sea, though each stroke was
growing feebler than the last.

Then Soma dived, and when he came to the surface
the blackness of night had swallowed up canoe and man
alike. This was the last the world ever saw of this old
hero, who died to revive a false and waning faith which
to him was as the Lamp of Truth. What leagues of sea
and silence he yet passed through before Death claimed
him was never known, nor whither the canoe with its
ghastly freight was drifted. The great spaces of that
vast sea are so wide and calm that it may have floated
on for years unseen with the crumbling bones and
grinning skull of what once was Paori crying out to
the unknown gods, who perhaps, after all, took him to
themselves as he had said.

CHAPTER XII

THE course of Christian's love had so far run smoothly enough; since the fight with Tama-iru that chief had ceased to torment Utamè, and she and North had met without let or hindrance. To a certain extent since their quarrel Tama-iru had tried to make himself agreeable to North, but Christian disliked the fellow too much to ever accept these advances, and he was not deceived as to his real feelings by any such friendly overtures. At the time of Paori's mysterious vanishing—for it always remained the deepest mystery, as neither Soma nor North, to whom he had confided the secret, ever breathed one word of the matter—Tama-iru had been away in Oneroa on a visit to his uncle Faäori's people. But he had been back for two or three days in Otorangi, and Christian thought he could detect a suppressed look of triumph in his face, though he had no reason for assuming it, as matters went on as usual. He brought news, however, that struck a chill to the hearts of Christian and Utamè, and that was that Faäori's son Rongo was coming very shortly to claim his affianced bride.

It was perhaps this information, which was as disastrous to him as to North, that made Tama-iru decide to act for himself without delay. One morning after the usual prolonged swim in the sea, and when the first meal had been eaten at Motuiti's house, Christian took Soma aside and said that he had promised to meet Utamè by the river and take her to one of their favourite spots. This place was where the forest opened out in a little sunny glade in which the river formed a deep clear pool, overhung on one side by a tree-grown cliff. Soma knew it well, and said that later in the day he would try to meet them there. They started out together, these two good friends, and to allay suspicion as to Christian's errand, walked towards the forest as though bent on pigeon-snaring. There they separated, North hurrying towards the little river and Soma turning off with a smile, which spoke of a similar business.

Christian found Utamè waiting on the bank of the stream with all the loves shining in her sunny eyes, and he hastened to where she stood in the shadow. She had grown more beautiful in these last few months, though North would have said from the first that that was impossible. Love had given her face a fresh significance, and now with the brightness and joyousness of the girl a woman's tenderness was mingled. She ran to meet Christian with a little inarticulate cry of love, and their silence for a moment was eloquent of the steady, honest passion that filled those two young savage hearts to overflowing. Christian looked down at Utamè's upturned face and saw that her deep eyes were dim with tears, but the next moment, taking her lover's hand, she laughed them away, shaking her head. Her eyes were always April skies, now bright with laughter and now dim with tears. Their canoe lay hidden some short distance up the stream, so they turned, and hand in hand entered the forest.

The day passed quickly enough for these two, there

was so much to be done and so much to be said. It took some time to reach the particular spot they had decided upon visiting, for Christian poled and paddled the canoe very slowly up stream; then, as they had no food with them, they had to find a meal of wild bananas, which had all the luscious, strange woodland scent and flavour that uncultivated fruit often has. These they gathered in a little rocky valley some way back from the river. Once or twice heavy rain fell, for although for the most part hot and sunny, the weather had been showery for the last few days. Then these two children had to shelter till once more the hot sun shone again.

A little after mid-day they returned to the river, that Soma might not miss them should he come to join them, and there they ate their mid-day meal of fruit and coco-nuts, which Christian climbed the palms to get. Then in the rosy silence of a little bower of hibiscus and palms that grew above the stream these two lovers sat hand in hand as quiet as the silenced birds, who had ceased their song for the glory of the mid-day heat. They spoke little, for they needed no words. Love was enough.

Over the rippling sea of sapphire the west wind laughed from the sun, warm and soft and caressing as lovers' hands; it stirred the tendrils of Utamè's soft hair, and fluttered the pale pink petals of the garland that lay upon her soft bosom, which slowly rose and fell as she breathed like one that dreams. It laughed as it lifted the little curls of Christian's hair, and whispered in his ear, ' Love, love, love ; time and the earth, at least for this hour, are the possessions of you two. Seize them, never let them slip.' But this message was not needed.

Slowly the light grew fainter—it could not be said to fade—and through the mass of hibiscus flowers, that covered the bushes to one side of them as though with living fire, the sun shone with a crimson glory, and first one bird and then another awoke to song, and the day-long quiet of the tropic forest ending, music as perfect as the silence took its place. They had risen to go home, and were standing on the little cliff above the pool that the stream made there, when Utamè called North's attention to her reflection in the water below them.

'Do you see my spirit down there in the water?' she said, waving her hand to her picture in the stream.

'Is that your spirit?' answered Christian.

'That is one of them; I have two. You have two. There is one,' she said, pointing to her reflection, 'and here is the other, always close to me,' and she indicated her elongated shadow on the ground.

'Are those your spirits? where do they come from?'

'Raä, the sun, gives them to us; that is why they faint when he goes into the sea. But they are always with us.'

'How do you know?' said Christian.

'You are foolish,' answered the girl seriously. 'Can you not see them at night? Take a torch and look into the water and there you are also. Dance in the firelight, and there at your feet, all black, you are dancing again.'

'But it is not you.'

'Yes, it is I. Do they not grow old as I grow old? and when I die, that one,' pointing to her shadow, with tears in her eyes at the thought of her own death, 'will vanish for ever. But that other,' and she pointed to the figure in the water which pointed back at her, ' that will linger for a long time near the place where I shall die, and then it will go away, I know not where.'

They were talking so earnestly that they had not noticed the rustling of the leaves behind them and the slight crackling of twigs caused by a light and rapid step, so that for a moment they were startled and alarmed by the sudden appearance of Soma, who burst upon them unawares through the dense foliage of the hibiscus trees. He ran to them in a state of great excitement, and almost breathless from the speed with which he had hurried from the town, and his face showed only too plainly that he was bearer of unexpected and perhaps alarming news.

' What is it ? ' asked Christian, stepping forward, the smile of welcome fading from his face.

' We must make haste,' gasped Soma, ' or all will be discovered. Tama-iru has been watching, and when he saw us leave the town he hurried to the house of Ngawa, your father, Utamè, and found that Utamè had gone out alone to the river. He has watched you for days, and thinks he will catch you now. I had only just come back from where I had been,' he went on, with a half smile and a glance at Christian, ' and Okotai, whom I met, told me that Tama-iru had been to Ilo and told him all that he thought. Ilo and Tama-iru and some others have left the town to find you, and are coming up the river. And Ilo's face is black against Papalangi tëa, for he thinks his *tabu* is broken.'

For a moment, in the extremity of their danger—for to be caught meant death to both Christian and Utamè —they looked blankly at one another. The girl was the first to recover her wits, and with all a woman's ingenuity came to the rescue; her thoughts were entirely devoted to Christian's safety, and her plan was formed with this object.

'Were you seen in the town?' she asked of Soma.

'Only Okotai saw me. He told me of Tama-iru's doings.'

'Can you trust him?'

'He will not speak; he is a friend of Soma and of Papalangi tëa.'

'Then you two must take the canoe and go down the river and meet Ilo. When he speaks, say that you have been alone together all the day.'

'But what will you do?' asked Christian anxiously.

'I will go home to the house of my father, gathering many flowers as I go, and will say that I have been alone to the forest to get fresh garlands for all the house. When they come in I will be weaving them with Sobele. I will say I have been there a long time. Sobele will say the same.'

'How can you get back?' asked North.

'I know a path through the forest. I will run. Talk much with Ilo and the men. Keep them on the river, and I will be at the *fale* before them. What's that? Quick, quick, I hear the sound of paddles.'

She did not hesitate for a moment, and appeared to have no fear; the sudden emergency seemed to summon up unknown latent energy and courage in her bosom, so that she was the calmest of the three. '*Vave ange!*' (quick, quick) she said, turning, even as she spoke, to begin her more difficult part of the work. She had not gone many steps before she ran back to say to Soma, 'Wash off all that dirt; you look too hot, and they will see you have been running.'

With this she darted across the glade and into the thick shelter of the forest. The two men only waited until Utamè had disappeared to hurry down the little cliff and along the side of the river to where the canoe lay moored; into this they sprang, and casting her off, Christian propelled her with a few quick strokes of the paddle out into the stream. They had barely reached the middle of the current when Soma said—

'They are upon us; I hear their voices.'

'Into the water,' whispered Christian, 'or they will see you are hot from running. Swim about the canoe.'

He had no sooner spoken than Soma had glided silently over the side of the rocking canoe, and was swimming with long lazy strokes up the stream. The next moment two large canoes rounded a bend in the stream, and Ilo and Tama-iru and their men were upon them. Soma turned and swam towards Ilo's canoe, and lifting his face, from which the cool water had washed away all trace of heat and fatigue, he asked him in the most natural manner—

'*Kalanga* (hallo), Ilo, what brings you to the river?'

'We come for the girl,' answered the chief.

'What girl?' asked Soma. 'Have you not girls enough in Otorangi?' and he laughed as he spoke, for Ilo had many wives.

'We seek Utamè e Ngawa, the tabued,' said Ilo angrily, but with a look of doubt at Tama-iru, who was in the next canoe.

'*Utamè!*' said Soma with the utmost astonishment; 'she is not here.'

'She is with the Papalangi tëa!' shouted Tama-iru, almost beside himself with rage and disappointment.

'What is the matter?' said Christian simply, as though surprised at hearing his name mentioned. He had brought his canoe up alongside that of Ilo, and spoke so calmly and smiled so lightly and pleasantly as to quite deceive the angry old chief. If quickness of sympathy and alertness of observation are the chief essentials of an actor's character, Christian possessed them abundantly, and upon this occasion turned them to the greatest advantage, for he acted the little comedy—which might have such tragic issues for all of them—so naturally as to carry conviction on the very face of it.

'Have you the girl with you?' said Ilo, with a softer manner.

'No, Ilo-cki, I have no one with me but Soma e Motuiti.'

'Then what are you doing on Mimi-Roruto?' asked Tama-iru.

'We are chiefs,' said Soma quickly and angrily, 'and can go where we please. We came for our pleasure,' he added, pointing with one wet arm to the canoe, where all could see the pigeon snares and nooses with which they had started out in the morning.

'When did you last see the girl?' interrupted Ilo.

To North's astonishment Soma answered, with a sudden inspiration, to strengthen their story by a corroboration of Utamè's, should they question her—

'This morning as I started I saw the girl going to the forest. She said she went to gather flowers for the garlands.'

'We will go to the house of Ngawa, and if this be so, it is proved truth that you speak, Soma. Then, too, it is proved that Tama-iru is a liar and a fool.'

With this intention the two canoes turned and began to paddle down stream. Christian and Soma, to carry out their assumed character of indifference, did not attempt to follow them, but Soma could not resist a parting shot at Tama-iru, who sat, the picture of impotent anger, in the prow of the first canoe.

'*Mata ho toë*, Tama-iru—good-bye' (literally—' your face again '), 'Tama-iru; you are a true friend to Faäori's son, to protect his *tabu* so well,' he called out with a meaning that the treacherous fellow could not fail to understand.

When the canoes were out of sight the two friends hurried back, a prey to too keen an alarm for Utamè to linger longer on the river. Rain fell heavily again as they reached the town, and all the people were driven indoors, so that they could gain no news from any one. It was some time after sunset before Ilo and Tama-iru were back in Otorangi, and as they and their party retired to the large house of the chief at the back of the town, they were unable to learn anything of what had happened at Ngawa's house. After night-fall Christian's anxiety became such that he could no longer rest in inaction, and against the advice of Soma, he started out to try to learn from Utamè herself that all was well with her. He took the beach path, which was much longer than the one through the town, but as at this hour it was quite deserted, he chose it in preference to the more frequented road. He hurried along the heavy track, consumed with anxiety and filled with a strange presentiment of evil, at which, at another time, he would have been the first to laugh. But to-night seemed bodeful; what might the shadows not hide? The sudden rush and patter of the heavy rain-drops shaken from the palms upon the shrubs below by a gust of ocean wind sounded like footsteps of unseen ghosts, and the quick gleam of some great burnished leaves, as the wind flashed them in the moonlight, was like a spirit's vanishing.

He had to pass one place as he skirted the bay where once the great god Rupe had claimed at the first launching of canoes his sacrifice of human lives, and on the same spot now the people of Otorangi buried many of their dead. Tall dark casuarina trees, with sweeping tresses of fine pinelike needles, surrounded all the place, and the slow and solemn swaying of their gnarled and twisted boughs, the sighing of the wind amongst their ancient boles, and the moving shadows of their branches over the silent graves below, made it seem a fitting place for the haunting souls of murdered men. Filled with many a wild sea superstition, from which scarce any man of the time was quite free, Christian, half scornful of himself, hurried past. Maybe some strange influence of wickedness and cruelty hung about that place of death—who knows?

It is often said that the unfeeling earth does not remember all the deeds of darkness and of sorrow that have taken place upon it; but this is not so. The wind is always mourning for the sorrow that the world has seen; men forget it, and live on gaily upon the very spot where some long-past tragedy was played; but the air that once, perchance, was breathed by the very actors in the play remembers all the grief and sadness of it and sighs still. And so the sea, after its wild moments of storm and passion, is always sobbing out its vain regret for the beautiful strong men and fair women it has drowned, and for the happiness and love it has broken and destroyed. Nature remembers —it is we who forget.

THE rain that fell as North and Soma returned to the town from the river had ceased at sunset; and the now slow and again breeze-hastened dripping of the water from the loftier trees, the low rustle of the freshened plants that edged Utamè's little rock-bound bay, and the tinkling and ripple of the swollen brook that flowed into the sea there, as it fell from ledge to ledge of rock, sounded like the treble of some strange overture, to which the low grave sound of the falling sea added its harmony of bass. It almost seemed that Nature had herself arranged a solemn introduction to the tragedy about to be played on that sea-swept stage.

The sun had set and the pearly twilight, that in those tropic lands lasts so short a time, had fled; the pure, rain-washed sky, so overcast before, was now an infinite space of clear air, through which the unrisen moon poured a flood of softened radiance. The eastern sky glowed brighter, and through its blue a golden stain crept up, until the rounded moon, like an Orient pearl, rose to her nightly realm. At first her level beams were veiled by the rising and falling of the reef-broken surf, which shone and glittered like a cataract of crystal and molten silver; but soon she rose above this cloud of spray, and shone down regally upon the deserted shore.

For some time the beach was solitary, but before long there was a rustle in the bushes that grew above the sand, and then, parting their wet branches and gleaming in the moonlight with the moisture that in places lay upon her, Utamè glided to the silent sands. Since the day that Christian first saw her there she was changed from the artless girl to the consciousness of womanhood; her rounded face was somewhat thinned by the passion that consumed her, but she held her head erect and moved with the grace of a queen. Her black and waving hair was crowned with the scarlet flowers of the hibiscus, that, even in the pale moonlight, glowed like flames about her head.

She thought that all the difficulties and dangers of the day were over, and had come to the sea in the security of the night to bathe and refresh her weary body after the effort and strain of the last few hours. Unconscious of the presence of her determined enemy —for such she considered her unwelcome lover— Utamè stepped down from the little pile of creeper-covered rocks, and smiling, as she remembered that other moonlight night that was the beginning of her happiness, she stepped upon the beach.

Tama-iru, frustrated in the bold stroke for revenge that he had planned and attempted to carry out, had determined, in the slow journey back to the town from Ngawa's house, not to be foiled in his love. He conceived his plan rapidly, and as promptly made all the necessary arrangements, which were but simple, to execute it. Almost directly after his return with Ilo to the town he quietly collected all his men, and telling them to place a little food and water in his own canoe, he bade them put to sea and await him in the lagoon on the farther side of the reef of rocks that

formed the more distant side of Utamè's bay. His
men were anxious to return to Oneroa, their own part
of the island, and willingly and quickly obeyed the
orders of their chief.

It is a strange thing that jealous people always
wish to know the very thing which when known
will make them miserable. But so it is; and the
wretched Tama-iru, whose savage heart suffered all the
agony of uncontrolled jealousy and unrequited love,
was no exception. He had watched and spied upon
Utamè so closely that he was almost as well acquainted
with her usual habits as Christian himself; and
feeling sure that North would not risk another meeting that night, and thinking that Utamè would in
all probability go to her favourite haunt, he had
placed himself in hiding amongst the rocks, from
whence he could see the whole of the beach of the
little bay. Had the girl failed to appear he had
determined upon summoning his men, when all Ngawa's
household slept, with them fall upon the women's
house, and seize upon and carry off the girl. He had
considered all the risk, and thought the prize was
worth it. He had been hiding there an hour or more
before the girl appeared, for she had waited till the
moon was up and until the beach was deserted. His
heart beat thickly and his eyes were hot with watching when at last Utamè stepped to the sand through
the rustling bushes.

Perhaps the excitement and danger of the day had
unnerved her, for there was an unusual hesitation in
her manner, and she looked this way and that to see
that the shore was quite solitary before she let go the
slender branches of the shrubs which she grasped in
either hand. At last, reassured by the silence, she

walked towards the margin of the sea, passing within a yard or two of where Tama-iru lay concealed

There is very little rise and fall in the tides upon the shores of the Coral Islands, but at that hour the water was at flood, and came creaming amongst the rocks and small rounded boulders that formed the end of the projecting reef. Before she had left the house Utamè had put on the thick black girdle of fringe that the women always wear when bathing, so that she had nothing to do but remove the short full skirt that the long piece of *tappa* made when folded round her waist. This she slipped off, and for one brief moment before she plunged into the water she stood, save for her flowing *hau*, nude in the eye of the moon.

Just as she was stepping into the water she heard behind her the sudden rustling of the bushes that Tama-iru's movements made as he started up to leave his place of concealment; she turned, and instantly recognised the passion-hurried man as he rushed towards her. Utamè gave one wild glance around to see what chance there was of escape by flight, and saw that there was none; then the courage that she had inherited from a long line of warrior ancestors came to her aid for her protection. Like a hawk she stooped and seized upon a heavy jagged stone, which she placed in her long waist-cloth that was lying at her feet. The folds of this she twisted with one or two quick turns, and with the ends of her improvised weapon in her hands she rose to her feet.

'Stand still!' she cried. 'I will kill you if you come one step nearer.' And the tones of her voice were so imperious that for a moment Tama-iru paused.

'What do you want?' she said.

'You,' he replied; 'and you I will have. My men

and my canoe await me round those rocks, and I will take you to my tribe and win Faäori's leave to make you my wife.'

'I will not go.'

'You shall.   You have no white lover here to protect you.'

'No; but with the help of the gods I will protect myself.'

'It is useless.   They will not help you, and you are but a girl.   The *muanu* (the luck) of Tama-iru is strong to-night.'

'Do not move,' she said, with such grim determination in her tone that he might have been warned; but blinded by fate he rushed towards her.

She stood there like a slim young palm, so young and slight she looked; but she was ready to do battle for her freedom and her lover.   Her body was thrown lightly back to give greater strength to her blow, and raising her arms she whirled her improvised weapon round her head like a flash of light.   Tama-iru bent his head as he sprang upon her, meaning to avoid her attack, but she lowered her arms slightly, and as his hand grasped her flowing hair she struck him a crashing blow on his left temple with all the strength of her young womanhood, and, as Goliath before David, he fell dead at her feet.

Her heart was hardened by the hate of this man that was in it, so that it was with no useless tremblings, though she breathed thick and fast, that Utamè stooped over her fallen foe and found that he was dead.   She had all her life been too well acquainted with death in its more terrible forms to be alarmed by the mere corpse of the man, and she knew that she had still much to do to save her lover's and her own life. She knew Tama-iru's rank, and she knew that the men who awaited him so near at hand would be searching for their chief before long, and that they would have small respect for her did they find him lying there. Her first thought was a womanly one— to fly; but a moment's reflection taught her that the body of the dead man would most certainly be found, and as his errand was probably known by some, she would be suspected of his death. She stood there for a moment or two as motionless as though carved in stone, and then untwisting her rough sling, the ends of which still lay in her hands, she let fall the stone and replaced her dress. Then, without looking in his distorted face, the brave woman—who felt that her whole future lay in the safety of the next few moments, and who knew that her lover's happiness as well as her own was in her hands—stooped, and grasping the dead man by his still warm wrists (in the clutched fist of one he still held a little strand of her own hair), she dragged him to the reef of rocks, on one side of which the water lay clear and deep.

It was no light task, for Tama-iru was a well-grown man; but the girl possessed in her despair a strength that was not her own, and disregarding the blows and bruises that her delicate limbs received as she slipped and fell among the rocks, she pushed and pulled the body of the dead man with a strength and fury that nothing but desperation could have summoned up. She had reason for what she did.

Every tribe and every family of a tribe in Omëo had a sort of titular deity that was peculiar to itself, and which for other tribes and other families had no sacredness whatever. These lesser gods were always represented by some bird, beast, or fish, and that family to which each creature was sacred could neither molest nor eat the animal which for it represented its special family god. Beyond this their honouring went no further, and no worship was mingled with their respect. The house of Ngawa had always held the great shark sacred, and not only never joined in the hunting of it, but often fed them, in times of sorrow or anxiety, with food thrown from the shore. This family possessed the famous shark charm which they used to protect themselves and their companions when fishing for pearl-shell off the reef or when swimming in the sea in dangerous localities. Soma had often told North of the power that they possessed over the savage creature, saying that the charm could summon him to the surface from where he lay lurking among the corals. Christian had always held the statement in honest scepticism, although Utamè had herself assured him of the truth of it.

To-night Utamè had determined upon calling the sharks to her aid, and by their help to rid herself of the damning evidence of Tama-iru's dead body. When she had dragged the corpse of her enemy to the side of the rock where deep water lay, she rose to her feet and chanted, rather than sang, the words of her weird charm. Her voice was clear and penetrating, and, for all her terror, quite steady. The words were uttered with a strange ringing rhythm or cadence, though tune, strictly speaking, there was none. These were the words she chanted—

> *Aengaru te atu e;*
> *Anga-tama marama.*
> *E tu ru e tama e,*
> *Gua kai.   Ua piri tanga.*
>
> *Tu-u me mothe, fonua ho aii*
> *Tu-u, kou nofo fu.   Tu-u anga-tama.*

She paused, and then, as nothing came and the still surface of the water was unmoved, she repeated in a louder tone and with all the confidence of an often-corroborated belief, the words of her spell. Almost before the last syllable was uttered the silver moonlight quivered on the water and the terrible black fin showed above the sea. She bent over the water in her eagerness and, in a lower voice, crooned the verses over again; and, as though impelled by some strange fascination, the huge creature glided through the water like a moving shadow till it stopped close under the rock on which she stood.

'*Gi heni, anga-tama,*' she said, '*e tama e, gua fuagi-kai e Utamè.*' (Here, father shark, eldest son, is food, the gift of Utamè.)

With these words she stepped back, and rolling the dead body to the verge she pushed it over into the sea. It fell with a dull and heavy splash. The triangular black fin disappeared as the huge shark rolled over to seize its prey; a second afterwards all that was mortal of Tama-iru was pulled beneath the surface and disappeared for ever.

No sooner was the danger over and her task done than all the heroic vanished from poor, miserable Utamè; she sank down, sitting on her heels, and covering her face with her hands to hide everything from her burning sight, she shook and trembled like a *kuru* leaf. It was at that moment that Christian arrived on the scene of the finished tragedy; as he leaped lightly over the rocks that surrounded the little bay he saw at a short distance from him the kneeling figure of Utamè, black against the silver water. He called her softly by her name, and the girl sprang up, and with a suppressed shriek of joy she flew to him, and throwing her arms round his waist, sank on the sand sobbing like a child.

It was some time before North could calm her sufficiently for her to explain to him what had caused this outburst; but she was able to do so at last, and he could not have said at that moment whether his admiration of her courage and devotion or his pity for her suffering were the greater. He could hardly realise the possibility of so young a girl as Utamè overcoming and killing in fair fight a great strong man such as Tama-iru was, and he asked her, as he clasped her tighter in the arms which, for all his chivalric love for her, had been useless for her protection that night—

'But did you slay him all alone ?'

'I did it with my two hands.' Then looking down at her hastily-adjusted dress, she saw a great stain of blood disfiguring one side of it. She gave a shriek and started up, plucking at the cloth as she cried—

'See, see, it is black with his blood! I cannot wear it.'

'Give it to me,' said Christian, 'and you take my *tappa*. I have my *mahi*,' and he slipped off his outer garment of cloth, which was only put on at night for warmth or on ceremonious occasions.

With hands that quivered so that she could hardly make the folding of the dress to support it, Utamè put on the *tappa* that North gave her and, with a shudder of disgust and fear, let fall her own blood-stained garment. It was curious how all her feminine weakness returned to her now that the necessity for courage had disappeared; seeing her then, trembling all over and every now and then shaken by a sob that she could not repress, it seemed impossible to believe that she was the heroine of half an hour before,—that she who sickened at the thought of her bloody dress could have slain a man and have flung him to the sharks.

She became quieter at last, soothed by the presence and the love of Christian, who felt that he could almost worship this noble woman who could dare and do so much for him and for their love ; and after a little time, clinging to him for protection as a child does to its father, she told him what had happened since she had left him and Soma on the river.

She had run home, she said, almost all the way, only stopping here and there to snatch masses of blossom and bright foliage from the bushes and trees as she passed. She paused when she neared the houses to regain her breath, and then passed quickly through the banana garden at the back of her father's house to the smaller house of the women, which was to one side of it. Here she only stopped to drink from one of the great hollow bamboos that the women had just brought up from the river, and went in. The noise of her entrance was drowned by the merry *too-too* of the *tappa*-making in front of the house. She laid down her fragrant burden, and passing through the other doorway (being a women's sleeping-house, the sides were closed in), she found her friend and servant Sobele beating away at her strip of white cloth on the springy palm-trunk that is used for this purpose. This woman was a slave who had been captured by Ngawa in a successful raid on the neighbouring island of Vei-tatei, and whom he had given to his daughter as an attendant.

Utamè rapidly explained to her the part she had to play ; all that she had to do was to say that her mistress had been in the house for some time, and that

she had gone out in the morning to gather flowers for
the wreaths that men and women alike wear round
their necks. This she promised to do. Whilst Utamè
put on an unspotted *tappa* and removed all signs of
her hurried flight through the forest, Sobele, keeping a
keen eye open for the approach of Ilo and Tama-iru,
began hurriedly to weave the garlands.

Almost before Utamè was ready Sobele called out,
'They are here,' so quickly had they paddled from the
river, and with a catlike spring the girl had seized one
of the unfinished wreaths and was seated amongst the
flowers by her servant's side. 'Sing,' she whispered;
and when Ilo burst into the house, for the *tabu* laid
upon it had no power over him, he found the two
women calmly plaiting the blossoms together singing
one of their curious two-part songs. It was not
etiquette for them to rise in the presence of a chief, but
they laid down their work and stopped singing with an
air of the utmost surprise.

'Tama-iru-eki,' shouted out the old chief angrily,
'come here and question the women. It is the thought
of Ilo that you lie, and that a wife for Tama-paru's
(Tama-iru's father) son is what you seek rather than
one for Faäori's son.'

Tama-iru, quailing before the keen eye of the old
chief who had begun to have such shrewd suspicions of
him, came into the house and questioned Sobele as to
her mistress's doings that day.

'After first food Utamè-eki went out to gather many
flowers for the wreaths. *Gi-noutolu gua* (here they
are),' she said, pointing to the heaped-up blossoms on
the mat before them.

'Where did you go?' asked Tama-iru of Utamè.

'To Ma-aune,' said the girl without a blush, naming

a part of the island in a directly opposite position to the river.

As the day is not separated into hours in Omëo, morning, noon, and evening being the only divisions, Tama-iru could not ask, 'How long has she been in the house?' so that he had to make use of a periphrasis, by the employment of which they often are only able to express themselves.

'Has she breathed much since she and the flowers were at the house?'

'Yes, Tama-iru-eki, she has breathed much; she was tired and she slept,' answered the woman.

'It is as Soma e Motuiti said!' exclaimed Ilo. 'Come away, Tama-iru; you have lied to me. It is you who would break Faäori's *tabu*, and my *tabu*.' Thus speaking, he angrily ordered the men back to their canoes and left the house.

Utamè was ignorant of what he meant when Ilo said that it was as Soma had told them, but she wisely held her peace; and a few moments afterwards Sobele, who went out to watch them, saw them all put off for Otorangi.

By the time that Utamè had finished her long story she was quite calm again, and it was she who recalled to Christian that they still were in danger from Tama-iru's men, who were waiting, doubtlessly impatiently, the return of their dead master. This was like the sound of trumpets to the war-horse, and made North once more the man of action, who was eager to be up and doing. He gently unclasped Utamè's hands, the tight grasp of which upon him was now the only sign of her fear, and rose to his feet. He was like those generals who in time of danger seem to think in flashes, who see what must be done for the safety of their arms by a sort of inspiration rather than by any course of reasoning. He saw all the advantages that might be gained by acting rapidly, by which means, as in all good generalship, what appeared present disaster might be turned to future success. He turned to Utamè and said—

'You know the news that Tama-iru brought back with him from Oneroa. Rongo is making ready to come to demand his wife from Ilo and your father Ngawa.'

'It is so,' she said.

'Well, we must be gone before he comes. To-night has made our plan quite plain. You must leave your father's house, and as Tama-iru has disappeared, Ilo-eki and all Otorangi will think that he has seized you and carried you off.'

'Yes,' said the girl, with quick apprehension of North's meaning, 'but his men yonder. They will say that Tama-iru never joined them.'

'They must be sent away, but who is to do it?' said Christian, pressing his forefinger to his lip, as was his way when he thought deeply. 'They will not obey me, for they must know their master's enmity towards me.'

'Sobelo must do it,' said Utamè with energy, all her courage returning with the necessity for action. 'I will fetch her. Wait here. I will tell her what to say.'

So saying she ran off towards the house, leaving North in doubt as to the message she would invent. Although the distance to Ngawa's houses was not great, and the girl both went and came very quickly, it seemed an eternity to Christian, who was waiting there the prey to such keen anxiety, until she was back again with her determined little slave. The two were talking earnestly as they again reached the shore, the servant asking questions, and Utamè evidently impressing over and over again the exact form of the message to be delivered to the crew of the canoe. Until that night Christian had never fully appreciated the bright intelligence and strength of character of the woman he loved. She came up to him with a quick step, followed by Sobele at a little trot.

'Sobele understands what she is to say,' she whispered.

'Yes, I understand,' repeated the little woman, with a slight accent that showed her foreign birth.

'Let us follow her to the rocks,' said Christian; 'she may want my help.'

With this they all three walked round the little curve of the bay to the great jutting reef of tumbled limestone rock beyond which the canoe was lying. When they had scrambled to the top of this, Utamè and North lay down and hid amongst the huge fern and creeper-covered stones, whilst Sobele went on a few yards farther, from whence she could see Tama-iru's men lying at a short distance from shore. She stood up in the moonlight with a boldness that her fat little figure and inferior position scarcely promised, and in a clear voice hailed the canoe.

'*Kalanga, kau takanga Tama-iru!*' she shouted. (Hallo, you followers of Tama-iru, do you hear me?)

A cry from the canoe answered that they did.

'I have a message for you from Tama-iru-eki,' she said.

'What is that message? Who are you?' asked a voice which sounded nearer; the canoe had evidently come towards the rocks.

'I am Sobele, the slave of Utamè e Ngawa.'

'I know her,' a voice was heard to say down below.

'Is that you, Iruru?' quickly said Sobele. 'I bear a message from your chief. He says that you must not wait for him, but set sail (*felou*) at once for Oneroa without going back to Otorangi. He says you are to say to Rongo-eki that he will be with him soon.'

'Why is he staying behind without us?' asked a sceptical voice.

'He did not say I was to tell you, but I will say it to you, Iruru. He has seized Utamè e Ngawa, and has carried her away to the mountains, and I am to go with her. You are to go away at once, and Ngawa-eki and Ilo-eki will think he has gone back to his own land.'

For some moments there was the sound of discussion in the canoe, and then a voice cried out—

'We will do as our master says.'

Directly afterwards the listeners could hear the rumble of the heavy mast sail being hauled up with its yard, and then the sound of the paddles striking the water together told them that the canoe was under way.

Christian breathed a sigh of relief as the canoe struck out to sea, and cautiously lifting his head he saw it quickly making its way in the direction of Oneroa.

'And now,' he said, when he had thanked the brave Sobele for the way she had served them that night, 'you two must go back to the house, and Utamè, you must sleep well, for it is not yet night-noon,' looking up at the moon as he spoke to see if she had begun to sink. 'I must see Soma and ask his help, and then, before dawn, I will be back to take you away to a place of safety where Rongo cannot find you should he come to take you before Tama-iru's men get to Oneroa.'

He gave his orders quietly, and Utamé, who, as all women, civilised or savage, so quickly do, had learned the meaning of the calm look of determination when it shows itself on a usually smiling and careless face, instantly obeyed him without objection or hesitation. She flung her dimpled arms round his neck, and kissing him, turned to the house without a word. Christian watched this dear woman till she vanished through the trees, and then turned with a happy heart and hurried back to the town.

CHAPTER XIV

As Christian walked back to the town his brain was
busy and his heart was full, for side by side with his
love for Utamè had grown that other graver love for
his friend which bound the two men together with
links of steel; and now that the hour had struck for
the fulfilment and fruition of his hopes in one direction, it knelled a separation from the man on whose
fidelity and strength of friendship he had grown to
rely with a trust that had never and could not ever
be shaken. The love of women is as the breath of
one's life, but the love of a friend is a staff in the
hand through life's rough places, and often, without
the comfort of its support, the walker therein would
stumble and fall. At the thought of leaving him
North's heart swelled and the clear stars were blurred
in the deep purple vault above him, and he knew at
this moment how strongly and finally his friendship
and love for this true-eyed, great-hearted savage had
entwined themselves in the strands of his life.

He had become a rich man in this last year, and
to-night, even in the hurry of his return to the town,
he paused in the deep-brooding silence of sea and
moonlight, which made a sort of silver heaven of the
great Pacific, and hugged his treasures to his soul, and,
unlike a miser of gold and wealth, was the better for it.

'I am rich,' he thought, 'with the greatest of riches. Wealth could not purchase what is mine by God's free gift, and riches untold could never tempt me to sell what many hold so cheap. Mine, too, is a treasure that I shall take with me if there be a Beyond, for it is a treasure of priceless love; not only love received, but love that I have loved and given. True love, pure love, is like charity; it blesses him that receives, but far more him that gives it.'

As he neared the house of Motuiti the silence of the sleeping town awed and impressed him as the night and silence of the sea and forest never could; the deathlike quiet of those living souls around him had something terrible in it that struck a chill to his heart. The whole town slept, husbands and wives, youths and maidens, old men and children, each with his true self before himself, waiting, grinning grimly, to be recognised. We are told that we must know ourselves. Philosophers preach it, and men say the lesson is too hard to be learned, or the riddle too dark to be solved. Yet there is a way of gaining that knowledge that is not too difficult. Remember in the morning the dreams of the night, and what you are in them know yourself truly to be. It is the real 'you' who thinks and acts in them, undisguised by any self-made, self-placed mask. You do not do all the foolish things or the wicked ones that you act in dreams, because, and *only* because, you are never in the circumstances of the dream surroundings; but all the potentialities for good or ill are in the waking man as strongly as in the dream one. The spirit which informs the sleeper and the waker are alike, but in sleep it is not controlled by fear or reason or other considerations which in part restrain it when awake. Could

all a man's dreams be known we should know him
for what he is; to ourselves our dreams are plain, and
we can in them recognise ourselves for what we are.
In dreams no bold man is ever timid, no coward ever
brave; the mean man cannot dream that he is generous,
nor the noble that he is base.

It seemed strange to Christian, with the wild thrill
in his blood, caused by what had so lately happened,
and by what was so soon to be done, that all these
men should lie so quiet and sleep so sound for all the
hurry of life, the passion, and the tragedy of death
that had been played out so fiercely so short a time
before, so little a distance away.   His emotions were
so aroused and his sensibilities so acute that night that
he thought that he should have stirred and waked
were any such wild drama played whilst he were
sleeping near.   He hurried across the *bara*, keeping in
the shadows as much as possible for all the silence of
the sleeping town, and crept lightly up to the platform
on which his friend's house stood.   As he stood in the
moonlight the interior of the house seemed to be quite
black; he stooped his head at the cave, and entering
the darkness, suddenly felt two strong warm arms
thrown round his night-chilled body.

'Hush,' whispered a voice in his ear, and he knew
that it was Soma.   'Why have you been so long?   I
have been waiting.'

Christian began to tell him, but he was stopped by
Soma saying, 'Come to our end of the house; some of
the men are still awake, I think, and no one must
hear.'

When they had carefully walked through the house
to the raised fern-covered end where their and Motuiti's
mats were spread, Christian told all his exciting story.

Soma listened in silence without any expression of surprise; perhaps such scenes of savage heroic self-defence and sudden death were not so terrible and astonishing to him as to North; all that he said was, 'It is well; she should have brave men for sons.'

'We must get away before morning,' said Christian. 'It must be thought that Tama-iru has taken her.'

'You must take her away,' said Soma, quietly laying his arm round North's shoulder; 'and, Kliss, you must leave Soma behind.'

It was not much to say, and there was no fuss and palaver in his way of saying it, but Christian knew from his own heart what the separation meant to Soma, and what it cost him to speak so calmly of what he felt so much.

'Cannot you come too?' he said impulsively, forgetting that he had decided how much better it was in every way for Soma to remain behind.

'No,' answered Soma, 'you two must go away alone. I will stay here; and lest men say you have deserted us and gone with Tama-iru, I will tell them that I know where you are and that all is well.'

'They will ask whither has Papalangi tëa gone.'

'And I will answer,' whispered Soma with a laugh, 'that you have gone to make love to a beautiful girl a long way off. Then they will laugh and nod their heads and say, "We know; we are not old men yet." The truth shall hide the truth.'

'Where shall I take her? where will she be safest?'

'I have thought,' said Soma, 'that you and she will be safe with Venga on Monoriro. She is of Utamè's clan. It was she who sent me to search for you below Hu-hu-e-Rupe ("Rupe's fork," as they call one of the southern constellations.) Utamè knows the path, though it is not easy to find. It was she who led me to Monoriro when I thought Maraki called me and that I should die.'

'You are right,' said North, admiring the shrewdness of the man. 'You are right, and perhaps the *kahua* that old Paori gave me will gain me a welcome too.'

'Now you must sleep,' said Soma. 'You have far to go to-morrow, and the path is steep. I will watch, and will wake you so that you and Utamè may be away before the sunrise.'

This the faithful fellow did, sitting there calmly through the hours of darkness till the setting of the stars in the western sea warned him that the sun was not far off. Then he roused Christian and gave him a tall carved walking staff, which he said he would want later on, and food in a basket of palm leaf. They started off together in the cold air of the hour that precedes the sunrise, for as the night shivers off to her under world she strikes a chill on all those who watch her going. Christian, just awakened, shuddered as they stepped from the warm house into the cold breath of the dying night, and without a word Soma turned and went back. The next moment he appeared with a warm *tappa*, which he threw on North's shoulders, and walked on as though such willing service were the most ordinary thing in life.

It did not take them very long to walk to Ngawa's house, and they arrived still talking earnestly. Sobele, who was on the watch, heard the quick, firm tread of the young men's feet, and ran in to wake her mistress. In a few moments Utamè joined them. She was ready to depart, and carried a little bundle in her hand ; she greeted Soma, and then stood quite calmly, with her little hand on Christian's sturdy arm, whilst they told her what they had decided.   Her love was so great that all difficulties disappeared before it; the one, the only thing that existed for her was the comely man before her, and when he held out his arms and took her to himself, she surrendered her heart and her brain and her will, with her youth and beauty.   With her—happy, savage, natural woman—as with Christian, there could be no half measures in a love such as theirs; and it was her happiness, as well as what she felt to be her duty, to receive and obey the instructions of the man.

'Am I to take Sobele?' she asked.

'No; it is best to leave her behind.   Soma will tell her what to say.'

'It is time to go,' said Soma.

'Where are we going?' said Utamè.   She had not asked before; all places were alike to her if only she had her lover with her; and her confidence in him was like a child's trust in its father.

'To Monoriro, to the house of Venga,' North answered.   'She will take us in, and there I will leave you in safety—for a short time,' he added, as he felt, rather than saw, a cloud pass over the happiness of the girl's face.

'She is a terrible old woman—so wise,' said the girl; 'but she loves me and will take us in.'   Then she said with sudden jealousy, 'Why must you leave me?'

'I must come back to Soma——'

'I hate Soma,' interrupted the girl.

'And try to make Ilo take off his *tabu*, so that we can always live together.'

Utamè's hand crept higher up Christian's arm, and he pressed it to his side.

'Look,' said Soma, 'the day is not far off. You must go, my *ofa-namu*. Be not too long away from Soma; he will neither sleep nor rest till your hand is in his again.' So saying he embraced Christian, and giving him the *uma* on his forehead he gently pushed him off in the direction of the path.

'*Kiodofa, ofa-namu au*,' said Christian with a sigh, as he turned to leave his friend.

'*Kiodofa*,' murmured Soma, and turning sharply on his heel, he walked back through the darkness to the house, with Sobele following closely for her instructions.

CHAPTER XV

NIGHT was shivering off and day was shivering in as North and Utamè reached the edge of the forest. The eternity-long combat was once more fought out between the eternal enemies day and night: enemies that, since the first day dawned, have never met each other face to face. Eternally defeating and eternally defeated, the day and night had once more fought out the endless battle, so soon to be renewed, and the beaten night was driven out to wait once more in the under-world her twelve hours' victory again. The night, grown sullen towards her end, shuffled slowly off, drawing her long robes of cloud behind her as though whisking away her very train from the touch and sight of the victor, but she was not quick enough—the dignity of her retreat left her open to insult—for already in the east, and in the west too, with fainter glow, the clouds had put on their heralds' coats, and with loud trumpetings of colour hailed the coming of the new monarch. False courtiers they, for but an hour before they wore the sable livery of the night.

But it was still so dark in the shadow of the forest that Christian and Utamè could not see their way, and they had to pause for a time before their journey was well begun. They had, however, escaped unobserved from the neighbourhood of the houses, and were already sufficiently deep in amongst the trees of the great woods to be perfectly hidden.

Until now the silence of the night had reigned undisturbed by voice of bird or buzz of insect; but now, although it was still quite black amongst the trunks of the trees, the silence was broken by the first flutterings and the earliest musical calls of the birds which perhaps, had seen from their lofty eyries in the topmost branches the promise of day glimmering in the east. One by one they awoke, till all the woods were ringing with their music. At first the day grew lighter very slowly, but as the sun neared the horizon it became perceptibly brighter every moment; all the sky was flushed with colour; next the gray of the topmost crags of the mountains caught the radiance and was flushed with a rosy glory; and then, like the flash of a sword, the edge of the sun gleamed above the horizon. Every bush and every tree, each leaf and each flower, glittered then with pendent gems of rain and dew.

It was but a moment before the whole sun had sprung above the sea line, and the glorious blaze of the tropic day had flooded all the island. It seemed that the eager sun was in such haste to enter on his kingdom that he could not pause upon its threshold, but must rush into it with such speed as to help him up the steep ascent of his most royal road. Through the dark woods he opened up broad golden pathways, flooding every hollow, bathing every hillside with his wealth of happiness and beauty. Insects chirped and whirred, great languid butterflies, slowly waving their gorgeous vans, floated from their shelters to warm themselves in his bright rays. Birds, almost as brightly coloured, preened their gay feathers or flew down to the streams for their bath. Buds of flowers, only waiting for his coming, opened their heart of fragrance to the day, and new leaves, so tenderly green, which were packed and curled away quite tightly only the night before, unfurled their verdant banners at his first touch. Yesterday's flowers, their mission ended, fell in little heaps of scarcely faded petals beneath the bushes at the light shaking of the morning breeze from the sea, and the new formed blossoms, shaking down a tear of regret as they opened their perfumed buds, replaced with their new glory the lost beauty of last night.

Standing there with this dear comrade beside him, with the cool daybreak breeze—the wings of the morning—fanning the fresh sea air about them, with new life bursting into being all around them, Christian felt for the first time that absolute oneness with nature which it is sometimes, but too rarely, our privilege to feel. He held Utamè's little soft hand in his as they walked gently along the path she chose, and forgetting all anxieties, all dangers past or to come, he felt himself breathe largely of the inner, deeper life of nature. A new life seemed before him, on which he was entering with heart and brain washed clean and pure in the flood of all this beneficence and beauty.

Christian felt very near to God in that time of intimate connection with nature and the fulness of life. The heaven of theology is nearer to some men in their sorrow than in their joy—they do not want it when they are glad; but to others of us the Giver of everything seems nearer when He gives us royally than when He stints us of His bounty. And that is natural enough, for He meant man to be happy, and we are closer to Him and more like Him then than when we are in grief. So it was with Christian, who only prayed when sufficiently at one with Him to be glad, for his prayer was never petition but always thanksgiving.

That day, before the heat had come, the air was so fresh and invigorating, with all the crispness and strength of the sea in it, the rapture of life was so intoxicating, and the beauty of the morning world so great, that Christian sang aloud, as the birds did, from the delight of life and the ecstasy of love that flooded his whole heart.   It was impossible for these two young, strong, and beautiful creatures to be sad, lost, as it were, in all that enchantment of nature of which they had become a part; for happiness was mixed in the very air with the golden sunshine of it.

Taking Utamè's bundle from her and slinging it with his own upon his back, Christian put his arm round her little waist, and side by side they turned deeper into the cool forest.   The path was narrow and broken, and the dewy ferns on either hand shook from their fronds little sparkling showers as they moved; and the golden sunlight piercing through the verdant roof above them burnished into brightness the polished leaves of the great wild arums, or shining on the gorgeous flowers, fixed in their cups of dew-wet leaves, made them glow like jewels set in flames.

Sometimes down the little hills they raced hand in hand, for very gladness of life and solitude and freedom, until, laughing and out of breath, they stopped, and Christian, throwing his arms round the panting girl, would kiss fresh beauty into her happy face, and she, with godlike innocence, kissed the man again. Youth was in their blood and youth was in the air, and the sense of escape from observation to a solitude peopled but by themselves gave a dash and a recklessness to their spirits that were indescribably exhilarating. They laughed as they looked in each other's eyes, and their souls expanded in this new freedom as a flower does to the sun. Christian thought that his heart beat quicker there than in his native country; the blood which beforetimes coursed with so calm and steady a flow now poured through his veins with a finer, quicker spirit; and his soul seemed to take on colour, as his face and body did, from the glorious sunshine.

The path they had been following for some hours, from which several others had branched off to different little towns and plantations, began before mid-day to become so indistinct and overgrown that North had doubts as to his powers of tracing it, and fearing that they might lose their way hopelessly in the vastness of the trackless and entangled forest he asked Utamè what they must do.

'Go on,' she answered.

'Yes; but I cannot see the way.'

'What does that matter? Are you different from me? I do not want to see the path. I know that the mountain is there,' she said, pointing in a certain direction, 'and I have been to it once with Soma and once with my father when I was little. I cannot forget it.'

Christian tried to make her explain, but all she said was, 'I do not know how. I feel it here. I know I am right.'

She was so confident of her own powers that Christian thought it best to trust to them; indeed, it was the only thing to do. He knew the wonderful instinct that these people possess, which is one of the many natural gifts that civilisation destroys. It appeared that she was right, for early in the afternoon they struck a beautiful little stream which flowed rapidly down to the sea. It was so shaded and over-arched with trees that it almost seemed to have tunnelled itself a way through the mass of the forest growth. Here Utamè was quite sure of her route, and said that they must follow the course of the stream through its little valley right into the heart of the hills before they began the ascent of the great fire mountain Monoriro, where, in the shade of its smoke, and shaken by earthquakes, Venga the priestess lived.

Here they rested for a time and ate part of the food which Soma had insisted upon their taking. They drank from the clear stream, Utamè making a cup of her little dimpled hands, and slept through the greatest heat of the day in the dense shade of the motionless trees. The whole place was full of the murmurous sound of flowing water, as the stream rippled and splashed over its rocky bed, and, when all the birds were hushed in the torrid splendour of the heat at high noon, Utamè said that she should sleep too. She lay down and placed her cheek upon her hand, and only opening her eyes once or twice to smile at Christian, fell asleep like a little child.

For some time Christian sat by her side and watched her as she slept. He was filled with an infinite tenderness for this slight creature who had dared so much for the love of him, and with it was mingled a feeling half of manly pride at having won her, and half a sentiment of almost paternal protec-tion. He watched the slow rise and fall of her young rounded bosom, where the light fell on the polished skin, and wondered why was it so beautiful; he saw the long black lashes that curled so thickly and lay so lightly on her cheek, and wished to see the deep loving eyes that the envious lids hid from him. One little hand lay palm upwards on the moss, the fingers slightly curved with the lassitude of sleep, and he tried to riddle some meaning from the delicate lines that were traced thereon. He thought that never had she looked so beautiful as now that she lay there in the soft shadow sleeping so lightly and soundly before him, because filled with the utter confidence that his presence gave. He softly kissed her shoulder, and though she did not wake she smiled through her sleep, as though she were aware that her lover and dear master had touched her. Then, too, for Christian the shadows grew darker, and the voice of the stream sang him to sleep and rippled and murmured to him in his dreams.

By the time they awoke the sun was long past the zenith, and when they stood in open spaces their shadows no longer formed a little black circle round their feet but had lengthened out upon the ground. But open spaces were few and far between, and the forest growth was here so dense and interwoven with a wild mass of creepers and tangled vines that the path, which had almost vanished for some time, now disappeared altogether. Utamè said that it would be much the wiser plan to take to the stream and follow its course, as that was quite the easiest manner of progression now that they were getting amongst the hills.

Picking Utamè up in his great arms, this giant with the heart of a child waded into the water and would have carried her thus the rest of the way; indeed, he felt a strange delight in giving up his strength and his body to her service. But the girl was the wiser—as is generally the case in such matters—and insisted upon being put down. By this time they had begun to get amongst the mountains; the path became more difficult, as the bed of the stream was very rocky, and as its descent was now very steep it was often interrupted by waterfalls and rapids. After they had passed a certain deep little pool which lay black in the shadow of the surrounding trees, into which the stream fell as a cascade down an inaccessible wall of rock, Utamè said—

'Here we leave the stream. Our road lies yonder.'

She pointed as she spoke to a little gravelly patch of ground between two great rocks that lay half in the water, and wading to it Christian found that there was a very narrow track that led back into the forest in the direction of the mountain. Night was coming on very quickly by the time they left the stream; already the shadow of the mountain, which, buried as they were in the thickness of the forest growth, was quite invisible to them, lay all across the valley, and they knew that darkness would be upon them before an hour was passed.

'We cannot reach the mountain to-night, can we?' asked Christian with some little anxiety in his voice.

'No,' answered Utamè cheerfully. 'When I came before with Soma we got there at sunset, but we did not rest once all the day, and, Kliss, you and I have rested often,' added the girl with a smile.

'Why did you not tell me?'

'Oh, I liked to rest,' said Utamè with true Polynesian carelessness. 'What does it matter? Not far off are the grass houses where Kulana and Tama-he lived before the Pangu men came here and drove them off.'

'We will go there,' said Christian decisively; 'but, my poor girl, what will you have to eat?'

'Are you all like that in *Papalangi* land?' she asked. 'Do you never know how or where to find food? I will show you. Near the houses will be bananas or a *talo* swamp. I can get a fire and we can cook our food. We are safe now; we can find food; why should we hurry? I am happy here.'

This happy philosophy of the girl consoled North, who had no anxiety for himself, so they left the stream quite cheerfully, and taking the little track, which was so much overgrown as to be almost indistinguishable from the rest of the thickly covered ground, they set out in search of the houses Utamè had spoken of. They lay but a short way back from the stream in a little clearing, where Nature, having for a short time been left to herself, was quickly reasserting her sway. The two or three houses still standing were greatly dilapidated, but still offered all the shelter that a tropical night requires, and with very little difficulty they found the *talo* patch where many plants were still growing; with these and some coco-nuts and a pile of ripe bananas, which they found all golden and luscious on a plant at the back of the house they had chosen, there were all the requisites for a good meal.

In all these preparations Utamè proved herself to be the better man; she knew where to find everything and how to prepare the food when they had found it. She it was who made the fire. This was a proceeding which Christian was never tired of watching; there was something wonderful in the change of motion and energy into heat that was novel and delightful still, for all that he had seen the process many times. At this time, though he had tried over and over again, he had not been able to learn the knack, so that all that he could do was to find suitable pieces of wood for Utamè to work with. These consisted of one large, very dry piece and one slender, hard, and pointed piece, which the girl held in her two hands and worked up and down on the larger piece till she had worn a long narrow groove in it. Bearing almost her entire weight upon this, she worked rapidly and more rapidly, till a faint filmy smoke arose from the heated timber, and finally, in the little heap of dry wood dust worn from the sides of the groove a tiny spark of fire was born from death and decay. This was carefully nursed with the girl's breath, till she raised the smallest of small flames, with which she set her dry leaves and tinder a-fire.

There was something curiously suggestive to Christian in this re-birth to a strange new life of the dead and worthless timber. It seemed almost an act of creation, or as though the fire-maker endowed the dead matter before her with a spark from her own vital flame.

But the gay chatter of the girl as she gave him instructions to help her, and sent him running hither and thither for different things she wanted, left Christian small time for such reflections. It was quite dark by the time that the food was ready, and they had to eat it by the fitful light of the little fire; but this they did not mind; they did not fear the dark, and when Christian had swept out the house with a bundle of twigs and leaves to clear it of centipedes or any other unpleasant companions, they were ready for sleep Through a ragged hole in the roof of thatch Christian could see a patch of clear dark sky, and he watched, for a long time before he slept, the stately march of the lustrous stars, which seemed that night to glow with an added tenderness, across the vault of heaven.

CHAPTER XVI

Next morning, long before sunrise, Utamè slipped out noiselessly from the house, and, retracing the little path to the stream, bathed in the clear cold pool into which the waterfall poured; she came back as cool and fresh as a young brown Naiad, and wakened North by shaking little drops of water from her hair on to his face. He sprang up wide awake at once, with that sense of buoyancy and wellbeing that only the young and strong and healthy know when first they wake, and on learning where the girl had been he started off like a deer along the dewy path, and stripping himself of his one garment as he ran he plunged headlong into the deep black pool. Although he could not see it for the thickness of the forest, he knew by the brightness of the daylight that the sun was rising as he left the pool. By the time he was back at the little dreamful house Utamè had prepared their somewhat fragmentary and rudimentary breakfast, and in a few minutes they left the place and were once more on their way.

For some time, perhaps for the distance of a mile, the character of the scenery was the same luxuriant forest growth as that through which they had passed the day before, but suddenly, so suddenly as to come as a shock almost to Christian, the whole prospect was changed. Only a few yards before them the bright

sunshine was pouring itself through the thickly growing trees into the green shadow of the forest, and walking on towards the light they found that the forest
ended abruptly in a narrow line of scorched and burnt
trees. Before them, like a great black river, lay a
gigantic stream of solid tumbled lava, all twisted into
waves and ropes and contorted in an agonised confusion
of hard metallic billows just as the fiery, slow-creeping
flood had consolidated into stone.

Before them lay the mother mountain, which Christian now, for the first time, saw in all her majesty of
stern and forbidding barrenness ; it rose in a great
broken cone high into the air, every crag and shattered
precipice clearly defined against the unstained blue of
the sky. Around it all the hills were forest-covered
with a growth as luxuriant as that which they were
leaving, and, for some little way up its steep sides, the
green vesture spread in the deep valleys which scored
its sacred flanks, but all the topmost heights were bare.
A cold and solitary remoteness seemed to crown the
mountain, as though, now that its fiery work was ended,
it rested with a scornful pride and dignity on its self-
made grandeur, for no smoke rose from that uppermost
crater, its fires were extinct, and its molten lake, having
burst in some wild turbulent heaving of its proud
waves the wall that confined it, had poured down a
flood of liquid fire into the green valleys below. This
last work of devastation must have taken place thousands
of years ago, for soft rain and softer airs had wrought
their patient charm upon the once fiery rocks and
softened them and broken them up to the sweeter uses
of nature, and forest trees and palms and filmy ferns
had once more covered the awful scar with a beautiful
cicatrice of verdant vegetation. But the mountain was

not dead; the great god Rorutu still made it his home, and the fires that now were long since cold in the lofty summit raged as fiercely and played their world-forming part as thoroughly on a black lower shoulder of the mountain as ever they had done from the height. From this great buttress of the mountain, which lay straight in front of Christian and Utamè as they paused amongst the charred and blackened stumps of trees at the edge of the forest, a curious silvery cloud of steam rose high into the air, where it hung, a heavy, constantly dissipated but always renewed mass that was ominous of what lay beneath.

'That,' said Utamè, pointing to it, 'is Rorutu's breath; at night time it is red and fiery, and it moves and changes with shadows.'

'Is that where Venga lives?'

'Yes, always in its shadow; sunshine only falls upon her house in the morning and the evening. It is just there she lives,' added the girl, quickly pointing to a sudden outburst of flame and fiery vapour that glowed red even in the daylight. The next moment a low hoarse roar reached them, and the ground trembled.

'Rorutu moves,' said the girl simply.

'And is that where I must leave you?' asked North.

'Yes,' answered the girl cheerfully; 'it is but for a little time, and I shall be safe with Venga. The gods protect her always.'

The stream of lava before them, as was evident from the burnt forest through which it flowed, had proceeded from the present active crater; it had come there, Utamè said, when she was a little girl. Nothing grew upon it; the whole length of it was black and

bare and barren, and in many places it was as bright
and glittering as glass.　For some little distance they
picked their way along this stony and uneven road,
but they soon left it, as it wounded their bare feet
to walk upon it.　The climbing now became serious,
for the ascent was steep.　They had been mounting gradually all the day before, so that they were
already very high above sea-level, and now Christian
noticed that the character of the vegetation changed.
The trees were no longer lofty and luxuriant, but
became more and more stunted, until towards noon
they had dwindled down to bushes and a sort of
scrubby undergrowth; the tropical appearance of nature
had vanished, no palms, except a very small and
prickly one, grew at that height, and soon even these
poor plants no longer thrived, and nothing but a coarse
turf of harsh grass sparsely covered the black and
crumbling shaly soil.　In places even this poor grass
was absent, and from amongst the tumbled rocks light
jets of steam were issuing, which had stained the earth
around them with sulphur of every shade from brown
to lemon colour.　These signs of the activity of the
volcano became more frequent as they approached the
edge of the precipitous cliff, at the bottom of which
Utamè said the lake of fire lay.　At intervals of about
half an hour the loud roar and rush of an explosion
would be heard, and the slight trembling of the earth
that North thought he had felt at .a lesser height
became more and more perceptible.

It was late in the afternoon when they reached the
edge of the great hollow crater, at the bottom of which
the surging lake of liquid fire beat incessantly in a
foam of molten lava against its shores, for although
the distance traversed was not very great, the diffi-

culties of climbing with bare feet over the now jagged
and now crumbling rocks and hills of loose cinders,
were so numerous that their painful progress had been
of the slowest. The sun poured down its noonday
heat upon them untempered by any shadow, and since
they had left the forest in the morning they had not
found water once, so that both of them were almost
exhausted before they reached the end of their task.
They hardly spoke, for their tongues and lips were
dry and parched, yet neither of them gave way to any
expression of fatigue or annoyance, for fear of discour-
aging the other ; but Christian could tell by Utamè's
flagging step that, brave though she was, she could not
hold out much longer. At the very end of the ascent,
under pretence of assisting her in difficult places, he
more than half supported her, and time after time he
found some reason or excuse for resting for a moment
where some great rock threw a grateful black shadow
on the black ground.

At last they reached the edge of the great crater,
and looked down to where, five hundred feet below
them, the sacred lake of fire tossed its waves and threw
its glowing fountains of liquid lava in the trembling
superheated air. Utamè looked upon the wonderful
scene with a savage's indifference, which was only
tempered with an expression of relief at having so
nearly attained their goal, but for Christian its awful
and unearthly beauty had such a terrible fascination,
that he forgot thirst, fatigue, and everything else as he
gazed into the great black gulf with its central heart
of restless fire.

The whole of the bottom of the huge depression
that the crater formed was filled with gigantic black
rocks, tumbled in every direction in the wildest con-

fusion, so that it resembled a vast city overthrown by the sudden stroke of an earthquake. In the midst of this desolation, confined by low overhanging cliffs, above which the lava sometimes rose and flowed over, lay the lake of fire, boiling, surging, and dashing its waves against the rocks. The colour of the lava was a curious golden crimson, with a marvellous burnished iridescence that no words can describe; every now and then a glorious violet colour suffused it with a fleeting flush, and where the lava curved itself to beat and break upon the rocks at the margin the shadows were of a glowing purple. This was the sacred lake; here Rorutu lived, and the awfulness, beauty, and wildness of it was such that North could not wonder that the worshippers of the deity had thought it worthy of being his home. The whole lake throbbed as with the heart-beat of the god.

Every now and then, as the molten waves dashed themselves in fiery spray upon the confining cliff, and licked with tongues of liquid fire about the rocks, great fragments would detach themselves and fall with a sullen plunge into the lake, where, with a rapturous leaping of flashing drops, and a sudden play of jewel-like fire, they would be swallowed up for ever. The lake never rested; it boiled like some immense infernal pot, or crisped itself to waves as though in that windless calm, where, for once, the tropic sun was impotent, a gale were blowing that must shake the rocks. It was so wonderful, so awful in its hellish beauty, so stupendous and miraculous, that it impressed itself upon Christian, from the first moment, as something sacred, so that it was almost with awe that he prepared to descend.

He had lost all idea of the flight of time, and stood gazing at it, fascinated, as they say men are by the weird, unearthly beauty that glows in the eyes of serpents; he had forgotten his fatigue, and was lost in the wonder of it, when at last poor, patient Utamè spoke.

'What is the matter, Kliss? your face is white, and you do not speak;' and she put out her hand and shook his arm to rouse him.

'My poor girl, I forgot.'

'I have been sitting here so long. I did not speak, did I? I am so thirsty now. Let us go.'

'Which is the way?'

'Straight down. There is Venga's house; do you not see?' She pointed as she spoke to a little bamboo and thatch building not very far from the margin of the lake, but at a little height above it, which, in his observation of the greater glories of the spectacle below him, Christian had not noticed.

The descent, though rough, was not very difficult, for the sides of the crater wall were often of crumbling ashes in which their feet got a firm hold, and they quickly reached the bottom. Here Christian found a little pool of clear, sweet water that was condensed from one of the innumerable jets of steam that escaped through a crevice in the rock; Utamè and he drank long and deeply, and the girl told him that it was from that source that Venga got all the water she wanted, for there was no spring or brook on that part of the mountain.

Although the distance that divided them from Venga's house was not great, when once they had reached the bottom of the crater wall, it took them some time to pick their way amongst the dangers of the place. It almost seemed a tempting of Providence to trust themselves so near the edge of the seething lake, but they had to approach it very closely once or twice to avoid the great black cracks and fissures that crossed their path, which yawned to an unknown depth, and from which pale ghostly clouds of steam arose and wuthered off in some strange current of hot mephitic air. The silence of the place, in the long intervals between the explosions from the red-edged open mouth of a secondary smaller crater some little distance from the lake, was in itself appalling, for such a scene of terror as the boiling, spouting lava presented ought to have been accompanied by noises as awe-inspiring as itself. But a complete silence lay upon that place of blasted desolation except for the rare noise of the falling of a fragment of the undermined lake edge, and a low, seething, bubbling sound which the lava made as great sullen bubbles formed themselves upon the surface and then burst with a loose, soft flapping of their molten lips. This sound, however, could only be heard when quite close to the lake.

When at last these two weary wanderers in this land of terror reached the little house of the old priestess, no sign of life was heard within. Before the door, for the house was enclosed on all sides with rough reed-work, was piled a heap of food—bananas, yams, *talo*, and coco-nuts, and two live fowl, with their scaly legs tied with a scrap of sinnet. All this was brought, Utamè said, by pilgrims to the holy place. They listened for a moment, and hearing nothing, the girl ventured into the house.

CHAPTER XVII

Directly afterwards Utamè came out of the house
with a scared look upon her face; she ran to where
North stood, and said—

'She sleeps, but her eyes are open and white.'

Almost before she had finished speaking a harsh
and extraordinarily loud voice at the doorway of the
house made them turn round with a violent start, and
there before them, haggard, dishevelled, and thin to
attenuation, the old priestess stood, upright as a dart,
and with eyes which seemed to glow from beneath her
thick gray brows with something of Rorutu's fire.

'I do not sleep,' she said. 'Venga was with the
god who said that you Utamè e Ngawa, and you
l'apalangi tüa, were coming to the mountain.'

The old woman spoke with the tone of sincerity
and conviction that she always used in uttering the
messages with which she said she was inspired, and
which had gained for her the great repute as a prophetess that she possessed. She was a shrewd and
very clever old woman, who received news from all
parts of the island by the devotees who flocked to the
shrine of fire, and was so generally well informed, even
of private matters, that she was able by a clever re-
tailing of her gossip to astonish almost any one who
visited her. Of Utamè's passion for North she was

already well informed through Tama-iru, who had visited her to induce her to remove by her spells the man whom he suspected too truly of being his rival. It was through similar channels of information that she had known, two years before, of Soma's despairing condition when he lost his first friend, and having stored in her retentive memory some rumour of white people visiting the islands to the west, she had sent him thither with the hope that a big change in his life might work a cure in him.

'Tell me what you want of me,' the loud-voiced old priestess went on to say. 'Do you come to sacrifice ?'

Utamè, who at first had been alarmed at the sudden apparition in the doorway, now remembered that, for all her loud voice and piercing eye, Venga had treated her with womanly kindness upon the two former occasions that she had seen her, and she determined to throw herself upon her generosity at once and say what was their request. In the simplest and most natural manner in the world she ran to her, and putting her young rounded arms about the withered neck of the old woman, she said—

'You are a prophetess. Don't you know what we want ? We want you to take care of me while Papalangi tëa goes back to Otorangi.'

'I will take care of you, for the blood of Makea flows in your veins as well as in mine. The man I cannot take in, for I have a charm (*sou-ayi*) working against him that he shall not live.'

Utamè uttered a piercing shriek as Venga said these last words, and rushed from the old woman to Christian's side, as though her presence could ward off all ill from him.

North wanted to laugh, but he stopped himself, fearing to insult the priestess, for he knew of what these dreaded and often fatal charms consisted. A little piece of food left after eating, the skin of a banana the fruit of which the doomed man had consumed, or a piece of his hair or nails was given to the sorcerer, who buried the object, whatever it might be, with strange incantations, taking good care that the fated man should know what had been done. So strong were the superstitious terrors of these people that, unless the charm were taken off, the man generally sickened and often died from sheer fright; each case but corroborating the fatal power of the witchcraft.

Stooping down to the frightened girl, Christian whispered something in her ear, and leaving her where she was, he approached Venga with a smile on his boyish face. Perhaps there was enough of the woman left in the old priestess to let her notice the comeliness of the young man, and the ease and strength with which he walked, and that these things were in his favour, for she allowed him to come near and speak to her without interruption, though her face was still stern.

'Is this thing true?' he asked.

'I have said it,' replied Venga.

'Then,' said Christian boldly, 'it is against the will of your gods and against the wish of your priests.'

'What do your words hide?' said the woman, meaning 'What do you mean?'

'My words say what is the truth, and for a sign of it behold what Paori, the old priest of Otorangi, gave to me for my protection, saying that all true followers of Rongo and Rorutu would aid me and shelter me if I showed it them.'

As he spoke he slipped his hand down into the narrow folds of his *mahi*, and produced the little worn stone figure that his dying friend had given him. The expression of Venga's face changed from sternness to one of eager interest directly she saw what North held in his hand.

'Did Paori give you that? It is one of the figures that Mokunga, Rorutu's son, made in memory of his father. You can come to no ill so long as you have that. Paori gave it because you were worthy. It is a sign.' The old woman was now all excitement, and the natural hospitality of the Omëans beamed from her face. 'Come to the mats,' she said, entering the little house. 'The way is long; you must eat.'

Hardly had they entered and seated themselves on the very fine mat she unrolled for them than she suddenly remembered that the charm was still doing its evil work, and as the frequently fatal success of her own witchcraft had reacted upon her, she had grown to have a firm belief in its efficacy, so that it was with the greatest earnestness that she hurried off.

'Come with me,' she said; 'the *sou-agi* must be taken off before you eat or drink.'

Christian followed her out of the house, and with difficulty kept pace with her, such was the surprising ease and speed with which the old woman crossed the rough lava rocks. At a short distance from the house, on a shaly slope, they came upon a series of little mounds of ashes and lava rock, decorated with odd slips and plumes of dried palm branches and withered fern. It looked like a miniature cemetery. To one of these little heaps, careful to avoid touching the others, Venga darted, and plucking up the dry branches she carefully broke each one, muttering some words

in a low tone to herself as she did so.   Next with her
shrivelled fingers she dispersed the little heap of dirt,
and taking out a mouldy and decaying piece of *talo*
and the rough rind of some fruit that Christian had
eaten, she said that they must be burnt.   The priestess
did not seem easy in her mind until they had reached
the house, and the rotten fragments were consumed in
her cooking fire.

After this she gave them food, saying that now
that the *sou-agi* was taken off, Christian's meal might
do him some good.   She talked a great deal, asking
many shrewd questions of both North and Utamè, and
then, seeing the state of fatigue that both her guests
were in, she said they might sleep in safety.

When Christian awoke it was nearly midnight, but
a ruddy glow filled all the place, so that it was easy to
see everything for some short distance.   The noise of
the explosion that had aroused him failed to disturb
Utamè, who was sleeping the deep sleep of physical
exhaustion, and Venga was nowhere to be seen.

He went out, drawn by an irresistible attraction to
the lake, and stumbling across the rough ground he
reached the little cliff that edged it.   If it were a
wonderful and awful scene by daylight, what were its
terrors when multiplied a thousandfold by the night!
The playing, constantly changing colours of the lava,
as it moved with its mysterious internal ebb and flow,
that even in the full blaze of daylight had been marvellous and bewildering, were intensified till he could
have thought the hollow crater was filled with molten
jewels; and where the sudden fountains arose in unexpected parts of the lake, the wonderful hues of the
liquid lava in other places were paled by their greater
magnificence.   It was awful, it was wonderful, it was

fascinating, for it possessed that terrible attraction that all things powerful for evil have for the souls of men. It is not the beauty of his shining scales that makes the fascination of the serpent—it is the knowledge that death, sudden and terrible death, lies behind those enigmatic jaws. Just so with the lava pool. It was not the glory of its shifting colours, nor the splendour of its fiery waves, that fixed North's gaze and thoughts; it was the knowledge of the evil it had done and the ills that remained for it to do.

In face of this relentless and irresistible force of nature that, careless of human well- or ill-being, played its part, blind as fate, and as regardless of man's prayer or execration, pouring its fires into cultivated valleys, and swallowing the human lives thrown to it for sacrifice or propitiation without change as without remorse, Christian felt that strange pagan feeling well up in his heart that deep down in our natures is in all of us. Since the day that man first felt some blind dim stirring of his soul within him as it strove to understand what even yet it has failed to grasp, there have been the same ideas in us of the enmity of the great wild forces of nature—storm and fire, thunder and earthquake—drawn up in array against the human race.

North felt all this inherent paganism that night as he stood upon the cliff edge, with the heat of the lava scorching his naked body, watching with shaded eyes the blinding glories of the restless fire. It was rising, Venga had said, and shortly would overflow and pour down its molten flood into some peaceful valley, no one could tell which, that, ignorant of its impending ruin, was happily sleeping as though in perfect safety. Here before his very eyes the old

Earth was preparing catastrophe and ruin; deep from her fiery womb she was drawing the elements of ill which shortly would carry devastation and despair, and perhaps an awful death, to whole families and villages of hapless men. He could understand at that moment how it was that the islanders had endowed the place with an evil personality, and understand, too, the wild terror that prompted them, in times when this peril threatened them, to choose the fairest, manliest, and most noble of their youths, and decorating him with flowers, fling him from the black rock of sacrifice, whilst the priests and people howled out the name 'Rorutu,' into the seething pit as a propitiation to the angry god. How many young lives had thus been wasted, he thought, since that mountain fire was first deified!—wasted without reward, for the lava rose in the crater and the stream of it poured down the hillside none the less angrily for the sacrifice.

Christian never knew how long he stood lost in the contemplation of this beautiful, horrible object, but at last an awful sense of fear of it grew upon him, and suddenly he was conscious of his solitude—lost, as it were, in the immensity of night and surrounded with the lava's bloody glow. It was not fear of any tangible object that beset him, though he had strange terrible impulses to throw himself down into that awful heart of fire, but a terror of the unseen, unfelt 'might-be.' The appalling stillness of the soundless air, the strange wild flickering of light from unseen flames, the sudden gushes of a hotter blast of vapour, and lastly, the awful lurkings of black shadows that sped away and flung themselves down again at the foot of the rocks as the hellish light flared up and now died down again, all conspired against him; he was alone there facing Nature in one of her weirdest, cruellest aspects, and the contest was too much for him. He felt himself too small.

He knew that he could not endure much more of this ordeal, and turning his back on the lava-pool —which went on sparkling, gleaming, and flashing with its iridescent magnificence unchanged though its only spectators were the night and the mother-mountain towering above it—he fled. In his hurry to get away from the scene he had begun to dread he did not notice the direction he took, and in a few moments, when he asked himself where the house of Venga lay, he found that he had entirely lost his way. For some time he hurried this way and that in the hope of seeing some landmark that might guide him back, but it was useless, and recognising the impossibility of finding his way by night through the black mazes of the huge volcanic rocks, he determined to stay there until daybreak.

Christian seated himself to wait for the morning with the patience that some great souls have at their command. He knew that there was no pushing on of the finger of God's great clock, and was content to wait till the stars in their march overhead had ticked off the hours till the day. He accepted the inevitable, and, as so many have done before him, he found it after all the softest of beds to lie on. Although so young in years he still was older than most men live to be, for life had no blank spaces in it for him. Every minute of time had for him sixty heart-beats of living in it, each one of which he experienced. He had learned to value his days too, and to do and to live and to enjoy in them as much as possible, for he knew that the longer he lived the shorter and shorter grew the days and the quicker and quicker passed the nights, for all the stir and activity of the fuller life he gained with years, and all the added love of them. The poetic heart of the man was deep and all his passions strong, so that the cup which Life held to his lips was full, and the draught was sweet to his strong youth.

But patience! a night is coming long enough for all to rest in. How will it feel at the end when, looking back on it, the spasm of life we have known shows bare and empty for all we have accomplished, and so very short? Shall we hail with joy the dark night coming, or shall we struggle for a little longer of the daylight? It is a long night to look forward to that lies between the day we die and the dawn of the Day of Judgment. Well, we shall sleep soundly, and our dreams—if dream we do—are perhaps the makings of our own hands now.

In youth the shortness of life is its greatest sorrow; in age that we have so misspent it. The first all thoughtful souls must feel, Christian among them, but he determined, if possible, to avoid the second, for he felt that of all sorrows the most unendurable is repentance that comes too late.

The night passed slowly, for Christian did not sleep—the few hours' rest he had had were enough to restore to him all his vigour, and he sat there facing the stars with nothing between him and their beauty but the millions of miles of pure ether, through which he sent his fancy flying with the godlike speed that is thought's own. What dreams of immortal beauty bathed his true heart in those star-drawn hours! Life pulsed itself in music worthy of the royal progress of his emancipated mind; his soul expanded its great wings and flew upwards, till he seemed to touch the Infinite.   Ah, Christian, poor dumb Christian, you were a poet, almost a prophet, then !

Of all God's gifts to men imagination is the noblest, for itself creates the beauty that is the happiness of mortals ; and Christian, our poor shiftless, careless wanderer on the earth, had this great boon, which often bore him heavenward.

At last the night was ended,—as all nights, even happiest ones, must end,—the light of the friendly stars was slowly withdrawn, the darkness gently melted off, and the great vault of the sky became so blue, so intensely, clearly, purely blue that one might have thought it the sapphire foundation of the second great wall of the city of God.

Christian rose, and felt for the first time that he was chilled to the bone.   Mounting a heap of tumbled rocks he looked for the house, and as soon as the light was strong enough he saw it not very far off.   Thither he hurried, to find Utamé at the doorway in the greatest state of alarm at his absence.   She was too happy at his return to be angry, and taking him by his cold and dew-wet arm she led him into the silent house.

CHAPTER XVIII

THAT day Christian left Monoriro, but not before Venga had shown him another great marvel of the mountain, which to Christian was more wonderful even than the crater and the lava pool. This was the series of colossal statues that stood on artificial terraces, built, with infinite labour, of huge blocks of stone. These great figures were almost exactly alike, and were all erected on a hillside, some distance from the volcano, which was covered with rocks of a sort of gray granite, and from whence, across the miles of dark green forest, the open sea could be seen. The whole of this mountain side was covered with the remains of this lost art, for the Omëans possessed no knowledge of working in stone, and the statues on Monoriro were as full of mystery to them as to North. These immense and impressive works must have been produced by a nation of giants, but of this mighty race, whether ancestors or no of the Omëans, the people had not the vaguest knowledge or even the faintest tradition.

The vanished race which had carved these dumb guardians of their tombs buried their dead in stone chambers in the great terraces on which they stood, and so sacred were these last resting-places of the mighty dead still held by the Omëans that Venga would not allow North to enter one of them from which the huge stone that sealed the entrance had fallen away. It was a strange fancy which prompted this departed people to sleep their last sleep thus high up towards the heaven which, perhaps, they hoped to reach; and the poetry which made them choose this one spot, from whence the open ocean could be seen—a fitting emblem of infinity—was recognised by North as in silence he faced this strange assembly of sleepless kings.

The figures were of vast proportions, being from thirty to forty feet in height, and although of rude execution, they possessed those elements of grandeur which colossal size and solemn dignity of aspect bestow. To add to their mystery, they were unlike any type of man that was known to Christian, and it pleased him to think that in these great carved rocks he saw a lasting memorial of the vanished race who, with a boldness of conception that in itself was grand, had seized upon the great crags of the mountain, and not knowing their own impending fate, had carved a monument for all time in their own image. The general contour of the face was square, the nose was thick but pure in outline, the upper lip short and thin, and the eyes were deeply set beneath an overhanging and thoughtful brow. The whole expression was solemn, and as of one who watches. From the great hollows of the eyes the eyeballs, which had probably been made of the black volcanic glass that was common on the mountain, had fallen out, but Christian could tell from the direction of the faces that the steady glance of all these gods or kings was fixed for ever skywards. It was the same with every figure on the mountain; their gaze was always to the stars. There were very many of these vast impressive figures, mostly standing erect, though some had fallen from their thrones. They were all alike; all turned their sightless gaze to heaven, and all without exception faced the north, where, league upon league before them, stretched the limitless expanse of open sea. What did they wait for? What was the message for which they had waited so patiently through the ages?

It almost seemed to North that he stood before the works of an earlier race of men than that of the seed of Adam, and in their dumb presence he felt the mighty force of artistic creation which had enabled those rude primeval sculptors to carve these images from the living rocks, which they had so impressed with their own awe and wonder as to leave their fleeting emotion written there in stone for all succeeding time. There before him those sightless Samsons stood that day, as they had stood throughout the ages, unmoved and patient, scorched by the tropic sun, drenched by the tropic rains, and beaten on by every wind of heaven, to tell at last, perhaps, the story of another world and of the vanished race which carved and set them there in the great solitude of the burnt and wasted mountain.

The joy of the artist of our era—whatsoever the method of his expression—is not so much in the perfection of his work as in the knowledge that he has gladdened and made beautiful some moments of the span of life—contracting even from its beginning—of those who look upon his creation. The dead-and-gone men who had carved the Titans of Monoriro had had another object; the intention of their work was stern and solemn, though perhaps they wished, in some strange way, in the quietness and patience of the figures, to speak of hope as well; and they had succeeded, for the awe and solemnity was as fresh and living that day in Christian's heart, before those silent witnesses of a long lost civilisation, as in those of the unknown men who had endowed them with their spirit.

The moment of parting which had now come to Christian and Utamè was a very bitter one, for although they both looked forward to a speedy reunion, they knew that the term of their separation was an indefinite one. Depending as it did upon Christian's power of persuasion over Ilo, the head chief, or resting upon the even more insecure footing of chance, it was probable that they might not see each other again for a long time. Though both loved equally well, and though the hearts of both were wrung with the bitterest anguish, it was perhaps the woman who would suffer most. As usual it was she who must sit and wait whilst he was up and doing. One thought only could fill her days and nights until she held her lover in her arms once more, while a hundred varied incidents, the mere affairs of active human life, must occupy his mind and keep his thoughts from dwelling too constantly on the loved woman who was away.

It was time for him to go: the sun was already at some height above the horizon, and all the mountain mist, which like a veil had floated about the great figures of the sightless gods, had drifted off. It was useless lingering. Christian seized Utamè in his great arms, lifting her from the ground in the passion of his embrace, and, whilst tears filled his tender eyes, he pressed her breathless to his breast and kissed her, as a man can only kiss one woman in a lifetime. Utamè threw her arms round his sunburnt neck and clung to him despairingly, as though she could never let him go. Her body was shaken by a storm of sobs, and tears ran down her cheeks; all that she held dear in life was going with him. Christian whispered something in the little ear that was so near his lips, and a smile, a memory of a smile, played for a moment on her face like a rainbow in a storm.

Perhaps it was suggested by what he said, or maybe it was prompted by her own fears, but suddenly she freed herself from Christian's arms, and with a jealousy that he loved to see, she grasped his hand and dragged him before one of the great stern figures of the mountain, in the long morning shadow of which they almost stood.

'Swear,' she said, 'that you will love no other woman down in Otorangi. Swear that you will not even kiss a woman until Utamè is with you again.'

'I could not love another woman,' he said; 'you have all my heart and all my worship.' And he swore it, laying his hand on the gigantic god as though to call him witness to his oath, and the girl's mind was relieved.

They now walked back to where Venga stood with a quiet smile on her wrinkled face, as though from the passionless calm of her old age she could look back on her own more stormy youth, and from her memory draw excuses for the two poor young things before her. There was a tone of tenderness in her loud voice, for women—even old women—never forget their girlhood, as she turned to North and said—

'Now go, the sun is getting up. You will come back to Monoriro. Venga will have taken care of your wife.'

This was the first time the word had been used to

Christian, and he felt a thrill as he heard it, and looking at Utamè he saw that she was blushing through her tears. He seized the girl in his arms once more for a last embrace, and then leaving her sobbing as though her heart would break, he tore himself away. He looked back once as he reached the turn of the hillside, and saw that Utamè, covering her face with her two hands, was stumbling along, being led by the old woman; she had not the courage to look upon him again, but Venga turned her head and silently waved him farewell. As he began his descent of the mountain the two women were out of sight in a moment, and with a strange new feeling of loneliness in his heart, Christian went on his way.

Before he had left her, Venga had pointed out to North the best road down the rough track of the lava stream, and following her instructions he reached in an hour the little path through the forest along which he and Utamè had travelled so happily so short a time before. Everything reminded him of his late gay companion, whose bright spirits and girlish talk had beguiled the way for him; every little place where they had rested on their journey was sacred to him, and seemed redolent still of the love that had been born there and had breathed itself for good into the world. How could he but remember, when every fibre of him and every pulse of his heart still thrilled at the memory of her touch and of her smile!

Although at that time memory was painful, accentuating his loneliness and reminding him each moment of what he had lost, Christian would not have forgotten had it been within his power to do so. The heart grows hard in forgetting, and it is more the remembering of past sorrows and joys that keeps it tender, and retains the capacity for love alive in it, than any fresh emotions can do. It is the recollection that he has loved much that keeps alight the fire of passion in a man's heart; without memory the love of a man for a woman, that he would only feel in her presence, would be nothing more than lust.

The whole long day was hot and fatiguing, but he hardly rested once, such was his anxiety to leave the forest, the oppressive stillness and silence of which weighed upon him with an inexpressible sadness. Even in the hottest hours of the day, when every bird was silent in the drowsy woods, and when even the flowers were drooping with a languor that was expressive of repose, he did not rest. In all the breathless forest he seemed to be the only living thing, except in one or two open spaces, where the falling of some gigantic tree, loaded with rich festoons of luxuriant creepers and strangely blooming, gorgeous parasitic flowers, had made a little clearing where the sunlight poured into the green gloom; there, slowly floating from flower to flower, or bathing their palpitating wings in the sunshine, as though to show their beauty better, one or two butterflies were to be seen.

Christian had no difficulty in finding his way. How could he forget? Here they had stopped to drink; he almost thought he could see Utamè's little footprints yet at the damp margin of the stream where she had stooped to fill her hollowed hands for him; here she had found a great bush of the *somala* flowers, which filled the whole space round it with its subtle and delicate perfume. She had gathered some of the white blossom, and looking up at him, had asked if he remembered it. There they had rested and slept. Every spot along the way recalled some incident to him of his innocent girl lover. His heart and mind were full of her, and this separation from her in the very height of their happiness made him aware how deep this love had sent its fibres and how firmly they had rooted themselves.

Early in the afternoon the wind had risen, and although still enough on the ground, to which the breeze could not penetrate, Christian could hear the rush of it high overhead and the rustling of the branches. He was glad of the change, for the monotony of the forest silence had become oppressive. The sun had set before he left the forest, but fortunately he had not much farther to travel, for after dark he could hardly have found his way; however, enough of twilight lingered for him to reach the open ground above the town. With what delight he stepped out into the fresh life-giving wind, which, blowing straight upon him from the south, had, for all its leagues of travel across the great wilderness of sea, something of the coldness in it of the ice-fields round the Pole. He stood at the skirt of the breathless forest behind him and drank his fill of it, as though he were athirst and it were water which could quench his drouth.

Night had come by the time he had reached the shore, to which he hurried that he might greet the sea, which sang a welcome to him, he thought, in its well-known, well-loved voice; the waves were breaking crisply on the sand, and the great free southern rollers beating on the reef cast up a huge and misty surf. The great round orb of the golden moon had risen in the east, and growing paler and more silvern as she mounted in her royal road, tinged the topmost crests of the tall black palms that lined the distant beach with a glory all her own. The sky was clear, for all the rushing wind, and the stars shone out in the zenith undimmed by the radiant moon.

But Christian did not linger on the shore longer than was necessary for him to cool his weary and bruised feet in the rising tide; he knew that Soma would be anxiously awaiting him, and he was so eager to clasp the dear fellow's hand in his again, and to unburden himself of all the secrets of his joy and sorrow, that he forgot his fatigue and hurried to the town. Whilst still some way out of Otorangi he was greeted by a faint, far-away sound of music, so soft and distant as barely to be heard; so delicate was it that he scarce could call it audible, it more resembled the gentle touches of a loved hand in one's hair than mere vulgar sound. It was music, but music so chastened by night and remoteness as to be like some strange emotion existing in the ocean air, and independent and quite outside of himself. It was so fitful and intermittent, too, as the south wind rose or fell, that Christian at first had to hold his breath to hear it; but the slight sounds swelled fuller as he approached the town, and he recognised the sweet singing of the girls' voices as they made music for the dance.

Just outside the town there was a little mound which the people called *Fetama geti*, and having climbed that, and being now almost within shouting distance of the performers, he looked down into the *bara* and saw the girls, each one with a lighted torch in her hand, dancing—like a swarm of fire-flies on a summer night—one of their most intricate and rhythmical dances. It was a most beautiful sight, for all the girls were young and graceful, with their dark wavy hair falling over their nude young shoulders, and their bright eyes gleaming in the ruddy torchlight; but North would not wait to watch it. He ran down the slope, and mingling with the crowd, looked eagerly amongst the seated spectators for the face of his friend, but not finding him there, he turned from the square and hurried to Motuiti's house.

CHAPTER XIX

Love in the heart of man is like fire which produces
the two effects of light and heat with one effort, for it
has its two qualities also, neither of which detracts
from the other, as they are totally dissimilar in
character—the love of man and the love of woman.
These two exist side by side, for one is friendship and
the other passion. The first has something of the
higher heaven in it, for it is calm, steady, and passionless; noble, pure, and unbounded, it seeks no reward,
and its only return is in kind. The love for the
woman is as strong and more ardent, inasmuch as it
has its reward. Love in friendship is love only, and
is self-expressive; whereas the love for the woman,
the love that fills one's heart and satisfies it, that
floods one's brain and stretches to its fullest every limb
and nerve and muscle, finds its last, its highest expression outside of itself. A man who loves a woman
truly, wholly, does not love her for her womanhood
alone; she is his friend too, and is bone of his bone, a
part of him; but the last expression of his love for her
must always be unspoken. Generous, self-sacrificing,
and spiritual, without jealousy because passionless, the
love of man for man burns brightly and with an unwavering flame, whilst the love of man for woman is a tenfold
stronger fire that sometimes leaves an ash behind it.

By Christian's heart the double flame was fed, whilst in Soma's a single one consumed it, so North's absence had left him solitary. For much more than a year now they had been inseparable companions, so that with his *ofa - namu* away the poor Omëan had found time hang heavy on his hands, and all that usually made his life happy was very savourless and dull. He had spent most of the time alone, going over in his mind all that they had done together, and looking forward to North's return ; and a life that is passed in memory and anticipation is apt to be barren in the present.

As Christian was hurrying to the house he was met by two girls, whom he knew very well, who, hand-in-hand, were swooping like two swallows towards the *bara* to join in the dance. They knew him at once, and barred his way with outstretched hands, and with bright smiles of recognition they began talking quickly, asking question after question without waiting for an answer.

'Here is our Papalangi. Where have you been ? Soma has told us you have gone to make love to a foreigner' (*i.e.* not one of their tribe). 'Who is she ? What is she like ? Do you know Utamè e Ngawa has gone away ? Tama-iru has taken her away to Oneroa.'

North did not answer these questions, but asked for the news of Soma, and where he was.

'We think Soma is bewitched,' said one of the girls, lowering her voice ; 'he has hardly left the house since you went away. He has not even been to see Ta-iiara here, and you know he is fond enough of doing that.'

Ta-iiara turned away her head and tried to laugh.

'To-night is a great dance,' she said. 'You must come. Take my *lalote*,' and she slipped off the great garland of flowers that hung down to her bosom and threw it round North's neck.

Chris laughed and shook his head. 'I cannot come; I am tired. I must find Soma.'

'Make him come back to me,' whispered Ta-üara so low that her companion did not hear her.

'I promise that,' said North.

'Oh, that's always the way with you and Soma,' said the other girl. 'You are like two *hiva* birds, never apart. You will both love the same girl some day, and then what about *ofa-namu*?' She tossed her head wickedly, and seizing hold of Ta-üara's hand, darted off towards the dancing ground.

In another moment North had reached the house, which was all silent and deserted, as all the men, and probably Motuiti himself, had gone to the great dance in the *bara*. The strong moonlight entered the house but a very little way, as the eaves of the roof were so low; the shadows of the short side-posts lay slanting and clearly defined on the floor, and then the rest of the large room lay in deep shadow. Christian entered the house quite quietly, but not so softly that the silent man sitting alone in the shadow failed to hear him; he must have heard some faint sound, and looking up have seen North's figure as he stooped to come in.

'*Kohai alu gua?*' (who is that?) said Soma, not too pleasantly, and with a suddenness that made Chris start.

To this North made no answer, but guided by the voice he walked across the room to where Soma lounged on the mats.

'Who is that?' said Soma again, and louder.

'You need not shout, *ofa-namu-ou*,' said Christian

quietly, and stretching out his hand to feel his way, he felt it grasped in a grip of iron, and with a shout of savage delight, notwithstanding Chris's warning, that might have been heard at the other end of the town, Soma sprang to his feet.

'Papalangi tëa! It is my Papalangi;' and he seized Christian in his great arms as though he were a child. 'You are back? You are well? Are you tired? Are you hungry? Do you thirst? Sit down; sit here on my mats. I must get a torch. Ah, I am happy!' The words of welcome and delight rolled out of his great throat in a perfect torrent of deep affectionate chest-tones.

'All those things I am, Soma-ou; but I am happy too,' and he tried to laugh, but it somehow stuck in his throat. 'Utamè is safe, and I am back again with you.'

'Ah! I am glad she is safe,' said Soma; 'I had forgotten the woman.'

'There are many things to tell,' began North.

'Not now. *Mea-kai mo mea-inu, lea mui-mui,*' said Soma, quoting an Omëan proverb. 'Food and drink and talking afterwards. I will call the men.'

'No, do not call the men,' said Chris. 'Give me what there is in the cook-shed and·water from the bamboos, and then we can talk as long as we wish.'

'Stay still,' said Soma, as Christian began to move towards the cooking shed. 'Sit there. The way has been long. I will find the food.'

He quickly brought food and water and a little torch of candle-nuts that he had lighted at the smouldering fire, which feebly lit the house with its flickering flame. Soma watched North with his faithful spaniel eyes whilst he ate, as though it were enough for him to have his friend with him once more.

'Now, tell me what has happened whilst I have been away,' said Chris. 'What have you done? Tell me of that first.'

'The days have been long and I have been sad. But I have forgotten that now,' he said brightly, slapping North on the shoulder with Herculean affection. 'I said to myself,' he added, pointing to his breast with one great finger, 'I have my *ofa-namu* with me always, and then I was glad. I have finished the carving on the war club for you. It shall be called *Malohi papa-langi*—the strength of the stranger.'

'It is true, Soma, I was with you and you were with me, although we were apart. I will not leave you again. My blood lives in you. If you have a son,' Christian added with a laugh, 'it will be mine too.'

'Do not laugh,' said Soma, 'for that is true. In Omëo the children of *ofa-namus* cannot marry ; they are brother and sister.'

'What is thought of Utamè's going away ?'

'They all think that Tama-iru has taken her, and Ilo-eki and Ngawa, the girl's father, are angry against him. If he were a great chief they would make war on him, but they think that Faäori, whose *tabu* he has broken and whose son's wife he has stolen, will punish him enough, for they believe he has gone back to Oneroa.'

'Hush!' whispered North, 'they are coming back.'

'They have seen the light. They have no thought where you have been. When they ask, laugh and shake your head and look sly (*lota-butu*). They will believe what I have told them.'

All further talk was put an end to then, for Motuiti and his dependants returned from the dance, and seeing Christian there, they overwhelmed him with many questions. To appear wiser than the others the old chief laughed and said he knew all about it, and Chris, going to sit on his mat, begged him not to tell.

For some little time after North's return things went on much as usual. There was at first much excitement and talk over Utamè's disappearance, but in a few days this calmed down, for although tabued to Faäori's son, she was only the daughter of one of the lesser chiefs. Other things of importance to the little community, such as the launching and trial of North's boat, occurred, and in the interest of the present moment the last week's excitement was forgotten. Soma and North returned to their old ways of life, and though never without a dull ache at the heart at the loss of Utamè, Christian was not selfish enough to let his own sorrow destroy all the happiness of his friend. He meant to return to the mountain to see Utamè before very long, and as he daily became a greater favourite with Ilo, to whom he was of service in a hundred ways, he began to have some hopes of inducing him to take off his *tabu* from the girl. He cheered himself with this expectation, and as no rumours came to the town of Utamè's presence on Monoriro, he knew that Venga had kept her word, and had been enabled to hide her from all prying eyes. For Soma this was an entirely happy time: he had Chris with him always, and when he went to see Ta-üara, as North had no difficulty in persuading him to do, he found he was forgiven.

CHAPTER XX

Like Janus, Time has two faces: one of them is stern and dreaded by us as the stealer of our youth and the curtailer of our joys, whilst the second is benignant and compassionate as the healer of wounds, the softener of sorrow, and the deadener of memory. This latter is the Time of old age, the promiser of peace. But Christian did not fear the one and had not seen the other; each day that he awoke to health and happiness seemed a new birth to him, the world was as fair and life as joyous as though he had but then first known them. Empty and vacant his days would have been to some, but they were full of interest and of living for him. Sometimes he worked hard, and then all his energies were concentrated on the task in hand, but he could amuse himself or be idle with just as good a will. Idleness! it was scarcely idleness to be purely and simply happy. What were the use of doing more—of doing anything—when it was happiness enough to exist, to lie in the warm shadows and breathe love and beauty at every breath, and let Life flow over one like a great warm wave?

Two months had passed since his return from Monoriro, and in that time the only drawback to his happiness—certainly a great one—was the absence of Utamè, and that drawback was about to vanish, as he hoped to visit the mountain with Soma in two days' time. Since his return Soma had often urged upon him the wisdom of finding another sweetheart, which would have been strictly in accordance with Omëan ideas of right, but Chris's heart was so filled with the love of Utamè that other women were no more than voices and shadows to him.

'What do I want with anybody else?' he said to Soma. 'I have Utamè and I have you.'

'But Utamè is away,' said Soma with an air of conviction. 'And I go away too sometimes,' he added with a laugh.

'So you think then, Soma-ou, that if you went away for a long time I should take another friend?'

'That is another thing,' the Polynesian answered. 'Utamè is only a woman. All women are the same as other women. Some are beautiful, some are not—that is the difference. But with men it is not so. Every man is different from another. When you take your friend that is for always. That is what the *ofa-namu* is for. We are always together. If I die I live on in you. As long as your heart beats Soma is alive. Are you not glad?' he added, with the light of a savage devotion in his eyes

'It is that which makes me glad,' said Chris quietly. 'And when I die Papalangi tëa will still live on in Soma.'

'We shall be together till the first one of us dies,' said the Omëan fiercely. 'If you are killed in battle I shall live long enough to slay him who struck you; if you are drowned at sea, that one wave is big enough for two; and if you live to be old in Omëo, when you die I shall be tired too, and will sleep with you.'

The two months since the death of Tama-iru had passed without any sign having been made by his own people in Oneroa that they had any suspicions as to his end, and as, of course, every one in Otorangi except the four actors in the drama, Christian, Soma, Utamè, and her servant Sobele, was totally ignorant of his death, they were unprepared for the terrible news that came into the town one night. All the town had gone to sleep ; even those who had been talking late after the *ava* drinking had at last gone to their homes, when the whole population was startled from its slumber by the terrible sound of the great alarm drum booming through the place. This great boat-shaped drum of hollow wood, which was never sounded except upon most important occasions, stood outside the house of Ilo, the chief of Otorangi, and at the very first sound of it everybody in the town started up from sleep. As the violent drumming continued, every man, woman, and child rushed out of doors to the *bara*, many of them in their haste not stopping to cover themselves with any protection from the chilly night air.

Motuiti's house, which was on the bank of the stream, was some little distance from Ilo's, so that when Soma and North arrived there, although Soma had stretched out a great arm in the darkness to where Chris lay, and had aroused him at the first stroke of the drum, a little crowd had already assembled. It was a dark night, and no one could see the face of his neighbour, and as every one was ignorant as yet of the meaning of the sudden summons, their voices were awestruck and alarmed. In a few minutes two or three men came round from the back of the house bearing great flaming torches of dried sugar-cane, which cast a broken light on the faces of the anxious people. Ilo's house was already quite full of men, and when Christian and North came upon the scene they could hear a loud voice talking excitedly inside the building.

In another moment all these people came pouring out of the chief's house, blinking as they came into the torchlight, and last of all came Ilo himself, a great, tall, fine-looking fellow, closely followed by a shrivelled and wrinkled but erect old woman. It was she whose ringing voice had been heard in the house, and the moment the torchlight fell upon her face Christian recognised Venga; she looked weary and very anxious, but the courage of the old woman, which had brought her so far, still shone undimmed in her eyes. As Ilo and the old priestess stooped and came out of the house into the torchlight, every voice in the crowd was hushed, for they all knew that it must be news of the most vital importance to them that had induced the chief to summon a meeting of the people at that unusual hour.

Ilo stood at the edge of the little platform or terrace on which his house was built, and, facing the people, began to speak, but even in that moment of anxiety and peril there was no unseemly haste in his words. His chief-like dignity would have been imperilled, and his people's respect might have been lost for ever, had he forgotten to be calm. Venga stood behind him; she would have gone back into the house had he not signed to her to stay where she was.

'*Kou tangata Omëo*,' he began. 'Men of Omëo, this night heavy news has come to us. Venga e Monoriro has come to bring it us. Out of friendship to us has she come. To the mountain yesterday two men of Oneroa came to make sacrifice to Rorutu, and they told to Venga what she has come to tell us. Without rest or food she has come from the mountain to give us warning. The men of Oneroa are upon us. We were ignorant of offence, but Faäori e Oneroa has made ready his great war canoes and he will be upon us this night or to-morrow. Tama-iru, who has stolen Utamè from amongst us, has not gone back to Oneroa, and Rongo and Faäori think that we have slain him, and they come for revenge. I for one am glad of it,' said the old savage, with a tone of hatred in his voice which was very expressive; 'we owe them many a grudge. Shall it be said that the men of Otorangi forget an injury? Are we thus tame and cowardly as not to rejoice at a chance of slaying our enemies in battle? Who amongst us cares for these last many months of peace? It is in battle that a man lives. Can we forget how our grandfathers were treacherously slain by these same men of Oneroa under their chief Taulo? We slew many of them in our return attack, but we are not equal yet. Do you forget how in warfare with the Pangu men our friends of Oneroa turned upon us and joined with the enemy? These things are not spoken of whilst they think we still are friends, but they never are forgotten. The blood of our fathers calls aloud for the blood of those who slew them; they have drunk much but are not satisfied yet.

'Which amongst you has not his club and his spear ready?' cried the chief with louder voice and a still more excited manner. 'Which of you is not prepared to fight? Let him stay amongst the women. He can put on the *vulu* (the woman's dress); he will not need the *mahi*. Say, chiefs and men of Otorangi, shall we not make ready this night? Shall we not receive them with a shout of welcome to the battle when they come? And shall we not slay every man among them that dares put his foot upon our beach ?   Shall we not give our thirsty clubs to drink ?   Shall not our hands tear out the hearts of those base men and leave their bodies naked there for the children and the women to laugh at ?   Speak, chiefs and men of Otorangi.'

All this speech was listened to in voiceless silence by the crowd of men; the only sign they made of the intense state of excitement into which their chief's speech had worked them was the heavy, almost panting breathing of some of the men, and every now and then a little guttural inarticulate sound of assent or dissent that some man amongst them uttered unconsciously. As Ilo ended, the feelings of the crowd, which had been so respectfully repressed during his speech, vented themselves in a loud roar of approval of what he had said.

'You are right,' 'We will be ready,' 'Their bones whiten already,' 'To the canoe-shed,' were amongst the answering shouts that North could distinguish amidst the volume of sound, and the cries seemed to Chris but echoes of his own thoughts, for he had caught the wild contagion of blood from the crowd around him which seemed literally to quiver with excitement.   He turned to Soma, whose eyes were dancing with a martial ardour, and said—

'Shall we tell them where Tama-iru is ?   That he is dead ? '

'No,' replied Soma; 'it would be useless; the *kau Oneroa* have long wanted a reason for war and so have we.   If Tama-iru is dead it matters not by whose hand he fell.   You will fight, my Papalangi ? '

'Fight ? ' said Chris, feeling that he had only lived thus long to fight.   'Yes, till I drop dead.'

'Come, let us get our clubs.   *Malohi Papalangi* that I carved for you is thirsting for some strong man's blood, and *Puku-nu*—that is what mine is called—has long been idle. Then whilst we are getting ready the great canoes the women and young children will be carrying away all the fine mats and bales of *tappa* to the woods, where they will hide them from the Oneroa men in case we are driven back.'

'Driven back!' said North, as they began to run towards the house; 'they shall never do that were they ten times as strong.'

And in truth he felt all that he said. There was born in him that wild desire for battle that at some moment of our lives we all have felt,—a craving for a personal hand-to-hand struggle which means death to the beaten one. He threw himself into the coming fight as ardently as he did into whatever he laid his hand to, and he felt the great muscles of his arms and chest stretch themselves to tautness as he imagined he had his enemy in his grasp, and was crushing him to death by mere exertion of his strength.

'We will fight side by side,' he said to Soma as they neared the house, and Soma grasped his arm for answer. It almost seemed to him then that he had the strength of two men, such was his absolute trust and reliance on his friend, and to the savageness of his pleasure in the coming struggle was added the delight of knowing that side by side with him this blood brother of his would be fighting too. Who knows, he might have to defend his friend's life with his own, and the very thought of it made him clench his teeth till his jaws swelled big, as he felt the strength move in him that he knew he should have at his command if a struggle came in which the prize was the life of the man he loved.

By this time all the town was lighted; fires had

been made in many places by the boys, of the dry husks
of coco-nuts, and tall torches were burning outside most
of the houses, so that every one could see quite well
enough to make all necessary preparations.   It was
a scene of the greatest excitement.   Chiefs were
running from house to house to see that every man
had arms; women and girls and children were hastily
making bundles of their most precious mats and cloths,
and already a long procession was forming itself of these
female porters who were bearing off their wealth to a
secure and secret place in the forest.   But nowhere
was there any sign of fear; old and young alike were
possessed with a courage that spoke well for their
chances in battle.   The boys could not be induced to
help the women to carry off the property to the woods,
—that, they said, was women's work; they armed themselves, too, as well as they could, and hung about the
bara or attached themselves to any little group of men
who might be talking of the one absorbing question.
From his infancy an Omëan boy is taught that courage
is the first of all the virtues, and to be called a coward
is worse than to be called murderer or thief; so that it
was natural that boys, who were mere children in years,
should have a spirit and courage that would not have
disgraced their fathers.

When North and Soma entered the house they found
that Motuiti was already there, singing quietly in his
old voice as he got down dusty bundles of spears from
the rafters and untied the thongs that bound them.

'How did you get here so quickly?' said Soma to
the old man.   'We have run all the way and have
just come.'

'I knew what all that talking meant,' said Motuiti
dryly, 'and did not stop to listen.   I knew it was war.

Who with did not matter. Motuiti came back to get ready the arms for his men.'

So long as Motuiti remained young enough and strong enough to fulfil all the duties of a chief it would have been considered most presumptuous and unfilial for Soma to interfere in any of the affairs belonging to his office, so that as soon as they had found their own arms they left the house again to Motuiti and his following, which now was crowding in. Soma was instinctively turning to the beach, where already a little crowd had gathered round the great canoe-sheds, but Chris stopped him and said—

'I must speak to Venga now. I could not when all the people were around her.'

'About Utamè?' asked Soma with a tone of quiet surprise in his voice, that at a time such as this North could stop to think about a girl.

Retracing their steps to Ilo's house they found the old woman, wide awake and talking fast to one of Ilo's wives, although she was almost exhausted by the long and difficult journey she had just accomplished. Directly she recognised North she rose and came over to where he and Soma stood, and lowering her loud voice to a sort of strident whisper, she said in answer to Christian's anxious question—

'Yes, the girl is well. As the sun rises every morning she says, "He will come to-day." And when you do not come she smiles and says, "He will come to-morrow, mother."'

Chris felt himself blush with tenderness as the old woman gave him this little detail of Utamè's life in the most matter-of-fact manner. He had hardly time to give Venga a message for the girl, saying that he was on the point of coming the next day when the news of war had come, when loud cries of 'Soma, Soma e Motuiti!' from the beach summoned them away. Only staying to ask Venga to tell Utamè that he loved her just the same and had kept his promise to her, he rushed away with his friend, who was calling him with the utmost impatience.

In the space of an hour from the time that Venga arrived with her news everything was ready in Otorangi for the expected attack of the Oneroa men, and Ilo, wishing his enemies to think him unprepared, ordered every light to be put out in the town and every one to remain quite silently at his post. The first part of the order was strictly obeyed; each fire was scattered and every torch extinguished, but it was impossible to make so many excited men hold their tongues, and through the darkness a murmur of talk, and in some places of laughter, made itself heard. The time passed very slowly to the waiting men, but no one in all the town closed an eye in sleep, and quietly the night waned without any attack being made by the expected enemy. An hour or so before dawn Ilo, who knew something of the probable tactics of the Omëans, ordered a meal for all the men, which, that they should not leave their stations along the beach, was brought to them from their houses by the women.

CHAPTER XXI

When at last that night of watching drew to a close, when the fingers of morning began to fine away the darkness from the world, Ilo, who, as a good general should, had been walking from one post to another all the long night through, ordered all the women and sleepy children back to the houses, and said that every man must conceal himself as well as possible among the rocks of the shore or the bushes which fringed it. His orders were exactly obeyed, and when the dim light grew strong enough for anything to be seen, the town and the whole beach looked as solitary as though the place was sleeping deeply as on every other day. Each eye was anxiously turned towards the lagoon as the day broke, but the calm sea was absolutely deserted, and some of the younger men thought that all danger for that morning was past, when just before the sun rose three great canoes with their mat sails spread swept round the forest-covered point of land that formed the eastern side of the bay. A loud murmurous exclamation rose along the shore, which showed that they had been seen almost simultaneously by all the hidden men.

From where he was crouching Ilo shouted out—the distance of the canoes was still so great that there was no danger of being overheard by them—that every man

should keep himself hidden until the moment when
the enemy should begin to disembark, and that no one
was to stir until he gave the order. The canoes
travelled quickly, for not only was the light breeze in
their favour, but the men on board, knowing that day
was so near at hand, redoubled their exertions.

At last the canoes were so close to land that the
Otorangi men could see that there were only enough
men in each one to manage it, and that all the crowd
of armed warriors they expected to see in them was
absent. At first they could not understand the meaning of this, but in another moment loud shrieks from
the town of ' *Kotou gohu*—the enemy is on us!'
made plain the trick that the Oneroans had played
upon them. They had landed their men in the night
some little distance up the coast, then had sent the
canoes down the lagoon to the front of the town to
make the Otorangi men think they were to be attacked
from the sea, so that, whilst the attention of the
enemy was thus concentrated on the shore, the whole
armed force of the attacking party might enter the
town in the rear and take it at once by surprise. All
this elaborate preparation had been made on the chance
—always a very possible one in Polynesian warfare—
that the party to be attacked had somehow been informed of the enemy's intention, as had been the case
in the present instance. The scheme had succeeded
admirably, for all the plans of Ilo were upset by this
most unexpected turn, and in great disorder his men
rushed from their hiding-places on the beach back to
the town.

By the time that North and Soma, who were
amongst the foremost of the party, reached the *bara*, a
scene of the greatest confusion was taking place in

the town; the enemy was already entering it, and a crowd of frightened children and women with babies in their arms were rushing across the square towards the gardens and forests on the other side, in which, with an animal-like instinct, they intended to hide. The attacking party, under the command of a strikingly tall chief, who wore a singular and very large head-dress of a sort of fine basket-work covered with small feathers, seeing the Otorangi men spring up as though by magic from the ground, paused and formed itself in an irregular but solid line. Seeing this, Ilo, who recognised the disadvantage at which he was placed by the straggling of his men, most of whom had not yet had time to collect together, shouted in stentorian tones a command to halt.

'Why does he not let us attack them?' said Soma, his voice actually ringing with impatience.

'Because he knows it would be foolish for our straggling men to throw themselves on that compact mass,' answered Chris, whose judgment remained cool, although his heart was beating fast and his face was flushed with excitement.

In a few moments all, or nearly all, of Ilo's men were collected in the *bara*, and the two little forces stood facing each other, with a look of grim determination on the savage faces which showed that small mercy was to be expected on either side. The Oneroans were a splendid lot of men; like the Otorangi warriors, naked, except for the savage ornaments that heightened their martial appearance, and armed with clubs and spears, and some few of them with bows and arrows. Even at that moment Chris could not help noticing the beauty of their symmetrical forms and admiring the expression of courage, almost of delight, in their fine faces. It seemed as true of them as of his party, that war and bloodshed were as the breath of their nostrils, and he felt with them, as the old savage and unregenerate nature in him surged over and drowned all nobler feelings, that truly a man only really lived in war time and in fighting. Object or reason for the quarrel was of no importance, so that the struggle and the fighting were to be had. He felt nothing but that he was a great strong animal, and a fighting animal too; and the strength and beauty of his enemies only made him feel the more eager to get at them, to have them beneath his hands, and to make a fair trial of strength against strength, and skill against skill with them. He could hear next to him the deep panting breaths of Soma, that seemed pumped up by the throbbing of his great eager heart, and he felt his breath hot on his neck when his friend turned and said something to him that he did not hear. To his surprise he found that he was panting too.

For a very short time the enemies faced each other without making a movement, each waiting for the other to begin the attack, and then the Oneroans let fly a few arrows into the line of Ilo's men, which seemed to sting them instantly into action.

' *Now*,' cried Soma, ' they are dead men.'

Shouting an oath, that was like the roar of the lion as he springs, Christian, side by side with Soma, rushed to the attack. The lust of blood was upon him, and he laughed loud and wildly from the rapture of thus letting his passions go free.

With a roar of deep bass voices that shook the air with the terror of it, the two forces left their positions at the same moment and rushed upon each other with savage fury. Christian did not seem to touch the ground as he ran, such was the wild exhilaration that possessed him; he only saw the mass of men before him for his slaying, and leaped upon them with his club in air.

Each line kept well together, and they met with a loud thud of naked bodies and a crash of clubs. Some fell on either side at the first rough onset, pierced by the barbed spears that some of the men of each party carried. For a moment a grim silence prevailed, but it was for only one moment; the next the air was filled with yells and groans and howls as blows were given and received, or some strong man received his death and shouted in his agony.

The sun had risen into a blue and peaceful sky as the fight began, and the whole *bura* was flooded with the warm brightness of the earliest hour of the tropical day; a few yards off, at the edge of the forest, the birds were singing till the town was sweet with their woodland music. Only a foot or two above the heads of the surging mass of men two fragile butterflies of a delicate blue, like two bits of the sky blown down by the wind, circled round one another in swift and giddy flight, now close together and then suddenly apart, as love or coyness impelled them. Nature was in her sweetest, gayest mood. At the edge of the gardens, ready to start into the woods at any sign of danger, the women stood with agonised faces, holding back their struggling naked little children by the hand, watching their men as they fought.

From the first moment, whilst still neither party had made the attack, Chris had singled out his man. This was a tall savage with a short curling black beard and shaggy throat, who, although not the leader of the Oneroans, from his chief-like bearing and the value

of the ornaments he wore, must have been a man of
some importance.   When the forces came in collision
these two were not directly opposite to one another,
and for the first few moments North fought desperately
with those who were immediately in front of him,
feeling a thrill of terrible delight as one man went
down with a blood-curdling shriek before him and was
trampled under foot by his own people.   But in a short
time he saw the man he had singled out at a little
distance to one side of him, and perhaps there was
something magnetic in the glance he threw upon him,
for the Oneroan, with that strange intuition which
enables us to recognise an enemy, seemed to know
what was passing in North's mind, for with one push
of his great arm he shoved a young man of his own
party on one side and took his place in front of
Christian.

By this time the two compact bodies had opened
out somewhat, that each man might have free play of
his weapons without damaging his own right and left
hand neighbours; and the battle, which had at first
been general, divided itself in little groups and sometimes into single combat between two champions of
either side.   In this manner North and the Oneroan
were separated from the other combatants, and with an
evil light in their eyes they rushed upon one another.
Although Chris was a tall and a very strong man,
his opponent was taller and, judging by the immense
development of the muscles of his arms and shoulders,
stronger, but North was lighter and quicker on his
feet.   The Oneroan was armed with a very heavy
curved club, the concave side of which was sharp, and
the back broad and solid to give strength to it and
weight to the blow; whilst Christian's weapon was a

short-handled club of the common sort, in the use of which he was better practised, and which he had taken the precaution to attach to his wrist by means of a tough band of sinnet.

Seeing the nature of his antagonist's weapon, North knew that he must depend chiefly upon his agility, and springing upon him he aimed a violent blow at his neck; but the Oneroan, lifting his left arm, received it on the inner part of it, whence it glided with a dull thud on to his breast. The fellow never wavered, though Chris had used his full force, and without losing a second he swung his own great weapon round, which was already raised in air; but by springing back Chris avoided the stroke. Before his enemy had time to lift his club again North closed with him once more, and grasping his short mace with both hands, struck the Oneroan so crashing a blow on the right shoulder that he dropped his club and staggered back a pace or two before he could recover himself. His first movement was to regain his weapon, but North was too quick for him, and had seized it, and whirling it round his head, flung it to a distance.

The man stood for a second as though dazed, and then, with a splendid courage, rushed empty-handed on his foe. Christian, seeing him thus defenceless, with a natural instinctive chivalry that showed the character of the man, as such unconscious and impulsive acts always do, slipped the noose from his wrist and dropped his own club. Weaponless, the two men closed in a hand-to-hand struggle that filled the heart of North with a savage joy. The Oneroan clipped Chris round the chest with so close a grip that it would have crushed a less strong man; but twining

one leg between those of his antagonist North managed
a clever wrestler's fall and threw him to the ground.
They fell as one man, for the Polynesian never loosed
his hold, but he was underneath.

North now began to grow savage; his temper went,
and he felt his strength rising with his passion, for he
failed to unclasp the grasp of the Oneroan round his
chest, and he began to feel his breathing growing short
and distressed. Had his ribs not been of iron they
must have been crushed in. His arms were still both
free, though his adversary, who was lying on his back,
had managed to throw his great legs round North's
and firmly to imprison them. For a moment or so
they rolled about the ground in their violent struggles,
Christian's grasp slipping several times on the sweating body of his opponent, but at last he succeeded in
getting a firm hold of his throat with both hands.
Nothing that the Oneroan now did could make him let
go, and he saw the handsome face of his antagonist
grow dark and swollen as the writhing man struggled
for breath. But even then, when he felt death near at
hand, he never relaxed his grip on North. He hoped
still to conquer, and Chris felt the iron circle round
him becoming each second tighter and less bearable,
and his own face grew a dull and livid crimson as he
no longer could get air into his lungs.

In another moment, however, when he was at the
last pitch of endurance, Chris suddenly felt that the
stifling grasp was relaxed, and filling his freed chest
with air, he looked down at the man whose life was
in his hands. The hands and arms that had almost
crushed the life out of him were now feebly plucking
and tearing at Chris's wrists to try to force them
from his throat, but in vain. Looking into the face of

his still conscious enemy he saw the swollen and bursting lips move, and he thought he could read a dumb prayer for life in the bloodshot eyes; and the tenderness and mercy which were natural to his heart, but which had been for the time expelled by sterner feelings, stole back into it. He shook the brute out of himself, and with an oath that was almost a sob he loosed his grasp of the man's throat, and said in Omëan:

'Yes, you shall live. I will not kill you.'

It may have been an absurd act of chivalry, but Christian was chivalrous, and it seemed natural enough to him. He helped the man to sit up, and, in a moment's time, to rise unsteadily to his feet. All this time the Oneroan never said a word, but gazed fixedly at North as though to impress his face on his memory, and then, as he staggered off to join a little detachment of his own forces, he said—

'*Tonuia na he tou;* the fight was a fair one. You gave Mäutara his life. He is your man.'

North did not know what he meant by that last part of his sentence; indeed in the noise that was going on he paid no heed to what he said.

Meanwhile the tide of battle had flowed this way and that upon the spacious field of the *bara*, and when Chris looked round, at the end of his own personal struggle, during which he had entirely forgotten the fact that a battle was raging round him, he found that he was separated by some little distance from the main body of belligerents. He could not tell how the fortunes of the day were going, so stooping and picking up his club he slipped the thong of it round his wrist, and still panting from his late contest, ran towards the centre of the affray. He had not gone many yards, leaping the contorted bodies of the dead or wounded that he passed, when he heard a hoarse and husky voice, which he seemed to recognise, cry out behind him for help.

He turned and, with a momentary shiver that chilled his flesh, he saw Soma, still erect and fighting, but on the point of being overpowered by a little party of four Oneroans, which for a moment longer he kept at bay.

With a howl of rage and despair Chris raced towards them, scarcely touching the ground as he ran, and with the full impetus gained by his speed he crashed upon the men. One man fell from the mere force with which Chris rushed against him, to rise again the next moment; but another one, who had raised his club for a death-blow to Soma, fell like a log, with his skull split open by the first blow that North made. As he had said, he felt he had the strength of ten men now that the life of his friend, his *ofa-namu*, was at stake. It was well that he came then, for Soma was weaponless; he had broken his famous *Paku-nu* and the neck of a man at the same time, and the pieces of the club lay battered and bloodstained by the side of the man it had killed.

A new light shone in Soma's face as Christian came to his aid; his very presence seemed to give him fresh courage and new strength. It was not a time for talking, with three men—for the one that Chris had first knocked down had risen to his feet and returned to the attack—engaging two, one of whom was unarmed, but Soma could not repress a sort of howl of joy.

'I knew you would come in time.'

'Yes,' said North simply.

Chris engaged one of the two men who were

attacking Soma, giving and receiving many a hard knock which would ache badly enough by and by, but which in the heat of battle he scarcely felt. He could have managed to hold his own with this fellow, breathed though he was by his struggle with Mäutara, but his antagonist was joined by the man he had knocked down in his first onset, and he felt himself being slowly overpowered. As they fought they gradually moved away from Soma and his adversary, till there was some distance between them. He determined to bring the struggle to a conclusion one way or another; so, seizing his club in both hands, leaving his body unprotected and exposed to the blows of his second assailant, he closed with the man he had first engaged, and swinging his club round his head like a flash of light, brought it down crashing on the left side of his enemy's face. Clapping his hand to his shattered jaw the man turned with a dull howl of anguish and fled.

Seeing the fate of his companion Chris's second man left him and rushed to the rescue of the third Oneroan, who was left with the defenceless Soma, hoping to overpower him at once, and then for the two to finish with North. He started too late. Soma's adversary, little knowing the gigantic strength of his foe, and seeing him with empty hands, had thought to make short work of him. He rushed in an unguarded manner upon Soma, aiming a blow at his head with his jagged and heavy club. But Soma was not the man to let himself be killed in this simple fashion. He suddenly dropped as the club was swung, and falling to the earth, seized the Oneroan by his ankles, and with one swift and violent jerk threw him to the ground. Before he had time even to attempt to rise

Soma had both hands firmly imbedded in his thick bushy hair, and crushing his head into the hard and stony earth, he literally, by sheer strength, ground the life of the man out of him.[1] It was a frightful sight; but in the field of battle, with Death ready to tap every man on the shoulder, there is no time to think what is terrible or not, and Chris had no feeling but one of delight in the courage and the noble strength of his friend.

The last of the four Oneroan men, seeing that Soma had great difficulty in getting to his feet—he was bleeding profusely from a wound in the thigh, from which part of the barbed head of a broken spear was projecting—rushed past North with a long spear that he had snatched up from the ground, poised to pierce Soma in his exposed side. Chris darted after him, but the Oneroan was the fresher man, and he could not overtake him to strike him with his club. The distance that separated them from Soma was not more than twenty or thirty yards, and the point of the Oneroan's spear was within a foot or two of Soma's naked side, when Chris managed to grasp the long handle of the spear that projected behind the bearer of it, and as he raised the end of it the point was lowered, and, with the whole impetus of the man's running, the spear was driven deep into the breast of the Oneroan who lay dead at Soma's feet.

Seeing that his blow was frustrated, and that North was close on his heels, this fellow did not pause in his flight, but ran lightly past Soma towards the centre of the *bara*; he got off scot-free, as Christian was too exhausted to follow him, even had he wished to leave Soma unprotected again. Neither of them spoke for

---

[1] A fact.

a moment, for both were panting for breath; but at last, wiping away with a shaking hand the sweat that was pouring down his face, Soma pointed to Christian's chest, down which a stream of blood was flowing from a torn and abraded wound.

'What is that?' he asked.

'What?' said North, looking down; and then, as he saw that he was wounded, a comical look came into his face, and he added, 'I don't know. I never felt it. I did not know I was wounded. It is nothing, so let me see what I can do for you. Why, Soma, you have half a spear in your leg.'

'Yes,' said the islander, 'that fellow there did it, but I broke his neck in return.'

'Can you walk?'

'No, not with this wood in me.'

North was anxious to stop the bleeding, which was very profuse, but nothing could be done whilst the spear was still in the wound. Soma saw this and said—

'Help me, Papalangi, and I will take it out.'

Seating himself with North's assistance, he grasped the broken piece of spear, but the barbed head, which was buried in the flesh, prevented it from being pulled out. He bore the excruciating pain of it like a Stoic, but he could not help the natural colour of his face changing. Christian saw that Soma could not do it himself, and knowing that if the enemy came upon him in that helpless condition he would be instantly clubbed, he determined upon performing a very rough operation himself then and there. He made Soma lie down on one side, and then said to him—

'I must do it. The pain will be very great.'

'If you do it I can smile,' said Soma quite calmly.

Knowing that it was the barbed sides of the spear that prevented it being pulled out, Chris saw at once that the only thing to be done was to push the spear right through the thick part of the thigh; and this he did. The agonising pain that he knew he must be inflicting made him sick, but he saw it was Soma's only chance, and he went on with it. The work took some little time, for the muscles of his thigh were like iron, but he never stirred; he only gripped one of North's legs—he was kneeling beside him—till his nails pierced the flesh, and all he said was—

'Is it nearly finished?'

When the spear was extracted, and Chris had seen as well as he could that no splinters were remaining, he brought the edges of the wounds together, and tearing up his *mahi* he bound the leg tightly, and managed to stanch the bleeding.

'Now,' said North, 'that is done. I must get you off somewhere. Can you stand?'

'Yes,' said Soma somewhat faintly, and he staggered to his feet.

'If you can't,' said Chris, 'get on my back, and I can carry you to the edge of the forest, where you will be safe whoever wins.'

But this plan was never executed. The two men had been too much occupied with their own fighting to notice how the day had gone, and neither of them knew to which side victory leaned; but at this moment loud and ringing shouts from the square informed them that one side or the other had conquered. They were not long in doubt, for directly afterwards all that remained of the attacking party were seen to be running full speed across the *bura* towards where their canoes lay at a stone's throw from the shore.

The Oneroans in their flight had to pass the very spot where North and Soma were standing, and some of their young men, enraged by defeat, made ready to club them as they passed; but the Oneroan chief, who had apparently passed scatheless through the affray with the exception of the loss of his feathered helmet, howled out—

'Take them to the canoes. They shall be for a sacrifice.'

Four or five men seized Christian and Soma, and they were carried along in the hurrying crowd to the water's edge. Here Chris did make some efforts at escape; but seeing that Soma, half fainting from loss of blood, had not the strength to follow him, he let himself be pushed through the shallow water to the side of the great double canoe, on to which both he and Soma were hustled and thrown.

The Otorangi men followed their enemies into the sea and succeeded in capturing one canoe; but they were beaten off, with some loss, from the other two, which in wild and fearful haste paddled off towards Oneroa.

CHAPTER XXII

THE breeze which had helped the canoes on their way to the town had fallen dead at sunrise, so that the Oneroans had to depend entirely upon their paddles for their safety, and for some little time, until they had put some distance between them and the shore, no attention was paid to anything else. The men who had been left in charge of the canoes were insufficient in number to paddle them back when loaded as they now were, so that many of the men who had been fighting had to help in the work, exhausted as they were. But the speed was allowed to be slackened, as the Otorangi men, satisfied with their victory and the capture of the one canoe, made no attempt to follow the flight of their enemies; indeed it would have been useless, for although the canoes were ready they were not launched, and it would take some time to get them afloat.

The heat was now very great, and all the men were parched with thirst, so that Mäutara, who was one of the minor chiefs and was in command of this canoe, ordered a number of coco-nuts, which lay in a heap at the end of the canoe, tied together in bunches by strips of their own fibrous husks, to be opened and passed round. All the men drank, and at a word from the chief, in spite of the protests of some of the men, both Christian and Soma were given to drink also.

The sea was of glass, and so blue that the canoe seemed floating in sky brought earthwards; it was so smooth and still—for the reef cut off the heart-beat of the open ocean—that, looking down through fathoms of clear water, Christian could see the gorgeous weeds and brilliant corals at the bottom in every detail as though quite close at hand. Now and then some little fish that was bolder than his fellows rose to the surface and sucked and nibbled with a tiny sound, as though athirst for air, and then the smooth water for far around would ripple into spreading rings. The sea was as clear as the air—down through which we shall look, perhaps, some time and watch the ways of our late fellows as men now look at fishes, and find the surface of that ethereal ocean all rippled into circles, too, by the movements of the men below.

The canoes kept close in shore, so close that they could hear all the woodland sounds across the water and smell the perfumes of the flowers. At times, when forest-crowned cliffs, from which were drooping pendent trees and trails of delicate green vines, edged the shore, the canoes passed over the bright reflections in the water of all the beauties of the land. As point after point was passed and fresh little bays were entered the loveliness only increased, for new vistas of the verdant interior opened out in the valleys, which ran back, as though for shelter and protection, to the mass of the mountains which lay blue in the distance through the summer haze.

Towards those mountains Christian's gaze was oftenest turned, for there in the shelter of that great volcanic cone, which he could recognise always by its unwavering column of cloud, lived the one woman to whom his heart cleaved, and who, in his sorrow perhaps more than in his joy, was never absent from his thoughts for long together. But it was hardly sorrow that Christian felt that day as the pictured shore glided dreamlike past them; it was all so beautiful that his happy nature could not give way to despair, although he and his friend were defenceless and prisoners in the hands of enemies suffering from the mortification of defeat. Hope, the fragrant herb— it was almost a weed in North's heart that choked by its luxuriance the benefits gained from experience— sprang up again uninjured and blossomed with many a promise. They were not dead, at any rate, and life and hope were almost synonymous with Christian.

Sleep, the death in life of every day, had thrown his soft and downy wing about the wearied Soma; forgetful of heat and wounds and weakness, he lay by Chris's side on the deck that stretched from side to side of the double canoe. North rested the head of the sleeping man upon his knee. Here was one cause, at any rate, for Christian's happiness. Captive, bound, bruised, and weary though he was, his heart was filled with an heroic joy as he felt by his side the warm and living flesh of this one chosen friend of his whom he had rescued from death by the strength of his right arm and the high courage of his heart. By saving his life he had forged a link in the chain that bound him to Soma stronger than any of the rest. What mattered what the future might bring him, the present was his; and the double life he lived—his own and that other which was dearer—felt all the warmer and the sweeter now that both of them had felt the cold breath of Death blow about them and the chill of his hand fall numb upon their hearts.

It was not until well on into the afternoon that the

canoes came in sight of the town of Oneroa, for it was a still and windless day, and the men at the paddles were too weary to make any speed. The heat had been almost intolerable to Christian, though the Polynesians were not incommoded at all by it, and he ached in every limb. The wound in his chest, though not deep or dangerous, became feverish and very painful, so that he was almost as glad as his enemies when they at last drew near the town. Soma had slept on well beyond noon and woke up like a giant refreshed.

The town of Oneroa, unlike Otorangi, was not situated in the curve of a bay. All the temples and houses had been built on a narrow and rocky promontory that ran out abruptly from the shore for some distance into the lagoon; it divided by its rocky reef two small and sandy bays. There were only slight signs of vegetation on this spur of land, but a few slanting coco-nuts broke the monotony of it. The gardens were all on the mainland. This curious site for a town had evidently been chosen for the facilities it offered for defence, for by building a strong palisade as a fortification across the narrow neck where the promontory joined the mainland, the town was easily made secure from all land attack. This was what had been done.

On its sea faces the promontory was in places so steep, although rising but six or seven feet above the water, that some of the houses actually overhung the sea, being supported on stout piles driven in amongst the submerged rocks. It was only possible to land from the canoes in one place, access to which was gained by passing through a somewhat narrow channel that could easily be defended; but once having passed between the rocks of this passage there was a small landlocked harbour, in which the canoes could safely lie at anchor.

Although, until lately, there had been peace between the Oneroans and the people of Otorangi for some years, Soma had never visited the town, so that it was with the keenest interest, though his life was not worth many hours' purchase, that he examined it in every detail as the canoes neared the shore.

There was a crowd of anxious people standing on every available space of land from which the approach of the canoes could be witnessed; but they waited in absolute silence, as they could tell by the demeanour of the returning warriors that they came back defeated and not elate with victory. All the occupants of the canoes preserved an equal silence, which was not broken until the leading canoe was deftly brought alongside a sort of clumsy jetty of loose blocks of stone that ran along part of one side of the little natural harbour. On this was standing a group of old and disabled men, chiefs and priests and decrepit warriors, headed by the hoary and fierce-looking head chief of Oneroa—the famous Faiiori.

This old man, with eyes blazing and his whole face quivering with passion, demanded in angry tones an account of the expedition and why it had thus disastrously terminated. His anger made him forgetful of all chief-like decorum, or he would never have questioned the chief, under whose command the expedition had been undertaken, before the public; but his impatience was too great to brook any delay. This young chief was nephew to Faiiori and was a man of renowned courage, but he was literally shaking with fear as he stepped from the prow of the canoe and faced the passionate old man. The first words that Faiiori addressed to him as he stepped ashore were not calculated to restore his self-possession. All he said was—

'You, Tana e Irua, back again alive ? None but cowards come back from a defeat.'

'Our surprise was no surprise,' stammered the miserable Tana. 'We were expected.'

'Then,' said the old man quickly, 'your plans were made as badly as you carried them out.'

In the presence of this raging old man, in whose absolute hands their lives were placed, Christian and Soma felt sure as to their fate ; it was only a question of 'when'; and though both of them were men of tried courage, they were but mortal, and their youth was strong within them, so that both felt the horror of the death that was thus brought so near to them in cold blood, as they had never felt it in times of danger or of battle. All the men had landed from the canoes by this time, and Soma and North amongst them. Both men stood quite calmly, and with steady eyes determined to meet Death grimly ; but though their quietness might deceive their captors, neither of them could hide from the keen eyes of the other all traces of the emotion he felt.

'A man dies but once,' whispered Soma.

'I wish it had been in battle,' answered North.

Whilst they were speaking old Faäori ended his harangue.

'Oneroa would not be mourning her defeat and her dead sons,' he said, 'if I, your chief, and these old warriors had been with you. You young men have the courage of women and the strength of children. The brave ones you have left behind you on the field of battle. How many of my men are slain ? '

Tana told him the number of the dead, and said

that as many or more of the Otorangi men had been killed by them.

'Ngako told fables,' said the old man scornfully, making use of a well-known proverb. Then suddenly pointing to North and Soma, of whom he seemed to have taken no notice before, he said—

'Who are those two men? I have not seen them before.'

'They are two prisoners we have caught. We brought them for a sacrifice to Rorutu,' said Tana eagerly, hoping to propitiate the old man.

'They are better warriors than yourselves,' said Faäori viciously, 'or they would not have driven you back. I will talk with them. You, Mäutara, take them to your house and give them food and all things that they want. They are brave men. Keep them safe,' he added savagely, as Mäutara, the young chief whose life Christian had spared, beckoned to them to follow him.

This most unexpected clemency on the part of the old chief, who was famous for his ferocity and cruelty, probably originated more from a desire to humiliate the conquered chief than from any real magnanimity, but the two prisoners, whatever its origin, were happy enough to receive even this much of mercy. It might be no more than a short reprieve, but every hour gained was an advantage and increased their chances of escape, with thoughts and hopes of which their minds were already occupied.

Without further delay Christian and Soma were marched off from the landing-place into the town, where they were the objects of the intensest popular interest, women and children, and such of the men as had been unable to find standing-room on the little quay, greeting them with jeers and addressing them in terms of the greatest obloquy and insult. The feelings of the whole town were naturally greatly excited against these two prisoners taken from a victorious enemy, and the people began to give vent to them not only by taunts and gibes of the most brutal nature, but ultimately by throwing stones and other missiles at the defenceless men. But Miiutara—whose throat was black and livid from the partial strangling he had undergone at Chris's hands—kept his word to North, and proved himself to be 'his man' by putting a stop to these demonstrations. He stood still for a moment and shouted out—

'Do no harm to these men. Faäori-eki has put his *tabu* on them.'

The words were magical, for although black looks met them on every side, no further attempt to injure them was made.

They found the town of Oneroa, now that they came to enter it, even more different from anything they had yet seen than, from the sea view of it, they expected it to be. The promontory on which it was built was so narrow that the numerous houses, great and small, of which the place consisted had had to be built so close together that there was but very little space between them; in many instances the buildings joined. The only open space was the long and irregular street that ran from end to end of the town, and this was in no part of any great width. To Soma, who was accustomed to the more spacious ways of Otorangi, it seemed almost impossible that so many people could live in so confined a space. The buildings were almost identical in form and construction with those of Otorangi, the only difference being in those cases where the houses were partly built out over the water, and there some alterations in construction were necessary.

The house to which Mäutara led them was a fairly large one, built, in what seemed to North to be, the very thickest and most populous part of the town ; into this they were told to enter, and, nothing unwilling, they went in. Here Mäutara, with usual Polynesian hospitality to any one beneath his roof, and forgetting that these men were his prisoners, invited them to the mats and to sit. He had ordered two of his men to come to guard the entrance of the house to prevent any chance of the escape of his charges, but they had not yet arrived, and he seized the opportunity of being for a moment alone with Soma and North, to say to the latter—

' Remember, I am your man. Let no one know. I will do all I can for you.'

' And for my brother ? ' said Chris.

' Ah, that is impossible. He is nothing to me.'

' He is my *ofa-namu.*'

' That is different,' said Mäutara, recognising this strange bond as a sufficient reason ; ' for him also I will do what I can.'

' If you cannot help us,' said Soma, speaking for the first time, ' you can warn us if we are in danger.'

' That I will do, but you must help me by never showing that I am your man.'

This they readily promised, and then all further talk was put an end to by the entrance of the two men whom Mäutara had sent for.

CHAPTER XXIII

For some days Christian and Soma were kept to the house in close confinement; although they were not bound, the strict watch that night and day was kept upon them gave them no chance of escape. Mäutara, who saw them daily, kept them well supplied with every necessary, as ordered by Faäori, but he never relaxed the seeming severity of his manner and appearance. But one morning, when they had been perhaps a week in Oneroa, by which time both men were longing for exercise and change of scene, Mäutara came in with the welcome news that they were to go to Faäori's house to be questioned on some matter of which, in a quick whisper, he said he was ignorant.

'Faäori is an angry man,' he went on. 'Do not try to go against him. Do what he asks.'

'We will,' laughed Chris, 'we are not fools. Come, Soma;' and then in English he added, 'Hurrah, for the open air. Thank God for this sunshine.'

The enforced idleness and perfect rest of the last few days had had one good result,—the wound in Soma's thigh was almost entirely cured; his wholesome flesh had healed wonderfully with no other remedy than pure water and clean bandages, so that by this time he could walk quite well again. He was, however, still slightly lame, so that it was with his

hand resting on Chris's shoulder that he walked down
the sunny street towards the house of the chief.
They were already well known in the town, as almost
every inhabitant of it had gratified his curiosity by
paying them a visit at some time or other, and Faäori
himself was almost the only Oneroan who had not had
some talk with this strange and wonderful white man,
of whose prowess in war many of the returned warriors had spoken.   It was from no lack of interest in
Christian that Faäori had not sent for him long before,
for he had questioned the chiefs of the expedition, and
even the fighting men, very closely about the doings of
this white man ; but the old warrior had been brought
up in stricter days, when a chief's dignity was much
sterner and more reserved than it had since become.
He knew he had the men safely in his power, and his
pride made him unwilling to appear either surprised or
curious about them ; but now that his self-respect was
satisfied he had sent for the two prisoners.

The change from the dulness of the house in which
they had been so closely kept, to the life and bustle of
the clean-swept town, was delightful to both men, and
though they were being led to the presence of the man
who might order their death at any moment, and
though they were followed by three stalwart Oneroans,
who were armed with clubs to prevent any attempt at
escape, their natural good spirits and light-heartedness
were not quenched.   Death had been near to them so
many times in one form or another that at last they
had lost their fear of him.   Many of the women who
were employed in their household work ran out of their
houses to see them pass, and most of them had a look
of pity in their faces and some few smiled ; but one girl,
—one of the most beautiful creatures, Christian thought,

that he had ever seen,—who stood plaiting with deft fingers a long string of sinnet, having felt the glance of Soma upon her, looked up once at the comely straight-limbed Polynesian, and overcome with confusion at what she read in his eyes, dropped her work and hurriedly entered the house.

'Ah ha, Soma-eki,' laughed Christian, who out of the tail of his eye had seen the very ardent look of admiration that his companion had cast upon the girl, 'you are the same Soma in Oneroa as in Otorangi! Well, even I think she is worthy of you.'

North was right; there was a royal splendour of colour and a rare perfection of face and form about this Polynesian woman which, joined to the stately grace of her movements, seemed to make her a fit mate for the noble specimen of strength and manliness that walked beside him; there was something satisfactory to Christian, who had a most exalted opinion of the worth of his *ofa-namu*, in the thought of this noble couple.

'Yes,' said Soma slowly, with a softened lustre in his eyes that spoke of more than admiration, 'she is very beautiful.'

One of the great charms of the Omëan language is the poetic discrimination that exists in it, that distinguishes qualities and feelings which in our coarser speech is expressed by one word. An example of this fineness was shown in Soma's last speech: the word *oëoëtua*, 'beautiful,' means nothing but the peculiar beauty of women; the beauty of men is *toleka leka*, which expresses also, with strange poetic insight, the tallness, strength, and grace of forest trees.

Poor Soma, who was as romantic and passionate as the rest of his race, walked the remaining distance to

Faiiori's house lost in a dream which the soul-moving beauty of the girl had cast upon him. He did not even ask her name of his guards, with whom they were upon the most friendly terms; but Christian, who had a fellow-feeling, made the inquiry in the interest of Soma, and found that she was named Viara, and that she was the daughter of a man who had been drowned when out diving for pearl-shell at the edge of the reef, his long hair becoming entangled with the branching coral which held him till he died.

The distance between the house they were confined in and that of Faiiori was not great, but it was long enough to do this piece of work for Soma. They found the house of the chief a very large one, and one of those the end of which was built out over the sea; the sides of it were, unlike the majority of the Otorangi houses, closed in with reed-work, but the whole seaward face of it was open. The beauty of this arrangement was the first thing that struck North when they entered the place; the house was in shadow, with a marvellous picture at the end of it of bright blue and glowing light framed in the dark woodwork of the house-posts and eaves.

The man they had been summoned to see was sitting with his back towards them tying on a shell fish-hook to a plaited line, for work of this kind is not considered menial by the greatest chiefs, and for some few minutes he took no notice of them. At last, when he thought he had sufficiently impressed them by his dignity, he turned to the men, who had sat down at once, as all must do before a chief, and said—

'Have you had food and all that you want?'

Soma, who took upon himself the post of spokesman, said that they had.

'You are brave men and fought well,' said Faäori.

'What can the old fox want?' said North to himself, 'that he speaks so fair;' for there was a crafty look in the chief's eyes that meant more than he wished to show. Faäori asked them one or two more civil questions, as though determined to prove that he was friendly, to all of which Soma replied in the style befitting a chief.

'What are your names?' next asked the old man.

'Soma e Motuiti and Papalangi tëa.'

'Does not the Papalangi speak as we speak in Omëo?'

'Now we are coming to it,' thought Chris, as he himself answered in the affirmative.

From that moment all Faäori's attention was paid to North. 'Come here and sit upon the mats,' he said. 'You men,' he shouted out in a loud voice, 'chew the *ava!*'

Christian and Soma walked across the house towards the open end of it and seated themselves, as invited, on the edge of the chief's mat. They could feel the cool air of the sea blow upon them there, and the smell of it was like a tonic to them; and below the thin flooring of mat-covered bamboos they could hear the sound of the water as it rippled amongst the piles and whispered in and out of the stones of the beach.

The Oneroan chief screwed up his face to a smile that he meant to be prepossessing as he began to talk to North, but it very ill concealed the character of the man or his feelings towards his prisoners.

'You are from a far island?'

'Yes,' answered Chris; 'many moons' voyage from Omëo.'

'Are the canoes of your people the same as ours?'

'No,' said North, with a little smile; 'they are much bigger, and different in shape.'

Faäori seemed to attach much importance to his answer to this question, and he gave almost a sigh of relief when North replied as he did.

'Ah! then my men spoke truly when they said that they had seen a very strange and wonderful canoe at Otorangi.'

Christian saw that he had fallen unwittingly into some sort of trap when he spoke so unguardedly, and began to regret his statement; but the next questions that the chief put to him began to give him a notion of what it was he wanted.

'Who was it that built that beautiful canoe, and in what way is it better than those we use?'

'It does not need the *raca-tolu* (the heavy outrigger attached to all Polynesian canoes), and it sails much quicker.'

'Can you make one?' asked the old chief eagerly.

'I made the one your people saw. If you will give me timber and skilful canoe-makers to work for me I can make you one.'

'You have said it,' said Faäori quickly.

'I cannot build it alone; this man Soma e Motuiti must be with me; he is wiser than I,' said Chris, thinking that the chief might revenge himself upon one of them if he thought the other could do what he wished by himself.

'You have said it,' again remarked Faäori.

'No, I have not said it yet,' answered Chris, knowing that this was the form of a solemn promise. 'We cannot do anything whilst kept prisoners as you have kept us. Let us be free men.'

Faäori waited and thought a moment, and then he

said, ' You can go free within the town, but you must not go beyond the *a-lëo* ' (the palisade that divided the promontory from the mainland).

Thinking that he had made a much better bargain than he ever expected, and feeling sure that Faäori would concede no more, Chris struck his breast with his open hands, in Omëan fashion, and bowing his head he said—

' You have said it, Faäori-eki ; I have said it.'

So the bargain was struck.

The business part of their visit being over, they only stayed long enough to drink the *ava* which had been made for them, and they shortly afterwards left the house. Faäori, whatever his thoughts might have been, was on this occasion as good as his word, and gave orders from where he sat to the men who had acted as guards to the prisoners. They rose from where they had been squatting at the entrance to the house and went off into the town. From that moment Christian and Soma were free to come and go in any part of the promontory, but they were conscious that in a quiet way their movements were always watched ; and if ever they appproached the *a-lëo*, which was formed of a mass of great felled trees and close wattle-work, they found several men placed there to guard it and to prevent their leaving the town.

The work began almost at once, for Faäori was anxious to possess this new canoe, which he hoped to use against his victorious enemies, for thoughts of revenge for his defeat already occupied his mind. Next morning a body of skilled carpenters and wood-fellers were sent out to the forest to cut down such trees as Christian should select for his purpose. He was sent with them, carefully guarded, to make choice of the timber, but Soma was not allowed to go with him, as Faäori, knowing the relationship between them, thought that one would not endeavour to escape without the other, and in this he showed that he knew his men.

The party, carrying their stone axes and slow-burning torches, passed through the only opening in the *a-lëo*—which in times of danger could be quickly and efficiently closed by the timber lying close by for the purpose—and reached the shore of the little right-hand bay. Crossing the hot sand of the shore, plunging into all the sun-warmed pools of water that the tide had left, they scrambled up the convolvulus-covered bank at the sea limit, and passing through a sort of scrub of the black-trunked, yellow-flowering hibiscus and pandanus trees, they quickly got amongst the cool shadows of the great wood. It was different from the forest round Otorangi, and more park-like, for the undergrowth was not so wild and luxuriant and the trees were not so crowded together, so that in places the sunlight poured through the leafy roof overhead; whereas in Otorangi the forest was almost always buried deep in green shadow.

The Oneroans with Christian, although cursing the men of Otorangi almost as often as they spoke of them, did not seem to regard him with any jealousy or dislike; knowing that he was not an Otorangan, they accepted him willingly enough. The man whose duty it was to look after North was a young chief with a merry face and a light heart, who seemed to think more about playing boyish tricks than keeping a strict watch over his charge. He seemed to recognise a kindred spirit in Christian, and beguiled the way by recounting to him many of his adventures, nearly all of which had a comic interest. Such was his love of fun, that even his love affairs—of which he spoke with perfect candour—had often been spoiled by the chance of playing some outrageous joke upon his *inamorata*.

The *vesi* trees that they had come to fell mostly grew in a little valley between two bluff headlands, from which, as they throve quite close to the sea margin, it was easy to float them to the promontory of Oneroa. North chose the trees that seemed most suitable to his purpose, and the long and tedious work of felling them was set about at once. As chopping down great living trees with the stone axes, which were the only ones known to the Omëans, was a very slow proceeding, the tree-cutters always had recourse to fire, which they applied to the trunk as soon as they had nicked a deep ring round the bole of the tree. It was usually by fire, too, that the great boughs of the trees were burnt off when they were felled.

Polynesians never work very hard, so that it was several days before the wood began to be floated across the bay to the place on the rocky promontory where, from time immemorial, the canoes of Oneroa had been built; but as soon as the first fine timber was brought in, Chris and his assistants set to work on it to chip and burn and split it down to the proper shape for the keel of his boat.

CHAPTER XXIV

Soma, in North's absence at the wood felling, used his newly gained liberty for a very different purpose. As was to be expected, the first thing he did after he parted from Chris at the *a-lëo* was to go to the house before which he had seen the girl Viara standing. In Omëo, as in other lands, although there are the strictest laws of etiquette upon the subject of marriage, no man has been able to frame any for the guidance of courtship and love-making; each man is by nature more or less a proficient in that mystery, and in Polynesia, where the art of Love stands before all others, not only in repute but in practice, most men are skilful, not merely in its broad main lines, but in its tricks and wiles as well.

The town was fairly empty at that hour of the morning, for the men had mostly gone to their work in the gardens on the mainland or to the different occupations of their daily life, so that there were but few people in the street. With his usual air of ease and self-possession, that so well became the handsome fellow, Soma walked up to the house in which Viara lived, and without hesitation stooped and went in. There was no one in the house, but the air was filled with the busy humming sound of the mallet as it fell on the flattened palm-trunk where the *tappa* was being made, so that he knew the women were not far off; and as he heard none of the gay chatter that nearly always accompanies this work when two or three women get together, he thought that the girl he sought was alone. He crossed the empty house, and looking out into a little green enclosure at the back of it, he saw Viara busily at work swinging the heavy four-sided mallet with one graceful arm, whilst with the other she moved the cloth about that all parts should receive the blows.

This little enclosed court was a pleasant place where the sun shone quietly, and its coarse green turf of harsh and wiry grass was all dappled with light moving shadows cast by two tall coco palms, that were rare in the town; it was shut in by closely crowded houses, and the only entrance to it was the way that Soma had come. In one corner of the very irregular little square a great bush of *ilu-ilu* grew, and beneath it the ground was thickly covered with the pale pink petals of its flowers.

The girl was singing a monotonous song as Soma slipped from the house, and this and the dull ringing of her mallet on the springy palm-trunk covered any slight sound that his bare feet made as he walked. Without saying a word he seated himself close to the girl, who saw and recognised him at once, but beyond the start she made at his sudden appearance, she gave no sign of noticing him. Her singing ceased certainly, and perhaps she began to beat her cloth a little quicker than before, but she neither looked at him nor spoke. This did not seem to disconcert our Soma in the least; he edged himself a little nearer to her, a very little at a time, and began to speak.

'I saw you yesterday. My name is Soma e Motuiti.'

' Viara e Uru,' said the girl in a very low voice.

This was a piece of strategy on Soma's part, for, according to Omëan laws of politeness, if any one names himself to another, that other has to do the same, and Soma reckoned on this to make the girl speak and so break the ice.

' I said in myself, " She is very beautiful. I will go to the house of her father." ' All this time, by degrees that would have been imperceptible to any one but himself and the girl, Soma was drawing nearer. ' The flowers of that *ilu-ilu* have not so sweet a scent —are not so soft '—and as he spoke the last words his hand lightly touched her shoulder for a moment. Still Viara said nothing, but she glanced at him once through the long lashes of her drooped lids, and the look she gave was not exactly one of annoyance. It rather emboldened Soma than otherwise, for in love-making an inch is as good as an ell, for he seized her hand and held it for a moment, and would have kept it longer had not the girl said—

' They will hear I am not beating the *tappa*. They will come back to see why.'

Soma, seeing that she did not want their meeting to be interrupted, quickly took the hint and loosed her hand, when the beating was resumed in a hurried, intermittent fashion. But he was no laggard in love ; the tropical sun of Polynesia had warmed the blood that flowed in his veins, and he did not let the necessity of the girl's work come in his way; he boldly put one arm round her smooth waist, and found that it in no way interfered with her labour.

' You have a wife in Otorangi,' suddenly said Viara, moving as though to free herself.

' No,' said Soma, ' I am *tai ohana* ' (unmarried).

‘ You are old enough,’ she said. ‘ It is not your fault.’

‘ I had not seen Viara e Uru,’ Soma whispered.

‘ Where did you find that white (*tëa*) man ?   They say in the town he is your *ofa-namu*.’

‘ It is true.’

‘ Can a man who is *ofa-namu* marry ? ’ said the girl slyly, pausing for a moment in her work and looking round.

‘ He is married ; why should not I ? ’

The girl shook back her silky hair from her face and flashed her dark eyes upon Soma ; all she said was—

‘ Why not ? ’

Once loosed, Viara’s tongue wagged freely enough, as question after question suggested itself. There was plenty of Mother Eve in the girl—perhaps the South Sea Paradise kept alive the first woman’s characteristics —and curiosity, the origin of most good, if of much evil, made her forget her shyness. Not that shyness is a leading Omëan defect, for their natural and free lives have prevented the growth of much timidity ; besides there was a fund of liveliness and humour in the girl which would not let her sit mum-chance with a young and handsome lover by her side. Soma had seen and done so much, too, that was novel and interesting that to hear him talk of the wonders of his long voyage fascinated the girl, and the swing of her mallet grew slower and slower as she became more and more absorbed, until at last it ceased altogether.

But the cunning Soma understood his business ; it was not all give—he managed to get confidence for confidence, and learned a good deal from Viara. Her father was dead, she said, and his brother, when he took all the property that was left, took the daughter as well, and she now lived in his family, and worked for him. Her mother had married again, and was living—Viara said this with a sly smile, though her eyes were cast down—in a house the back of which joined the side of the one in which Soma and North had been imprisoned.

'I have heard you and the Papalangi talking when I have been to my mother's house. I could have put my hand through the reeds of the two houses and almost have touched you.'

'Why did not you?'

'I had not seen you then,' said the girl, unconscious of her naïve confession.

'But you have now!' said Soma quickly, giving, as may be imagined, the girl's waist a little squeeze as he spoke with the arm that had not ceased to lie around it.

'Well,' said Viara, with a sideway glance at his bending head, and an artful, attractive little smile, 'I may put out my arm another time.'

With this half promise Soma had to be satisfied for that time, for there was a little sound within the house of the approach of some one, and with a quick and not too gentle a push the girl moved away from his side, and resumed her work with a sudden violence and rapidity that were very ill designed to cover her recent idleness. Soma sprang to his feet as silently as a shadow, and when the old woman, who acted as a sort of duenna to the women in Uru's house, appeared in the little courtyard, across which the long shadows of the palms had now moved half way, he was looking on at the girl's work from a little distance in the most nonchalant manner. Seeing the girl so busily occupied, and that the young man stood at so respectful a distance, the old lady, unmindful of the wiles of her own youth, appeared to suspect nothing, or at any rate was good-naturedly blind to the doings of her charge.　After a few commonplace remarks to the old woman, Soma innocently went away.

This was the first of many meetings.

CHAPTER XXV

THREE months passed, and Christian and Soma were still prisoners in Oneroa; they had almost unlimited freedom within the town, but were never allowed to go beyond the bounds of it together, unless accompanied by a band of Oneroans, who acted as a guard to prevent their making any attempts at escape. Many and many a plan had North contrived in the long still hours of the night, but something was always wanting for the success of them, and one after another had fallen to the ground. Soma was all this time the same loving, faithful, and devoted friend to him that he had been from the first—no cloud had come between them to obscure the clear and steady daylight of their affection; but the very thing that made Chris so eager to return to Otorangi was what made Soma willing, nay, desirous, to stay in Oneroa. The love of a woman was what swayed both hearts, for North had never for a moment forgotten the girl whom he regarded as his wife, and Soma, the great Hercules, was daily becoming faster bound to this Omëan Omphale of his. But circumstance, as it so often does when we think it is we who are deciding, determined their course of action for them.

The boat, upon which North and the men under

him had been working incessantly since the day it was begun, was now almost finished; it had been built with the utmost labour, as all the timbers had had to be split, and then patiently chipped to the required form by stone implements. However, it was at last approaching completion, and perhaps from the very demands it had made upon his patience, North had begun to bestow a sort of affection upon the production of his hands. So much so that just of late he had banished from his mind the idea of escape, which he decided he would not attempt, at any rate till the boat was complete. But the behaviour of Faäori for the last few days had begun to make him waver in this determination. The old chief, seeing that the desired boat was all but finished, had begun to remove the light of his countenance from them, and the principal men of the town, who took their whole tone from him, had changed their former courtesy to a brusqueness and inhospitality which were very evident. Neither of the men relished this alteration of manner, and once or twice Christian, who had a better command over his temper, had been unable to prevent Soma from expressing in a peculiarly forcible manner his opinion of the character of the Oneroans.

The young chief Mäutara, whose life Chris had spared, was unable to openly befriend them,—it would have been risking his own life to no purpose,—but on several occasions he had visited them at night and cautioned them to be wary in their dealings with Faäori, as their lives were again in danger. It was for this reason that North at this time began to expatiate to Faäori upon the difficulties of sailing this new canoe of his, saying that it would be quite useless to him unless he first could explain to him the management ·

of the boat. By this means he hoped to at least delay any attempts upon their lives.

This was the condition of affairs one night when, tired out by a long and arduous day's work, he and Soma walked back to their house from the little ship-yard where the boat still lay unlaunched. Both men felt an unwonted fatigue; a strange lassitude was upon them, for the weather had been oppressive and hot, and a dead and windless calm had lain upon the day from morning till evening. There had been no clouds, but an unusual haze had covered the whole sky, which, though it gave an unnatural pallor to the daylight, had seemed to have the effect of increasing the heavy and lowering heat. The whole town appeared to feel this strange influence, for it was unusually quiet, and even the wash of the water among the stones and rocks of the little promontory was silent as the tide rose without a ripple.

All day Christian had noticed the curious oily still-ness of the sea, which had been so smooth that the rocks and trees of the mainland had been reflected in it as perfectly as though it were a sheltered forest pool. No tremor ruffled its burnished surface except now and again, as the tide flowed in from the reef, when one long ripple moved across it and crept upon the sand of the bay, leaving the water as motionless and undis-turbed as before. Sometimes, too, a heavy broad-winged leaf, loosened and made yellow by the long continued heat and drought, would come falling down in wide swoops through the languid air from one of the overhanging trees, and reaching the water at last, would spread faint widening rings about it.

Now that night was come, heavy clouds had formed themselves low down on the horizon in the west and south, into which the dull red sun was hurrying, as though himself tired of this long weary day. Soma had called North's attention to them before they left the shore to enter the town.

'The wings of the rain are spread,' he said, 'and soon the storm will be here.'

There had been no fall of rain since they had been in Oneroa, and all the earth, in bare places, was burnt and cracked by the heat; the dark green of the forest trees was marked in many places with sere and yellow branches, though, as a rule, the leaves retained their colour. The sun could not penetrate into the thick-nesses of the forest, where some moisture still lingered. The gardens and plantations had suffered much not-withstanding all the careful irrigation that was practised, and the broad leaves of the plantains and bananas hung shrivelled and limp. There was no actual dearth of water in the town, for a stream flowed out into the bay from the cloud-capped mountains of the interior, but the land cried aloud for rain.

For all the quiet of the place it appeared to North that an air of unusual excitement prevailed; men were hurrying about with an appearance of importance and haste, and little groups of people were standing talking in the street, which, as this was the usual time for eating, was in itself an uncommon occurrence. North noticed that all these men ceased speaking when he and Soma approached, and he thought, too, that they were regarded with even less favour than had been their portion of late. They saw, as they passed it, that Faäiori's house was full of men, and they could hear voices raised in excited dis-cussion in it, though they failed to catch what was being said.

'What does all this mean?' asked North of Soma. 'Don't you see that something has happened?'

'Yes,' said Soma, with a perfectly impassive face and looking straight before him, 'I see. Do not look at them. Shut your eyes to it. Do not talk till we get to the house.'

Since they had left the boat darkness had come rapidly on, and the last view they got of the sea as they passed an opening to it near the house, showed them that the evil augury of the sky had increased its angry promise. The sun had sunk behind the black mass of clouds, tinging its abrupt topmost line with an edge of livid red, and it seemed to North that a greater space of sky was overcast than had been half an hour before. The dull-coloured sea was still perfectly calm, for not a breath of the great raging wind that probably lay behind the south-western darkness had reached them yet, but far off on the horizon the whole wide ocean was as black as ink.

All their end of the town appeared to be deserted; the men had gone towards Faäori's house, and only a few women, busy preparing the evening meal, and a lot of noisy, naked children, whom even the heavy day and the approaching storm had failed to repress, were about. Soma and North entered the empty house, which was now almost entirely dark, and Soma, without resuming their talk, began with an admirable philosophy to prepare their food; he lit a little wood fire in the small sunk hearth in the middle of the floor, to re-heat the cold *talo* which had been boiled in the morning.

'Soma,' said North, when at last the fire was made and the earthen jar placed upon it, 'something will happen to-night. It is not for nothing that Faäori's house is full.'

'No,' said Soma. 'We have waited too long; we ought to have gone before this.'

'We could not have passed the *a-lëo*.'

'We ought to have swum,—as we did before,' said Soma with a little smile.

'What fools we have been! But we have never been alone.'

'No, but we are now. Come;' and springing to his feet with sudden resolution, Soma was making for the door when a child, a boy of six or seven, with whom both men had often played, appeared at it. He was a straight well-grown little chap, quite naked, except for a necklace of bright red berries that harmonised beautifully with his brown colour, and with his head shaved perfectly clean, as is the fashion for all Omëan boys. It was a very unusual thing for this child to be about after dark, so drawing him into the narrow range of the firelight, Soma asked what it was he wanted.

'Come over here,' the child said, walking towards the shadowy end of the house; 'Mäutara said I was to let nobody see me speak to you.'

Directly that Soma heard the name of Mäutara he knew that the child must have been entrusted with some message that was perhaps of vital importance to them, and taking in his great palm the little brown hand that the child held out to him, he moved away from the tell-tale firelight. He knelt down on the floor by the side of the boy when they were well within the shadow, and asked what the message was that he had to give him. At this the little chap began to cry, and throwing his arms round the neck of his big playmate, he said in a jerky, half whispering voice—

'Are they going to kill you, Soma-ou? You and the Papalangi?'

'I hope not,' said Soma. 'Tell me what Mäutara said.'

This reminded the child that he had not delivered his message, and he stopped crying, rubbing his smooth little mouse-back head against Soma's cheek.

'Mäutara called me out of the house. Pilu was there and Tubu-fua. Mäutara said, "Go to my house where those men of Otorangi are. Let no one see you go. Say to them that Mäurata sent you." And then he said some things that I forget. Mäutara spoke so fast. But I know he said, "Tell them that to-night they must go. Tell them that Faäori has sworn a sacrifice." I don't know what he means.'

Though startled, Soma was not surprised by this news; he gently unclasped the boy's arms from his neck and giving him the *uma* he bade him go home, and then, as the child ran off into the outside darkness, he turned to Christian and said—

'*Ofa-namu-ou*, it is as we feared.'

'What message did the child bring?' asked North.

'It was from your man Mäutara. We are to be food for the gods.'

'What is the reason? Why has Faäori changed? What have we done?'

'Who knows?' said Soma. 'But so it is.'

'What must we do?' said North, more to himself than to his companion.

'Go at once,' answered Soma for him. 'We only risk our lives in trying to escape. It is certain death to stay.'

There was truth in this bold statement of their position, and Christian, as he always did in times of emergency, rose to the occasion, and was in spirit ready for anything. The presence of danger acted like a tonic on him, and as though it were a burden that he threw from his shoulders, he shook off the depression and lassitude that had oppressed him all day. There was a smile on his face and a little laugh in his throat as he turned to his companion and said—

'We are in a bad place, Soma-ou, but we have been in worse, and somehow we have managed to pull through. And so we will this time.'

But this time their luck seemed to have deserted them, for as the two men stepped out into the night they heard the dull and hurried sound of many men running towards them, the dull *thud, thud* and rustle of their naked feet sounding loudly in the stillness of the night. The wind had not come yet; the starlit sky overhead was still clear and blue, though a blackness as of the last day was mounting quickly in the heavens. Already light whirling wisps of vapour, torn from the edge of the advancing storm, were beginning to stretch long misty filaments, like wind-blown hair, across the still clear space of sky. These silent presages of the storm moved and were tossed with a wildness and speed that spoke of the force of the tempest that drove them.

'If they had but waited one half hour more,' said Christian to himself, casting one quick glance at the sky, 'they would have had enough to do without troubling about us.'

But the storm, for the sake of the two friends, came half an hour too late, for a crowd of eager hurrying men was about the house before Soma and North had time to hide themselves and all chance of doing so was gone. The two men, seeing that they were discovered, assumed an unconcern they were very far from feeling, and walked towards the band of Oneroans and demanded what it was that brought them there so hurriedly at that time of night.

'Go back into the house,' said the foremost of the party, which had come to a standstill upon finding the men they were seeking, as though uncertain of their next movements. 'Go back into the house. Faäori-eki will be here soon. You will know then.'

In another moment or two, when North and Soma had done as they were asked, a glimmer of torches shone into the place and Faäori with two other chiefs entered the house, followed by as many men as could come in. The two men were standing by one of the great central house-posts, and Chris, who thought he was something of a favourite with the savage old chief, walked towards him and asked why it was that Faäori and so many chiefs had come to their house.

A very evil light shone in the chief's eyes; he appeared to be as angry and excited as his following, and without noticing North's question he turned to one of the men who had first reached the house and said—

'Why have you waited? Did I not tell you what to do? take those men and bind them hand and foot.'

No sooner had he spoken than three or four men rushed forward to do his bidding, thinking to overpower the two defenceless men at once, but North at his first word had sprung back and given Soma a warning nudge, and as the men tried to seize them, North and Soma leaped upon them with clenched fists, felling two of them with their first furious and unexpected blows, pushed past the others, and made a sudden rush for the door. The attack was so sudden that they almost made good their escape, for Polynesians are so accustomed to abject obedience to their chiefs that they rarely make in such cases any attempt to resist ; but there were too many men in the house for them to evade, and in another moment both men, still struggling gallantly, were overpowered and borne to the ground. Before he fell Soma made one violent clutch at the only torch in the house, hoping that in the confusion and darkness they might still get away, but it was unsuccessful, and he only managed to burn the face and singe the hair of the man next the torchbearer.

Once upon the ground they were quite helpless, so many pairs of hands held them down that in a moment they were bound hand and foot without being able to resist. From where he lay Chris could see Mäutara, the man who had sent them the warning message, but he made no sign of recognising the prisoners, and North, for fear of implicating him, was as cautious and spoke no word. In the confusion of the struggle both men had received many blows and kicks, and both were breathless from their violent but futile struggles. Neither of them had any idea of the reason for this sudden change in Faäori's behaviour, and it appeared that they were not, at any rate at present, to be enlightened upon it, for in a few moments, after a short consultation with the men who accompanied him, Faäori ordered the house to be emptied of every one but the prisoners, and placing a strong guard at the door to prevent their escape, he hurried back into the town, where much had to be done in a short time to prepare for the rapidly coming hurricane.

CHAPTER XXVI

For a few minutes after North and Soma were left bound and panting on the floor, silence reigned in the emptied house; both men were so angry and confused by the sudden change in their condition that they did not know what to say—hardly what to think. North was the first to collect himself, and swearing a good round sailor's oath to relieve his mind, he sat up to try to do the same good office for his body; he found that his feet were so tightly tied at the ankles that the cord was cutting deeply into the already swelling flesh, and that his crossed wrists were fastened in the same manner. He could move his fingers, but that was all. Not daring to speak aloud to Soma, for fear of attracting the attention of the men who had been placed to guard the house, whose dark figures he could see dimly defined against the pale light of the doorway, he lay down again and quietly rolled across the floor to where he could hear Soma breathing.

A deathly silence lay upon the town, as though the coming storm were holding its breath for the howl and roar with which it would shortly burst upon it; now and then a sound of voices came to them from the other side of the promontory, where the people were hurriedly hauling their canoes into places of safety or securing their houses by passing stout ropes over them and attaching the ends to rocks or any available heavy weight. So silent was it that Chris could distinctly hear what the three or four men who were at the entrance to the house were saying, though their voices were lowered to a whisper that they might not be overheard by the prisoners. The first words that he caught seemed to refer to him and Soma, and thinking that he might learn something of importance, he stopped moving that he might hear the better.

'When did Faäori say it should be?' asked a boyish voice.

'He was angry and said, "I will do this thing to-morrow. Rongo, the god, shall not wait,"' answered one of the men.

'It is long since such a sacrifice was made.'

'That is why the god was not with us in Otorangi.'

'But why has Faäori waited so long?' asked the first speaker. 'I was over at Kaveka and did not hear the talking in his house.'

'Iruru, one of Tama-iru's men, has been back to Otorangi. He went by the land. He went back for a woman of the Otorangi called Sobele. She is his wife now, and she told him that Tama-iru, Faäori's nephew, was slain. Faäori will wipe out his blood with theirs.'

Here another and a rather louder voice, which North recognised as that of Nasili, one of his workmen, joined in with a laugh.

'At Rongo's stone, then, to-morrow I shall be revenged for all the work on that cursed (*kahe*) canoe.'

Even in that moment of peril these words had power to wound poor North, for he had been uniformly kind and considerate to this man, who had always seemed to be a harmless and good fellow.

After this Christian did not stop to hear more; he

had learned more than enough to convince him of the
absolute certainty of their death on the morrow were
they still in the power of the savage and now in-
furiated old chief.   Taking every precaution not to be
overheard, he rolled and shuffled across the floor until
he was alongside of Soma.   He found him lying perfectly rigid and still with the sullenness of despair
upon him, and when he spoke in answer to Chris's
questions there was a quiet hopelessness in his tones
that went to North's heart.   It is in times of this sort
that the superiority of the European shows itself; the
Polynesian fights boldly as long as he thinks he has
a chance of victory, but he has none of the moral
courage which struggles on as bravely against defeat
and disaster.   He is apt to accept misfortune in a
fatalistic spirit and as though inevitable, so that frequently he refuses to aid himself when he might better
his position, from the idea that to do anything is
useless.

It was in this condition that Chris found Soma;
he considered that all hope was gone, so he lay there
grimly awaiting the end.   He did not speak when
North reached the place where he lay, and Christian
had to push him in the side with his shoulder to make
him sit up.

'Did you hear what the men said?' asked
Christian.

'I heard,' said Soma, without moving.

'What are you going to do?'

'Nothing,' answered he in the same voice.

'Yes, you are,' said North savagely.   'Where are
you tied?'   He had learned by this time the character
of the Omëans, and he knew that to rouse Soma from
this fatalistic lethargy he must speak and act decisively;

besides this he felt somewhat angry at the helpless-
ness of his companion, who had never before failed him
in time of need.

'Where are you tied?' he repeated in a more
urgent whisper, for the house was so dark that it was
impossible to see for himself.

'My feet are tied,' said Soma, spurred to life by
the unusual tone of Christian's voice, 'and my hands
are also.   They are tied behind my back.'

Seeing that he had succeeded in rousing him, North,
in a more natural tone, said, 'Roll over on to your
face, Soma-ou, and I will try to untie them.'

Soma did as he was bid, and Christian with his
own bound hands, which had been tied in front of him,
tried, but in vain, to loosen the tight knots in the
sinnet cord with which Soma was fastened.   He had
been quite unable to make any impression on his own
bonds, but with an admirable pluck he was down in
a moment with his elbows on the floor, and with his
strong teeth began to tear and gnaw at the toughly
woven cords.   Soma, prone on the ground, turned his
head towards him, and with his unsupported cheek
pressing the mats, mumbled something about ' No use.
It is impossible.'   To which North answered, moving
his flushed and sweating face to Soma's ear, in a
whisper which in itself was exasperating to him,
excited as he was, and breathing quickly from his
exertions, ' It is of use.   Neither you, my friend, nor
I shall die this night for want of a little courage or a
little labour.   Lie still.   I shall be back in a moment.'

A new idea had struck him, and without a moment's
delay he began to execute it. Lying down again he
began to roll across the floor towards the little hearth
at which Soma had been preparing their food when

the child that had been sent by Mäntara to warn them had come into the house. The small fire had not been noticed when the excited men had poured into the house some short time before—it was unusual in Oneroa to have a hearth in the dwelling-house, but North and Soma had at first not been allowed to go to the cooking sheds, and they had continued to use the one originally made for them—and the embers and some small fragments of wood were still glowing.

Without a moment's hesitation he chose a stick of the wood which was burning brightest, and drawing it out of the embers with his bound hands, he placed it so that the glowing end was uppermost, then on this he put his two wrists so that the cord might be burnt through. He did not flinch, but held his hands steadily there, though the fire that burnt the sinnet charred his flesh at the same time till the tender skin stretched and cracked and shrivelled with the heat, and a sharp pungent smell rose from the burnt flesh. The agony was intense, and the self-control that he had to exert to keep his wrists over the fire, and at the same time to prevent himself from groaning aloud, seemed to make his sufferings greater. His toes and fingers were all cramped and contorted, and the perspiration was pouring from every limb and quivering muscle, but beyond a thick and gasping indrawn breathing, he made no sign of what he felt. Fortunately it was not for long, or he could not have endured the self-inflicted torment.

Soma groaned aloud when he saw what North was doing for him as well as for his own sake, and managed to propel himself worm-like to the hearth, entreating North to desist. Christian did not turn his head; his gaze was fixed too intently on the slow red charring of the cord, and all he said, in a whisper that was harsh and strident with pain, was—

'Be quiet, or I do it in vain.'

Just as Soma had wriggled to him the tough cord parted in several places, and Chris snatched his scorched hands away from the fire. Soma, down whose savage face childish tears of pity and compassion were pouring, stooped in his passionate devotion to kiss the wounded hands, but North, who even from Soma never could tolerate that sort of sentimentality, snatched them away, saying—

'*Ou-a fi koëni*' (*Anglice*, stop that).

Without waiting, as another man would have done, to examine his burns, Christian untwisted the burnt cords from his wrists, and then, before he finished freeing himself by untying his feet, turned to Soma, and making him lie down again that he could get at his hands, managed in a little time to undo the knots of his bonds with his strong fingers and teeth. All the time they could hear the murmur of the voices outside the house, which warned them never to raise their own above the faintest whisper. After some difficulty and much pain to his wounded hands, North managed to unfasten the last knot that tied his companion's wrists and ankles, and then Soma, stretching his great arms and legs till the joints cracked, turned to Chris and in a very short time succeeded in liberating his feet.

All this that they had now done was, however, nothing but the first step towards their liberty; they were hesitating for a moment and consulting as to what should be their next move when they heard a tiny rustling sound at one side of the house, as though some one were faintly and delicately scratching the reed-work that closed in the spaces between the house-posts. Soma laid a cautioning hand on North's shoulder and whispered quickly—

'Don't move. We are saved. It is Viara. That is the house of her mother.'

Almost as he spoke he began to creep silently towards the sound. But that night ill-luck seemed to pursue them, for as he was cautiously crossing the house he inadvertently kicked over the great rude earthen jar in which the food had been placed for cooking. This fell into the little hollow of the hearth and broke with a crash on the stones with which it was lined. North gave a great silent spring after Soma, and catching him by the shoulders whispered as quick as thought in his ear—

'Lie down and put your hands behind your back as you were. Say nothing; I will speak.'

The same instant the guard rushed into the house and demanded to know what the noise meant. They found both of their prisoners lying down in much the same position as that in which they had left them, and in the darkness of the house they could not detect the fact that they were no longer bound. Chris took upon himself to answer their question.

'What does that noise mean? It means that we have lost the supper we were cooking when you came and bound us. That fool of a Soma there said his feet were swelling. He stretched out his legs and kicked the pot over.'

The men laughed at this, and went back to their former position outside the house, with the exception of one, Nasili, North's former assistant, who was perhaps of a more suspicious nature, or probably enjoyed the sense of tyrannising over his former master.

This man said to the others as they went out of the house—

'I will stay here and watch our prisoners. His legs must have been looser than I left them if he can kick. I shall look at the sinnet.'

'Roko always smelt fire in a mist,' quoted one of the men from the doorway.

To say that North's heart stood still as he heard what Nasili said, little expresses the condition of anxiety he was in; he thought that immediate detection threatened them; but he need not have been alarmed. Soma's ears were open also, and as Nasili—who really had no suspicion as to the security of the prisoners—came near him, although he lay perfectly still, he prepared himself for his blow. There is very little magnanimity in the character of most Polynesians, and as Nasili stooped over his fallen enemy he could not resist taunting him with his approaching fate.

'Ha, my fine Otorangan, you will make a capital breakfast for Rongo to-morrow.'

The words were hardly out of his mouth before Soma's great arms sprang from behind him, and before the astonished and terrified Oneroan had time to give a cry he had him firmly in his grasp, with one gigantic hand upon his throat.

'If you make a sound I'll kill you,' he breathed hotly in the ear of the struggling man.

Christian was by his side instantly, and in a flash had secured his wildly waving arms with the very cord that he had taken from Soma's ankles. To his surprise he heard Soma give vent to a stifled little gurgle of laughter, and lifting his head to learn the reason he heard Soma whisper in his ear—

'Look in the ashes of the fire for the *talo* we were

going to eat. Nasili shall have a mouthful or two
instead.'

Not fully understanding his meaning Chris crept
softly to the hearth, and finding two or three great
lumps of the soft partly cooked vegetable, he brought
them back to Soma. Without taking his hand from
Nasili's throat, Soma took the *talo* from North, and
stooping to the ear of the half-suffocated man, he
whispered pleasantly—

'Come, Nasili, you must taste our cooking. Open
your mouth wide.' As the wretched fellow kept his
jaws firmly closed, Soma tightened his clutch about
his throat a little, and added, 'If you don't I'll strangle
you.'

This showed the superiority of persuasion over
force, for without more ado Nasili, baring his teeth
with a savage snarl, opened his mouth.

'Wider,' whispered Soma softly, and then, as the
Oneroan distended his great jaws, Soma crammed in
one piece of *talo* after another till North thought he
must choke; he said so to Soma, who very wisely
answered—

'If I don't put in enough he can move his tongue
and will swallow it all. He can sing again then.'

So he calmly proceeded to pack the great cavern
of Nasili's mouth till it could hold no more, and then
with a further length of the sinnet which had lately
bound them, and for which reason he seemed to doubly
enjoy the present use of it, he tied his jaws firmly
together.

'I wish we had a light,' he said as he finished his
work. 'Nasili never looked so funny' (*hoö-a*).

North was glad that Soma could accept Nasili's
treachery to them so lightly; he had always passed

as being their friend, and had, particularly to Christian, shown a degree of affection and confidence that had completely deceived him. Nothing can wound a true man so deeply as treachery and disloyalty from a friend, and yet, strangely enough, it is always the constant and stanch—who, from the very faithfulness and constancy of their own hearts, cannot believe in the untrustworthiness of a friend—who are oftenest deceived. How much better an open enemy than a false friend! One can respect the first, but the contempt for the last seems somehow to smirch one's own heart.

Before they left their captive they took the precaution of dragging him to one of the central house-posts, against which they seated him, and firmly tied him with his back to it that he might not wriggle across the floor as they had done. They then stepped across the house to the wall where they had heard the scratching of their friend; they listened for a moment, but could hear nothing. Thinking that she had perhaps been alarmed by the noisy entrance of Nasili and the other men, Soma began to make a little opening in the reed-work, through which he thrust his hand, and on the principle of nothing venture nothing win, he lightly ran the back of one of his nails across the reeds that formed the wall of the house which was not more than a foot from their own. In a moment they heard the sound of a light footstep crossing the floor of the next house, and then a soft voice, which they both recognised as that of Viara, although she spoke in a faint whisper, said—

'Is that you, Soma-ou?'

'We are both here,' he answered.

'You are dead men. Viara weeps. There is one way.'

'What is it?' eagerly whispered Soma.

'Cut through the screen; not here, lower down a little. Here is a knife. I have made a hole in the side of this house. You must come right through.'

As she spoke Soma felt the wooden handle of one of their obsidian-bladed knives thrust into his hand; and he managed—true lover that he was—to press in his for a moment the little hand that gave it him.

The reeds of which these screens are made are not woven, they are too thick and brittle to be much bent; they are cut of the length that will just reach from the eaves to the floor of the space they are to fill, and then are tied together perpendicularly by narrow strings of sinnet, which run longitudinally the whole length of the screen at distances of about six or eight inches. Once armed with the clumsy but keen-bladed knife, it was easy enough to cut the strings and make an opening, which it would have been almost impossible to do with their hands without much noise, in the short time they had at their disposal.

They effected their work in silence; not a reed cracked, and having made a hole large enough for them to pass through, they were just about to glide through it into the next house when a cheerful voice at the doorway—the approaching fate of the two prisoners evidently weighed but little on the minds of the guards—called out—

'You are very quiet, Nasili; are you going to sleep with your friends there?'

'Nasili is kind,' said the other voice; 'he does not want to wake them till breakfast time. Is not that so, Nasili?'

Fearing that if they got no answer the men would come into the house to know the reason and find their prisoners flown, Soma stepped lightly back into the house, and, with a wit and presence of mind that North could never sufficiently admire, hurrying to the hearth, snatched up a piece of the *talo*, which thus came to their assistance a second time, and filled his mouth with it. Having thus disguised his voice, he answered naturally enough and in rather a surly tone—

'I'm not asleep. I have found food, and am eating.'

'I am hungry,' said one of the men at the door. 'Let us go in, Mapai. We will eat too.'

With a boldness born of desperation Soma snatched up two or three lumps of the now cold vegetable and rushed to the door. With his mouth still full of food he said to the men—

'Here is the *talo*.'

The night had grown so dark that he might have ventured outside without being recognised, but he wisely kept on the safe side of prudence, and did not leave the house. The men took the food innocently enough, and he stepped back calmly into the house, and in another moment he and the exultant Christian had passed through the openings in the two walls, and, silently led by Viara, found themselves free on the rocky shore of the little promontory.

CHAPTER XXVII

ALTHOUGH it was not very long, not more than an hour, since they had last looked upon the sky, a terrible change had come over it. The torn and flying clouds that had edged the black mass of the mounting storm, like great waves of blackness rent from the heart of night, had swept across the zenith. It was as though some dire bird of infinite wing had pulsed across the heaven, eclipsing in its sombre flight all the glory of the stars. The darkness could almost be felt. Viara and the two men standing there in the open air shoulder to shoulder would not have known that each was not alone but for the sense of touch and the sound of each other's voice. The storm had not broken yet, and the silence in the midst of that appalling darkness, with the knowledge that the awful and devastating violence of a raging hurricane was only collecting its direst forces to break upon them at any moment, seemed to weigh like lead upon their hearts. The intense stillness of that moment as God held His breath was more awe-inspiring than the wildest shrieking of the winds and raging of the storm could be.

It seemed that everything had been done by the people in the town that could be thought of for their safety, and now they waited in terror-stricken silence for the hurricane to burst. Soma and North might have passed unchallenged through the town, but the darkness was such that they could not have found their way, and in all probability they would have walked straight into the arms of their enemies. But for this they would have made the venture there and then. They did not know for what they waited, but they stood still on the spot they first had reached when they left Viara's mother's house until something, they knew not what, should occur.

It was not for long. It was North who first heard it, for the other two were quietly talking in low whispers, and did not pay so much attention to what might happen. Poor souls, it was the last time that they ever spoke together. As Christian with uplifted face tried to pierce the darkness all around him, and strained his hearing for any sign of coming change, he noticed a very faint low roaring which slowly but steadily grew nearer. It came from the sea, as though the calm water were suddenly forced into wild waves, which growled deeply and hoarsely at the coming of the mighty raging wind. From the land across the bay, too, a low sound came as the vanguard of the storm seized the top branches of the trees, which, tearing and tossing in its grasp, shrieked with the ten myriad tiny voices of their leaves.

Louder and nearer came the wind, a few heavy drops of rain fell, and then suddenly, without any preliminary warnings of gusts of wind, the full fury of the hurricane burst upon the town. The rain fell in torrents, and was dashed with such force to the earth that it was worse than the heaviest hail; with this was mixed the driving scud of sea-water that was torn from the crests of the great waves, which, as though by magic, sprang up within the lagoon and came crashing on the rocky shore. No one could stand up in the face of this terrific gale, and Viara and the two men, grasping each other, flung themselves down amongst the great rocks of the shore where the rain beat on them till they could scarcely breathe, and every now and then some great billow, larger than his fellows, came crashing on the beach and surged over them as though to drown them on dry land. Soma and North did all that they could to protect the girl who had risked so much for them, but it was of little service; she bore it very bravely, and creeping close to Soma seemed to find comfort in his presence.

The lightning, which was almost incessant, rendered the intervals of darkness doubly black; but so terrific was the deep roaring of the wind that they could not hear the loudest thunder-clap. It is impossible to describe the frenzied violence of the tempest or the unutterable din of the one continuous howl and roar of the wind. Though every now and then North tried to make Soma hear by shouting his very loudest in his companion's ear, it was perfectly futile; no human voice could make itself heard above the din of all the elements let loose.

Christian thought it almost impossible that they could live the night through, for every few moments flying objects, boughs and branches torn from the forest across the bay, beat upon them, and of course they were unable to protect themselves from these unseen missiles. They crouched and cowered amongst the tumbled rocks on that side of the promontory, and it was doubtless the poor protection these afforded that saved their lives.

After some time the lightning, which at first had seemed to dart from all four quarters of the heavens at once, became rarer, though the stinging rain, that fell in one great cascade from the sky, showed no sign of ceasing. It was then that through the floods of rain Chris first noticed a strange pale fluctuating light that dimly shone along the shore; this was caused by the phosphorescence of the great waves which came thundering over the reef, and crossing the lagoon, broke on the beach in masses of wildly leaping spray, each drop of which glowed with its weird lamp of life.

So the first hour of that terrible night passed, the three desperate creatures crouching among the rocks as much isolated from the crowded town behind them as if a hundred miles away. Every living soul on the promontory might have been swept away into eternity without their knowing or hearing even a faint echo of their last despairing shrieks.

About midnight, as near as North could judge, when they were almost exhausted with the violence of the storm and all of them were stiff with the cold, a sudden change occurred. As abruptly as the storm had burst upon them there fell a deathly calm. The centre of the circular cyclone was passing over the town, and for the space of about ten minutes not a breath of air moved and not one drop of rain fell. The instantaneous change from the howling and roaring of the wind to that soundless calm—for except the beating of the waves on the rocks and the *drip, drip* of rain from trees or houses, there was no sound during that mysterious interlude—created a suspense and terrible anxiety that were almost worse than the raging of the hurricane. The clouds overhead had time to part, and for a few moments the tranquil stars shone out before the storm burst upon them once more with all its former fury, but from the opposite direction.

Short as was that little time of calm it was taken advantage of by the two determined men; they bore their lives in their own hands, and knowing the value that moments were to the success of their attempt, they sprang to their feet the instant the wind fell. Now that the torrents of rain had ceased, the faint phosphorescent light of the beating surf was enough for them to find their way into the town again. Soma picked up the almost senseless body of Viara, and kissing her passionately as he stumbled up the rocky way, he said a farewell that he little thought was an eternal one, and passing the entrance to her mother's house, which, like every other in the town, was almost in ruins, he left the girl there, and hurried along what had been the well-kept open street. Now everything was changed: the town was ruined, almost all the houses roofless, and masses of debris of all sorts blocked the open spaces.

Over and amongst all this rubbish North and Soma quickly made their way; hand-in-hand, like two children, that they should not lose one another in the darkness, they rapidly ran and scrambled towards the *a-lëo* that divided the promontory from the mainland. They passed many a terrified group of men and women crouched together and covering their crying children as well as they could, and once or twice they were called after, but they did not pause, and the hapless Oneroans had too much to think of in their own misfortunes to remember the prisoners who were awaiting death in the morning.

The opening in the *a-lëo* was not closed, and stumbling through this in a broken and breathless run, the two men found themselves on the mainland, free of the town from which they had hardly dared to hope they would escape with their lives. There was no time for speech; they could not tell how soon the hurricane would be upon them again, and they knew that to be caught in the forest, with trees and branches falling in all directions, was dangerous in the extreme, so with one accord they ran to the open space of the shore, taking, almost instinctively, the left-hand side, in which direction Otorangi lay.

Hardly had they left the strip of forest and reached the sandy shore of the bay before the storm with all its former violence was beating upon them once more; but what did they care in that moment for all the fury of wind or rain, for they were free.

Free! Ah, none but those who for a time have lost it can tell what a man's freedom is to him! Free! free! North could have shouted the word aloud with the delight and rapture that he felt in being his own master again. The very storm that tore and hustled about him might have been the balmiest, softest air that ever blew from out a summer heaven without giving him a greater joy. In truth, the force and wildness of it seemed fitting to his mad rapture. Let it buffet him as it would, let it try to beat the very life out of him, as it indeed seemed trying to do, it only served to rouse his manhood in him now that he was free. Restricted, watched, and imprisoned as he had been all these last long months, it was enough for him to feel that he could turn this way or that at his own free will, that all the earth was his once more. The very airs of heaven—storms from hell they might have been from their fury—seemed purer now that no man was his master. He felt that for the first

time since their capture he drew his breath as a man
should breathe.

A man can live and be happy in one house, even
in one room, from year's end to year's end, if he does
it of his own free will and with the knowledge that
he can leave it any moment that he chooses, but it
becomes the bitterest of torments if it be against his
will.   Imprison a man's body and, let poets say what
they may, his soul becomes imprisoned too ; his body
may be unhurt, but his spirit is crippled, and slowly
the integrity of his self-respect is wounded, not to be
cured again until he is his own master.

Christian had chafed bitterly against his confinement, and had become, for him, moody, silent, and de-
pressed under it, so that now, when by one bold stroke
they had regained the treasure of their liberty, a natural
reaction had set in.   He felt neither cold nor hunger
nor discomfort, his heart beat high, and his natural
cheerfulness and good spirits returned in such a flood
that for a time the man was 'fey.'   He laughed aloud
and sang, though none, not even himself, could hear a
sound of it, and if for a moment there were any lull
in the tempest, he shouted the wildest nonsense to his
somewhat melancholy companion.

Everything was as he wished it to be.   He would
not have had the storm one jot less strong ; he loved to
fight against it, and to use his strength and manhood to
conquer it ; the wind howled louder for him than he
could for himself, and the wild shouting of the thundering surf was no wilder than his own mad heart.   He
could not rest, and when Soma proposed to shelter in
the lee of a mass of rocks, he urged him not to stop,
but to buffet and struggle on along the beach, where
the phosphorescence of the breakers marked out their

way for them ; and he sang to himself as he staggered along and waved his arms in mockery of the black, tossing, tempest-torn masses of the groaning forest on their right hand, when, sometimes for a moment, they could define its outlines against the scudding sky.

Towards daylight they felt the fury of the storm begin to abate, and it rapidly decreased in violence, though a full gale of wind was still blowing when the blackness of the terrible night first was tempered with the cold gray of the coming dawn. They had made but little progress in those long hours, the force of the wind, which had veered round and blew directly in their faces, frequently keeping them at an absolute standstill, if not actually driving them backwards. They could throw themselves on to it and be borne up as though by a solid body. So that an hour before sunrise both men were completely worn out, and feeling sure that they had put a sufficient distance between themselves and their enemies,—even in the unlikely eventuality of their flight being detected and followed, —they, by the earliest dim light, looked out for a place of comparative shelter, where they flung themselves down side by side, and, notwithstanding rain, wind, and cold, fell asleep, and slept soundly until long after sunrise.

CHRISTIAN sprang to his feet the instant that he awoke, feeling his life as elastic and youthful as though just poured from the immortal sea, to which some day it must flow back. He looked down at his sleeping companion, who was lying, like a tired child, in the same position in which he had thrown himself down some hours before; he seemed, however, to miss North from his side, and awoke in a moment, looking round wondering. The wind was still high, though the sun was shining brightly through the broken clouds that, like flocks of great birds, were flying across the blue. The sea had not yet gone down; it had lost its angry look, but was still wild with its last night's passion, and its broad breast still heaved with sobs though its anger was spent. Great rolling waves came crashing on the beach, white-crested, majestic, beautiful, and clear, through which the warm sun shone, making fleeting caves of emerald and sapphire in the smooth hollows of their curves.

'Look there,' said Chris, pointing with one hand to the sea, whilst with the other he seized the wrist of the half-awakened Soma.

No more needed to be said; Soma sprang to his feet, his last night's sorrow forgotten, and the two happy savages ran headlong to the sea. They tore off their damp *mahis* and unfolded them, and weighting them with stones, left them to dry in the sun and wind whilst they plunged into the waves like sea-gods regaining their element. The surging force of the delicious water, the fresh and strong cool wind, the glowing sun, and the sweet rain-washed air, all seemed to have conspired together to make much of these two true sons of theirs. They swam boldly out to sea, battling with the great waves and then riding triumphantly to land on the backs of these splendid sea-horses. Life and happiness and health glowed in their veins and love warmed their hearts as they, laughing like two boys at the buffets of the waves, came staggering to the firm sand of the beach; crisp and fresh and hard, they stood there with the wind blowing about them and the water running down their smooth, healthy skins, as it does from marble. For very exuberance of joy in their liberty, Chris threw his arms round Soma in a boyish embrace and challenged him to a race along the beach.

Laugh your fill, Christian—you will not laugh again for many a long sad day; race, leap, stretch your grand limbs and fill your great chest, oh Soma—your strength is at its greatest, your youthful manhood is at its beautiful perfection, and your noble heart mature; not long shall these God-given gifts help to glorify the earth; all these shall weigh how light in your un-flinching hand when the time comes for their sacrifice.

Everywhere along the wave-ridged beach were strewn the signs of last night's storm; broken boughs, long palm branches, and tufts of shining leaves were mingled in a wild confusion with dark, curved lines of brown and purple sea-wrack. Far above the usual limit of high tide this debris of the sea lay piled, long ropes of gorgeous marine vegetation, deep olive-green and bright pink tresses of weed, amongst which mermaids might have played; gay shells and strange forms of life cast up from the mighty deep. In and out of these quickly-drying masses little bright-coloured crabs ran sideways down to the water, and lines of big-winged, slowly moving birds were seeking their food—an unexampled banquet—amidst the rubbish. Fruits from the forest and ripe and immature coco-nuts from the line of palms that edged the shore, lay there all shent in countless thousands, and once or twice they found a dead and battered bird. These last Christian could never pass; he would pick them up and dry them and set their dainty plumage as straight as his clumsy man's fingers would let him, and then he would bury them in a hasty hole in the sand. They were too sad a sight, he thought, for the beauty and vitality of that day.

The memory of that happy day remained bright and unfaded in North's heart as long as he lived; the blackness and the grief that lay ahead of him was unseen then, and when it came it only served to throw into greater brightness by its contrast the joy and blitheness of these hours. How happy they were, those two; how they laughed as they talked of their outwitted enemies; what plans for the future did they not make—that careless future which, like a sunny landscape, lies spread out before our untroubled youth! North was now to have no difficulty in making Ilo remove his *tabu* from Utamè, and he talked of their happiness as assured; Soma was to manage for Viara to join him in Otorangi. This was to be and that was to be. They arranged it all. Dreams, dreams, which an hour was to wreck.

The march back to Otorangi, although interrupted by no dangers, was a long one, and took them the whole day, for neither man knowing the way through the forest, they had to walk along the wind-swept beach the whole distance, and as the coast-line of that side of the island is broken into many bays, their journey was much longer than if they had been able to cut across the land. There was only one town of any importance between Oneroa and Otorangi, and that they wisely avoided by making a considerable detour and passing in the rear of it; they might in all probability have passed unchallenged through it, though it was one of Faäori's dependencies, on account of the confusion caused in it by the hurricane, but they did not wish to run the slightest risk of losing their newly-gained liberty. They managed to obtain sufficient food and drink on the shore and the edge of the forest without venturing near any inhabited place.

It was after sunset when they began to approach their own town, and the natural excitement that they both felt prevented them from noticing their fatigue. The sun had gone down in a solemn sky, all barred at the horizon with heavy banks of cloud, and now the serene moon was rising, sailing onwards to that unknown port for which she always steers, but which she never reaches.

They left the shore now and turned a little inland to gain the town more quickly, for by this time they knew every inch of the road, and in the warm shadows and silence of the woods they hurried on with the joy of home-coming in their hearts. The storm had been there before them, and signs of its violence were everywhere visible, though the devastation it had wrought seemed less complete than that which had fallen on

Oneroa; it was the edge of the cyclone that had struck
Otorangi, so that its force had not been so great.
They did not meet a soul until they were almost in
the town, but there they found many men still about
doing what they could to repair the last night's
damage.

It had been thought that both men had been killed
long before this by their enemies, so that the sudden
return of Soma was the cause of the wildest excitement and joy to his fellows. Even in that first
moment Christian noticed a change in their treatment
of him, for whilst glad shouts of 'Soma o Motuiti is
back!' 'The dead is living!' 'Here is our Soma!' surprised the silence of the night, no word of welcome was
raised for North, and he was looked upon askance by
one and all, though pityingly by some. This gave
him a strange and unhappy chill, for North, like all
emotionally quick men, instantly detected a change in
the feelings of those about him.

In his first excitement, and in the eager questionings
that he made as to what had occurred in the long
months of their absence, Soma failed to observe the
change in the demeanour of his friends to Christian,
and he led the way joyously to the house of his father.
The little river was so swollen by the torrents of rain
that it had far overflown its usual limits, and they had
to cross by means of the high stepping-stones that had
been useless during the whole time of North's presence
on the island.

Old Motuiti, told by a young man who ran on
ahead, of the return of the son he had so long thought
dead, was outside the house to welcome him, and
though he tried to preserve a chief-like calm, the nervous
working of his kind old face and the trembling of his

lips as his son clasped him in his arms for the *uma*, showed well enough the joy of the old fellow. He led them both into the house, and with a shaking voice called to the young men to bring food for the wanderers. There was no change in him, Christian saw; his kindness and hospitality were what they had always been, for by his adoption by the old chief, North had really become as a member of his own family. But whilst they ate with the appetite of young and healthy men he told them of the discoveries made by Ilo, through the slave girl Sobele, of Tama-iru's death, and of Utamé's flight to Monoriro with Christian. The head chief had been furiously angry with North for breaking *tabu* by taking away the girl, whom he entirely exonerated from the death of Tama-iru, as it was evident that she had slain him in self-defence; but North he held responsible for the attack on the town by the Oneroans, and the consequent loss of so many of his warriors who had been killed in the battle. The priests of the old worship had laid all the blame of this fatal engagement on North, and, though both they and Ilo had thought him dead, they had held him up to execration in the songs composed in commemoration of the battle, and had vowed a bitter vengeance if by chance he had escaped and should ever fall into their hands.

'And now that you are back, my son,' concluded the old man, addressing Christian, 'I fear you are in worse danger with Ilo than you were amongst the Oneroa men. Ilo will have your life.'

Chris laid his food down with a sigh. He had come back with a light heart expecting a welcome, and had found a sentence of death. He was, however, game to the core, and he sprang to his feet as lightly as though he had known no fatigue that day, and turning quietly to Soma, he said—

'There is no rest for Papalangi tëa; truly he is a stranger.   I must go.'

'It is best,' answered Soma; 'we must go.'

At first Christian did not know what he meant, but he saw at the first glance that Soma meant to accompany him.   He had felt discouraged at this sudden ruin of his hopes, but the words of his friend seemed to give him new courage, though his eyes, poor wanderer, were dimmed by this display of natural and unconscious generosity and devotion.

'I cannot take you from home again, Soma-ou,' said North.

'Where you are is my home, *ofa-namu-ou*,' was all that Soma said, but he spoke in so calm and determined a voice that Christian knew nothing would shake his resolve, and he was happy in the thought of that sturdy affection on which he might rely as on a rock.

'Where shall you go?' asked Motuiti, who had listened to their conversation without making any interruption.

'To Monoriro, first of all, to see Utamè,' answered North.

'But Utamè is here in Otorangi,' quickly said the old man.

'Then I will see her if I die for it,' said Christian passionately.   'Where is she?'

Before Motuiti could answer Soma made a quick sign for silence, and looking round across the ill-lighted house, North saw that four or five men had come silently up to it and were already entering.

'What is it that you want?' asked Soma angrily.

'We come from Ilo-cki,' answered one of the men. 'You and the Papalangi tëa are to come to his house at once.'

Both Christian and Soma knew that it would be useless to refuse to obey, so making a sign to Motuiti to follow them, they went out and walked across the moonlit *bara* to Ilo's house. The place was all lighted up with candle-nut torches and pine-gum burning on flat stones on the floor, and Christian could see by these preparations, and by the eager talking of the little group of men on the mats round Ilo, that a discussion of importance was taking place. He had little doubt of the subject of it when he recognised amongst the old men talking with the chief several of the principal priests of that part of the island. The manner of their reception convinced him that his fate had been decided as soon as his return to the town had become known. He knew that it was 'death,' but what manner of death remained to be told.

He experienced a curious sinking at the heart as he felt the looks of these previously friendly people turned upon him with an expression of hate and revenge painted upon their faces, different from anything that he had ever felt when in danger among enemies. It was not so much the death that threatened him as that he should come by it at the hands of old companions and friends,—here was the sting. He felt a hopelessness then that had been a stranger to him in all his previous straits; it seemed that in this struggle with men who before this had loaded him with kindness and benefits, all his old pugnacity was dead and a dull despair had taken its place.

They stood for a moment at the entrance to the house, uncertain what to do next, when from where he

sat Ilo called out to them to come in, inviting Soma
to the mats where he and his councillors sat, but
bidding North sit down at the doorway. Then Soma
showed his mettle and spoke up.

'What has the Papalangi tëa done that he should
sit in the doorway with slaves and not on the mats
with the chiefs? Is he not a son of the house of
Motuiti?'

'You speak truly, Soma-eki,' answered Ilo with a
wonderful dignity, and betraying no anger at Soma's
interruption. 'He is a son of your house. But he
has defied the gods, my ancestors, by breaking *tabu*
placed upon Utamè e Ngawa. He is no longer worthy
of a place amongst us chiefs. He is a dead man.
The thing is decided. Come sit with us and aid us
with your counsels.'

'He is my *ofa-namu*,' answered Soma, with a
boldness that did not seem to be displeasing to the old
chief, 'and I will not sit with those who wish his
death.' So saying he stepped to North's side and sat
down; etiquette would not allow him to remain standing in the presence of the sitting chiefs.

'You are a stranger,' said Ilo then, addressing
Christian, 'and may have laws unlike to ours in Omëo.
It is for this that I tell you that you are a dead man.
These priests of the great gods, whose own voices we
chiefs have heard, have said that through you all these
ills have fallen on Otorangi. You have broken *tabu*,
and the angry gods have sent the men of Oneroa upon
us, who have slain many of our warriors and young
men. They could not tell us why the gods had sent
the great storm on us that has destroyed our crops and
coco-nuts. But now the wise priests say the gods were
angry still because you lived.'

'How do you know,' interrupted Soma at this point, 'that the priests speak the will of the gods?'

'Did not some among us begin to doubt the power of the older gods, and give worship to Iro Vearu and Lomangatini? Did not Paori, the priest, tell us that the gods were angry, and that for a sign they would take him to themselves? Did they not do so? We therefore fear the gods and their anger. If we give them a life for a sacrifice they will spare ours and our children's. Rorutu has moved on his mats many times of late, and the earth has shaken. Monoriro has breathed red and waxed hotter for two moons, and Venga says the fire is high in the mountain and soon must pour down into the valleys. To him, into his fire will we cast this life.'

Ilo had become wrought up as he talked, and towards the end of his speech his voice was raised in loud tones, which excited the audience of chiefs and priests about him as the smell of blood affects a lion. Their eyes blazed, and they breathed loud and deep, and as Ilo finished an angry growl of savage voices was heard all round the house.

'To the mountain,' 'He is food for Rorutu,' 'His blood shall appease the god,' 'Into the fire with him,' and other cries of cruelty and brutality, which showed plainly enough that the savage lust for blood was stirred and awakened within them, and that nothing but the death of the demanded victim would satisfy it. The cry was taken up outside the house, and soon the *bara* was ringing with similar shouts of 'Death,' and 'To the great fire.'

Christian sat there as pale as death already, but he did not flinch for an instant before the gaze of all these passionate men; he did not attempt to say one word in self-defence; he knew that it would be useless, and he let this storm of anger and superstitious hatred surge about him without making a sign.   He possessed already that strange dignity which absolute hopelessness bestows.   He knew everything; hopes and fears could no longer disturb him; he knew the worst, and had nothing to dread now but the one quick step he would have to take,—the one strange second of agony that lay between this life and the nothingness called Death,—or another existence, perhaps, of which he knew nothing.   He was loath to leave this full, bright life, it is true, but death itself he had never feared, and beyond the mere moment of dying, which to his strong youth was terrible enough, he had nothing to dread.   All he thought then was of the agony of mind that Soma was suffering, and that perhaps Utamè—ah, God, how his heart leaped yet!—might hear these shouts which condemned her husband and true lover.

Christian had lived long enough on the island to grasp thoroughly the religious principles of the Omëans, and he knew how firm a hold in their hearts the strange theory of atonement, that their priests preached, had obtained.   He had seen it carried out in minor instances over and over again, how if a man robbed another and himself escaped punishment, it was meted out to some member of his family, who acted as scapegoat, and the aggrieved person was satisfied; even in cases of life and death he had known an innocent man struck dead, and the blood-price thus being paid, the guilty one had gone scot-free, purged of his crime by the other's death.   Knowing this, he was well aware that Ilo—and indeed every one in the island—thought that he was not only justified but meritorious in taking his life for those of the men whose death, in an indirect manner, he may have occasioned.

It almost seemed that the council of chiefs would end in general confusion, so excited were one and all, but an old priest seated next to Ilo called his attention to the fact that he had not said what was to be done with North. Reminded of his duty, Ilo in a few words gave orders that Christian should be strongly bound and be taken, well guarded, to the temple on the river bank—to the god of which, Rorutu, he was now dedicate—and that Soma should not be permitted to be with them. The next day, he said, they would start before sunrise for Monoriro to complete the sacrifice.

CHAPTER XXIX

ALTHOUGH he knew that this was his last night on
earth, and that his very breaths were numbered—as
truly are those of all us from the first sobbing one we
draw—Christian slept a deep, unbroken sleep. As he
had crossed the *bara*, to reach the temple where he
was to spend his short imprisonment, he had looked
about him with eyes still mindful of the beauty of
everything around, and he then made a sort of farewell
to life, of whose cup he had drunk so deep. His heart
was very full, for life, with youth and love and friendship still strong within him, was exceeding sweet
to him, and all he had for consolation now was the
knowledge that he had not wasted but had lived every
hour of it. But this scarcely made him more ready
for death.

His guards were talking busily as they led him to the
well-known building, but he paid no heed to them, his
thoughts were otherwhere,—with Utame and Soma for
the most part, but feeling his throat swell and his eyes
fill with tears, he would not let his mind dwell on
them, for fear lest his thoughts should unman him. It
was a perfect night, cooler than was usual in Omëo at
that time of year, and the storm-cleansed air was fresh
and clear. He looked upwards at the galaxy of stars
above him as he entered the dark old temple, and said

to himself with almost a smile, 'I may know your mysteries to-morrow.'

Binding him hand and foot, and fastening his wrists to the central post of the temple, his guards left him alone in the presence of the great hideous god, whose glittering eyes of shell had looked down upon his parting with the old priest Paori, and to whose name to-morrow he was to be offered up. The noise and excitement in the town gradually died away, and sleep, like a downy-winged night-bird, flew about the houses; not a sound broke the silence except the low, rapid murmurs of the flooded little river, and once, far away across the drowsy woods, towards Nareva, a faint echo of some lover's music. His very guards on watch around the house seemed sleeping too, but they watched well for all their silence.

Towards midnight, when the moon was hidden by the mass of the great central mountains, Soma, who had retired quietly to his father's house when his friend was separated from him, rose from the mats where, for the last hour and more, he had been lying feigning the sleep that was so distant from his hot eyes. Without disturbing any of the sleeping men about him, he crept from the house, and keeping clear of the open spaces of the town, where he might have been seen in the bright starlight by any watching man, he stole to the beach. He walked resolutely, as one whose mind is made up; and quickly, but without noise, he arrived at the place where a little crowd of small fishing canoes lay moored to posts driven into the sand. He carefully chose one, and untying its rope of fibre, dragged it through the shallow water to a part of the beach directly opposite the temple in which North lay. Here he pulled it a little way up

the sand that it might not float off, and then returned
to the town along the bank of the swollen stream.

He moved now with extreme caution, and when he
was near the guarded building he pulled the sharp
obsidian dagger from his *mahi*, and putting the light
wooden handle between his teeth, dropped on to his
hands. Creeping slowly on all fours he approached
the temple. Everything was quiet, and from the end
of the building, the side of which he had gained
without being observed, he could just distinguish in
the feeble light the forms of the men who were guard-
ing the place by lying across the entrance to it. He
thought they slept, and crept, with throbbing heart, till
he could have touched the feet of the nearest man.
They little thought how near to death they were in that
moment, for without one moment of compunction Soma
would have slain them one and all had he thought he
could do it noiselessly. What were the lives of these
men in the eyes of Soma when compared with that of
his love-brother ?

He hesitated for a moment whether it would not
be better to try to kill them one by one; but, on
reflection, he considered that, though he certainly could
slay the one beneath his hand, he must make some
noise and so disturb the others. He passed this man,
who was sleeping with his face turned up to the sky,
and holding his breath, he prepared to step across the
second man and enter the dark temple.

Alas, Soma, it was not to be ! As he lifted his foot
to step across this fellow, a great pair of arms were
stretched out, and before he knew what had happened,
he was tripped up and fell heavily to the ground. He
struggled violently to free himself, but in vain, for in
a second the other men were roused and held him

securely down. None of them spoke a word, and it all happened so silently, that Christian, worn out by the various fatigues and emotions of the day, slumbered heavily on, quite undisturbed by the struggle, and he never knew that this bold attempt had been made to set him at liberty.

Finding himself quite overpowered, Soma ceased struggling, and said sullenly and in a low voice—

'What are you going to do to me?'

'Nothing, Soma-eki,' answered one of the men. 'Ilo-eki warned us that you, perhaps, would do this thing. He said we were to watch well. We were to stop your going in, but that we were to do you no harm. You and the Papalangi were *ofa-namu*, he said, and what you would do for him would be right. You were to be sent back to your house.'

'I will go,' said Soma quietly; and without another word, with the wonderful self-control of a Polynesian, he rose and vanished into the darkness.

Although he slept soundly Christian awoke before daybreak, cramped and stiff from the constrained position in which he had passed the night, and with his hands and feet somewhat swollen from his bonds. For the first few seconds he could not remember where he was, and then in a flash memory adjusted itself, and he knew that the day had come on which he was to die. It is a strange experience to awake in the morning well and strong and hearty, and to know that the dawn of the day has come which is to be your last on earth. As he remembered this a savage fury possessed North for a time, and like a wild beast, he tore at his bonds, and with muttered oaths, strove to wrench his hands from the ropes that bound them. It was very hard to die. He quickly found that all this was useless, and he calmed himself with the strong self-command of which he had always been the possessor.

It was something very different from resignation that he felt—it was more a stony, thoughtless blank that he forced upon his mind to save himself from the agony of thinking. In this negative condition he watched, through the open entrance to the temple, the day slowly break over the dark mass of forest on the other side of the *bara*, and with his poet's eyes he witnessed—remembering with a dulled ache that it was for the last time—the daily miracle of the dawn. Colour, so infinitely pale and distant as to seem but a dream of day, stole imperceptibly into the sky; and light, like life made visible, broke upon the sleeping world.

He was sitting thus when they came to fetch him; he had not heard the first sounds of awakening in the town, and it was only when the figures of the men darkened the doorway as they came in that he was aware that the place was astir. Two or three men advanced together to untie his feet and hands, as though nervous for their safety, for they knew his great strength, and Christian could not help smiling at their timidity.

'I am not going to hurt you,' he said in his usual kindly voice. 'I could not if I wished; my hands and feet are numb.'

The sun was not yet risen when the party set out from the town, and the sea air was damp and almost cold, but every man, woman, and child was out of doors, and watched in perfect silence the little band start on its sacred way. Christian, whose one desire was to see, if only for a moment, the face of the girl he loved so passionately, looked this way and that for Utamè, with a hungry eagerness that was terrible to see; but she was nowhere visible—amongst all the well-known faces hers was not to be found. This was a sore trial to him, but his faithful heart never doubted that she was kept back by force—perfect love had cast out fear in his case, and he felt no pang of jealousy. After all, jealousy is only a form of humility; but Christian North, though modest, as all such lovable, simple-minded men are, had none of that quality of it.

However, he was not to leave the town without receiving from Utamè a token that was in itself a message. Chris and the party which was accompanying him were just passing between Rakatira's house and the place where the women painted the *tappa*, when a little boy ran forward, and thrusting something into North's hand, darted away again without a word. The men laughed, thinking it was a freak on the part of the child, but Christian looking down at the flowers thus strangely given, and breathing in their delicate, clear perfume, recognised the white *somala* blossom, and knew from whom they came.

Crossing the flooded and half-ruined gardens, and the bird-haunted space on the other side of them, they entered the silent woods at sunrise by the well-remembered path. Christian saw then how numerous was the party; for all the principal chiefs of the town, and the old priests he had seen the night before at Ilo's house, were accompanying him. He noticed too that all of them wore or carried their ceremonial dress as though bound for some festivity, and all were decorated with their most valuable ornaments. He knew what all this meant, and looking back in his memory, with a sort of impersonal interest, on the neglected, happy, brown-faced boy he could see playing

about the wharves in the old drowsy English seaport—
how far away all that seemed now—he smiled as he
thought of all this fuss being made about so very
unimportant a person.

It was in this reflective, half-dreamy state that he
remained all day; facts of the present moment were
shadowy to him compared with the brightness and
sharpness of his mental pictures. It appeared to
North that what he was doing was not real—it
seemed so impossible that he was marching to his
death—it felt to him that he was performing in
some pre-ordained tragedy of the plot of which he was
ignorant, and in which he had no personal interest,
but in which words and acts were suggested to him
when their time was come. Everything went smoothly
as though perfected by many rehearsals, and he, the
central figure of it all, seemed least conscious of any
as to what it portended. He felt and moved as he
had often done in dreams when, quite unconcerned, he
had acted in incredible dramas, and when impossible
things presented themselves with all the aspect of
probable and natural occurrences. He looked about
the marvellous stage on which he was playing his
part, and at the other actors grouped around him, as
a spectator might look on at some great religious
ceremony, in which his only interest was the beauty
of the processions and the stateliness of the old ritual.

They climbed all day, only stopping twice for food
and rest, and Christian ate what they gave him without
noticing that it was of the very best, and slept like a
child when, at the waterfall, the party halted for the
mid - day *siesta* during the hottest hour of the day.
He was treated with a curious deference by one and
all, as though something of the sacredness of the god

had already fallen on the sacrifice; but he did not observe it—the strangeness of it was only part of the dreamlike naturalness of everything that happened. He did not catch a glimpse of Soma all the day, but he felt sure that he should see his friend once more before the veil fell between them. He gathered, from something that one of the men said, that Ilo had forbidden him to accompany them, though old Motuiti, a most unwilling member of the party, was with Ilo and the other chiefs. The old man had a great affection for North, and had used all his influence to alter Ilo's mind, but to no purpose—the chief was inexorable.

CHAPTER XXX

IT was already sunset when the party reached the last
height of the mountain and stood on the crater edge,
and the heavenly glow of the evening sky was gradually
being replaced by the infernal red reflected from the
boiling lava lake. How well North remembered the
scene! It was quite unchanged since the day he
had bidden farewell to Utamè on the mountain,
with the exception that the volcano seemed to be in
even greater activity than then, and that the lava pool
had swollen to nearly double its former size, and was
now so full that it almost overflowed the edge of the
great hollow which contained it.

Many of the men had never visited Monoriro before,
and they stood, with awe-struck faces, looking down at
the fiery pit where Rorutu dwelt; but Ilo would not
let them linger; night was coming on, and it was
difficult and dangerous to cross the tumbled lava fields
at the bottom of the great cone in the dark. Before
he began to descend the steep shaly sides of the
cliff, Christian turned to look once more at the fair
prospect of the island lying below him, at the wooded
valleys already filling with cool, blue shadow, and at
the gray weather-worn peaks of the mountains, on
which for a moment longer the last rays of his last
sun still shone; once in the fatal hollow of the crater

cup he would look no more on valley or hillside, forest or free streams. Then he calmly stepped into the shadow of the pit.

They crossed over and amongst the great wild rocks and chasms of the bottom of the crater with much difficulty, as the short tropic twilight was almost gone, and men and leaders alike were weary with their long and toilsome journey. At one place they were going wrong, and, to the astonishment of everybody, Christian stopped them and pointed out the way. They could not understand a man helping those who were leading him to his death, but North knew that escape was impossible, and saw no reason why these jaded fellows should be put to all this extra labour for the want of a word from him. He felt that he was as good as dead already, and that the one hour longer of painful struggling over these rough rocks was not worth the purchase.

Night had quite come by the time they had stumbled to the edge of the lava lake, and, with one quick shudder of sickening anticipation as he realised the awfulness of the death before him, Chris saw how greatly the lava pool had spread beyond its former limits, and what a wild and violent state of ebullition it was in. Jets and fountains of the molten rocks were leaping from every part of it, and the gold and crimson waves, with their gem-like foam and spray of fire, were ceaselessly beating, with a roar of dull thunder, on the cliffs that penned them in, as though an infernal storm of wind were urging on their billows.

Scorched by the fearful heat, and with dry and burning eyes, Christian stood on the cliff, which rose about thirty feet above the lake, like one that was petrified by the horror of this awful place. He could

not help but gaze into the pit, which, like the mouth
of hell, stood a-gape to swallow him, though his body
shrank back with an instinctive dread of it. The
terror of it almost overcame the courage with which
he was prepared to meet his death, and it was only
by summoning all his manhood and resolution to his
aid that he regained his old spirit of daring, and could
face his fate without flinching, if not without fear.

So absorbed had Christian been that he had paid
no heed to what had been happening behind him at
some little distance, and it was not until Esoku came
up to him, and screening his face with his hand from
the intolerable heat and glare, took him by the arm
to lead him back to where Ilo was standing, that he
saw they had already begun their preparations for the
sacrifice. It came upon him then with a sudden and
bitter pang that the moment had come at last, and
though he walked firmly enough he felt his face grow
white and drawn, and for a moment he could hardly
breathe. In this little interval the chiefs had put on
their ceremonial dress, and were standing with the
priests near Venga's house, into which no one had
dared to venture without the old woman's invitation.
As he came up he heard the loud tones of the priestess's
voice come from the house, and he saw the heads of
all the little crowd turn in the direction of it, as though
they had not known until then that she was there.

'What do you here, Ilo-eki? And you also, chiefs
and priests?'

And then Christian, whose every sense seemed
quickened in those last moments by the extremity of
his danger, as though life at its last throe was intensified
tenfold, thought he heard a low voice say something in
faint remonstrance.

'My God!' he gasped.

Was it Soma's voice he recognised? Hush, *hush*; and he held his breath, and pressed his hand to his heart to stop its throbbing as he strained his ears to listen. It was Soma's voice, he was *sure* of it. How could he have thought that his blood-brother, his one friend, could have left him to die alone; and for one wild maddening moment hope entered his heart.

But no further sound came from the house, and as he looked the withered but majestic figure of the resolute old priestess appeared in the doorway and advanced towards them. Everything was plainly visible, for although there was no moon the ruddy glare from the boiling pit cast a bright but lurid light on all around.

'What do you here?' repeated Venga in her loud and thrilling voice, and Ilo made answer—

'We come to make a sacrifice to the god. His *tabu* has been broken. Many ills have come upon us, and we will make *soro* to him that his fire comes not into our valleys. Our sacrifice is a perfect man, he has no blemish. For him the gods may spare us, and Rorutu's fire flow not down into our valleys.'

Christian thought that Venga's eye rested upon his for a second with a hidden meaning before she answered the head chief; but she took no other notice of him, and only said—

'It is well that this be done; but, chiefs, it is now night, and nothing is prepared. Do this thing in the morning. By daylight all may be ready. You are tired. Come, eat; the food is cooked.'

But all her efforts to gain time were useless, for one of the priests, a brother to Ilo, fearing perhaps lest Ilo might relent thus far, interrupted the chief as he was about to speak, and said—

'This thing must not be. We will not eat, nor sleep, nor rest until the anger of the gods is turned from us.'

This seemed to be decisive, for without further parleying Ilo turned and gave instructions for everything to go on. Christian was surrounded by the priests, who were there to the number of eight or ten, and he was bathed and washed with the soft tepid water that the young men had collected from the rock pools, where it had condensed from the steam which issued from the crannies in many parts of the crater. A fresh *mahi* was given him to put on, and a long and beautifully painted robe of *tappa* was fastened round his waist, and his curly hair was combed out and scented and dressed. Then the priest who seemed to take the lead made a sign to one of the young men, and he brought a stout cord of sinnet, with which poor Christian—who had to clench his teeth and dig his nails into the palms of his hands till the blood dripped from them to keep himself from making any sign of nervousness or fear—was firmly bound with his hands behind his back. The same young man carried another rope to bind his legs when Christian had walked to the edge of the cliff.

They asked him then if he wanted anything, and he said, 'Some water,' for his lips and mouth were dry.

'This is indeed a man,' said Ilo to the priests. 'He is worthy of the gods, for not one muscle of him yet has trembled. He has shown no fear.'

All was then ready, and Ilo making a sign, two men seized Chris by the upper arms and made him walk towards the little cliff above the lake. They had proceeded some part of the very short distance when a man, who, it was easy to see, was not of their party, for he was naked but for his torn and travel-stained *mahi*, and wore no dress of ceremony, rushed past them, pressing Christian's shoulder with a burning hand in a swift and passionate embrace as he darted by.

He gained the edge of the overhanging cliff before they thought of stopping him, and then he turned and showed them the face of Soma, glorified with a new beauty and transformed with the splendour of his high resolve.

It was Christian who first, with a sudden inspiration, realised the heroic intention of his friend; with a violent spring he tried to free himself from the men who held him that he might reach Soma's side before it was too late, but they threw themselves upon him, and, bound as he was, he could not get away.

'Seize him,' cried North with a frenzied shout. 'My God, I cannot see him die!'

'Stand back,' shouted Soma, with a voice like a trumpet, so steady and clear was it, as some of the men started to run towards him. 'Stand back, or I will throw myself in before you can touch me.'

He was splendid in his beauty at that moment, standing there armed for victory in his fight with death, a victory to be won by his own defeat. Weaponless for the encounter, naked as he had come into the world, he stood there with the light of conquest already shining in his face, himself the weapon he must use in that contest in which even now he felt triumphant. The glow of the lava fires shone on him, throwing all his great rounded muscles into light and falling suavely on the curves of his noble form, and making his black hair gleam with an unwonted gold.   He stood there like a god himself in his beauty and in the grandeur of his sacrifice, whilst the love that prompted this atonement shone like a glory in his face.

He was a type of Love and Youth defeating Age, Superstition, and Death, and in that moment of high passion it seemed natural to him that he should be standing where he was.   He had loved so much, that a last sacrifice for it, whilst still in the prime of his early manhood and with the power for love unimpaired in his heart, was but the fruition of all that blossoming.

Soma raised his arm to silence the loud murmurs amongst the witnesses of this wild scene, and speaking in a calm and steady voice, he said—

'Chiefs, must this thing be?   Will the gods be satisfied with nothing less?'

'This thing must be,' answered Ilo for the rest of the party.   'The gods are angry; their *tabu* has been broken.   This man must die.'

At this the priests and other chiefs expressed their assent by cries of 'Rorutu, Rorutu,' 'To the great fire,' 'He must die;' and some of them began to urge North forward.

'Stand still,' shouted Soma.   'I have not ended. Ilo-eki and chiefs, you know the law of Omëo is the law of the gods.   Break it not.   That man is free; I take his sins upon myself.   The anger of the gods will be upon you if you harm him.'

All this was more than North could bear; he struggled like a netted lion to free himself and rush to the side of this hero who was taking death upon himself so lightly, but he was powerless in the hands of the men holding him.   Great sobs tore his breast as he cried out to his friend—

'Oh, Soma, Soma, *ofa-namu-ou*, come back. I will not have you do this thing.' His voice was hoarse, and great tears rolled down his cheeks.

But Soma only shook his head, even smiling a little; all he said was—

'It is true, we are *ofa-namu*. Shall it be said that Soma-e-Motuiti would not die for his blood-brother? It is easy to die. Always remember that I live in you. Farewell. We have been true brothers.'

As he ended, Christian by a sudden superhuman effort managed to tear himself away from the men who detained him, and rushed towards the cliff crying some strange incoherent entreaty to his friend. At the same moment, as he saw him start, Soma cried out—

'That was strongly done. *Manatui koi*—remember me.'

Christian was within twenty yards of him, but he was too late, for with his tender glance turned upon the man for whom he was dying, Soma sprang high into the air from the edge of the cliff, and fell without a cry into the waves of molten lava which seemed to leap to meet him. A low dull splash, scarcely to be distinguished from the heavy lapping of the lava, was all that was heard.

'*My God, oh my God!*' burst in a shriek from Christian's lips as he saw his friend leap into the pit, and as he cried in the bitterness of his heart, he fell like a log face downwards on the rocks.

Christian was quite senseless when the men who were close upon him picked him up and untied his hands; they carried him to Venga's house and wiped away, not unkindly, the blood from his bruised and bleeding face. But the old man Motuiti stood like one petrified with horror when the party had turned its back on the fatal place, on the spot where they had halted, and, dry-eyed and silent, made no sign. At last, when he was quite alone, the agony of the child-less man burst from his lips in a little cry—

'My son, my son, my only son.'

That night the mild-eyed stars shone down upon the mountain unchanged, undimmed, upon the valleys below, where the cool mists lay lightly on the breathing forests and on the awful heart of fire in the black crater cup, which played and flashed ten thousand changing hues of beauty as its wild fountains played and its waves broke heavily on the crumbling cliff.

On the serener heights above it the sightless kings of stone still turned their strained gaze to heaven as though searching for its God, and the inscrutable smile still curved their mysterious lips.

Next morning before sunrise the whole party left the mountain, leading North with them more dead than alive. He had not spoken since the time that he awoke from the merciful oblivion that for a time fell on him. He moved like one who dreams, but he thought and thought, and his brain and soul and body ached with the anguish of his loss. His friend was dead; the world was empty of him; never again would he look in those true eyes of his; never again would he hear the deep tones of his dear voice; never feel the loving pressure of his hand. Never again, never again.

Why had they let him live? He did not wish to live. He was careless of what they did with him; death had now for him no thrill of terror in it. So little did he care that he did not notice where he was or whither being taken. He lost himself in that strange forgetfulness of the present that all feel who enter newly into the waste silent kingdom of sorrow. Time stood still. He felt nothing, knew nothing, but when he was recalled to himself, his hand was always pressed upon his heart.

'Dead; lost; empty; empty; never again,' were the cries of his soul, and to those sad watchwords no happier thought made answer. The first stunning effects of an overwhelming irremediable sorrow is to make us ungratefully forgetful of other loves that are ours, and in this moment of abandonment to grief Christian had no heart to remember that Utamè was left to him. But even then, without knowing what it was, he missed something, a voice, a hand that could help him through this thick darkness. What that was he knew afterwards.

It was late in the evening of that same day that, footsore and weary, Ilo and his party got back to Otorangi, but the chiefs and priests had had time for council on the way, and they had determined what they must do with the man whom they thought had brought such ills upon them. They could not put him to death, though some of the more bloodthirsty had suggested it, for a substitute had offered himself and had thereby redeemed his life; but they could not allow him to live in their midst, and, perhaps, bring down fresh evil on them. Their minds were made up before they reached the town, and not a soul in it was ignorant of their intention half an hour after their return.

That night Christian was lodged in the temple, from which so short a time before he had been led out, as he thought, to certain death; they need not have guarded it, he had no thoughts of escape. They gave him food and drink, some of which he ate and drank mechanically, but no one spoke of what his fate was to be, and he had not sufficient interest to ask. Sleep had entirely deserted him, and he lay there wide-eyed all through the night, in that condition of half-expectancy of some spiritual experience which overwrought emotion leaves with us. But no sign came to him out of the void.

Dawn found him wakeful, and when they came to fetch him soon after light first glowed in the east they found him crouching on the mat where they had left him the night before. They told him to get up and follow them, and without a word he rose and left the house. The town was full of a cool, light vapour which rose waist high. He was led to the beach, where a good-sized double canoe lay ready for his embarking, on the tiny deck of which a heap of food and fresh coco-nuts and goods lay piled, partly covered with one or two mats and the sail. It was not their intention to starve him as well as drive him away. To this, through the crowd on the beach, he was taken and told to embark. No one said a friendly word, even the children shrank back from the tabued man; but just as he was wading through the shallow water to the canoe, an old man rushed forward, and throwing his arms round him, pressed his face, down which silent tears were pouring, to North's, and gave him the *umu*, and said 'Farewell!' It was Motuiti, Soma's father. Nothing could have touched Chris as this did, and tears for the first time filled his hot dry eyes as he returned the old man's embrace.

He entered the canoe, and found that it was attached to another one filled with stalwart paddlers who, at a word from the shore, cast loose the moorings,

and silently and swiftly towed Christian out towards
the reef. It did not take them long to gain the opening in the reef, and through this they towed him for
some way out to sea. Then they cast him off, and
the man who with a long-bladed paddle was steering
the canoe, turned and spoke to him for the first
time.

'You are free. Go where you will. We have kept
our word with Soma-eki. If ever you come back to
Omëo you are a dead man.'

The canoe then turned to the reef, and very soon
was hidden in the mist. Christian was alone. The
sea was calm, it just rippled softly against the side of
the canoe; the wind came softly from the west, and
overhead the sky was clear of clouds. As the canoe
vanished it seemed to Chris that everything real that
connected him with Omëo was ended, and that nothing
was left him but his sorrow. It might all have been
a dream but for the love and the grief which made
reality of it. The town and the valleys where his
happiness had passed were all hidden in mist; but the
mountain where sorrow was born was standing clear
above the vapoury veil; and there the air was calm,
and a radiance from the coming sun was in it. There
seemed to Chris a truth in this.

Christian felt the light breeze blowing, and saw
that the canoe was almost standing still in spite of it,
so, sailor-like, as if by instinct, he rose and walked to
where the mat-sail lay. As he stooped over it he heard
a tiny, wailing cry; for a moment he stood too much
surprised to move, and then in frantic haste he tore
aside the covering. There, in a little opening she had
made for herself the night before, when she had heard
of Christian's doom, lay Utamè, laughing, blushing,

crying, and radiant, with a tiny week-old baby at her breast.

In a second he was on his knees, with mother and child in his empty arms, thanking God in a broken voice.

The cold sea-mist seemed to melt and rise about them, though it still lay on the island, and they could see interspaces of pure sky between bright cloud vistas that led the eye through their long avenues to the glories of the morning where, with floods of radiant light, the sun was rising.

Christian, with new life in his heart, with these two lives to live for, raised the stout mat-sail, and the canoe moved on through the rippling water. There are islands over there; will they reach them?

Farther and farther towards the east the life-freighted bark drifted on, fainter and fainter grew the island behind them, until, as the sun rose, the canoe was lost to sight in the glories of his golden pathway on the water.

THE END

NEW NOVELS.

A CIGARETTE MAKER'S ROMANCE. By F. Marion Crawford, Author of 'Mr. Isaacs,' 'A Roman Singer,' 'Marzio's Crucifix,' 'Sant' Ilario,' etc. 2 vols. Globe 8vo. 12s. [*Shortly.*

THE TRAGIC MUSE. By Henry James, Author of 'The Europeans,' 'Daisy Miller,' 'A London Life,' etc. 3 vols. Crown 8vo. 31s. 6d. [*Nearly ready.*

PLAIN TALES FROM THE HILLS. By Rudyard Kipling. 1 vol. Crown 8vo. 6s.

MORE BYE WORDS. By Charlotte M. Yonge. 1 vol. Crown 8vo. 6s. [*Shortly.*

MRS. CRAIK'S (the Author of 'John Halifax, Gentleman') NOVELS AND TALES.

A New and Uniform Edition. Crown 8vo. 3s. 6d. each. In monthly volumes.

OLIVE. With Illustrations by G. Bowers. [*Ready.*

THE OGILVIES. With Illustrations by J. M'L. Ralston. [*Ready.*

AGATHA'S HUSBAND. With Illustrations by Walter Crane. [*Ready.*

HEAD OF THE FAMILY. With Illustrations by Walter Crane. [*Ready.*

TWO MARRIAGES. [*July.*

THE LAUREL BUSH. [*Aug.*

MY MOTHER AND I. With Illustrations by J. M'L. Ralston. [*Sept.*

MISS TOMMY. A Mediæval Romance. With Illustrations by Frederick Noel Paton. [*Oct.*

KING ARTHUR: Not a Love Story. [*Nov.*

MR. F. MARION CRAWFORD'S NOVELS.

Crown 8vo, Uniform Edition, price 3s. 6d. each.

Mr. Isaacs.	Marzio's Crucifix.
Dr. Claudius.	A Tale of a Lonely Parish.
A Roman Singer.	Paul Patoff.
Zoroaster.	

MACMILLAN AND CO., LONDON.

NEW NOVELS—Continued.

THE RING OF AMASIS: A Romance. By the Right Hon. the EARL OF LYTTON, G.C.B., G.C.S.I. Crown 8vo. 3s. 6d.

The *Pall Mall Gazette* says:—"It is impossible to deny the exquisite literary skill of large portions of this book, or the Poe-like command of the weird with which Lord Lytton enthrals his reader from first to last."

The *Saturday Review* says:—"On both sides of the book—the psychological and the supernatural—one thing strikes us very much—the amount of thought which is packed into very close compass. The book, indeed, is full of thought put into the tersest expression, and that expression is always of the happiest kind. The closeness of imagination and reflection may puzzle the hurrying reader, but it is not to the hurrying reader that the 'Ring of Amasis' can appeal. . . . A strong and exquisite piece of work."

A LOVER OF THE BEAUTIFUL. By the MARCHIONESS OF CARMARTHEN. 1 vol. Crown 8vo. 6s.

The *Athenæum* says:—"It recalls with a certain vividness the warmth and colour of Rossetti's pictures instinct with the poetry of the 'Vita Nuova.'"

The *Morning Post* says:—"It is a work of unusual promise."

The *Glasgow Herald* says:—"An excellent piece of work."

The *Scotsman* says:—"The story is beautiful throughout, and of absorbing interest."

THE MINER'S RIGHT. By ROLF BOLDREWOOD, Author of "Robbery Under Arms," etc. 3 vols. Crown 8vo. 31s. 6d.

The *Athenæum* says:—"It is distinguished by very much the same qualities as those which singled out the earlier narrative from its contemporaries. . . . The picture is unquestionably interesting, thanks to the very detail and fidelity which tend to qualify its attractiveness for those who like excitement and incident before everything else."

The *World* says:—"Full of good passages, passages abounding in vivacity, in the colour and play of life. . . . The pith of the book lies in its singularly fresh and vivid pictures of the humours of the goldfields—tragic humours enough they are, too, here and again. . . . The various types of humanity that strut, or in those days used to strut, across that strangest of the world's stages, an Australian goldfield, are capitally touched in, for he can draw a man as well as tell a story."

THE HERIOTS. By Sir HENRY S. CUNNINGHAM, K.C.I.E., Author of "The Cœruleans: a Vacation Idyll," "The Chronicles of Dustypore," "Wheat and Tares," etc. 3 vols. Cr. 8vo. 31s. 6d.

The *Academy* says:—"This is a work of genius. . . . 'The Heriots' leave us with a large circle of new friends, whose acquaintance it has been a privilege to make, and many of whose sayings it is pleasant to remember. Several of the characters may fairly claim to be original creations in English fiction."

The *Guardian* says:—"It is an eminently readable novel, as well as a singularly clever one."

The *Spectator* says:—"The most brilliant novel of the year. . . . A gallery where no single figure is devoid of interest or charm. 'The Heriots' is, in short, a book to be read, and it is impossible to imagine its being read without admiration."

WHEAT AND TARES. By Sir HENRY CUNNINGHAM, K.C.I.E., Author of "The Heriots," "The Cœruleans," etc. New Edition. Crown 8vo. 3s. 6d. [*Just ready.*

JOHN VALE'S GUARDIAN. By D. CHRISTIE MURRAY, Author of "Aunt Rachel," "The Weaker Vessel," etc. 3 vols. Crown 8vo. 31s. 6d.

The *Athenæum* says:—"It is in some respects the best novel Mr. Christie Murray has produced."

MACMILLAN AND CO., LONDON.

POPULAR NOVELS IN ONE VOLUME.

Macmillan's Three Shilling and Sixpenny Novels. New Volumes.

Schwartz. By D. CHRISTIE MURRAY, Author of "Aunt Rachel," etc. Crown 8vo. 3s. 6d.

Neighbours on the Green. By Mrs. OLIPHANT. Crown 8vo. 3s. 6d.

Robbery under Arms: A Story of Life and Adventure in the Bush and in the Goldfields of Australia. By ROLF BOLDREWOOD. Crown 8vo. 3s. 6d.

The Weaker Vessel. By D. CHRISTIE MURRAY. Crown 8vo. 3s. 6d.

Joyce. By Mrs. OLIPHANT. Crown 8vo. 3s. 6d.

Cressy. By BRET HARTE. Crown 8vo. 3s. 6d.

Faithful and Unfaithful. By MARGARET LEE, Author of "Dr. Wilmer's Love," "Lizzie Adriance," etc. Crown 8vo. 3s. 6d.

Reuben Sachs. By AMY LEVY, Author of "The Romance of a Shop." Crown 8vo. 3s. 6d.

Wessex Tales; Strange, Lively, and Commonplace. By THOMAS HARDY, Author of "The Woodlanders," etc. Crown 8vo. 3s. 6d.

Miss Bretherton. By Mrs. HUMPHRY WARD, Author of "Robert Elsmere." Crown 8vo. 3s. 6d.

A London Life. By HENRY JAMES, Author of "The American," "The Europeans," "Daisy Miller," "The Reverberator," "The Aspern Papers." Crown 8vo. 3s. 6d.

A Beleaguered City. By Mrs. OLIPHANT. Crown 8vo. 3s. 6d.

Castle Daly. By ANNIE KEARY. Crown 8vo. 3s. 6d.

The Woodlanders. By THOMAS HARDY. Crown 8vo. 3s. 6d.

The Cœruleans: A Vacation Idyll. By Sir HENRY CUNNINGHAM, Author of "The Chronicles of Dustypore," etc. Crown 8vo. 3s. 6d.

The Ring of Amasis. By LORD LYTTON. Crown 8vo. 3s. 6d.

Wheat and Tares. By Sir HENRY CUNNINGHAM. Crown 8vo. 3s. 6d.

Aunt Rachel. By D. CHRISTIE MURRAY. Crown 8vo. 3s. 6d.

Louisiana; and That Lass o' Lowrie's. By FRANCES HODGSON BURNETT. Crown 8vo. 3s. 6d.

Marooned. By W. CLARK RUSSELL, Author of "The Wreck of the 'Grosvenor,'" etc. New and Cheaper Edition, 1 vol. Crown 8vo. 3s. 6d.

UNIFORM WITH THE ABOVE.

A Year with the Birds. By W. WARDE FOWLER, Sub-Rector of Lincoln College, Oxford. With Illustrations by BRYAN HOOK. Crown 8vo. 3s. 6d.

Tales of the Birds. By the same. With Illustrations by BRYAN HOOK. Crown 8vo. 3s. 6d.

Storm Warriors; or, Lifeboat Work on the Goodwin Sands. By the Rev. JOHN GILMORE, M.A. Crown 8vo. 3s. 6d.

Tales of Old Japan. By A. B. MITFORD, Second Secretary to the British Legation in Japan. With Illustrations, drawn and cut on Wood by Japanese Artists. Crown 8vo. 3s. 6d.

. *Other Volumes to follow.*

MACMILLAN AND CO., LONDON.

Catalogue of Books

PUBLISHED BY

MACMILLAN AND CO.

BEDFORD STREET, COVENT GARDEN, LONDON

February, 1890.

ABBOT (Francis).—SCIENTIFIC THEISM. Crown 8vo. 7s. 6d.

ABBOTT (Rev. E. A.).—A SHAKESPEARIAN GRAMMAR. Extra fcp. 8vo. 6s.

—— CAMBRIDGE SERMONS. 8vo. 6s.

—— OXFORD SERMONS. 8vo. 7s. 6d.

—— FRANCIS BACON: AN ACCOUNT OF HIS LIFE AND WORKS. 8vo. 14s.

ABBOTT (Rev. E. A.) and RUSHBROOKE (W. G.).—THE COMMON TRADITION OF THE SYNOPTIC GOSPELS, IN THE TEXT OF THE REVISED VERSION. Crown 8vo. 3s. 6d.

ACLAND (Sir H. W.).—THE ARMY MEDICAL SCHOOL. An Address delivered at Netley Hospital. 8vo. 1s.

ACTS OF THE APOSTLES. The Greek Text of Drs. Westcott and Hort. With Notes by T. E. PAGE, M.A. Fcp. 8vo. 4s. 6d.

ADAMS (Sir F. O.) and CUNNINGHAM (C.)—THE SWISS CONFEDERATION. 8vo. 14s.

ADDISON.—By W. J. COURTHOPE. Crown 8vo. 1s. 6d.; sewed, 1s.

ADDISON, SELECTIONS FROM. Chosen and Edited by J. R. GREEN. 18mo. 4s. 6d.

ÆSCHYLUS.—PERSÆ. Edited by A. O. PRICKARD, M.A. Fcp. 8vo. 3s. 6d.

—— EUMENIDES. With Notes and Introduction, by BERNARD DRAKE, M.A. 8vo. 5s.

—— PROMETHEUS VINCTUS. With Introduction, Notes, and Vocabulary, by Rev. H. M. STEPHENSON, M.A. 18mo. 1s. 6d.

—— THE "SEVEN AGAINST THEBES." With Introduction, Commentary, and Translation, by A. W. VERRALL, Litt.D. 8vo. 7s. 6d.

—— THE "SEVEN AGAINST THEBES." With Introduction and Notes, by A. W. VERRALL and M. A. BAYFIELD. Fcp. 8vo. 3s. 6d.

—— AGAMEMNON. With Introduction, Commentary, and Translation, by A. W. VERRALL, Litt.D. 8vo. 12s.

—— THE SUPPLICES. Text, Introduction, Notes, Commentary, and Translation, by Prof. T. G. TUCKER. 8vo. 10s. 6d.

ÆSOP—CALDECOTT.—SOME OF ÆSOP'S FABLES, with Modern Instances, shown in Designs by RANDOLPH CALDECOTT. 4to. 5s.

AGASSIZ (Louis): HIS LIFE AND CORRESPONDENCE. Edited by ELIZABETH CARY AGASSIZ. 2 vols. Crown 8vo. 18s.

AINGER (Rev. Alfred).—SERMONS PREACHED IN THE TEMPLE CHURCH. Extra fcp. 8vo. 6s.

AINGER (Rev. A.).—CHARLES LAMB. Crn. 8vo. 1s. 6d.; sewed 1s.

AIRY (Sir G. B.).—TREATISE ON THE ALGEBRAICAL AND NUMERICAL THEORY OF ERRORS OF OBSERVATION AND THE COMBINATION OF OBSERVATIONS. Cr. 8vo. 6s. 6d.

—— POPULAR ASTRONOMY. With Illustrations. Fcp. 8vo. 4s. 6d.

—— AN ELEMENTARY TREATISE ON PARTIAL DIFFERENTIAL EQUATIONS. Cr. 8vo. 5s. 6d.

—— ON SOUND AND ATMOSPHERIC VIBRATIONS. With the Mathematical Elements of Music. 2nd Edition. Crown 8vo. 9s.

—— GRAVITATION. An Elementary Explanation of the Principal Perturbations in the Solar System. 2nd Edition. Cr. 8vo. 7s. 6d.

AITKEN (Mary Carlyle).—SCOTTISH SONG. A Selection of the Choicest Lyrics of Scotland. 18mo. 4s. 6d.

AITKEN (Sir W.)—THE GROWTH OF THE RECRUIT AND YOUNG SOLDIER. With a view to the selection of "Growing Lads" for the Army, and a Regulated System of Training for Recruits. Crown 8vo. 8s. 6d.

ALBEMARLE (Earl of).—FIFTY YEARS OF MY LIFE. 3rd Ed., revised. Cr. 8vo. 7s. 6d.

ALDIS (Mary Steadman).—THE GREAT GIANT ARITHMOS. A MOST ELEMENTARY ARITHMETIC. Illustrated. Globe 8vo. 2s. 6d.

ALEXANDER (C. F.).—THE SUNDAY BOOK OF POETRY FOR THE YOUNG. 18mo. 4s. 6d.

ALEXANDER (T.) and THOMPSON (A.).—ELEMENTARY APPLIED MECHANICS. Part II. Transverse Stress; upwards of 150 Diagrams, and 200 Examples carefully worked out. Crown 8vo. 10s. 6d.

ALLBUTT (Dr. T. Clifford).—ON THE USE OF THE OPHTHALMOSCOPE. 8vo. 15s.

ALLEN (Grant).—ON THE COLOURS OF FLOWERS, as Illustrated in the British Flora. With Illustrations. Crown 8vo. 3s. 6d.

ALLINGHAM (William).—THE BALLAD BOOK. 18mo. 4s. 6d.

AMERICAN JOURNAL OF PHILOLOGY. Edited by BASIL L. GILDERSLEEVE. Quarterly Parts. 4s. 6d. each.

AMIEL (Henri Frederic).—THE JOURNAL INTIME. Translated by Mrs. HUMPHRY WARD. 2nd Edition. Crown 8vo. 6s.

AN ANCIENT CITY, AND OTHER POEMS. Extra fcp. 8vo. 6s.

1

AN AUTHOR'S LOVE. Being the Unpublished Letters of PROSPER MÉRIMÉE'S "Inconnue." 2 vols. Ex. cr. 8vo. 12s.

ANDERSON (A.).—BALLADS AND SONNETS. Crown 8vo. 5s.

ANDERSON (Dr. McCall).—LECTURES ON CLINICAL MEDICINE. Illustrated. 8vo. 10s. 6d.

ANDERSON (L.).—LINEAR PERSPECTIVE AND MODEL DRAWING. Royal 8vo. 2s.

ANDOCIDES.—DE MYSTERIIS. Edited by W. J. HICKIE, M.A. Fcp. 8vo. 2s. 6d.

ANDREWS (Dr. Thomas), THE SCIENTIFIC PAPERS OF THE LATE. With a Memoir by Profs. TAIT and CRUM BROWN. 8vo. 18s.

ANGLO-SAXON LAW: ESSAYS ON. Med. 8vo. 18s.

ANTONINUS, MARCUS AURELIUS.—BOOK IV. OF THE MEDITATIONS. The Greek Text Revised. With Translation and Commentary, by HASTINGS CROSSLEY, M.A. 8vo. 6s.

APPLETON (T. G.).—A NILE JOURNAL. Illustrated by EUGENE BENSON. Cr. 8vo. 6s.

ARATUS.—THE SKIES AND WEATHER FORECASTS OF ARATUS. Translated by E. POSTE M.A. Crown 8vo. 3s. 6d.

ARIOSTO.—PALADIN AND SARACEN. Stories from Ariosto. By H. C. HOLLWAY-CALTHROP. Illustrated. Crown 8vo. 6s.

ARISTOPHANES.—THE BIRDS. Translated into English Verse, with Introduction, Notes, and Appendices. By Prof. B. H. KENNEDY, D.D. Crown 8vo. 6s.

—— HELP NOTES FOR THE USE OF STUDENTS. Crown 8vo. 1s. 6d.

ARISTOTLE ON FALLACIES; OR, THE SOPHISTICI ELENCHI. With Translation and Notes by E. POSTE, M.A. 8vo. 8s. 6d.

ARISTOTLE.—THE FIRST BOOK OF THE METAPHYSICS OF ARISTOTLE. Translated into English Prose, with marginal Analysis and Summary of each Chapter. By a Cambridge Graduate. 8vo. 5s.

—— THE POLITICS. Translated with an Analysis and Critical Notes by J. E. C. WELLDON, M.A. 2nd Edition. 10s. 6d.

—— THE RHETORIC. By the same Translator. Crown 8vo. 7s. 6d.

ARMY PRELIMINARY EXAMINATION, Specimens of Papers set at the, 1882-88. With Answers to the Mathematical Questions. Crown 8vo. 3s. 6d.

ARNOLD (Matthew).—THE COMPLETE POETICAL WORKS. New Edition. 3 vols, Crown 8vo. 7s. 6d. each.—Vol. I. Early Poems, Narrative Poems, and Sonnets.—Vol. II. Lyric and Elegiac Poems.—Vol. III. Dramatic and Later Poems.

—— ESSAYS IN CRITICISM. 6th Edition. Crown 8vo. 9s.

—— ESSAYS IN CRITICISM. Second Series. With an Introductory Note by LORD COLERIDGE. Crown 8vo. 7s. 6d.

—— ISAIAH XL.—LXVI. WITH THE SHORTER PROPHECIES ALLIED TO IT. With Notes. Crown 8vo. 5s.

ARNOLD (Matthew).—ISAIAH OF JERUSALEM. In the Authorised English Version, with Introduction, Corrections, and Notes. Crown 8vo. 4s. 6d.

—— A BIBLE-READING FOR SCHOOLS. The Great Prophecy of Israel's Restoration (Isaiah xl.-lxvi.) Arranged and Edited for Young Learners. 4th Edition. 18mo. 1s.

—— HIGHER SCHOOLS AND UNIVERSITIES IN GERMANY. Crown 8vo. 6s.

—— SELECTED POEMS. 18mo. 4s. 6d.

—— POEMS OF WORDSWORTH. Chosen and Edited by MATTHEW ARNOLD. With Portrait. 18mo. 4s. 6d.
Large Paper Edition. 9s.

—— POETRY OF BYRON. Chosen and arranged by MATTHEW ARNOLD. With Vignette. 18mo. 4s. 6d.
Large Paper Edition. 9s.

—— DISCOURSES IN AMERICA. Cr. 8vo. 4s. 6d.

—— JOHNSON'S LIVES OF THE POETS, THE SIX CHIEF LIVES FROM. With MACAULAY'S "Life of Johnson." With Preface and Notes by MATTHEW ARNOLD. Crown 8vo. 4s. 6d.

—— EDMUND BURKE'S LETTERS, TRACTS AND SPEECHES ON IRISH AFFAIRS. Edited by MATTHEW ARNOLD. Crown 8vo. 6s.

—— REPORTS ON ELEMENTARY SCHOOLS, 1852-82. Edited by the Right Hon. Sir FRANCIS SANDFORD, K.C.B. Cr. 8vo. 3s. 6d.

ARNOLD (T.)—THE SECOND PUNIC WAR. By the late THOMAS ARNOLD, D.D. Edited by WILLIAM T. ARNOLD, M.A. With Eight Maps. Crown 8vo. 8s. 6d.

ARNOLD (W. T.).—THE ROMAN SYSTEM OF PROVINCIAL ADMINISTRATION TO THE ACCESSION OF CONSTANTINE THE GREAT. Crown 8vo. 6s.

ARRIAN.—SELECTIONS. Edited by J. BOND, M.A., and A. S. WALPOLE, M.A. 18mo. 1s. 6d.

ART AT HOME SERIES. Edited by W. J. LOFTIE, B.A.

MUSIC IN THE HOUSE. By JOHN HULLAH. Fourth Edition. Crown 8vo. 2s. 6d.

THE DINING-ROOM. By Mrs. LOFTIE. With Illustrations. 2nd Ed. Cr. 8vo. 2s. 6d.

THE BEDROOM AND BOUDOIR. By Lady BARKER. With numerous Illustrations. 2nd Edition. Crown 8vo. 2s. 6d.

AMATEUR THEATRICALS. By WALTER H. POLLOCK and LADY POLLOCK. Illustrated by KATE GREENAWAY. Crown 8vo. 2s. 6d.

NEEDLEWORK. By ELIZABETH GLAISTER. Illustrated. Crown 8vo. 2s. 6d.

THE LIBRARY. By ANDREW LANG, with a Chapter on English Illustrated Books, by AUSTIN DOBSON. Crown 8vo. 3s. 6d.

ARNAULD, ANGELIQUE. By FRANCES MARTIN. Crown 8vo. 4s. 6d.

ARTEVELDE—ASHLEY.—JAMES AND PHILIP VAN ARTEVELDE. By W. J. ASHLEY, B.A. Crown 8vo. 6s.

ATKINSON (J. Beavington).—AN ART TOUR TO NORTHERN CAPITALS OF EUROPE. 8vo. 12s.

ATTIC ORATORS, SELECTIONS FROM THE. Antiphon, Andocides, Lysias, Isocrates, and Isaeus. Edited, with Notes, by Prof. R. C. JEBB, Litt.D. 2nd Edition. Fcp. 8vo. 6s.

ATTWELL (H.)—A BOOK OF GOLDEN THOUGHTS. 18mo. 4s. 6d.

AULUS GELLIUS (STORIES FROM). Edited by Rev. G. H. NALL, M.A. 18mo. 1s. 6d.

AUSTIN (Alfred).—SAVONAROLA: A TRAGEDY. Crown 8vo. 7s. 6d.

—— SOLILOQUIES IN SONG. Crown 8vo. 6s.

—— AT THE GATE OF THE CONVENT; AND OTHER POEMS. Crown 8vo. 6s.

—— PRINCE LUCIFER. Crown 8vo. 6s.

—— MADONNA'S CHILD. Crown 4to. 3s. 6d.

—— THE TOWER OF BABEL. Crown 4to. 9s.

—— ROME OR DEATH. Crown 4to. 9s.

—— THE GOLDEN AGE. Crown 8vo. 5s.

—— THE SEASON. Crown 8vo. 5s.

—— LOVE'S WIDOWHOOD: AND OTHER POEMS. Crown 8vo. 6s.

—— THE HUMAN TRAGEDY. Cr. 8vo. 7s. 6d.

AUTENRIETH (Dr. G.).—AN HOMERIC DICTIONARY. Translated from the German, by R. P. KEEP, Ph.D. Crown 8vo. 6s.

AWDRY (Frances).—THE STORY OF A FELLOW SOLDIER. (A Life of Bishop Patteson for the Young.) With a Preface by CHARLOTTE M. YONGE. Globe 8vo. 2s. 6d.

BABRIUS. With Introductory Dissertations, Critical Notes, Commentary, and Lexicon, by W. G. RUTHERFORD, LL.D. 8vo. 12s. 6d.

"BACCHANTE." THE CRUISE OF H.M.S. "BACCHANTE," 1879-1882. Compiled from the private Journals, Letters and Note-books of PRINCE ALBERT VICTOR and PRINCE GEORGE OF WALES. With Maps, Plans, Illustrations, and Additions, by the Rev. JOHN N. DALTON, Canon of Windsor. 2 vols. Medium 8vo. 2l. 12s. 6d.

BACON.—By the Very Rev. Dean CHURCH, Globe 8vo. 5s.; Crn. 8vo. 1s. 6d.; swd., 1s.

BACON'S ESSAYS AND COLOURS OF GOOD AND EVIL. With Notes and Glossarial Index, by W. ALDIS WRIGHT, M.A. With Vignette. 18mo. 4s. 6d.

—— ESSAYS. Edited by Prof. F. G. SELBY, M.A. Globe 8vo. 3s. 6d.

BACON (Francis).—AN ACCOUNT OF HIS LIFE AND WORKS. By E. A. ABBOTT. 8vo. 14s.

BAINES (Rev. Edward).—SERMONS: Preached mainly to Country Congregations. With a Preface and Memoir, by ALFRED BARRY, D.D., Bishop of Sydney. Cr. 8vo. 6s.

BAKER (Sir Samuel White).—ISMAILIA. A Narrative of the Expedition to Central Africa for the Suppression of the Slave Trade, organised by ISMAIL, Khedive of Egypt. Crown 8vo. 6s.

—— THE NILE TRIBUTARIES OF ABYSSINIA, AND THE SWORD HUNTERS OF THE HAMRAN ARABS. Crown 8vo. 6s.

—— THE ALBERT N'YANZA GREAT BASIN OF THE NILE AND EXPLORATION OF THE NILE SOURCES. Crown 8vo. 6s.

—— CYPRUS AS I SAW IT IN 1879. 8vo. 12s. 6d.

BAKER (Sir Samuel White).—CAST UP BY THE SEA: OR, THE ADVENTURES OF NED GRAY. With Illustrations by HUARD. Crown 8vo. 6s.

—— THE EGYPTIAN QUESTION. Letters to the *Times* and the *Pall Mall Gazette*. 8vo. 2s.

—— TRUE TALES FOR MY GRANDSONS. Illustrated by W. J. HENNESSY. Cr. 8vo. 7s. 6d.

BALFOUR (The Right Hon. A. J.)—A DEFENCE OF PHILOSOPHIC DOUBT. Being an Essay on the Foundations of Belief. 8vo. 12s.

BALFOUR (Prof. F. M.).—ELASMOBRANCH FISHES. With Plates. 8vo. 21s.

—— COMPARATIVE EMBRYOLOGY. With Illustrations. 2 vols. 2nd Edition. 8vo.—Vol. I. 18s.—Vol. II. 21s.

—— THE COLLECTED WORKS. Memorial Edition. Edited by M. FOSTER, F.R.S., and ADAM SEDGWICK, M.A. 4 vols. 8vo. 6l. 6s. Vols. I. and IV. Special Memoirs. May be had separately. Price 73s. 6d.

BALL (Sir R. S.).—EXPERIMENTAL MECHANICS. Illustrated. New Ed. Cr. 8vo. 6s.

BALL (W. W. R.).—THE STUDENT'S GUIDE TO THE BAR. 5th Ed. revised. Cr. 8vo. 2s. 6d.

—— A SHORT ACCOUNT OF THE HISTORY OF MATHEMATICS. Crown 8vo. 10s. 6d.

BALLIOL COLLEGE. PSALMS AND HYMNS FOR BALLIOL COLLEGE. 18mo. 2s. 6d.

BARKER (Lady).—FIRST LESSONS IN THE PRINCIPLES OF COOKING. 3rd Ed. 18mo. 1s.

—— A YEAR'S HOUSEKEEPING IN SOUTH AFRICA. Illustrated. Crown 8vo. 3s. 6d.

—— STATION LIFE IN NEW ZEALAND. Crown 8vo. 3s. 6d.

—— LETTERS TO GUY. Crown 8vo. 5s.

—— THE BED ROOM AND BOUDOIR. With numerous Illustrations. Crown 8vo. 2s. 6d.

BARNES.—LIFE OF WILLIAM BARNES, POET AND PHILOLOGIST. By his Daughter, LUCY BAXTER ("Leader Scott"). Cr. 8vo. 7s. 6d.

BARRY (Bishop).—FIRST WORDS IN AUSTRALIA. Sermons preached in April and May, 1884. Crown 8vo. 5s.

BARTHOLOMEW (J. G.).—ELEMENTARY SCHOOL ATLAS. 4to. 1s.

—— LIBRARY REFERENCE ATLAS OF THE WORLD. With Index to 100,000 places. Folio. 2l. 12s. 6d. net.

—— PHYSICAL AND POLITICAL SCHOOL ATLAS. Royal 4to. [*In the Press.*

BARWELL (Richard, F.R.C.S.).—THE CAUSES AND TREATMENT OF LATERAL CURVATURE OF THE SPINE. Crown 8vo. 5s.

—— ON ANEURISM, ESPECIALLY OF THE THORAX AND ROOT OF THE NECK. 3s. 6d.

BASTIAN (H. Charlton).—THE BEGINNINGS OF LIFE. 2 vols. Crown 8vo. 28s.

—— EVOLUTION AND THE ORIGIN OF LIFE. Crown 8vo. 6s. 6d.

—— ON PARALYSIS FROM BRAIN DISEASE IN ITS COMMON FORMS. Crown 8vo. 10s. 6d.

BATHER (Archdeacon).—ON SOME MINISTERIAL DUTIES, CATECHISING, PREACHING, &c. Edited, with a Preface, by C. J. VAUGHAN, D.D. Fcp. 8vo. 4s. 6d.

BATH (Marquis of).—OBSERVATIONS ON BULGARIAN AFFAIRS. Crown 8vo. 3s. 6d.

BEASLEY (R. D.)—AN ELEMENTARY TREATISE ON PLANE TRIGONOMETRY. With numerous Examples. 9th Ed. Cr. 8vo. 3s. 6d.

BEAUMARCHAIS. LE BARBIER DE SEVILLE, OU LE PRÉCAUTION INUTILE. Comedie en Quatre Actes. Edited by L. P. BLOUET, B.A., Univ. Gallic. Fcp. 8vo. 3s. 6d.

BECKER (B. H.).—DISTURBED IRELAND. Being Letters written during the winter 1880-81. Crown 8vo. 6s.

BEESLY (Mrs.).—STORIES FROM THE HISTORY OF ROME. Fcp. 8vo. 2s. 6d.

BELCHER (Rev. H.).—SHORT EXERCISES IN LATIN PROSE COMPOSITION AND EXAMINATION PAPERS IN LATIN GRAMMAR; WITH A CHAPTER ON ANALYSIS OF SENTENCES. 18mo. 1s. 6d.
    KEY (supplied to Teachers only). 3s. 6d.

—— SHORT EXERCISES IN LATIN PROSE COMPOSITION.—Part II. On the Syntax of Sentences. With an Appendix. 18mo. 2s.
    KEY (supplied to Teachers only). 18mo. 3s.

BENHAM (Rev. W.).—A COMPANION TO THE LECTIONARY. Crown 8vo. 4s. 6d.

BENTLEY.—By Professor JEBB. Crown 8vo. 1s. 6d. ; sewed, 1s.

BERLIOZ (Hector).—AUTOBIOGRAPHY OF. Translated by RACHEL (Scott Russell) HOLMES and ELEANOR HOLMES. 2 vols. Crown 8vo. 21s.

BERNARD (M.).—FOUR LECTURES ON SUBJECTS CONNECTED WITH DIPLOMACY. 8vo. 9s.

BERNARD (St.)—THE LIFE AND TIMES OF ST. BERNARD, ABBOT OF CLAIRVAUX. By J. C. MORISON, M.A. Crown 8vo. 6s.

BERNERS (J.)—FIRST LESSONS ON HEALTH. 18mo. 1s.

BETHUNE-BAKER (J. F.).—THE INFLUENCE OF CHRISTIANITY ON WAR. 8vo. 5s.

—— THE STERNNESS OF CHRIST'S TEACHING, AND ITS RELATION TO THE LAW OF FORGIVENESS. Crown 8vo. 2s. 6d.

BETSY LEE: A FO'C'S'LE YARN, AND OTHER POEMS. Crown 8vo. 7s. 6d.

BETTANY (G. T.).—FIRST LESSONS IN PRACTICAL BOTANY. 18mo. 1s.

BIGELOW (M. M.).—HISTORY OF PROCEDURE IN ENGLAND FROM THE NORMAN CONQUEST. The Norman Period, 1066-1204. 8vo. 16s.

BIKÉLAS.—LOUKIS LARAS ; OR, THE REMINISCENCES OF A CHIOTE MERCHANT DURING THE GREEK WAR OF INDEPENDENCE. Translated by J. GENNADIUS, Greek Minister in London. Crown 8vo. 7s. 6d.

BINNIE (the late Rev. William).—SERMONS. Crown 8vo. 6s.

BIRKBECK (William Lloyd).—HISTORICAL SKETCH OF THE DISTRIBUTION OF LAND IN ENGLAND. With Suggestions for some Improvement in the Law. Crown 8vo. 4s. 6d.

BIRKS (Thomas Rawson, M.A.).—FIRST PRINCIPLES OF MORAL SCIENCE ; OR, FIRST COURSE OF LECTURES DELIVERED IN THE UNIVERSITY OF CAMBRIDGE. Cr. 8vo. 8s. 6d.

BIRKS (Thomas Rawson).—MODERN UTILITARIANISM ; OR, THE SYSTEMS OF PALEY, BENTHAM, AND MILL EXAMINED AND COMPARED. Crown 8vo. 6s. 6d.

—— THE DIFFICULTIES OF BELIEF IN CONNECTION WITH THE CREATION AND THE FALL, REDEMPTION AND JUDGMENT. 2nd Edition. Crown 8vo. 5s.

—— COMMENTARY ON THE BOOK OF ISAIAH, CRITICAL, HISTORICAL, AND PROPHETICAL ; INCLUDING A REVISED ENGLISH TRANSLATION. 2nd Edition. 8vo. 12s. 6d.

—— THE NEW TESTAMENT. Essay on the Right Estimation of MS. Evidence in the Text of the New Testament. Cr. 8vo. 3s. 6d.

—— SUPERNATURAL REVELATION ; OR, FIRST PRINCIPLES OF MORAL THEOLOGY. 8vo. 8s.

—— MODERN PHYSICAL FATALISM, AND THE DOCTRINE OF EVOLUTION. Including an Examination of Mr. Herbert Spencer's "First Principles." Crown 8vo. 6s.

—— JUSTIFICATION AND IMPUTED RIGHTEOUSNESS. Being a Review of Ten Sermons on the Nature and Effects of Faith by JAMES THOMAS O'BRIEN, D.D., late Bishop of Ossory, Ferns, and Leighlin. Cr. 8vo. 6s.

BJÖRNSON.—SYNNÖVE SOLBAKKEN. Translated from the Norwegian, by JULIE SUTTER. Crown 8vo. 6s.

BLACK (William).—THE STRANGE ADVENTURES OF A PHAETON. Illustrated. Cr. 8vo. 6s.

—— A PRINCESS OF THULE. Crown 8vo. 6s.

—— THE MAID OF KILLEENA, AND OTHER TALES. Crown 8vo. 6s.

—— MADCAP VIOLET. Crown 8vo. 6s.

—— GREEN PASTURES AND PICCADILLY. Crown 8vo. 6s.

—— MACLEOD OF DARE. With Illustrations by eminent Artists. Crown 8vo. 6s.

—— WHITE WINGS : A YACHTING ROMANCE. Crown 8vo. 6s.

—— THE BEAUTIFUL WRETCH : THE FOUR MACNICOLS : THE PUPIL OF AURELIUS. Crown 8vo. 6s.

—— SHANDON BELLS. Crown 8vo. 6s.

—— YOLANDE. Crown 8vo. 6s.

—— JUDITH SHAKESPEARE. Crown 8vo. 6s.

—— GOLDSMITH. Cr. 8vo. 1s. 6d. ; sewed, 1s.

—— THE WISE WOMEN OF INVERNESS : A TALE. AND OTHER MISCELLANIES. Cr. 8vo. 6s.

—— WHITE HEATHER. Crown 8vo. 6s.

—— SABINA ZEMBRA. Crown 8vo. 6s.

BLACKBURNE.—LIFE OF THE RIGHT HON. FRANCIS BLACKBURNE, late Lord Chancellor of Ireland, by his son, EDWARD BLACKBURNE, one of Her Majesty's Counsel in Ireland. With Portrait. 8vo. 12s.

BLACKIE (Prof. John Stuart.).—GREEK AND ENGLISH DIALOGUES FOR USE IN SCHOOLS AND COLLEGES. 3rd Edition. Fcp. 8vo. 2s. 6d.

—— HORÆ HELLENICÆ. 8vo. 12s.

—— THE WISE MEN OF GREECE : IN A SERIES OF DRAMATIC DIALOGUES. Cr. 8vo. 9s.

—— GOETHE'S FAUST. Translated into English Verse. 2nd Edition. Crown 8vo. 9s.

BLACKIE (Prof. John S.).—LAY SERMONS. Crown 8vo. 6s.

—— MESSIS VITAE: Gleanings of Song from a Happy Life. Crown 8vo. 4s. 6d.

—— WHAT DOES HISTORY TEACH? Two Edinburgh Lectures. Globe 8vo. 2s. 6d.

BLAKE (J. F.)—ASTRONOMICAL MYTHS. With Illustrations. Crown 8vo. 9s.

BLAKE.—LIFE OF WILLIAM BLAKE. With Selections from his Poems and other Writings. Illustrated from Blake's own Works. By ALEXANDER GILCHRIST. New and Enlarged Edition. 2 vols. cloth gilt. Med. 8vo. 2l. 2s.

BLAKISTON (J. R.).—THE TEACHER: HINTS ON SCHOOL MANAGEMENT. Cr. 8vo. 2s. 6d.

BLANFORD (H. F.).—THE RUDIMENTS OF PHYSICAL GEOGRAPHY FOR THE USE OF INDIAN SCHOOLS. 12th Edition. Illustrated. Globe 8vo. 2s. 6d.

—— A PRACTICAL GUIDE TO THE CLIMATES AND WEATHER OF INDIA, CEYLON AND BURMAH, AND THE STORMS OF INDIAN SEAS. 8vo. 12s. 6d.

BLANFORD (W. T.).—GEOLOGY AND ZOOLOGY OF ABYSSINIA. 8vo. 21s.

BÖHM-BAWERK (Prof.).—CAPITAL AND INTEREST. Translated by W. SMART. 8vo.

BOLDREWOOD (Rolf).—ROBBERY UNDER ARMS: A STORY OF LIFE AND ADVENTURE IN THE BUSH AND IN THE GOLDFIELDS OF AUSTRALIA. Crown 8vo. 3s. 6d.

—— THE MINER'S RIGHT. 3 vols. 31s. 6d.

BOLEYN (ANNE): A Chapter of English History, 1527-1536. By PAUL FRIEDMANN. 2 vols. 8vo. 28s.

BONAR (James).—MALTHUS AND HIS WORK. 8vo. 12s. 6d.

BOOK OF GOLDEN DEEDS OF ALL TIMES AND ALL LANDS. By CHARLOTTE M. YONGE. 18mo. 4s. 6d. Edition for Schools. Globe 8vo. 2s. Abridged Edition. 18mo. 1s.

BOOLE (George).—A TREATISE ON THE CALCULUS OF FINITE DIFFERENCES. Edited by J. F. MOULTON. 3rd Edition. Cr. 8vo. 10s. 6d.

—— THE MATHEMATICAL ANALYSIS OF LOGIC. 8vo. Sewed, 5s.

BOTTOMLEY (J. T.). — FOUR-FIGURE MATHEMATICAL TABLES. Comprising Logarithmic and Trigonometrical Tables, and Tables of Squares, Square Roots and Reciprocals. 2s. 6d.

BOUGHTON (G. H.) and ABBEY (E. A.).—SKETCHING RAMBLES IN HOLLAND. With Illustrations. Fcp. 4to. 21s.

BOWEN (H. Courthope).—FIRST LESSONS IN FRENCH. 18mo. 1s.

BOWER (Prof. F. O.).—A COURSE OF PRACTICAL INSTRUCTION IN BOTANY. Cr. 8vo. 10s. 6d.

BRADSHAW (J. G.).—A COURSE OF EASY ARITHMETICAL EXAMPLES FOR BEGINNERS. Globe 8vo. 2s. With Answers. 2s. 6d.

BRAIN. A JOURNAL OF NEUROLOGY. Edited for the Neurological Society of London, by A. DE WATTEVILLE. Published Quarterly. 8vo. 3s. 6d. (Part I. in January, 1878.) Yearly Vols. I. to XII. 8vo, cloth. 15s. each.

BREYMANN (Prof. H.)—A FRENCH GRAMMAR BASED ON PHILOLOGICAL PRINCIPLES. 3rd Edition. Extra fcp. 8vo. 4s. 6d.

—— FIRST FRENCH EXERCISE BOOK. 2nd Edition. Extra fcp. 8vo. 4s. 6d.

—— SECOND FRENCH EXERCISE BOOK. Extra fcp. 8vo. 2s. 6d.

BRIDGES (John A.).—IDYLLS OF A LOST VILLAGE. Crown 8vo. 7s. 6d.

BRIGHT (John).—SPEECHES ON QUESTIONS OF PUBLIC POLICY. Edited by Professor THOROLD ROGERS. 2nd Edition. 2 vols. 8vo. 25s. With Portrait. Author's Popular Edition. Extra fcp. 8vo. 3s. 6d.

—— PUBLIC ADDRESSES. Edited by J. E. T. ROGERS. 8vo. 14s.

BRIGHT (H. A.)—THE ENGLISH FLOWER GARDEN. Crown 8vo. 3s. 6d.

BRIMLEY (George).—ESSAYS. Globe 8vo. 5s.

BRODIE (Sir Benjamin).—IDEAL CHEMISTRY. Crown 8vo. 2s.

BROOKE.—THE RAJA OF SARAWAK (Life of). By GERTRUDE L. JACOB. Portrait and Maps. 2 vols. 8vo. 25s.

BROOKE (Stopford A.).—PRIMER OF ENGLISH LITERATURE. 18mo. 1s. Large Paper Edition. 8vo. 7s. 6d.

—— RIQUET OF THE TUFT: A LOVE DRAMA. Extra crown 8vo. 6s.

—— POEMS. Globe 8vo. 6s.

—— MILTON. Fcp. 8vo. 1s. 6d. Large Paper Edition. 8vo. 21s.

—— POEMS OF SHELLEY. Edited by STOPFORD A. BROOKE, M.A. With Vignette. 18mo. 4s. 6d. Large Paper Edition. 12s. 6d.

BROOKS (Rev. Phillips).—THE CANDLE OF THE LORD, AND OTHER SERMONS. Cr. 8vo. 6s.

—— SERMONS PREACHED IN ENGLISH CHURCHES. Crown 8vo. 6s.

—— TWENTY SERMONS. Crown 8vo. 6s.

—— TOLERANCE. Crown 8vo. 2s. 6d.

BROOKSMITH (J.).——ARITHMETIC IN THEORY AND PRACTICE. Crown 8vo. 4s. 6d.

BROOKSMITH (J. and E. J.).—ARITHMETIC FOR BEGINNERS. Globe 8vo. 1s. 6d.

BROOKSMITH (E. J.).—WOOLWICH MATHEMATICAL PAPERS, for Admission in the Royal Military Academy for the years 1880—1888. Ed. by E. J. BROOKSMITH, B.A. Cr. 8vo. 6s.

BROWN (J. Allen).—PALÆOLITHIC MAN IN NORTH-WEST MIDDLESEX. 8vo. 7s. 6d.

BROWN (T. E.).—THE MANX WITCH: AND OTHER POEMS. Crown 8vo. 7s. 6d.

BROWNE (J. H. Balfour).—WATER SUPPLY. Crown 8vo. 2s. 6d.

BROWNE (Sir Thomas).—RELIGIO MEDICI; LETTER TO A FRIEND, &c., AND CHRISTIAN MORALS. Edited by W. A. GREENHILL, M.D. With Portrait. 18mo. 4s. 6d.

BRUNTON (Dr. T. Lauder).—A TEXT-BOOK OF PHARMACOLOGY, THERAPEUTICS, AND MATERIA MEDICA. 3rd Edition. Medium 8vo. 21s.

—— DISORDERS OF DIGESTION: THEIR CONSEQUENCES AND TREATMENT. 8vo. 10s. 6d.

BRUNTON (Dr. T. Lauder).—PHARMACOLOGY AND THERAPEUTICS; OR, MEDICINE PAST AND PRESENT. Crown 8vo. 6s.

—— TABLES OF MATERIA MEDICA: A COMPANION TO THE MATERIA MEDICA MUSEUM. 8vo. 5s.

—— THE BIBLE AND SCIENCE. With Illustrations. Crown 8vo. 10s. 6d.

BRYANS (Clement).—LATIN PROSE EXERCISES BASED UPON CAESAR'S "GALLIC WAR." With a Classification of Caesar's Phrases and Grammatical Notes on Caesar's Chief Usages. Pott 8vo. 2s. 6d.
    KEY (for Teachers only). 4s. 6d.

BRYCE (James, M.P., D.C.L.).—THE HOLY ROMAN EMPIRE. 8th Ed. Cr. 8vo. 7s. 6d.. Library Edition. 8vo. 14s.

—— TRANSCAUCASIA AND ARARAT. 3rd Edition. Crown 8vo. 9s.

—— THE AMERICAN COMMONWEALTH. 2nd Edition. 2 vols. Extra Crown 8vo. 25s.

BUCHHEIM (Dr.).—DEUTSCHE LYRIK. 18mo. 4s. 6d.

BUCKLAND (Anna).—OUR NATIONAL INSTITUTIONS. 18mo. 1s.

BUCKLEY (Arabella).—HISTORY OF ENGLAND FOR BEGINNERS. With Coloured Maps and Chronological and Genealogical Tables. Globe 8vo. 3s.

BUCKNILL (Dr.).—THE CARE OF THE INSANE AND THEIR LEGAL CONTROL. Crown 8vo. 3s. 6d.

BUCKTON (G. B.).—MONOGRAPH OF THE BRITISH CICADÆ, OR FETTIGIIDÆ. In 8 parts. Part I. 8vo. 8s.

BUMBLEBEE BOGO'S BUDGET. By a RETIRED JUDGE. Illustrations by ALICE HAVERS. Crown 8vo. 2s. 6d.

BUNYAN (John).—THE PILGRIM'S PROGRESS FROM THIS WORLD TO THAT WHICH IS TO COME. 18mo. 4s. 6d.

BUNYAN. By J. A. FROUDE. Crown 8vo. 1s. 6d.; sewed, 1s.

BURGON (Dean).—POEMS. Ex. fcp. 8vo. 4s. 6d.

BURKE (Edmund).—LETTERS, TRACTS, AND SPEECHES ON IRISH AFFAIRS. Edited by MATTHEW ARNOLD, with Preface. Cr. 8vo. 6s.

BURKE. By JOHN MORLEY. Globe 8vo. 5s. Crown 8vo. 1s. 6d.; sewed, 1s.

BURN (Robert).—ROMAN LITERATURE IN RELATION TO ROMAN ART. With Illustrations. Extra Crown 8vo. 14s.

BURNETT (F. Hodgson).—"HAWORTH'S." Globe 8vo. 2s.

—— LOUISIANA: AND THAT LASS O' LOWRIE'S. Two Stories. Illustrated. Cr. 8vo. 3s. 6d. Cheap Edition. Globe 8vo. 2s.

BURNS, THE COMPLETE WORKS OF. Edited by ALEXANDER SMITH. Globe 8vo. 3s. 6d.

—— THE POETICAL WORKS. With a Biographical Memoir by ALEXANDER SMITH. In 2 vols. fcp. 8vo. 10s.

BURNS. By Principal SHAIRP. Crown 8vo. 1s. 6d.; sewed, 1s.

BURY (J. B.).—A HISTORY OF THE LATER ROMAN EMPIRE FROM ARCADIUS TO IRENE, A.D. 390—800. 2 vols. 8vo. 32s.

BUTCHER (Prof. S. H.).—DEMOSTHENES. Fcp. 8vo. 1s. 6d.

BUTLER (Archer).—SERMONS, DOCTRINAL AND PRACTICAL. 11th Edition. 8vo. 8s.

—— A SECOND SERIES OF SERMONS. Ninth Edition. 8vo. 7s.

—— LETTERS ON ROMANISM. 2nd Ed., revised by Archdeacon HARDWICK. 8vo. 10s. 6d.

BUTLER (George).—SERMONS PREACHED IN CHELTENHAM COLLEGE CHAPEL. 8vo. 7s. 6d.

BUTLER'S HUDIBRAS. Edited by ALFRED MILNES. Fcp. 8vo. Part I., 3s. 6d. Part II. and III., 4s. 6d.

BYRON.—POETRY OF BYRON, chosen and arranged by MATTHEW ARNOLD. 18mo. 4s. 6d.
    Large Paper Edition. Crown 8vo. 9s.

BYRON. By Prof. NICHOL. Crown 8vo. 1s. 6d.; sewed, 1s.

CAESAR.—THE GALLIC WAR. Book I. Edited, with Notes and Vocabulary by A. S. WALPOLE, M.A. 18mo. 1s. 6d.

—— THE GALLIC WAR.—Books II. and III. Edited by W. G. RUTHERFORD, LL.D. 18mo. 1s. 6d.

—— THE INVASION OF BRITAIN. Being Selections from Books IV. and V. of the "De Bello Gallico." With Notes, Vocabulary, and Exercises, by W. WELCH, M.A., and C. G. DUFFIELD, M.A. 18mo. 1s. 6d.

—— SCENES FROM THE FIFTH AND SIXTH BOOKS OF THE GALLIC WAR. Selected and Edited by C. COLBECK, M.A. 18mo. 1s. 6d.

—— THE HELVETIAN WAR. Selected from Book I. of "The Gallic War," with Notes, Vocabulary, and Exercises, by W. WELCH and C. G. DUFFIELD. 18mo. 1s. 6d.

—— THE GALLIC WAR. Edited by the Rev. J. BOND, M.A., and A. S. WALPOLE, M.A. Fcp. 8vo. 6s.

—— THE GALLIC WAR.—Book IV. Edited, with Introduction, Notes, and Vocabulary, by CLEMENT BRYANS, M.A. 18mo. 1s. 6d.

—— THE GALLIC WAR.—Book V. Edited with Notes and Vocabulary, by C. COLBECK, M.A. 18mo. 1s. 6d.

—— THE GALLIC WAR.—Book VI. By the same Editor. With Notes and Vocabulary. 18mo. 1s. 6d.

—— THE GALLIC WAR—Book VII. Edited by the Rev. J. BOND, M.A., and A. S. WALPOLE, M.A. With Notes and Vocabulary. 18mo. 1s. 6d.

CAIRNES (Prof. J. E.).—POLITICAL ESSAYS. 8vo. 10s. 6d.

—— SOME LEADING PRINCIPLES OF POLITICAL ECONOMY NEWLY EXPOUNDED. 8vo. 14s.

—— THE SLAVE POWER. 8vo. 10s. 6d.

—— THE CHARACTER AND LOGICAL METHOD OF POLITICAL ECONOMY. Crown 8vo. 6s.

CALDERON.—SELECT PLAYS OF CALDERON. Ed. by NORMAN MACCOLL, M.A. Cr. 8vo 14s.

CALDERWOOD (Prof. H.).—HAND-BOOK OF MORAL PHILOSOPHY. 14th Edition. Crown 8vo. 6s.

—— THE RELATIONS OF MIND AND BRAIN. 2nd Edition. 8vo. 12s.

CALDERWOOD (Prof. H.).—THE PARABLES OF OUR LORD. 2nd Edition. Crown 8vo. 6s.

—— THE RELATIONS OF SCIENCE AND RELIGION. Crown 8vo. 5s.

—— ON TEACHING. 4th Ed. Ex. fcp. 8vo. 2s. 6d.

CALVERT.—SCHOOL-READINGS IN THE GREEK TESTAMENT. Edited, with Notes and Vocabulary, by A. CALVERT, M.A. Fcp. 8vo. 4s. 6d.

CAMBRIDGE.—COOPER'S LE KEUX'S MEMORIALS OF CAMBRIDGE. Illustrated with 90 Woodcuts in the Text, 154 Plates on Steel and Copper by LE KEUX, STORER, &c., including 20 Etchings by R. FARREN. 3 vols. Medium 8vo. Cloth, gilt tops.
A few copies, proofs, large paper, 4to, bound in half-levant morocco, with gilt tops.
Fifty copies of the Etchings by R. FARREN, from the "Memorials of Cambridge." Proofs, signed, in a Portfolio.

CAMBRIDGE SENATE-HOUSE PROBLEMS AND RIDERS, WITH SOLUTIONS:

1848—51. RIDERS. By JAMESON. 8vo. 7s. 6d.

1875. PROBLEMS AND RIDERS. Edited by Prof. A. G. GREENHILL. Cr. 8vo. 8s. 6d.

1878. SOLUTIONS BY THE MATHEMATICAL MODERATORS AND EXAMINERS. Edited by J. W. L. GLAISHER, M.A. 8vo. 12s.

CAMEOS FROM ENGLISH HISTORY. By the Author of "The Heir of Redclyffe." 6 vols. Extra fcp. 8vo. 5s. each.
Vol. I. Rollo to Edward II. II. The Wars in France. III. The Wars of the Roses. IV. Reformation Times. V. England and Spain. VI. Forty Years of Stuart Rule (1603—43). VII. The Rebellion and Restoration (1642—78).
[In the Press.

CAMERON (V. L.).—OUR FUTURE HIGHWAY TO INDIA. 2 vols. Crown 8vo. 21s.

CAMPBELL (Dr. John M'Leod).—THE NATURE OF THE ATONEMENT. 6th Edition. Crown 8vo. 6s.

—— REMINISCENCES AND REFLECTIONS. Ed., with an Introductory Narrative, by his Son, DONALD CAMPBELL, M.A. Cr. 8vo. 7s. 6d.

—— RESPONSIBILITY FOR THE GIFT OF ETERNAL LIFE. Compiled from Sermons preached at Row, in the years 1829—31. Cr. 8vo. 5s.

—— THOUGHTS ON REVELATION. 2nd Edition. Crown 8vo. 5s.

CAMPBELL (J. F.).—MY CIRCULAR NOTES. Cheaper issue. Crown 8vo. 6s.

CAMPBELL (Lord George).—LOG-LETTERS FROM THE "CHALLENGER." 7th Edition. Crown 8vo. 6s.

CAMPBELL (Prof. Lewis).—SOPHOCLES. Fcp. 8vo. 1s. 6d.

CANDLER (H.).—HELP TO ARITHMETIC. 2nd Edition. Globe 8vo. 2s. 6d.

CANTERBURY (His Grace Edward White, Archbishop of).—BOY-LIFE: ITS TRIAL, ITS STRENGTH, ITS FULNESS. Sundays in Wellington College, 1859—73. 4th Ed. Cr. 8vo. 6s.

—— THE SEVEN GIFTS. Addressed to the Diocese of Canterbury in his Primary Visitation. 2nd Edition. Crown 8vo. 6s.

CANTERBURY (Archbishop of).—CHRIST AND HIS TIMES. Addressed to the Diocese of Canterbury in his Second Visitation. Crown 8vo. 6s.

CAPES (Rev. W. W.)—LIVY. Fcp. 8vo. 1s. 6d.

CARLES (W. R.).—LIFE IN COREA. 8vo. 12s. 6d.

CARLYLE (Thomas).—REMINISCENCES. Ed. by CHARLES ELIOT NORTON. 2 vols. Crown 8vo. 12s.

—— EARLY LETTERS OF THOMAS CARLYLE. Edited by C. E. NORTON. 2 vols. 1814—26. Crown 8vo. 18s.

—— LETTERS OF THOMAS CARLYLE. Ed. by C. E. NORTON. 2 vols. 1826—36. Cr. 8vo. 18s.

—— GOETHE AND CARLYLE, CORRESPONDENCE BETWEEN. Ed. by C. E. NORTON. Cr. 8vo. 9s.

CARMARTHEN (Marchioness of). — A LOVER OF THE BEAUTIFUL. A Novel. Crown 8vo.

CARPENTER (Bishop W. Boyd).—TRUTH IN TALE. Addresses, chiefly to children. Cr. 8vo. 4s. 6d.

—— THE PERMANENT ELEMENTS OF RELIGION: Bampton Lectures, 1887. 8vo. 14s.

CARR (J. Comyns).—PAPERS ON ART. Cr. 8vo. 8s. 6d.

CARROLL (Lewis).—ALICE'S ADVENTURES IN WONDERLAND. With 42 Illustrations by TENNIEL. Crown 8vo. 6s.
People's Edition. With all the original Illustrations. Crown 8vo. 2s. 6d.
A GERMAN TRANSLATION OF THE SAME. Crown 8vo, gilt. 6s.
A FRENCH TRANSLATION OF THE SAME. Crown 8vo, gilt. 6s.
AN ITALIAN TRANSLATION OF THE SAME. Crown 8vo, gilt. 6s.

—— ALICE'S ADVENTURES UNDER-GROUND. Being a Facsimile of the Original MS. Book, afterwards developed into "Alice's Adventures in Wonderland." With 27 Illustrations by the Author. Crown 8vo. 4s.

—— THROUGH THE LOOKING-GLASS AND WHAT ALICE FOUND THERE. With 50 Illustrations by TENNIEL. Crown 8vo, gilt. 6s.
People's Edition. With all the original Illustrations. Crown 8vo. 2s. 6d.
People's Edition of "Alice's Adventures in Wonderland," and "Through the Looking-Glass." 1 vol. Crown 8vo. 4s. 6d.

—— THE GAME OF LOGIC. Crown 8vo. 3s.

—— RHYME? AND REASON? With 65 Illustrations by ARTHUR B. FROST, and 9 by HENRY HOLIDAY. Crown 8vo. 6s.

—— A TANGLED TALE. Reprinted from the "Monthly Packet." With 6 Illustrations by ARTHUR B. FROST. Crown 8vo. 4s. 6d.

—— SYLVIE AND BRUNO. With 46 Illustrations by HARRY FURNISS. Cr. 8vo. 7s. 6d.

CARSTARES (William).—A Character and Career of the Revolutionary Epoch (1649—1715). By R. H. STORY. 8vo. 12s.

CARTER (R. Brudenell, F.C.S.).—A PRACTICAL TREATISE ON DISEASES OF THE EYE. 8vo. 16s.

CARTER (R. Brudenell).—EYESIGHT, GOOD AND BAD. Cr. 8vo. 6s.

—— MODERN OPERATIONS FOR CATARACT. 8vo. 6s.

CASSEL.—MANUAL OF JEWISH HISTORY AND LITERATURE. Translated by Mrs. HENRY LUCAS. Fcp. 8vo. 2s. 6d.

CATULLUS.—SELECT POEMS. Edited by F. P. SIMPSON, B.A. Fcp. 8vo. 5s.

CAUCASUS: NOTES ON THE. By "Wanderer." 8vo. 9s.

CAUTLEY (G. S.).—A CENTURY OF EMBLEMS. With Illustrations by the Lady MARIAN ALFORD. Small 4to. 10s. 6d.

CAZENOVE (J. Gibson).—CONCERNING THE BEING AND ATTRIBUTES OF GOD. 8vo. 5s.

CHALMERS (J. B.).—GRAPHICAL DETERMINATION OF FORCES IN ENGINEERING STRUCTURES. 8vo. 24s.

CHALMERS (M.D.).—LOCAL GOVERNMENT. Crown 8vo. 3s. 6d. [English Citizen Series.

CHATTERTON: A BIOGRAPHICAL STUDY. By Sir DANIEL WILSON, LL.D. Cr. 8vo. 6s. 6d.

CHAUCER. By Prof. A. W. WARD. Crown 8vo. 1s. 6d.; sewed, 1s.

CHEYNE (C. H. H.).—AN ELEMENTARY TREATISE ON THE PLANETARY THEORY. Crown 8vo. 7s. 6d.

CHEYNE (T. K.).—THE BOOK OF ISAIAH CHRONOLOGICALLY ARRANGED. Crown 8vo. 7s. 6d.

CHILDREN'S GARLAND FROM THE BEST POETS. Selected and arranged by COVENTRY PATMORE. 18mo. 4s. 6d.

Globe Readings Edition for Schools. 2s.

CHOICE NOTES ON THE FOUR GOSPELS, drawn from Old and New Sources. Crown 8vo. 4 vols. 4s. 6d. each. (St. Matthew and St. Mark in 1 vol. 9s.)

CHRISTIE (J.).—CHOLERA EPIDEMICS IN EAST AFRICA. 8vo. 15s.

CHRISTIE (J. R.).—ELEMENTARY TEST QUESTIONS IN PURE AND MIXED MATHEMATICS. Crown 8vo. 8s. 6d.

CHRISTMAS CAROL, A. Printed in Colours, with Illuminated Borders from MSS. of the 14th and 15th Centuries. 4to. 21s.

CHRISTY CAREW. By the Author of "Hogan, M.P." Globe 8vo. 2s.

CHURCH (Very Rev. R. W.).—THE SACRED POETRY OF EARLY RELIGIONS. 2nd Edition. 18mo. 1s.

—— ST. ANSELM. Crown 8vo. 6s.

—— HUMAN LIFE AND ITS CONDITIONS. Cr. 8vo. 6s.

—— THE GIFTS OF CIVILISATION, and other Sermons and Lectures. Crown 8vo. 7s. 6d.

—— DISCIPLINE OF THE CHRISTIAN CHARACTER, and other Sermons. Crown 8vo. 4s. 6d.

—— ADVENT SERMONS. 1885. Cr. 8vo. 4s. 6d.

—— MISCELLANEOUS WRITINGS. Collected Edition. 5 vols. Globe 8vo. 5s. each.

Vol. I. MISCELLANEOUS ESSAYS. II. ST. ANSELM. III. DANTE: AND OTHER ESSAYS. IV. SPENSER. V. BACON.

CHURCH (Very Rev. R. W.).—SPENSER. Globe 8vo. 5s.; Crown 8vo. 1s. 6d.; swd., 1s.

—— BACON. Globe 8vo. 5s.; Cr. 8vo. 1s. 6d.; sewed, 1s.

CHURCH (Rev. A. J.).—LATIN VERSION OF SELECTIONS FROM TENNYSON. By Prof. CONINGTON, Prof. SEELEY, Dr. HESSEY, T. E. KEBBEL, &c. Edited by A. J. CHURCH, M.A. Extra fcp. 8vo. 6s.

CHURCH (A. J.) and BRODRIBB (W. J.).—TACITUS. Fcp. 8vo. 1s. 6d.

CICERO.—THE LIFE AND LETTERS OF MARCUS TULLIUS CICERO. Being a New Translation of the Letters included in Mr. Watson's Selection. By the Rev. G. E. JEANS, M.A. 2nd Edition. Crown 8vo. 10s. 6d.

—— THE ACADEMICA. The Text revised and explained by J. S. REID, M.L. 8vo. 15s.

—— THE ACADEMICS. Translated by J. S. REID, M.L. 8vo. 5s. 6d.

—— DE AMICITIA. Edited by E. S. SHUCKBURGH, M.A. With Notes, Vocabulary, and Biographical Index. 18mo. 1s. 6d.

—— DE SENECTUTE. Edited, with Notes, Vocabulary, and Biographical Index, by E. S. SHUCKBURGH, M.A. 18mo. 1s. 6d.

—— SELECT LETTERS. Edited by Rev. G. E. JEANS, M.A. 18mo. 1s. 6d.

—— THE SECOND PHILIPPIC ORATION. Edited by Prof. JOHN E. B. MAYOR. New Edition, revised. Fcp. 8vo. 5s.

—— PRO PUBLIO SESTIO. Edited by Rev. H. A. HOLDEN, M.A., LL.D. Fcp. 8vo. 5s.

—— THE CATILINE ORATIONS. Edited by Prof. A. S. WILKINS, Litt.D. New Edition. Fcp. 8vo. 3s. 6d.

—— PRO LEGE MANILIA. Edited by Prof. A. S. WILKINS, Litt.D. Fcp. 8vo. 2s. 6d.

—— PRO ROSCIO AMERINO. Edited by E. H. DONKIN, M.A. Fcp. 8vo. 4s. 6d.

—— STORIES OF ROMAN HISTORY. With Notes, Vocabulary, and Exercises by G. E. JEANS, M.A., and A. V. JONES. 18mo. 1s. 6d.

CLARK.—MEMORIALS FROM JOURNALS AND LETTERS OF SAMUEL CLARK, M.A. Edited by his Wife. Crown 8vo. 7s. 6d.

CLARK (L.) and SADLER (H.).—THE STAR GUIDE. Roy. 8vo. 5s.

CLARKE (C. B.).—A GEOGRAPHICAL READER AND COMPANION TO THE ATLAS. Cr. 8vo. 2s.

—— A CLASS-BOOK OF GEOGRAPHY. With 18 Coloured Maps. Fcp. 8vo. 3s. 6d.; swd., 3s.

—— SPECULATIONS FROM POLITICAL ECONOMY. Crown 8vo. 3s. 6d.

CLARKE (F. W.).—A TABLE OF SPECIFIC GRAVITY FOR SOLIDS AND LIQUIDS. (Constants of Nature, Part I.) 8vo. 12s. 6d.

CLASSICAL WRITERS. Edited by JOHN RICHARD GREEN. Fcp. 8vo. 1s. 6d. each.

EURIPIDES. By Prof. MAHAFFY.
MILTON. By the Rev. STOPFORD A. BROOKE.
LIVY. By the Rev. W. W. CAPES, M.A.
VERGIL. By Prof. NETTLESHIP, M.A.
SOPHOCLES. By Prof. L. CAMPBELL, M.A.
DEMOSTHENES. By Prof. BUTCHER, M.A.
TACITUS. By CHURCH and BRODRIBB.

CLAUSIUS (R.).—The Mechanical Theory of Heat. Translated by Walter R. Browne. Crown 8vo. 10s. 6d.

CLERGYMAN'S SELF-EXAMINATION Concerning the Apostles' Creed. Extra fcp. 8vo. 1s. 6d.

CLIFFORD (Prof. W. K.).—Elements of Dynamic. An Introduction to the Study of Motion and Rest in Solid and Fluid Bodies. Crown 8vo. Part I. Kinematic. Books I.—III., 7s. 6d. Book IV. and Appendix, 6s.

—— Lectures and Essays. Ed. by Leslie Stephen and Sir F. Pollock. Cr. 8vo. 8s. 6d.

—— Seeing and Thinking. With Diagrams. Crown 8vo. 3s. 6d.

—— Mathematical Papers. Edited by R. Tucker. With an Introduction by H. J. Stephen Smith, M.A. 8vo. 30s.

CLIFFORD (Mrs. W. K.).—Anyhow Stories. With Illustrations by Dorothy Tennant. Crown 8vo. 1s. 6d.; paper covers, 1s.

CLOUGH (A. H.).—Poems. New Edition. Crown 8vo. 7s. 6d.

—— Prose Remains. With a Selection from his Letters, and a Memoir by his Wife. Crown 8vo. 7s. 6d.

COAL: Its History and Its Uses. By Profs. Green, Miall, Thorpe, Rücker, and Marshall. 8vo. 12s. 6d.

COBDEN (Richard.).—Speeches on Questions of Public Policy. Edited by John Bright and J. E. Thorold Rogers. Globe 8vo. 3s. 6d.

COCKSHOTT (A.) and WALTERS (F. B.).—A Treatise on Geometrical Conics. Crown 8vo. 5s.

COHEN (D. Julius B.).—The Owens College Course of Practical Organic Chemistry. Fcp. 8vo. 2s. 6d.

COLBECK (C.).—French Readings from Roman History. Selected from various Authors, with Notes. 18mo. 4s. 6d.

COLENSO.—The Communion Service from the Book of Common Prayer, with Select Readings from the Writings of the Rev. F. D. Maurice. Edited by the late Bishop Colenso. 6th Ed. 16mo. 2s. 6d.

COLERIDGE.—The Poetical and Dramatic Works of Samuel Taylor Coleridge. 4 vols. Fcp. 8vo. 31s. 6d.
Also an Edition on Large Paper, 2l. 12s. 6d.

COLERIDGE. By H. D. Traill. Crown 8vo. 1s. 6d.; sewed, 1s.

COLLECTS OF THE CHURCH OF ENGLAND. With a Coloured Floral Design to each Collect. Crown 8vo. 12s.

COLLIER (John).—A Primer of Art. 18mo. 1s.

COLQUHOUN.—Rhymes and Chimes. By F. S. Colquhoun (née F. S. Fuller Maitland). Extra fcp. 8vo. 2s. 6d.

COLSON (F. H.).—First Greek Reader. Stories and Legends. With Notes, Vocabulary, and Exercises. Globe 8vo. 3s.

COLVIN (S.).—Landor. Crown 8vo. 1s. 6d.; sewed, 1s.

COLVIN (S.).—Selections from the Writings of Walter Savage Landor. 18mo. 4s. 6d.

—— Keats. Crown 8vo. 1s. 6d.; sewed, 1s.

COMBE.—Life of George Combe. By Charles Gibbon. 2 vols. 8vo. 32s.

—— Education: Its Principles and Practice as Developed by George Combe. Edited by William Jolly. 8vo. 15s.

CONGREVE (Rev. John).—High Hopes and Pleadings for a Reasonable Faith, Nobler Thoughts, Larger Charity. Crown 8vo. 5s.

CONSTABLE (Samuel).—Geometrical Exercises for Beginners. Cr. 8vo. 3s. 6d.

CONWAY (Hugh).—A Family Affair. Globe 8vo. 2s.

—— Living or Dead. Globe 8vo. 2s.

COOKE (E. T.).—A Popular Handbook to the National Gallery. Including, by special permission, Notes collected from the Works of Mr. Ruskin. With a Preface by John Ruskin, LL.D., D.C.L. Crown 8vo, half morocco. 14s.
Also an Edition on Large Paper, limited to 250 copies. 2 vols. 8vo.

COOKE (Josiah P., jun.).—Principles of Chemical Philosophy. New Ed. 8vo. 16s.

—— Religion and Chemistry. Cr. 8vo. 7s. 6d.

—— Elements of Chemical Physics. 4th Edition. Royal 8vo. 21s.

COOKERY. Middle Class Book. Compiled for Manchester School of Cookery. Fcp. 8vo. 1s. 6d.

CO-OPERATION IN THE UNITED STATES: History of. Edited by H. B. Adams. 8vo. 15s.

COPE (E. M.).—An Introduction to Aristotle's Rhetoric. 8vo. 14s.

COPE (E. D.).—The Origin of the Fittest. Essays on Evolution. 8vo. 12s. 6d.

CORBETT (Julian).—The Fall of Asgard: A Tale of St. Olaf's Day. 2 vols. 12s.

—— For God and Gold. Crown 8vo. 6s.

—— Kophetua the Thirteenth. 2 vols. Globe 8vo. 12s.

—— Monk. With Portrait. Cr. 8vo. 2s. 6d.
[English Men of Action.

CORE (T. H.).—Questions on Balfour Stewart's "Lessons in Elementary Physics." Fcp. 8vo. 2s.

CORFIELD (Dr. W. H.).—The Treatment and Utilization of Sewage. 3rd Edition, Revised by the Author, and by Louis C. Parkes, M.D. 8vo. 16s.

CORNAZ (S.).—Nos Enfants et Leurs Amis. Edited by Edith Harvey. Globe 8vo. 1s. 6d.

CORNELL UNIVERSITY STUDIES IN CLASSICAL PHILOLOGY. Edited by I. Flagg, W. G. Hale, and B. I. Wheeler. I. The CUM-Constructions: their History and Functions. Part I. Critical. 1s. 8d. nett. Part II. Constructive. By W. G. Hale. 3s. 4d. nett. II. Analogy and the Scope of its Application in Language. By B. I. Wheeler. 1s. 3d. nett.

CORNEILLE.—Le Cid. Ed. by G. Eugène Fasnacht. 18mo. 1s.

COSSA.—Guide to the Study of Political Economy. From the Italian of Dr. Luigi Cossa. Crown 8vo. 4s. 6d.

COTTERILL (Prof. James H.).—Applied Mechanics: An Introduction to the Theory of Structures and Machines. 2nd Edition. Med. 8vo. 18s.

COTTON (Bishop).—Sermons Preached to English Congregations in India. Crown 8vo. 7s. 6d.

COTTON and PAYNE.—Colonies and Dependencies. Part I. India. By J. S. Cotton. Part II. The Colonies. By E. J. Payne. Crown 8vo. 3s. 6d.

COUES (Elliott).—Key to North American Birds. Illustrated. 8vo. 2l. 2s.

COWELL (George).—Lectures on Cataract: Its Causes, Varieties, and Treatment. Crown 8vo. 4s. 6d.

COWPER.—Cowper's Poetical Works. Ed. by Rev. W. Benham. Globe 8vo. 3s. 6d.

—— **The Task:** An Epistle to Joseph Hill, Esq.; Tirocinium, or a Review of the Schools; and the History of John Gilpin. Edited by William Benham. Globe 8vo. 1s.

—— **Letters of William Cowper.** Edited by the Rev. W. Benham. 18mo. 4s. 6d.

—— **Selections from Cowper's Poems.** Introduction by Mrs. Oliphant. 18mo. 4s. 6d.

COWPER. By Goldwin Smith. Crown 8vo. 1s. 6d.; sewed, 1s.

COX (G. V.).—Recollections of Oxford. 2nd Edition. Crown 8vo. 6s.

CRAIK (Mrs.).—Olive. Illustrated. Crown 8vo. 6s.—Cheap Edition. Globe 8vo. 2s.

—— **The Ogilvies.** Illustrated. Crown 8vo. 6s.—Cheap Edition. Globe 8vo. 2s.

—— **Agatha's Husband.** Illustrated. Crown 8vo. 6s.—Cheap Edition. Globe 8vo. 2s.

—— **The Head of the Family.** Illustrated. Cr. 8vo. 6s.—Cheap Edition. Gl. 8vo. 2s.

—— **Two Marriages.** Globe 8vo. 2s.

—— **The Laurel Bush.** Crown 8vo. 6s.

—— **My Mother and I.** Illust. Cr. 8vo. 6s.

—— **Miss Tommy: A Mediæval Romance.** Illustrated. Crown 8vo. 6s.

—— **King Arthur: Not a Love Story.** Crown 8vo. 6s.

   *** Beginning on March 1st, 1890, and continued monthly, a uniform edition of Mrs. Craik's Novels will be issued, price 3s. 6d. each.*

—— **Poems.** New and Enlarged Edition. Extra fcp. 8vo. 6s.

—— **Children's Poetry.** Ex. fcp. 8vo. 4s. 6d.

—— **Songs of our Youth.** Small 4to. 6s.

—— **Concerning Men: and other Papers.** Crown 8vo. 4s. 6d.

—— **About Money: and other Things.** Crown 8vo. 6s.

—— **Sermons out of Church.** Cr. 8vo. 6s.

—— **An Unknown Country.** Illustrated by F. Noel Paton. Royal 8vo. 7s. 6d.

CRAIK (Mrs.).—Alice Learmont: A Fairy Tale. With Illustrations. 4s. 6d.

—— **An Unsentimental Journey through Cornwall.** Illustrated. 4to. 12s. 6d.

—— **Our Year: A Child's Book in Prose and Verse.** Illustrated. 2s. 6d.

—— **Little Sunshine's Holiday.** Globe 8vo. 2s. 6d.

—— **The Adventures of a Brownie.** Illustrated by Mrs. Allingham. 4s. 6d.

—— **The Little Lame Prince and his Travelling Cloak.** A Parable for Old and Young. With 24 Illustrations by J. McL. Ralston. Crown 8vo. 4s. 6d.

—— **The Fairy Book: The Best Popular Fairy Stories.** Selected and rendered anew. With a Vignette by Sir Noel Paton. 18mo. 4s. 6d.

CRAIK (Henry).—The State in its Relation to Education. Crown 8vo. 3s. 6d.

CRANE (Lucy).—Lectures on Art and the Formation of Taste. Cr. 8vo. 6s.

CRANE (Walter).—The Sirens Three. A Poem. Written and Illustrated by Walter Crane. Royal 8vo. 10s. 6d.

CRAVEN (Mrs. Dacre).—A Guide to District Nurses. Crown 8vo. 2s. 6d.

CRAWFORD (F. Marion).—Mr. Isaacs: A Tale of Modern India. Cr. 8vo. 3s. 6d.

—— **Doctor Claudius: A True Story.** Crown 8vo. 3s. 6d.

—— **A Roman Singer.** Crown 8vo. 3s. 6d.

—— **Zoroaster.** Crown 8vo. 3s. 6d.

—— **A Tale of a Lonely Parish.** Crown 8vo. 3s. 6d.

—— **Marzio's Crucifix.** Crown 8vo. 3s. 6d.

—— **Paul Patoff.** Crown 8vo. 3s. 6d.

—— **With the Immortals.** 2 vols. Globe 8vo. 12s. 1 vol. Crown 8vo. 3s. 6d.

—— **Greifenstein.** Crown 8vo. 6s.

—— **Sant Ilario.** Crown 8vo. 6s.

CREIGHTON (M.).—Rome. 18mo. 1s.

   [Literature Primers.

—— **Cardinal Wolsey.** Crown 8vo. 2s. 6d.

CROSS (Rev. J. A.).—Bible Readings Selected from the Pentateuch and the Book of Joshua. 2nd Ed. Globe 8vo. 2s. 6d.

CROSSLEY (E.), GLEDHILL (J.), and WILSON (J. M.).—A Handbook of Double Stars. 8vo. 21s.

   Corrections to the Handbook of Double Stars. 8vo. 1s.

CUMMING (Linnæus).—Electricity. An Introduction to the Theory of Electricity. With numerous Examples. Cr. 8vo. 8s. 6d.

CUNNINGHAM (Sir H. S.).—The Cœruleans: A Vacation Idyll. Cr. 8vo. 3s. 6d.

—— **The Heriots.** 3 vols. Cr. 8vo. 31s. 6d.

CUNNINGHAM (Rev. W.).—The Epistle of St. Barnabas. A Dissertation, including a Discussion of its Date and Authorship. Together with the Greek Text, the Latin Version, and a New English Translation and Commentary. Crown 8vo. 7s. 6d.

CUNNINGHAM (Rev. W.).—Christian Civilisation, with Special Reference to India. Crown 8vo. 5s.

—— The Churches of Asia: A Methodical Sketch of the Second Century. Crown 8vo. 6s.

CUNNINGHAM (Rev. John).—The Growth of the Church in its Organisation and Institutions. Being the Croall Lectures for 1886. 8vo. 9s.

CUNYNGHAME (Gen. Sir A. T.).—My Command in South Africa, 1874—78. 8vo. 12s. 6d.

CURTEIS (Rev. G. H.).—Dissent in its Relation to the Church of England. Bampton Lectures for 1871. Cr. 8vo. 7s. 6d.

——The Scientific Obstacles to Christian Belief. The Boyle Lectures, 1884. Cr. 8vo. 6s.

CUTHBERTSON (Francis). — Euclidian Geometry. Extra fcp. 8vo. 4s. 6d.

DAGONET THE JESTER. Cr. 8vo. 4s. 6d.

DAHN (Felix).—Felicitas. Translated by M. A. C. E. Crown 8vo. 4s. 6d.

"DAILY NEWS."—Correspondence of the War between Russia and Turkey, 1877. To the Fall of Kars. Cr. 8vo. 6s.

—— Correspondence of the Russo-Turkish War. From the Fall of Kars to the Conclusion of Peace. Crown 8vo. 6s.

DALE (A. W. W.).—The Synod of Elvira, and Christian Life in the Fourth Century. Crown 8vo. 10s. 6d.

DALTON (Rev. T.).—Rules and Examples in Arithmetic. New Edition. 18mo. 2s. 6d.

—— Rules and Examples in Algebra. Part I. New Ed. 18mo. 2s. Part II. 2s. 6d. Key to Algebra. Part I. Cr. 8vo. 7s. 6d.

DAMIEN (Father).—A Journey from Cashmere to his Home in Hawaii. By Edward Clifford. Crown 8vo. 2s. 6d.

DAMPIER.—By W. Clark Russell. With Portrait. Crown 8vo. 2s. 6d.

DANIELL (Alfred).—A Text-Book of the Principles of Physics. With Illustrations. 2nd Edition. Medium 8vo. 21s.

DANTE.—The Purgatory of Dante Alighieri. Edited, with Translations and Notes, by A. J. Butler. Cr. 8vo. 12s. 6d.

—— The Paradiso of Dante. Edited, with a Prose Translation and Notes, by A. J. Butler. Crown 8vo. 12s. 6d.

—— De Monarchia. Translated by F. J. Church. 8vo. 4s. 6d.

—— Dante: and other Essays. By the Dean of St. Paul's. Globe 8vo. 5s.

—— Readings on the Purgatorio of Dante. Chiefly based on the Commentary of Benvenuto Da Imola. By the Hon. W. W. Vernon, M.A. With an Introduction by the Very Rev. the Dean of St. Paul's. 2 vols. Crown 8vo. 24s.

DARWIN (Charles).—Memorial Notices, reprinted from Nature. By T. H. Huxley, G. J. Romanes, Archibald Geikie, and W. T. Thiselton Dyer. With a Portrait. Crown 8vo. 2s. 6d. [Nature Series.

DAVIES (Rev. J. Llewelyn).—The Gospel and Modern Life. 2nd Edition, to which is added Morality according to the Sacrament of the Lord's Supper. Extra fcp. 8vo. 6s.

—— Warnings against Superstition. Ex. fcp. 8vo. 2s. 6d.

—— The Christian Calling. Ex. fcp. 8vo. 6s.

—— The Epistles of St. Paul to the Ephesians, the Colossians, and Philemon. With Introductions and Notes. 2nd Edition. 8vo. 7s. 6d.

—— Social Questions from the Point of View of Christian Theology. 2nd Ed. Crown 8vo. 6s.

DAVIES (J. Ll.) and VAUGHAN (D. J.).—The Republic of Plato. Translated into English. 18mo. 4s. 6d.

DAWKINS (Prof. W. Boyd).—Early Man in Britain and his Place in the Tertiary Period. Medium 8vo. 25s.

DAWSON (Sir J. W.).—Acadian Geology, the Geological Structure, Organic Remains, and Mineral Resources of Nova Scotia, New Brunswick, and Prince Edward Island. 3rd Ed. 8vo. 21s.

DAWSON (James).—Australian Aborigines. Small 4to. 14s.

DAY (Rev. Lal Behari).—Bengal Peasant Life. Crown 8vo. 6s.

—— Folk Tales of Bengal. Cr. 8vo. 4s. 6d.

DAY (R. E.).—Electric Light Arithmetic. Pott 8vo. 2s.

DAY (H. G.).—Properties of Conic Sections proved Geometrically. Crown 8vo. 3s. 6d.

DAYS WITH SIR ROGER DE COVERLEY. From the Spectator. With Illustrations by Hugh Thomson. Fcp. 4to. 6s.

DEÁK (Francis).—Hungarian Statesman. A Memoir. 8vo. 12s. 6d.

DEFOE (Daniel). — The Adventures of Robinson Crusoe. Ed. by Henry Kingsley. Globe 8vo. 3s. 6d. [Globe Series. Golden Treasury Series Edition. Edited by J. W. Clark, M.A. 18mo. 4s. 6d.

DEFOE. By W. Minto. Crown 8vo. 1s. 6d.; sewed, 1s. [English Men of Letters Series.

DELAMOTTE (Prof. P. H.).—A Beginner's Drawing-Book. Progressively arranged. With upwards of 50 Plates. 3rd Edition. Crown 8vo. 3s. 6d.

DEMOCRACY: An American Novel. Crown 8vo. 4s. 6d.

DEMOSTHENES.—Adversus Leptinem. Ed. Rev. J. R. King, M.A. Fcp. 8vo. 4s. 6d.

—— The Oration on the Crown. Edited by B. Drake, M.A. 7th Ed. Fcp. 8vo. 4s. 6d.

—— The First Philippic. Edited by Rev. T. Gwatkin, M.A. Fcp. 8vo. 2s. 6d.

DEMOSTHENES.—By Prof. S. H. Butcher, M.A. Fcp. 8vo. 1s. 6d.

DE MAISTRE.—La Jeune Sibérienne et le Lépreux de la Cité d'Aoste. Edited, with Notes and Vocabulary, by S. Barlet, B.Sc. Globe 8vo. 1s. 6d.

DE MORGAN (Mary).—THE NECKLACE OF PRINCESS FIORIMONDE, AND OTHER STORIES. Illustrated by WALTER CRANE. Extra fcp. 8vo. 3s. 6d. Also a Large Paper Edition, with the Illustrations on India Paper. 100 copies only printed.

DE QUINCEY. By Prof. MASSON. Crown 8vo. 1s. 6d. ; sewed, 1s.

DEUTSCHE LYRIK.—THE GOLDEN TREASURY OF THE BEST GERMAN LYRICAL POEMS. Selected and arranged by Dr. BUCHHEIM. 18mo. 4s. 6d.

DE VERE (Aubrey).—ESSAYS CHIEFLY ON POETRY. 2 vols. Globe 8vo. 12s.

—— ESSAYS, CHIEFLY LITERARY AND ETHICAL. Globe 8vo. 6s.

DE WINT.—MEMOIR OF PETER DE WINT. By WALTER ARMSTRONG, B.A. Oxon. Illustrated by 24 Photogravures from the Artist's pictures. Super-Royal 4to. 31s. 6d.

DICEY (Prof. A. V.).—LECTURES INTRODUCTORY TO THE STUDY OF THE LAW OF THE CONSTITUTION. 3rd Edition. 8vo. 12s. 6d.

—— LETTERS ON UNIONIST DELUSIONS. Crown 8vo. 2s. 6d.

—— THE PRIVY COUNCIL. Crown 8vo. 3s. 6d.

DICKENS (Charles). — THE POSTHUMOUS PAPERS OF THE PICKWICK CLUB. With Notes and numerous Illustrations. Edited by CHARLES DICKENS the younger. 2 vols. Extra crown 8vo. 21s.

DICKENS. By A. W. WARD. Crown 8vo. 1s. 6d. ; sewed, 1s.

DIDEROT AND THE ENCYCLOPÆDISTS. By JOHN MORLEY. 2 vols. Globe 8vo. 10s.

DIGGLE (Rev. J. W.).—GODLINESS AND MANLINESS. A Miscellany of Brief Papers touching the Relation of Religion to Life. Crown 8vo. 6s.

DILETTANTI SOCIETY'S PUBLICATIONS.—ANTIQUITIES OF IONIA. Vols. I. II. and III. 2l. 2s. each, or 5l. 5s. the set. Part IV., folio, half morocco, 3l. 13s. 6d.

—— PENROSE (Francis C.). An Investigation of the Principles of Athenian Architecture. Illustrated by numerous engravings. New Edition. Enlarged. Folio. 7l. 7s.

—— SPECIMENS OF ANCIENT SCULPTURE : EGYPTIAN, ETRUSCAN, GREEK, AND ROMAN. Selected from different Collections in Great Britain by the Society of Dilettanti. Vol. II. Folio. 5l. 5s.

DILKE (Sir C. W.).—GREATER BRITAIN. A RECORD OF TRAVEL IN ENGLISH-SPEAKING COUNTRIES DURING 1866-67. (America, Australia, India.) 9th Edition. Crown 8vo. 6s.

—— PROBLEMS OF GREATER BRITAIN. Maps. 2 vols. 8vo. 36s.

DILLWYN (E. A.).—JILL. Crown 8vo. 6s.

—— JILL AND JACK. 2 vols. Globe 8vo. 12s.

DOBSON (Austin).—FIELDING. Crown 8vo. 1s. 6d. ; sewed, 1s.

DODGSON (C. L.).—EUCLID. Books I. and II. With Words substituted for the Algebraical Symbols used in the first edition. 4th Edition. Crown 8vo. 2s.

DODGSON (C. L.).—EUCLID AND HIS MODERN RIVALS. 2nd Edition. Cr. 8vo. 6s.

—— SUPPLEMENT TO FIRST EDITION "EUCLID AND HIS MODERN RIVALS." Crown 8vo. Sewed, 1s.

—— CURIOSA MATHEMATICA. Part I. A New Theory of Parallels. 2nd Ed. Cr. 8vo. 2s.

DONALDSON (Prof. James).—THE APOSTOLICAL FATHERS. A CRITICAL ACCOUNT OF THEIR GENUINE WRITINGS, AND OF THEIR DOCTRINES. 2nd Ed. Cr. 8vo. 7s. 6d.

DONISTHORPE (Wordsworth). — INDIVIDUALISM : A SYSTEM OF POLITICS. 8vo. 14s.

DOWDEN (Prof. E.).—SHAKSPERE. 18mo. 1s.

—— SOUTHEY. Crown 8vo. 1s. 6d. ; sewed, 1s.

DOYLE (J. A.).—HISTORY OF AMERICA. With Maps. 18mo. 4s. 6d.

DOYLE (Sir F. H.).—THE RETURN OF THE GUARDS : AND OTHER POEMS. Cr. 8vo. 7s. 6d.

DREW (W. H.).—A GEOMETRICAL TREATISE ON CONIC SECTIONS. 8th Ed. Cr. 8vo. 5s.

DRUMMOND (Prof. James).—INTRODUCTION TO THE STUDY OF THEOLOGY. Crown 8vo. 5s.

DRYDEN : ESSAYS OF. Edited by Prof. C. D. YONGE. Fcp. 8vo. 2s. 6d.

—— POETICAL WORKS. Edited, with Memoir, Revised Text, and Notes, by W. D. CHRISTIE, C.B. Globe 8vo. 3s. 6d. [Globe Edition.

DRYDEN. By G. SAINTSBURY. Crown 8vo. 1s. 6d. ; sewed, 1s.

DU CANE (Col. Sir E. F.).—THE PUNISHMENT AND PREVENTION OF CRIME. Crown 8vo. 3s. 6d.

DUFF (Right Hon. Sir M. E. Grant).—NOTES OF AN INDIAN JOURNEY. 8vo. 10s. 6d.

—— MISCELLANIES, POLITICAL AND LITERARY. 8vo. 10s. 6d.

DUMAS.—LES DEMOISELLES DE ST. CYR. Comédie par ALEXANDRE DUMAS. Edited by VICTOR OGER. 18mo. 1s. 6d.

DÜNTZER.—LIFE OF GOETHE. Translated by T. W. LYSTER. With Illustrations. 2 vols. Crown 8vo. 21s.

—— LIFE OF SCHILLER. Translated by P. E. PINKERTON. Illustrations. Cr. 8vo. 10s. 6d.

DU PRÉ (A. M. D.).—OUTLINES OF ENGLISH HISTORY. Globe 8vo. In 2 Parts.

DUPUIS (Prof. N. F.).—ELEMENTARY SYNTHETIC GEOMETRY OF THE POINT, LINE, AND CIRCLE IN THE PLANE. Gl. 8vo. 4s. 6d.

DYER (J. M.).—EXERCISES IN ANALYTICAL GEOMETRY. Crown 8vo. 4s. 6d.

EADIE (Prof. John).—THE ENGLISH BIBLE : AN EXTERNAL AND CRITICAL HISTORY OF THE VARIOUS ENGLISH TRANSLATIONS OF SCRIPTURE. 2 vols. 8vo. 28s.

—— ST. PAUL'S EPISTLES TO THE THESSALONIANS, COMMENTARY ON THE GREEK TEXT. 8vo. 12s.

—— LIFE OF JOHN EADIE, D.D., LL.D. By JAMES BROWN, D.D. 2nd Ed. Cr. 8vo. 7s. 6d.

EAGLES (T. H.).—CONSTRUCTIVE GEOMETRY OF PLANE CURVES. Crown 8vo. 12s.

EASTLAKE (Lady).—FELLOWSHIP: LETTERS ADDRESSED TO MY SISTER-MOURNERS. Cr. 8vo. 2s. 6d.

EBERS (Dr. George).—THE BURGOMASTER'S WIFE. Translated by CLARA BELL. Crown 8vo. 4s. 6d.

—— ONLY A WORD. Translated by CLARA BELL. Crown 8vo. 4s. 6d.

ECCE HOMO. A SURVEY OF THE LIFE AND WORK OF JESUS CHRIST. 20th Edition. Crown 8vo. 6s.

ECONOMICS, THE QUARTERLY JOURNAL OF. Vol. II. Part II. January, 1888. 8vo. 2s. 6d. Part III. 2s. 6d. Part IV. 2s. 6d. Vol. III. 4 parts, 2s. 6d. each. Vol. IV. Part I. 2s. 6d.

EDGAR (J. H.) and **PRITCHARD** (G. S.).— NOTE-BOOK ON PRACTICAL SOLID OR DESCRIPTIVE GEOMETRY, CONTAINING PROBLEMS WITH HELP FOR SOLUTION. 4th Edition, Enlarged. By ARTHUR G. MEEZE. Globe 8vo. 4s. 6d.

EDWARDS (Joseph). — AN ELEMENTARY TREATISE ON THE DIFFERENTIAL CALCULUS. Crown 8vo. 10s. 6d.

EDWARDS-MOSS (J. E.).—A SEASON IN SUTHERLAND. Crown 8vo. 4s. 6d.

EGGLESTON (E.). — THE HOUSEHOLD HISTORY OF THE UNITED STATES AND ITS PEOPLE. Illustrations and Maps. 4to. 12s.

EICKE (K. M.).—FIRST LESSONS IN LATIN. Extra fcp. 8vo. 2s.

EIMER (G. H. T.).—ORGANIC EVOLUTION. Translated by J. T. CUNNINGHAM, M.A. 8vo.

ELDERTON (W. A.).—MAP DRAWING AND MAP MAKING. Globe 8vo.

ELLERTON (Rev. John).—THE HOLIEST MANHOOD, AND ITS LESSONS FOR BUSY LIVES. Crown 8vo. 6s.

ELLIOT (Hon. A.).—THE STATE AND THE CHURCH. Crown 8vo. 3s. 6d.

ELLIOTT.—LIFE OF HENRY VENN ELLIOTT, OF BRIGHTON. By JOSIAH BATEMAN, M.A. 3rd Edition. Extra fcp. 8vo. 6s.

ELLIS (A. J.).—PRACTICAL HINTS ON THE QUANTITATIVE PRONUNCIATION OF LATIN. Extra fcp. 8vo. 4s. 6d.

ELLIS (Tristram).—SKETCHING FROM NATURE. With Illustrations by H. STACY MARKS, R.A., and the Author. 2nd Edition. Crown 8vo. 3s. 6d.

EMERSON.—THE LIFE OF RALPH WALDO EMERSON. By J. L. CABOT. 2 vols. Crown 8vo. 18s.

—— THE COLLECTED WORKS OF RALPH WALDO EMERSON. 6 vols. (1) MISCELLANIES. With an Introductory Essay by JOHN MORLEY. (2) ESSAYS. (3) POEMS. (4) ENGLISH TRAITS; AND REPRESENTATIVE MEN. (5) CONDUCT OF LIFE; AND SOCIETY AND SOLITUDE. (6) LETTERS; AND SOCIAL AIMS, &c. Globe 8vo. 5s. each.

ENGLAND (E. B.).—EXERCISES IN LATIN SYNTAX AND IDIOM. Arranged with reference to Roby's School Latin Grammar. Crown 8vo. 2s. 6d.

KEY to the above. Crown 8vo. 2s. 6d.

ENGLISH CITIZEN, THE.—A Series of Short Books on his Rights and Responsibilities. Edited by HENRY CRAIK, C.B. Crown 8vo. 3s. 6d. each.

CENTRAL GOVERNMENT. By H. D. TRAILL, D.C.L.

THE ELECTORATE AND THE LEGISLATURE. By SPENCER WALPOLE.

THE POOR LAW. By the Rev. T. W. FOWLE.

THE NATIONAL BUDGET; THE NATIONAL DEBT; TAXES AND RATES. By A. J. WILSON.

THE STATE IN RELATION TO LABOUR. By W. STANLEY JEVONS, LL.D., F.R.S.

THE STATE AND THE CHURCH. By the Hon. ARTHUR ELLIOTT, M.P.

FOREIGN RELATIONS. By SPENCER WALPOLE.

THE STATE IN ITS RELATION TO TRADE. By Sir T. H. FARRER, Bart.

LOCAL GOVERNMENT. By M. D. CHALMERS.

THE STATE IN ITS RELATION TO EDUCATION. By HENRY CRAIK, C.B.

THE LAND LAWS. By Sir F. POLLOCK, Bart. 2nd Edition.

COLONIES AND DEPENDENCIES.
Part I. INDIA. By J. S. COTTON, M.A.
II. THE COLONIES. By E. J. PAYNE.

JUSTICE AND POLICE. By F. W. MAITLAND.

THE PUNISHMENT AND PREVENTION OF CRIME. By Colonel Sir EDMUND DU CANE.

ENGLISH HISTORY, READINGS IN.— Selected and Edited by JOHN RICHARD GREEN. 3 Parts. Fcp. 8vo. 1s. 6d. each. Part I. Hengist to Cressy. II. Cressy to Cromwell. III. Cromwell to Balaklava.

ENGLISH ILLUSTRATED MAGAZINE, THE. — Profusely Illustrated. Published Monthly. Number 1. October, 1883. 6d. Vol. 1. 1884. 7s. 6d. Vols. II.—VI. Super royal 8vo, extra cloth, coloured edges. 8s. each. Cloth Covers for binding Volumes, 1s. 6d. each.

—— Proof Impressions of Engravings originally published in *The English Illustrated Magazine*. 1884. In Portfolio 4to. 21s.

ENGLISH MEN OF ACTION. — Crown 8vo. With Portraits. 2s. 6d. each.

The following Volumes are Ready:

GENERAL GORDON. By Col. Sir W. BUTLER.

HENRY V. By the Rev. A. J. CHURCH.

LIVINGSTONE. By THOMAS HUGHES.

LORD LAWRENCE. By Sir RICHARD TEMPLE.

WELLINGTON. By GEORGE HOOPER.

DAMPIER. By W. CLARK RUSSELL.

MONK. By JULIAN CORBETT.

STRAFFORD. By H. D. TRAILL.

WARREN HASTINGS. By Sir ALFRED LYALL.

PETERBOROUGH. By W. STEBBING.

The undermentioned are in the Press or in Preparation:

WARWICK, THE KING-MAKER. By C. W. OMAN.

DRAKE. By JULIAN CORBETT.

ENGLISH MEN OF ACTION—*contd.*

MONTROSE. By MOWBRAY MORRIS.

MARLBOROUGH. By Col. Sir WM. BUTLER.

CAPTAIN COOK. By WALTER BESANT.

RODNEY. By DAVID HANNAY.

CLIVE. By Colonel Sir CHARLES WILSON.

SIR JOHN MOORE. By Colonel MAURICE.

SIR CHARLES NAPIER. By Col. BUTLER.

SIR HENRY HAVELOCK. By ARCHIBALD FORBES.

ENGLISH MEN OF LETTERS.—Edited by JOHN MORLEY. Crown 8vo. 2s. 6d. each. Cheap Edition. 1s. 6d.; sewed, 1s.

JOHNSON. By LESLIE STEPHEN.

SCOTT. By R. H. HUTTON.

GIBBON. By J. COTTER MORISON.

HUME. By T. H. HUXLEY.

GOLDSMITH. By WILLIAM BLACK.

SHELLEY. By J. A. SYMONDS.

DEFOE. By W. MINTO.

BURNS. By Principal SHAIRP.

SPENSER. By the DEAN OF ST. PAUL'S.

THACKERAY. By ANTHONY TROLLOPE.

MILTON. By MARK PATTISON.

BURKE. By JOHN MORLEY.

HAWTHORNE. By HENRY JAMES.

SOUTHEY. By Prof. DOWDEN.

BUNYAN. By J. A. FROUDE.

CHAUCER. By Prof. A. W. WARD.

COWPER. By GOLDWIN SMITH.

POPE. By LESLIE STEPHEN.

BYRON. By Prof. NICHOL.

DRYDEN. By G. SAINTSBURY.

LOCKE. By Prof. FOWLER.

WORDSWORTH. By F. W. H. MYERS.

LANDOR. By SIDNEY COLVIN.

DE QUINCEY. By Prof. MASSON.

CHARLES LAMB. By Rev. ALFRED AINGER.

BENTLEY. By Prof. JEBB.

DICKENS. By A. W. WARD.

GRAY. By EDMUND GOSSE.

SWIFT. By LESLIE STEPHEN.

STERNE. By H. D. TRAILL.

MACAULAY. By J. COTTER MORISON.

FIELDING. By AUSTIN DOBSON.

SHERIDAN. By Mrs. OLIPHANT.

ADDISON. By W. J. COURTHOPE.

BACON. By the DEAN OF ST. PAUL'S.

COLERIDGE. By H. D. TRAILL.

SIR PHILIP SIDNEY. By J. A. SYMONDS.

KEATS. By SIDNEY COLVIN.

ENGLISH POETS. Selections, with Critical Introductions by various Writers, and a General Introduction by MATTHEW ARNOLD. Edited by T. H. WARD, M.A. 4 vols. Crown 8vo. 7s. 6d. each. Vol. I. CHAUCER TO DONNE. II. BEN JONSON TO DRYDEN. III. ADDISON TO BLAKE. IV. WORDSWORTH TO ROSSETTI.

ENGLISH STATESMEN (TWELVE). Crown 8vo. 2s. 6d. each.

WILLIAM THE CONQUEROR. By EDWARD A. FREEMAN, D.C.L., LL.D. [*Ready.*

HENRY II. By Mrs. J. R. GREEN. [*Ready.*

EDWARD I. By F. YORK POWELL.

HENRY VII. By JAMES GARDINER. [*Ready.*

CARDINAL WOLSEY. By Prof. M. CREIGHTON. [*Ready.*

ELIZABETH. By E. S. BEESLEY.

OLIVER CROMWELL. By FREDERIC HARRISON. [*Ready.*

WILLIAM III. By H. D. TRAILL. [*Ready.*

WALPOLE. By JOHN MORLEY. [*Ready.*

CHATHAM. By JOHN MORLEY.

PITT. By JOHN MORLEY.

PEEL. By J. R. THURSFIELD.

ESSEX FIELD CLUB MEMOIRS. Vol. I. REPORT ON THE EAST ANGLIAN EARTHQUAKE OF 22ND APRIL, 1884. By RAPHAEL MELDOLA, F.R.S., and WILLIAM WHITE, F.E.S. Maps and Illustrations. 8vo. 3s. 6d.

ETON COLLEGE, HISTORY OF, 1440—1884. By H. C. MAXWELL LYTE, C.B. Illustrations. 2nd Ed. Med. 8vo. Cloth, 21s.

EURIPIDES.—MEDEA. Edited by A. W. VERRALL, Litt.D. 8vo. 7s. 6d.

—— HIPPOLYTUS. Edited by J. P. MAHAFFY, M.A., and J. B. BURY. Fcp. 8vo. 3s. 6d.

—— HECUBA. Edited by Rev. JOHN BOND, M.A., and A. S. WALPOLE, M.A. 18mo. 1s. 6d.

—— IPHIGENIA IN TAURIS. Edited by E. B. ENGLAND, M.A. Fcp. 8vo. 4s. 6d.

—— MEDEA. Edited by A. W. VERRALL, Litt.D. Fcp. 8vo. 3s. 6d.

—— ION. Edited by M. A. BAYFIELD, M.A. Fcp. 8vo. 3s. 6d.

EURIPIDES. By Prof. MAHAFFY. Fcp. 8vo. 1s. 6d.

EUROPEAN HISTORY, NARRATED IN A SERIES OF HISTORICAL SELECTIONS FROM THE BEST AUTHORITIES. Edited and arranged by E. M. SEWELL and C. M. YONGE. 2 vols. 3rd Edition. Crown 8vo. 6s. each.

EUTROPIUS. Adapted for the Use of Beginners. With Notes, Exercises, and Vocabularies. By W. WELCH, M.A., and C. G. DUFFIELD, M.A. 18mo. 1s. 6d.

EVANS (Sebastian). — BROTHER FABIAN'S MANUSCRIPT, AND OTHER POEMS. Fcp. 8vo, cloth. 6s.

—— IN THE STUDIO: A DECADE OF POEMS. Extra fcp. 8vo. 5s.

EVERETT (Prof. J. D.).—UNITS AND PHYSICAL CONSTANTS. 2nd Ed. Globe 8vo. 5s.

FAIRFAX.—LIFE OF ROBERT FAIRFAX OF STEETON, Vice-Admiral, Alderman, and Member for York, A.D. 1666—1725. By CLEMENTS R. MARKHAM, C.B. 8vo. 12s. 6d.

FAITH AND CONDUCT: AN ESSAY ON VERIFIABLE RELIGION. Crown 8vo. 7s. 6d.

FARRAR (Archdeacon).—THE FALL OF MAN, AND OTHER SERMONS. 5th Ed. Cr. 8vo. 6s.

FARRAR (Archdeacon).—The Witness of History to Christ. Being the Hulsean Lectures for 1870. 7th Edit. Cr. 8vo. 5s.

—— Seekers after God. The Lives of Seneca, Epictetus, and Marcus Aurelius. 12th Edition. Crown 8vo. 6s.

—— The Silence and Voices of God. University and other Sermons. 7th Ed. Cr. 8vo. 6s.

—— In the Days of thy Youth. Sermons on Practical Subjects, preached at Marlborough College. 9th Edition. Cr. 8vo. 9s.

—— Eternal Hope. Five Sermons, preached in Westminster Abbey. 28th Thousand. Crown 8vo. 6s.

—— Saintly Workers. Five Lenten Lectures, delivered at St. Andrew's, Holborn. 3rd Edition. Crown 8vo. 6s.

—— Ephphatha; or, The Amelioration of the World. Sermons preached at Westminster Abbey. Crown 8vo. 6s.

—— Mercy and Judgment. A few Last Words on Christian Eschatology. 2nd Ed. Crown 8vo. 10s. 6d.

—— The Messages of the Books. Being Discourses and Notes on the Books of the New Testament. 8vo. 14s.

—— Sermons and Addresses delivered in America. Crown 8vo. 7s. 6d.

—— The History of Interpretation. Being the Bampton Lectures, 1885. 8vo. 16s.

FARREN (Robert).—The Granta and the Cam, from Byron's Pool to Ely. Thirty-six Etchings. Large Imperial, cloth gilt.
A few Copies, Proofs, Large Paper, of which but 50 were printed, half morocco.

—— Cambridge and its Neighbourhood. A Series of Etchings. With an Introduction by John Willis Clark, M.A. Imp. 4to.

—— A Round of Melodies. A Series of Etched Designs. Oblong folio, half morocco.

—— The Birds of Aristophanes. 13s. net. Proofs.

—— The Battle Ground of the Eights. The Thames, the Isis, and the Cam. Oblong 4to, cloth.

—— Cathedral Cities: Ely and Norwich. With Introduction by E. A. Freeman, D.C.L. Col. 4to.
Proofs on Japanese paper.

—— —— Peterborough. With the Abbeys of Crowland and Thorney. With Introduction by Edmund Venables, M.A. Col. 4to. 2l. 2s. net. Proofs, folio, 5l. 5s. net.
The Edition is limited to 125 Small Paper and 45 Large.

—— The Eumenides of Æschylus. As performed by Members of the University at the Theatre Royal, Cambridge. Oblong 4to. Small size, 10s. 6d. net. Large size, India Proofs, 21s. net. On Whatman paper, 27s. net.

—— The Oedipus Tyrannus of Sophocles. As performed at Cambridge. Oblong 4to. Prints, 10s. 6d. net. Proofs, 21s. net.

FASNACHT (G. Eugène).—The Organic Method of Studying Languages. I. French. Extra fcp. 8vo. 3s. 6d.

—— A Synthetic French Grammar for Schools. Crown 8vo. 3s. 6d.

FAWCETT (Rt. Hon. Henry).—Manual of Political Economy. 7th Edition, revised. Crown 8vo. 12s.

—— An Explanatory Digest of Professor Fawcett's Manual of Political Economy. By Cyril A. Waters. Cr. 8vo. 2s. 6d.

—— Speeches on some Current Political Questions. 8vo. 10s. 6d.

—— Free Trade and Protection. 9th Edition. Crown 8vo. 3s. 6d.

FAWCETT (Mrs. H.).—Political Economy for Beginners, with Questions. 7th Edition. 18mo. 2s. 6d.

—— Some Eminent Women of Our Times. Short Biographical Sketches. Cr. 8vo. 2s. 6d.

FAWCETT (Rt. Hon. Henry and Mrs. H.).—Essays and Lectures on Political and Social Subjects. 8vo. 10s. 6d.

FAY (Amy.).—Music-Study in Germany. With a Preface by Sir George Grove, D.C.L. Crown 8vo. 4s. 6d.

FEARNLEY (W.).—A Manual of Elementary Practical Histology. Cr. 8vo. 7s. 6d.

FEARON (D. R.).—School Inspection. 6th Edition. Crown 8vo. 2s. 6d.

FERREL (Prof. W.).—A Popular Treatise on the Winds. 8vo. 18s.

FERRERS (Rev. N. M.).—A Treatise on Trilinear Co-ordinates, the Method of Reciprocal Polars, and the Theory of Projections. 3rd Ed. Cr. 8vo. 6s. 6d.

—— Spherical Harmonics and Subjects connected with them. Crown 8vo. 7s. 6d.

FIELDING.—By Austin Dobson. Crown 8vo. 1s. 6d.; sewed, 1s.

FINCK (Henry T.).—Romantic Love and Personal Beauty. 2 vols. Cr. 8vo. 18s.

FIRST LESSONS IN BUSINESS MATTERS. By a Banker's Daughter. 2nd Edition. 18mo. 1s.

FISHER (Rev. Osmond).—Physics of the Earth's Crust. 2nd Edition. 8vo. 12s.

FISKE (John).—Outlines of Cosmic Philosophy, based on the Doctrine of Evolution. 2 vols. 8vo. 25s.

—— Darwinism, and other Essays. Crown 8vo. 7s. 6d.

—— Man's Destiny Viewed in the Light of his Origin. Crown 8vo. 3s. 6d.

—— American Political Ideas Viewed from the Stand-point of Universal History. Crown 8vo. 4s.

—— The Critical Period in American History, 1783—89. Ex. Cr. 8vo. 10s. 6d.

—— The Beginnings of New England; or, The Puritan Theocracy in its Relations to Civil and Religious Liberty. Crown 8vo. 7s. 6d.

FISON (L.) and HOWITT (A. W.).—Kamilaroi and Kurnai Group. Group-Marriage and Relationship and Marriage by Elopement, drawn chiefly from the usage of the Australian Aborigines, also the Kurnai Tribe, their Customs in Peace and War. With an Introduction by Lewis H. Morgan, LL.D. 8vo. 15s.

FITZGERALD (Edward).—LETTERS AND LITERARY REMAINS OF. Ed. by W. ALDIS WRIGHT, M.A. 3 vols. Crown 8vo. 31s. 6d.

FITZ GERALD (Caroline).—VENETIA VICTRIX, AND OTHER POEMS. Ex. fcp. 8vo. 3s. 6d.

FLEAY (Rev. F. G.).—A SHAKESPEARE MANUAL. Extra fcp. 8vo. 4s. 6d.

FLEISCHER (Dr. Emil).—A SYSTEM OF VOLUMETRIC ANALYSIS. Translated by M. M. PATTISON MUIR, F.R.S.E. Cr. 8vo. 7s. 6d.

FLEMING (George).—A NILE NOVEL. Gl. 8vo. 2s.

—— MIRAGE. A Novel. Globe 8vo. 2s.

—— THE HEAD OF MEDUSA. Globe 8vo. 2s.

—— VESTIGIA. Globe 8vo. 2s.

FLITTERS, TATTERS, AND THE COUNSELLOR; WEEDS; AND OTHER SKETCHES. By the Author of "Hogan, M.P." Globe 8vo. 2s.

FLORIAN'S FABLES. Selected and Edited by Rev. CHARLES YELD, M.A. Illustrated. Globe 8vo. 1s. 6d.
[*Primary French and German Readers.*

FLOWER (Prof. W. H.).—AN INTRODUCTION TO THE OSTEOLOGY OF THE MAMMALIA. With numerous Illustrations. 3rd Edition, revised with the assistance of HANS GADOW, Ph.D., M.A. Crown 8vo. 10s. 6d.

FLÜCKIGER (F. A.) and HANBURY (D.). —PHARMACOGRAPHIA. A History of the principal Drugs of Vegetable Origin met with in Great Britain and India. 2nd Edition, revised. 8vo. 21s.

FO'C'SLE YARNS, including "Betsy Lee," and other Poems. Crown 8vo. 7s. 6d.

FORBES (Archibald).—SOUVENIRS OF SOME CONTINENTS. Crown 8vo. 6s.

FORBES (Edward).—MEMOIR OF. By GEORGE WILSON, M.D., and ARCHIBALD GEIKIE, F.R.S., &c. Demy 8vo. 14s.

FORBES (Rev. Granville).—THE VOICE OF GOD IN THE PSALMS. Crown 8vo. 6s 6d.

FORBES (George).—THE TRANSIT OF VENUS. Crown 8vo. 3s. 6d. [*Nature Series.*

FORSYTH (A. R.).—A TREATISE OF DIFFERENTIAL EQUATIONS. Demy 8vo. 14s.

FOSTER (Prof. Michael).—A TEXT-BOOK OF PHYSIOLOGY. With Illustrations. 5th Ed. 3 Parts. Part I., comprising Book I. Blood— The Tissues of Movement, the Vascular Mechanism. 8vo. 10s. 6d. — Part II., comprising Book II. The Tissues of Chemical Action, with their Respective Mechanisms—Nutrition. 10s. 6d.
4th Edition. Part III., comprising Book III. The Central Nervous System and its Instruments. Book IV. The Tissues and Mechanisms of Reproduction. 8vo. 7s. 6d.

—— PRIMER OF PHYSIOLOGY. New Edition. 18mo. 1s. [*Science Primers.*

FOSTER (Prof. Michael) and BALFOUR (F. M.) (the late).—THE ELEMENTS OF EMBRYOLOGY. Edited by ADAM SEDGWICK, M.A., and WALTER HEAPE. With Illustrations. 3rd Edition, revised and enlarged. Crown 8vo. 10s. 6d.

FOSTER (Michael) and LANGLEY (J. N.). —A COURSE OF ELEMENTARY PRACTICAL PHYSIOLOGY AND HISTOLOGY. 6th Edition, enlarged. Crown 8vo. 7s. 6d.

FOTHERGILL (Dr. J. Milner).—THE PRACTITIONER'S HANDBOOK OF TREATMENT; OR, THE PRINCIPLES OF THERAPEUTICS. 3rd Edition, enlarged. 8vo. 16s.

—— THE ANTAGONISM OF THERAPEUTIC AGENTS, AND WHAT IT TEACHES. Crown 8vo. 6s.

—— FOOD FOR THE INVALID, THE CONVALESCENT, THE DYSPEPTIC, AND THE GOUTY. 2nd Edition. Crown 8vo. 3s. 6d.

FOWLE (Rev. T. W.).—THE POOR LAW. Cr. 8vo. 3s. 6d. [*English Citizen Series.*

—— A NEW ANALOGY BETWEEN REVEALED RELIGION AND THE COURSE AND CONSTITUTION OF NATURE. Crown 8vo. 6s.

FOWLER (Rev. Thomas).—LOCKE. Crown 8vo. 1s. 6d.; sewed, 1s.

—— PROGRESSIVE MORALITY: AN ESSAY IN ETHICS. Crown 8vo. 5s.

FOWLER (W. W.).—TALES OF THE BIRDS. Illustrated. Crown 8vo. 3s. 6d.

—— A YEAR WITH THE BIRDS. Illustrated. Crown 8vo. 3s. 6d.

FOX (Dr. Wilson).—ON THE ARTIFICIAL PRODUCTION OF TUBERCLE IN THE LOWER ANIMALS. With Plates. 4to. 5s. 6d.

—— ON THE TREATMENT OF HYPERPYREXIA, AS ILLUSTRATED IN ACUTE ARTICULAR RHEUMATISM BY MEANS OF THE EXTERNAL APPLICATION OF COLD. 8vo. 2s. 6d.

FRAMJI (Dosabhai).—HISTORY OF THE PARSIS: INCLUDING THEIR MANNERS, CUSTOMS, RELIGION, AND PRESENT POSITION. With Illustrations. 2 vols. Med. 8vo. 36s.

FRANKLAND (Prof. Percy).—A HANDBOOK OF AGRICULTURAL CHEMICAL ANALYSIS. Founded upon "Leitfaden für die Agricultur-Chemische Analyse," von Dr. F. KROCKER. Crown 8vo. 7s. 6d.

FRASER.—SERMONS. By the Right Rev. JAMES FRASER, D.D., Second Bishop of Manchester. Edited by Rev. JOHN W. DIGGLE. 2 vols. Crown 8vo. 6s. each.

FRASER — HUGHES. — JAMES FRASER, SECOND BISHOP OF MANCHESTER: A Memoir. By T. HUGHES. Crown 8vo. 6s.

FRASER-TYTLER. — SONGS IN MINOR KEYS. By C. C. FRASER-TYTLER (Mrs. EDWARD LIDDELL). 2nd Ed. 18mo. 6s.

FRATERNITY: A Romance. 2 vols. Cr. 8vo. 21s.

FREDERICK (Mrs.).—HINTS TO HOUSEWIVES ON SEVERAL POINTS, PARTICULARLY ON THE PREPARATION OF ECONOMICAL AND TASTEFUL DISHES. Crown 8vo. 1s.

FREEMAN (Prof. E. A.).—HISTORY OF THE CATHEDRAL CHURCH OF WELLS. Crown 8vo. 3s. 6d.

—— OLD ENGLISH HISTORY. With 5 Col. Maps. 9th Edition. revised. Extra fcp. 8vo. 6s.

—— HISTORICAL ESSAYS. First Series. 4th Edition. 8vo. 10s. 6d.

FREEMAN (Prof. E. A.). — HISTORICAL ESSAYS. Second Series. 3rd Edition. With Additional Essays. 8vo. 10s. 6d.

—— —— Third Series. 8vo. 12s.

—— THE GROWTH OF THE ENGLISH CONSTITUTION FROM THE EARLIEST TIMES. 5th Edition. Crown 8vo. 5s.

—— GENERAL SKETCH OF EUROPEAN HISTORY. With Maps, &c. 18mo. 3s. 6d.

—— EUROPE. 18mo. 1s. [Literature Primers.

—— COMPARATIVE POLITICS. Lectures at the Royal Institution. To which is added "The Unity of History." 8vo. 14s.

—— HISTORICAL AND ARCHITECTURAL SKETCHES: CHIEFLY ITALIAN. Illustrated by the Author. Crown 8vo. 10s. 6d.

—— SUBJECT AND NEIGHBOUR LANDS OF VENICE. Illustrated. Crown 8vo. 10s. 6d.

—— ENGLISH TOWNS AND DISTRICTS. A Series of Addresses and Essays. 8vo. 14s.

—— THE OFFICE OF THE HISTORICAL PROFESSOR. Inaugural Lecture at Oxford. Cr. 8vo. 2s.

—— DISESTABLISHMENT AND DISENDOWMENT. WHAT ARE THEY? 4th Ed. Cr. 8vo. 1s.

—— GREATER GREECE AND GREATER BRITAIN: GEORGE WASHINGTON THE EXPANDER OF ENGLAND. With an Appendix on IMPERIAL FEDERATION. Cr. 8vo. 3s. 6d.

—— THE METHODS OF HISTORICAL STUDY. Eight Lectures at Oxford. 8vo. 10s. 6d.

—— THE CHIEF PERIODS OF EUROPEAN HISTORY. Six Lectures read in the University of Oxford, with an Essay on GREEK CITIES UNDER ROMAN RULE. 8vo. 10s. 6d.

—— FOUR OXFORD LECTURES, 1887. FIFTY YEARS OF EUROPEAN HISTORY—TEUTONIC CONQUEST IN GAUL AND BRITAIN. 8vo. 5s.

—— WILLIAM THE CONQUEROR. Crown 8vo. 2s. 6d. [Twelve English Statesmen.

FRENCH COURSE.—See p. 37.

FRENCH READINGS FROM ROMAN HISTORY. Selected from various Authors. With Notes by C. COLBECK. 18mo. 4s. 6d.

FRIEDMANN (Paul).—ANNE BOLEYN. A Chapter of English History, 1527—36. 2 vols. 8vo. 28s.

FROST (Percival).—AN ELEMENTARY TREATISE ON CURVE TRACING. 8vo. 12s.

—— THE FIRST THREE SECTIONS OF NEWTON'S PRINCIPIA. 3rd Edition. 8vo. 12s.

—— SOLID GEOMETRY. 3rd Edition. 8vo. 16s.

—— HINTS FOR THE SOLUTION OF PROBLEMS IN THE THIRD EDITION OF SOLID GEOMETRY. 8vo. 8s. 6d.

FROUDE (J. A.).—BUNYAN. Crown 8vo. 1s. 6d.; sewed, 1s.

FURNIVALL (F. J.).—LE MORTE ARTHUR. Edited from the Harleian MS. 2252, in the British Museum. Fcp. 8vo. 7s. 6d.

FYFFE (C. A.).—GREECE. 18mo. 1s.

GAIRDNER (Jas.). HENRY VII. Crown 8vo. 2s. 6d.

GALTON (Francis). — METEOROGRAPHICA; OR, METHODS OF MAPPING THE WEATHER. 4to. 9s.

GALTON (F.).—ENGLISH MEN OF SCIENCE: THEIR NATURE AND NURTURE. 8vo. 8s. 6d.

—— INQUIRIES INTO HUMAN FACULTY AND ITS DEVELOPMENT. 8vo. 16s.

—— RECORD OF FAMILY FACULTIES. Consisting of Tabular Forms and Directions for Entering Data. 4to. 2s. 6d.

—— LIFE HISTORY ALBUM: Being a Personal Note-book, combining the chief advantages of a Diary, Photograph Album, a Register of Height, Weight, and other Anthropometrical Observations, and a Record of Illnesses. 4to. 3s. 6d.—Or, with Cards of Wools for Testing Colour Vision. 4s. 6d.

—— NATURAL INHERITANCE. 8vo. 9s.

GAMGEE (Prof. Arthur).—A TEXT-BOOK OF THE PHYSIOLOGICAL CHEMISTRY OF THE ANIMAL BODY, including an account of the Chemical Changes occurring in Disease. Vol. I. Med. 8vo. 18s. [Vol. II. in the Press.

GANGUILLET (E.) and KUTTER (W. R.). —A GENERAL FORMULA FOR THE UNIFORM FLOW OF WATER IN RIVERS AND OTHER CHANNELS. Translated by RUDOLPH HERING and JOHN C. TRAUTWINE, Jun. 8vo. 17s.

GARDNER (Percy).—SAMOS AND SAMIAN COINS. An Essay. 8vo. 7s. 6d.

GARNETT (R.).—IDYLLS AND EPIGRAMS. Chiefly from the Greek Anthology. Fcp. 8vo. 2s. 6d.

GASKOIN (Mrs. Herman). — CHILDREN'S TREASURY OF BIBLE STORIES. 18mo. 1s. each. — Part I. Old Testament; II. New Testament; III. Three Apostles.

GEDDES (Prof. William D.).—THE PROBLEM OF THE HOMERIC POEMS. 8vo. 14s.

—— FLOSCULI GRÆCI BOREALES, SIVE ANTHOLOGIA GRÆCA ABERDONENSIS CONTEXUIT GULIELMUS D. GEDDES. Cr. 8vo. 6s.

—— THE PHAEDO OF PLATO. Edited with Introduction and Notes. 2nd Ed. 8vo. 8s. 6d.

GEIKIE (Archibald).—PRIMER OF PHYSICAL GEOGRAPHY. With Illustrations. 18mo. 1s.

—— PRIMER OF GEOLOGY. Illust. 18mo. 1s.

—— ELEMENTARY LESSONS IN PHYSICAL GEOGRAPHY. With Illustrations. Fcp. 8vo. 4s. 6d.—QUESTIONS ON THE SAME. 1s. 6d.

—— OUTLINES OF FIELD GEOLOGY. With numerous Illustrations. Crown 8vo. 3s. 6d.

—— TEXT-BOOK OF GEOLOGY. Illustrated. 2nd Edition. 7th Thousand. Med. 8vo. 28s.

—— CLASS-BOOK OF GEOLOGY. With upwards of 200 New Illustrations. Cr. 8vo. 10s. 6d.

—— GEOLOGICAL SKETCHES AT HOME AND ABROAD. With Illustrations. 8vo. 10s. 6d.

—— THE SCENERY OF SCOTLAND. Viewed in connection with its Physical Geology. 2nd Edition. Crown 8vo. 12s. 6d.

—— THE TEACHING OF GEOGRAPHY. A Practical Handbook for the use of Teachers. Globe 8vo. 2s.

—— GEOGRAPHY OF THE BRITISH ISLES. 18mo. 1s.

GEOMETRY, SYLLABUS OF PLANE. Corresponding to Euclid I.—VI. Prepared by the Association for the Improvement of Geometrical Teaching. 9th Ed. Cr. 8vo. 1s.

GIBBON. By J. C. MORISON. Crown 8vo. 1s. 6d. ; sewed, 1s.

GILMAN (N. P.).—PROFIT-SHARING BETWEEN EMPLOYER AND EMPLOYÉ. A Study in the Evolution of the Wages System. Crown 8vo. 7s. 6d.

GILMORE (Rev. John).—STORM WARRIORS ; OR, LIFEBOAT WORK ON THE GOODWIN SANDS. Crown 8vo. 3s. 6d.

GLADSTONE (Rt. Hon. W. E.).—HOMERIC SYNCHRONISM. An Inquiry into the Time and Place of Homer. Crown 8vo. 6s.

—— PRIMER OF HOMER. 18mo. 1s.

GLADSTONE (J. H.).—SPELLING REFORM FROM AN EDUCATIONAL POINT OF VIEW. 3rd Edition. Crown 8vo. 1s. 6d.

GLADSTONE (J. H.) and TRIBE (A.).— THE CHEMISTRY OF THE SECONDARY BATTERIES OF PLANTÉ AND FAURE. Crown 8vo. 2s. 6d.

GLAISTER (Elizabeth). — NEEDLEWORK. Crown 8vo. 2s. 6d.

GLOBE EDITIONS. Gl. 8vo. 3s. 6d. each.

THE COMPLETE WORKS OF WILLIAM SHAKESPEARE. Edited by W. G. CLARK and W. ALDIS WRIGHT.

MORTE D'ARTHUR. Sir Thomas Malory's Book of King Arthur and of his Noble Knights of the Round Table. The Edition of Caxton, revised for modern use. By Sir E. STRACHEY, Bart.

THE POETICAL WORKS OF SIR WALTER SCOTT. With Essay by Prof. PALGRAVE.

THE POETICAL WORKS AND LETTERS OF ROBERT BURNS. Edited, with Life and Glossarial Index, by ALEXANDER SMITH.

THE ADVENTURES OF ROBINSON CRUSOE. With Introduction by HENRY KINGSLEY.

GOLDSMITH'S MISCELLANEOUS WORKS. Edited by Prof. MASSON.

POPE'S POETICAL WORKS. Edited, with Memoir and Notes, by Prof. WARD.

SPENSER'S COMPLETE WORKS. Edited by R. MORRIS. Memoir by J. W. HALES.

DRYDEN'S POETICAL WORKS. A revised Text and Notes. By W. D. CHRISTIE.

COWPER'S POETICAL WORKS. Edited by the Rev. W. BENHAM, B.D.

VIRGIL'S WORKS. Rendered into English by JAMES LONSDALE and S. LEE.

HORACE'S WORKS. Rendered into English by JAMES LONSDALE and S. LEE.

MILTON'S POETICAL WORKS. Edited, with Introduction, &c., by Prof. MASSON.

GLOBE READERS, THE.—A New Series of Reading Books for Standards I.—VI. Selected, arranged, and Edited by A. F. MURISON, sometime English Master at Aberdeen Grammar School. With Original Illustrations. Globe 8vo.

Primer I.	…	…	(48 pp.)	3d.
Primer II.	…	…	(48 pp.)	3d.
Book I.	…	…	(96 pp.)	6d.
Book II.	…	…	(136 pp.)	9d.
Book III.	…	…	(232 pp.)	1s. 3d.
Book IV.	…	…	(328 pp.)	1s. 9d.
Book V.	…	…	(416 pp.)	2s.
Book VI.	…	…	(448 pp.)	2s. 6d.

GLOBE READERS, THE SHORTER.—A New Series of Reading Books for Standards I.—VI. Edited by A. F. MURISON. Gl. 8vo.

Primer I.	…	…	(48 pp.)	3d.
Primer II.	…	…	(48 pp.)	3d.
Standard I.	…	…	(92 pp.)	6d.
Standard II.	…	…	(124 pp.)	9d.
Standard III.	…	…	(178 pp.)	1s.
Standard IV.	…	…	(182 pp.)	1s.
Standard V.	…	…	(216 pp.)	1s. 3d.
Standard VI.	…	…	(228 pp.)	1s. 6d.

₊ This Series has been abridged from the "Globe Readers" to meet the demand for smaller reading books.

GLOBE READINGS FROM STANDARD AUTHORS. Globe 8vo.

COWPER'S TASK : An Epistle to Joseph Hill, Esq. ; TIROCINIUM, or a Review of the Schools ; and the HISTORY OF JOHN GILPIN. Edited, with Notes, by Rev. WILLIAM BENHAM, B.D. 1s.

GOLDSMITH'S VICAR OF WAKEFIELD. With a Memoir of Goldsmith by Prof. MASSON. 1s.

LAMB'S (CHARLES) TALES FROM SHAKSPEARE. Edited, with Preface, by Rev. ALFRED AINGER, M.A. 2s.

SCOTT'S (SIR WALTER) LAY OF THE LAST MINSTREL : and the LADY OF THE LAKE. Edited by Prof. F. T. PALGRAVE. 1s.

MARMION : and THE LORD OF THE ISLES. By the same Editor. 1s.

THE CHILDREN'S GARLAND FROM THE BEST POETS. Selected and arranged by COVENTRY PATMORE. 2s.

A BOOK OF GOLDEN DEEDS OF ALL TIMES AND ALL COUNTRIES. Gathered and narrated anew by CHARLOTTE M. YONGE. 2s.

GODFRAY (Hugh). — AN ELEMENTARY TREATISE ON LUNAR THEORY. 2nd Edition. Crown 8vo. 5s. 6d.

—— A TREATISE ON ASTRONOMY, FOR THE USE OF COLLEGES AND SCHOOLS. 8vo. 12s. 6d.

GOETHE—CARLYLE.—CORRESPONDENCE BETWEEN GOETHE AND CARLYLE. Edited by C. E. NORTON. Crown 8vo. 9s.

GOETHE'S LIFE. By Prof. HEINRICH DÜNTZER. Translated by T. W. LYSTER. 2 vols. Crown 8vo. 21s.

GOETHE.—FAUST. Translated into English Verse by JOHN STUART BLACKIE. 2nd Edition. Crown 8vo. 9s.

—— —— Part I. Edited, with Introduction and Notes ; followed by an Appendix on Part II., by JANE LEE. 18mo. 4s. 6d.

—— REYNARD THE FOX. Translated into English Verse by A. DOUGLAS AINSLIE. Crown 8vo. 7s. 6d.

—— GÖTZ VON BERLICHINGEN. Edited by H. A. BULL, M.A. 18mo. 2s.

GOLDEN TREASURY SERIES. — Uniformly printed in 18mo, with Vignette Titles by Sir J. E. MILLAIS, Sir NOEL PATON, T. WOOLNER, W. HOLMAN HUNT, ARTHUR HUGHES, &c. Engraved on Steel. Bound in extra cloth. 4s. 6d. each.

THE GOLDEN TREASURY OF THE BEST SONGS AND LYRICAL POEMS IN THE ENGLISH LANGUAGE. Selected and arranged, with Notes, by Prof. F. T. PALGRAVE.

GOLDEN TREASURY SERIES—*contd.*

THE CHILDREN'S GARLAND FROM THE BEST POETS. Selected by COVENTRY PATMORE.

THE BOOK OF PRAISE. From the best English Hymn Writers. Selected by ROUNDELL, EARL OF SELBORNE.

THE FAIRY BOOK: THE BEST POPULAR FAIRY STORIES. Selected by the Author of "John Halifax, Gentleman."

THE BALLAD BOOK. A Selection of the Choicest British Ballads. Edited by WILLIAM ALLINGHAM.

THE JEST BOOK. The Choicest Anecdotes and Sayings. Arranged by MARK LEMON.

BACON'S ESSAYS AND COLOURS OF GOOD AND EVIL. With Notes and Glossarial Index by W. ALDIS WRIGHT, M.A.

THE PILGRIM'S PROGRESS FROM THIS WORLD TO THAT WHICH IS TO COME. By JOHN BUNYAN.

THE SUNDAY BOOK OF POETRY FOR THE YOUNG. Selected by C. F. ALEXANDER.

A BOOK OF GOLDEN DEEDS OF ALL TIMES AND ALL COUNTRIES. By the Author of "The Heir of Redclyffe."

THE ADVENTURES OF ROBINSON CRUSOE. Edited by J. W. CLARK, M.A.

THE REPUBLIC OF PLATO. Translated by J. LL. DAVIES, M.A., and D. J. VAUGHAN.

THE SONG BOOK. Words and Tunes Selected and arranged by JOHN HULLAH.

LA LYRE FRANÇAISE. Selected and arranged, with Notes, by G. MASSON.

TOM BROWN'S SCHOOL DAYS. By AN OLD BOY.

A BOOK OF WORTHIES. By the Author of "The Heir of Redclyffe."

GUESSES AT TRUTH. By TWO BROTHERS.

THE CAVALIER AND HIS LADY. Selections from the Works of the First Duke and Duchess of Newcastle. With an Introductory Essay by EDWARD JENKINS.

SCOTTISH SONG. Compiled by MARY CARLYLE AITKEN.

DEUTSCHE LYRIK. The Golden Treasury of the best German Lyrical Poems. By Dr. BUCHHEIM.

CHRYSOMELA. A Selection from the Lyrical Poems of Robert Herrick. By FRANCIS TURNER PALGRAVE.

POEMS OF PLACES—ENGLAND AND WALES. Edited by H. W. LONGFELLOW. 2 vols.

SELECTED POEMS OF MATTHEW ARNOLD.

THE STORY OF THE CHRISTIANS AND MOORS IN SPAIN. By CHARLOTTE M. YONGE.

LAMB'S TALES FROM SHAKSPEARE. Edited by Rev. ALFRED AINGER, M.A.

SHAKESPEARE'S SONGS AND SONNETS. Ed. with Notes, by Prof. F. T. PALGRAVE.

POEMS OF WORDSWORTH. Chosen and Edited by MATTHEW ARNOLD.
Large Paper Edition. 9s.

POEMS OF SHELLEY. Edited by STOPFORD A. BROOKE.
Large Paper Edition. 12s. 6d.

GOLDEN TREASURY SERIES—*contd.*

THE ESSAYS OF JOSEPH ADDISON, Chosen and Edited by JOHN RICHARD GREEN.

POETRY OF BYRON. Chosen and arranged by MATTHEW ARNOLD.
Large Paper Edition. 9s.

SIR THOMAS BROWNE'S RELIGIO MEDICI; LETTER TO A FRIEND, &c., AND CHRISTIAN MORALS. Ed. by W. A. GREENHILL, M.D.

THE SPEECHES AND TABLE-TALK OF THE PROPHET MOHAMMAD. Translated by STANLEY LANE-POOLE.

SELECTIONS FROM WALTER SAVAGE LANDOR. Edited by SIDNEY COLVIN.

SELECTIONS FROM COWPER'S POEMS. With an Introduction by Mrs. OLIPHANT.

LETTERS OF WILLIAM COWPER. Edited, With Introduction, by Rev. W. BENHAM.

THE POETICAL WORKS OF JOHN KEATS. Edited by Prof. F. T. PALGRAVE.

LYRICAL POEMS OF LORD TENNYSON. Selected and Annotated by Prof. FRANCIS T. PALGRAVE.
Large Paper Edition. 8vo. 9s.

IN MEMORIAM. By LORD TENNYSON, Poet Laureate.
Large Paper Edition. 8vo. 9s.

THE TRIAL AND DEATH OF SOCRATES Being the Euthyphron, Apology, Crito and Phaedo of Plato. Translated by F. J. CHURCH.

A BOOK OF GOLDEN THOUGHTS. By HENRY ATTWELL.

PLATO.—PHAEDRUS, LYSIS, AND PROTAGORAS. A New Translation, by J. WRIGHT.

THEOCRITUS, BION, AND MOSCHUS. Rendered into English Prose by ANDREW LANG.
Large Paper Edition. 8vo. 9s.

BALLADS, LYRICS, AND SONNETS. From the Works of HENRY W. LONGFELLOW.

GOLDEN TREASURY PSALTER.—THE STUDENT'S EDITION. Being an Edition with briefer Notes of "The Psalms Chronologically Arranged by Four Friends." 18mo. 3s. 6d.

GOLDSMITH. By WILLIAM BLACK. Crown 8vo. 1s. 6d.; sewed, 1s.

GOLDSMITH. — THE MISCELLANEOUS WORKS OF OLIVER GOLDSMITH. With Biographical Essay by Prof. MASSON. Globe 8vo. 3s. 6d.

—— ESSAYS OF OLIVER GOLDSMITH. Edited by C. D. YONGE, M.A. Fcp. 8vo. 2s. 6d.

—— THE TRAVELLER AND THE DESERTED VILLAGE. With Notes by J. W. HALES, M.A. Crown 8vo. 6d.

—— THE VICAR OF WAKEFIELD. With a Memoir of Goldsmith by Prof. MASSON. Globe 8vo. 1s.

—— THE TRAVELLER AND THE DESERTED VILLAGE. Edited, with Introduction and Notes, by ARTHUR BARRETT, M.A. Gl. 8vo. 1s. 6d.

GONE TO TEXAS.—LETTERS FROM OUR BOYS. Edited, with Preface, by THOMAS HUGHES, Q.C. Crown 8vo. 4s. 6d.

GOODWIN (Prof. W. W.).—SYNTAX OF THE GREEK MOODS AND TENSES. New Edition. 8vo. 14s.

GOODWIN (Prof.).—A GREEK GRAMMAR. New Revised Edition. Crown 8vo. 6s.

—— A SCHOOL GREEK GRAMMAR. Crown 8vo. 3s. 6d.

GORDON (General). A SKETCH. By REGINALD H. BARNES. Crown 8vo. 1s.

—— LETTERS OF GENERAL C. G. GORDON TO HIS SISTER, M. A. GORDON. 4th Edition. Crown 8vo. 3s. 6d.

GORDON. By Colonel Sir WILLIAM BUTLER. With Portrait. Crown 8vo. 2s. 6d.

GORDON (Lady Duff).—LAST LETTERS FROM EGYPT, TO WHICH ARE ADDED LETTERS FROM THE CAPE. 2nd Edition. Cr. 8vo. 9s.

GOSCHEN (Rt. Hon. George J.).—REPORTS AND SPEECHES ON LOCAL TAXATION. 8vo. 5s.

GOSSE (E.).— GRAY. Cr. 8vo. 1s. 6d. ; swd., 1s.

GOW (Dr. James).—A COMPANION TO SCHOOL CLASSICS. Illustrated. 2nd Ed. Cr. 8vo. 6s.

GOYEN (P.).—HIGHER ARITHMETIC AND ELEMENTARY MENSURATION, for the Senior Classes of Schools and Candidates preparing for Public Examinations. Globe 8vo. 5s.

GRAHAM (David).—KING JAMES I. An Historical Tragedy. Globe 8vo. 7s.

GRAHAM (John W.).— NEÆRA : A TALE OF ANCIENT ROME. Crown 8vo. 6s.

GRAND'HOMME. — CUTTING OUT AND DRESSMAKING. From the French of Mdlle. E. GRAND'HOMME. 18mo. 1s.

GRAY (Prof. Andrew).—THE THEORY AND PRACTICE OF ABSOLUTE MEASUREMENTS IN ELECTRICITY AND MAGNETISM. 2 vols. Crown 8vo. Vol. I. 12s. 6d.

—— ABSOLUTE MEASUREMENTS IN ELECTRICITY AND MAGNETISM. 2nd Edition, revised. Fcp. 8vo. 5s. 6d.

GRAY (Prof. Asa).—STRUCTURAL BOTANY; OR, ORGANOGRAPHY ON THE BASIS OF MORPHOLOGY. Crown 8vo. 10s. 6d.

—— THE SCIENTIFIC PAPERS OF ASA GRAY. Selected by CHARLES S. SARGENT. 2 vols. 8vo. 21s.

GRAY (Thomas).— Edited by EDMUND GOSSE. In 4 vols. Globe 8vo. 20s. Vol. I. POEMS, JOURNALS, AND ESSAYS.—II. LETTERS.—III. LETTERS. — IV. NOTES ON ARISTOPHANES ; AND PLATO.

GRAY. By EDMUND GOSSE. Crown 8vo. 1s. 6d. ; sewed, 1s.

GREAVES (John).—A TREATISE ON ELEMENTARY STATICS. 2nd Ed. Cr. 8vo. 6s. 6d.

—— STATICS FOR BEGINNERS. Gl. 8vo. 3s. 6d.

GREEK ELEGIAC POETS. FROM CALLINUS TO CALLIMACHUS. Selected and Edited by Rev. H. KYNASTON. 18mo. 1s. 6d.

GREEK TESTAMENT.—THE NEW TESTAMENT IN THE ORIGINAL GREEK. The Text revised by Prof. B. F. WESTCOTT, D.D., and Prof. F. J. A. HORT, D.D. 2 vols. Crown 8vo. 10s. 6d. each.—Vol. I. Text; II. Introduction and Appendix.

THE NEW TESTAMENT IN THE ORIGINAL GREEK, FOR SCHOOLS. The Text Revised by B. F. WESTCOTT, D.D., and F. J. A. HORT, D.D. 12mo. cloth. 4s. 6d.—18mo. roan, red edges. 5s. 6d.

GREEK TESTAMENT—continued.

SCHOOL READINGS IN THE GREEK TESTAMENT. Being the Outlines of the Life of our Lord as given by St. Mark, with additions from the Text of the other Evangelists. Edited, with Notes and Vocabulary, by A. CALVERT, M.A. Fcp. 8vo. 4s. 6d.

THE GREEK TESTAMENT AND THE ENGLISH VERSION, A COMPANION TO. By PHILIP SCHAFF, D.D. Crown 8vo. 12s.

THE ACTS OF THE APOSTLES. Being the Greek Text as Revised by Drs. WESTCOTT and HORT. With Explanatory Notes by T. E. PAGE, M.A. Fcp. 8vo. 4s. 6d.

THE GOSPEL ACCORDING TO ST. MATTHEW. Greek Text as Revised by Drs. WESTCOTT and HORT. With Introduction and Notes by Rev. A. SLOMAN, M.A. Fcp. 8vo. 2s. 6d.

GREEN (John Richard).—A SHORT HISTORY OF THE ENGLISH PEOPLE. With Coloured Maps, Genealogical Tables, and Chronological Annals. New Edition, thoroughly revised. Cr. 8vo. 8s. 6d. 150th Thousand. Also the same in Four Parts. With the corresponding portion of Mr. Tait's "Analysis." 3s. each. Part I. 607—1265. II. 1204—1553. III. 1540—1689. IV. 1660—1873.

—— STRAY STUDIES FROM ENGLAND AND ITALY. Crown 8vo. 8s. 6d.

—— HISTORY OF THE ENGLISH PEOPLE. In 4 vols. 8vo.—Vol. I. With 8 Coloured Maps. 16s.—II. 16s.—III. With 4 Maps. 16s.—IV. With Maps and Index. 16s.

—— THE MAKING OF ENGLAND. With Maps. 8vo. 16s.

—— THE CONQUEST OF ENGLAND. With Maps and Portrait. 8vo. 18s.

—— READINGS IN ENGLISH HISTORY. In 3 Parts. Fcp. 8vo. 1s. 6d. each.

—— ESSAYS OF JOSEPH ADDISON. 18mo. 4s. 6d.

GREEN (J. R.) and GREEN (Alice S.).— A SHORT GEOGRAPHY OF THE BRITISH ISLANDS. With 28 Maps. Fcp. 8vo. 3s. 6d.

GREEN (Mrs. J. R.).—HENRY II. Crown 8vo. 2s. 6d.

GREEN (W. S.).—AMONG THE SELKIRK GLACIERS. Crown 8vo. 7s. 6d.

GREENHILL (Prof. A. G.).—DIFFERENTIAL AND INTEGRAL CALCULUS. Cr. 8vo. 7s. 6d.

GREENWOOD (Jessy E.). — THE MOON MAIDEN : AND OTHER STORIES. Cr. 8vo. 3s 6d.

GREENWOOD (Principal J. G.).—THE ELEMENTS OF GREEK GRAMMAR. Cr. 8vo. 5s. 6d.

GRIFFITHS (W. H.).—LESSONS ON PRESCRIPTIONS AND THE ART OF PRESCRIBING. New Edition. 18mo. 3s. 6d.

GRIMM'S FAIRY TALES. A Selection from the Household Stories. Translated from the German by LUCY CRANE, and done into Pictures by WALTER CRANE. Cr. 8vo. 6s.

GRIMM.—KINDER-UND-HAUSMÄRCHEN. Selected and Edited, with Notes and Vocabulary, by G. E. FASNACHT. Gl. 8vo. 2s. 6d.

GUEST (M. J.).—LECTURES ON THE HISTORY OF ENGLAND. Crown 8vo. 6s.

GUEST (Dr. E.).—ORIGINES CELTICÆ (A Fragment) and other Contributions to the History of Britain. Maps. 2 vols. 8vo. 32s.

GROVE (Sir George).—A DICTIONARY OF MUSIC AND MUSICIANS, A.D. 1450—1889. Edited by Sir GEORGE GROVE, D.C.L. In 4 vols. 8vo, 21s. each. With Illustrations in Music Type and Woodcut.—Also published in Parts. Parts I.—XIV., XIX.—XXII. 3s. 6d. each; XV. XVI. 7s.; XVII. XVIII. 7s.; XXIII.—XXV., Appendix, Edited by J. A. FULLER MAITLAND, M.A. 9s. [Cloth cases for binding the volumes, 1s. each.]

—— PRIMER OF GEOGRAPHY. Maps. 18mo. 1s.

GUILLEMIN (Amédée).—THE FORCES OF NATURE. A Popular Introduction to the Study of Physical Phenomena. 455 Woodcuts. Royal 8vo. 21s.

—— THE APPLICATIONS OF PHYSICAL FORCES. With Coloured Plates and Illustrations. Royal 8vo. 21s.

—— ELECTRICITY AND MAGNETISM. A Popular Treatise. Translated and Edited, with Additions and Notes, by Prof. SYLVANUS P. THOMPSON. Royal 8vo. [In the Press.

GUIDE TO THE UNPROTECTED, In Every-day Matters relating to Property and Income. 5th Ed. Extra fcp. 8vo. 3s. 6d.

GUIZOT.—GREAT CHRISTIANS OF FRANCE. ST. LOUIS AND CALVIN. Crown 8vo. 6s.

GUNTON (George).—WEALTH AND PROGRESS. Crown 8vo. 6s.

HADLEY (Prof. James).—ESSAYS, PHILOLOGICAL AND CRITICAL. 8vo. 14s.

HADLEY—ALLEN.—A GREEK GRAMMAR FOR SCHOOLS AND COLLEGES. By Prof. JAMES HADLEY. Revised and in part Rewritten by Prof. FREDERIC DE FOREST ALLEN. Crown 8vo. 6s.

HAILSTONE (H.).—NOVAE ARUNDINES; OR, NEW MARSH MELODIES. Fcp. 8vo. 3s. 6d.

HALES (Prof. J. W.).—LONGER ENGLISH POEMS, with Notes, Philological and Explanatory, and an Introduction on the Teaching of English. 12th Ed. Ex. fcp. 8vo. 4s. 6d.

HALL (H. S.) and KNIGHT (S. R.).—ELEMENTARY ALGEBRA FOR SCHOOLS. 5th Ed., revised. Gl. 8vo. 3s. 6d. With Answers, 4s. 6d.

—— ALGEBRAICAL EXERCISES AND EXAMINATION PAPERS to accompany "Elementary Algebra." 2nd Edition. Globe 8vo. 2s. 6d.

—— ARITHMETICAL EXERCISES AND EXAMINATION PAPERS. Globe 8vo. 2s. 6d.

—— HIGHER ALGEBRA. A Sequel to "Elementary Algebra for Schools." 3rd Edition. Crown 8vo. 7s. 6d.

—— SOLUTIONS OF THE EXAMPLES IN "HIGHER ALGEBRA." Crown 8vo. 10s. 6d.

HALL (H. S.) and STEVENS (F. H.).—A TEXT-BOOK OF EUCLID'S ELEMENTS. Globe 8vo. Book I. 1s.; I. II. 1s. 6d.; I.—IV. 3s.; III.—VI. 3s.; I.—VI. and XI. 4s. 6d.; XI. 1s.

HALLWARD (R. F.).—FLOWERS OF PARADISE. Music, Verse, Design, Illustration. Royal 4to. 6s.

HALSTEAD (G. B.).—THE ELEMENTS OF GEOMETRY. 8vo. 12s. 6d.

HAMERTON (P. G.).—THE INTELLECTUAL LIFE. 4th Edition. Crown 8vo. 10s. 6d.

HAMERTON (P. G.).—ETCHING AND ETCHERS. 3rd Edition, revised. With 48 Plates. Colombier 8vo.

—— THOUGHTS ABOUT ART. New Edition. Crown 8vo. 8s. 6d.

—— HUMAN INTERCOURSE. 4th Edition. Crown 8vo. 8s. 6d.

—— FRENCH AND ENGLISH: A COMPARISON. Crown 8vo. 10s. 6d.

HAMILTON (John).—ON TRUTH AND ERROR. Crown 8vo. 5s.

—— ARTHUR'S SEAT; OR, THE CHURCH OF THE BANNED. Crown 8vo. 6s.

—— ABOVE AND AROUND: THOUGHTS ON GOD AND MAN. 12mo. 2s. 6d.

HAMILTON (Prof. D. J.).—ON THE PATHOLOGY OF BRONCHITIS, CATARRHAL PNEUMONIA, TUBERCLE, AND ALLIED LESIONS OF THE HUMAN LUNG. 8vo. 8s. 6d.

—— A TEXT-BOOK OF PATHOLOGY, SYSTEMATIC AND PRACTICAL. Illustrated. Vol. I. 8vo. 25s.

HANBURY (Daniel). — SCIENCE PAPERS, CHIEFLY PHARMACOLOGICAL AND BOTANICAL. Medium 8vo. 14s.

HANDEL. LIFE OF GEORGE FREDERICK HANDEL. By W. S. ROCKSTRO. Crown 8vo. 10s. 6d.

HARDWICK (Ven. Archdeacon). — CHRIST AND OTHER MASTERS. 6th Edition. Crown 8vo. 10s. 6d.

—— A HISTORY OF THE CHRISTIAN CHURCH. Middle Age. 6th Edition. Edited by Prof. STUBBS. Crown 8vo. 10s. 6d.

—— A HISTORY OF THE CHRISTIAN CHURCH DURING THE REFORMATION. 9th Edition. Revised by Prof. STUBBS. Cr. 8vo. 10s. 6d.

HARDY (Arthur Sherburne).—BUT YET A WOMAN. A Novel. Crown 8vo. 4s. 6d.

—— THE WIND OF DESTINY. 2 vols. Globe 8vo. 12s.

HARDY (H. J.).—A LATIN READER FOR THE LOWER FORMS IN SCHOOLS. Gl. 8vo. 2s. 6d.

HARDY (Thomas). — THE WOODLANDERS. Crown 8vo. 3s. 6d.

—— WESSEX TALES: STRANGE, LIVELY, AND COMMONPLACE. Crown 8vo. 3s. 6d.

HARE (Julius Charles).—THE MISSION OF THE COMFORTER. New Edition. Edited by Prof. E. H. PLUMPTRE. Crown 8vo. 7s. 6d.

—— THE VICTORY OF FAITH. Edited by Prof. PLUMPTRE, with Introductory Notices by the late Prof. MAURICE and by the late Dean STANLEY. Crown 8vo. 6s. 6d.

—— GUESSES AT TRUTH. By Two Brothers, AUGUSTUS WILLIAM HARE and JULIUS CHARLES HARE. With a Memoir and Two Portraits. 18mo. 4s. 6d.

HARMONIA. By the Author of "Estelle Russell." 3 vols. Crown 8vo. 31s. 6d.

HARPER (Father Thomas). — THE METAPHYSICS OF THE SCHOOL. In 5 vols. Vols. I. and II. 8vo. 18s. each; Vol. III., Part I. 12s.

HARRIS (Rev. G. C.).—SERMONS. With a Memoir by CHARLOTTE M. YONGE, and Portrait. Extra fcp. 8vo. 6s.

HARRISON (Frederic).—THE CHOICE OF BOOKS. Globe 8vo. 6s.
Large Paper Edition. Printed on hand-made paper. 8vo. 15s.
—— OLIVER CROMWELL. Crown 8vo. 2s. 6d.

HARRISON (Miss Jane) and VERRALL (Mrs.).—MYTHOLOGY AND MONUMENTS OF ANCIENT ATHENS. Illustrated. Cr. 8vo. 16s.

HARTE (Bret).—CRESSY: A Novel. Crown 8vo. 3s. 6d.
—— THE HERITAGE OF DEDLOW MARSH: AND OTHER TALES. 2 vols. Globe 8vo. 12s.

HARTLEY (Prof. W. Noel).—A COURSE OF QUANTITATIVE ANALYSIS FOR STUDENTS. Globe 8vo. 5s.

HARWOOD (George).—DISESTABLISHMENT; OR, A DEFENCE OF THE PRINCIPLE OF A NATIONAL CHURCH. 8vo. 12s.
—— THE COMING DEMOCRACY. Cr. 8vo. 6s.
—— FROM WITHIN. Crown 8vo. 6s.

HASTINGS (Warren). By Sir ALFRED LYALL. With Portrait. Crown 8vo. 2s. 6d.

HAUFF.—DIE KARAVANE. Edited, with Notes and Vocabulary, by HERMAN HAGER, Ph. D. Globe 8vo. 3s.

HAVELOCK (Sir Henry). By ARCHIBALD FORBES. With Portrait. Crn. 8vo. 2s. 6d.

HAWTHORNE (Nathaniel). By HENRY JAMES. Crown 8vo. 1s. 6d. ; sewed, 1s.

HAYWARD (R. B.).—THE ELEMENTS OF SOLID GEOMETRY. Globe 8vo.

HEARD (Rev. W. A.).—A SECOND GREEK EXERCISE BOOK. Globe 8vo.

HEINE. SELECTIONS FROM THE REISEBILDER AND OTHER PROSE WORKS. Edited by C. COLBECK, M.A. 18mo. 2s. 6d.

HELLENIC STUDIES, THE JOURNAL OF.—Vol. I. 8vo. With Plates of Illustrations. 30s.—Vol. II. 8vo. 30s. With Plates of Illustrations. Or in 2 Parts, 15s. each.—Vol. III. 2 Parts. 8vo. With Plates of Illustrations. 15s. each.—Vol. IV. 2 Parts. With Plates. Part I. 21s. Part II. 15s. Or complete, 30s.—Vol. V. With Plates. 30s.—Vol. VI. With Plates. Part I. 15s. Part II. 15s. Or complete, 30s.—Vol. VII. Part I. 15s. Part II. 15s. Or complete, 30s.—Vol. VIII. Part I. 15s. Part II. 15s.—Vol. IX. 2 Parts. 15s. each.—Vol. X. 30s.
The Journal will be sold at a reduced price to Libraries wishing to subscribe, but official application must in each case be made to the Council. Information on this point, and upon the conditions of Membership, may be obtained on application to the Hon. Sec., Mr. George Macmillan, 29, Bedford Street, Covent Garden.

HELPS.—ESSAYS WRITTEN IN THE INTERVALS OF BUSINESS. Edited by F. J. ROWE, M.A., and W. T. WEBB, M.A. Gl. 8vo. 2s. 6d.

HENRY II. By Mrs. J. R. GREEN. Crown 8vo. 2s. 6d.

HENRY V. By the Rev. A. J. CHURCH. With Portrait. Crown 8vo. 2s. 6d.

HENRY VII. By J. GAIRDNER. Cr. 8vo. 2s. 6d.

HENSLOW (Rev. G.).—THE THEORY OF EVOLUTION OF LIVING THINGS, AND THE APPLICATION OF THE PRINCIPLES OF EVOLUTION TO RELIGION. Crown 8vo. 6s.

HERODOTOS.—Books I.—III. Edited by A. H. SAYCE, M.A. 8vo. 16s.
—— SELECTIONS FROM BOOKS VII. and VIII. THE EXPEDITION OF XERXES. Edited by A. H. COOKE, M.A. 18mo. 1s. 6d.
—— THE HISTORY. Translated into English, with Notes and Indices, by G. C. MACAULAY, M.A. 2 vols. Crown 8vo. 18s.

HERRICK. — CHRYSOMELA. A Selection from the Lyrical Poems of ROBERT HERRICK. Arranged, with Notes, by Prof. F. T. PALGRAVE. 18mo. 4s. 6d.

HERTEL (Dr.).—OVERPRESSURE IN HIGH SCHOOLS IN DENMARK. With Introduction by Sir J. CRICHTON-BROWNE. Cr. 8vo. 3s. 6d.

HERVEY (Rt. Rev. Lord Arthur).—THE GENEALOGIES OF OUR LORD AND SAVIOUR JESUS CHRIST. 8vo. 10s. 6d.

HICKS (W. M.).— DYNAMICS OF PARTICLES AND SOLIDS. Crown 8vo. 6s. 6d.

HILL (Florence D.).—CHILDREN OF THE STATE. Ed. by FANNY FOWKE. Cr. 8vo. 6s.

HILL (Octavia).—OUR COMMON LAND, AND OTHER ESSAYS. Extra fcp. 8vo. 3s. 6d.
—— HOMES OF THE LONDON POOR. Sewed. Crown 8vo. 1s.

HIORNS (Arthur H.).—PRACTICAL METALLURGY AND ASSAYING. A Text-Book for the use of Teachers, Students, and Assayers. With Illustrations. Globe 8vo. 6s.
—— A TEXT-BOOK OF ELEMENTARY METALLURGY FOR THE USE OF STUDENTS. Gl. 8vo 4s.
—— IRON AND STEEL MANUFACTURE. A Text-Book for Beginners. Illustr. Gl. 8vo. 3s. 6d.

HISTORICAL COURSE FOR SCHOOLS. Edited by EDWARD A. FREEMAN. D.C.L.
Vol. I. GENERAL SKETCH OF EUROPEAN HISTORY. By E. A. FREEMAN. With Maps, &c. 18mo. 3s. 6d.
II. HISTORY OF ENGLAND. By EDITH THOMPSON. Col. Maps. 18mo. 2s. 6d.
III. HISTORY OF SCOTLAND. By MARGARET MACARTHUR. 18mo. 2s.
IV. HISTORY OF ITALY. By the Rev. W. HUNT, M.A. With Coloured Maps. 18mo. 3s. 6d.
V. HISTORY OF GERMANY. By JAMES SIME, M.A. 18mo. 3s.
VI. HISTORY OF AMERICA. By J. A. DOYLE. With Maps. 18mo. 4s. 6d.
VII. HISTORY OF EUROPEAN COLONIES. By E. J. PAYNE, M.A. With Maps. 18mo. 4s. 6d.
VIII. HISTORY OF FRANCE. By CHARLOTTE M. YONGE. Maps. 18mo. 3s. 6d.

HOBART. — ESSAYS AND MISCELLANEOUS WRITINGS OF VERE HENRY, LORD HOBART. With a Biographical Sketch. Edited by MARY, LADY HOBART. 2 vols. 8vo. 25s.

HOBDAY (E.). — VILLA GARDENING. A Handbook for Amateur and Practical Gardeners. Extra crown 8vo. 6s.

HODGSON (F.).—MYTHOLOGY FOR LATIN VERSIFICATION. 6th Edition. Revised by F. C. HODGSON, M.A. 18mo. 3s.

HODGSON. — MEMOIR OF REV. FRANCIS HODGSON, B.D., SCHOLAR, POET, AND DIVINE. By his Son, the Rev. JAMES T. HODGSON, M.A. 2 vols. Crown 8vo. 18s.

HOFMANN (Prof. A. W.).—THE LIFE WORK OF LIEBIG IN EXPERIMENTAL AND PHILOSOPHIC CHEMISTRY. 8vo. 5s.

HOGAN, M.P. Globe 8vo. 2s.

HOLE (Rev. C.).—GENEALOGICAL STEMMA OF THE KINGS OF ENGLAND AND FRANCE. On a Sheet. 1s.

—— A BRIEF BIOGRAPHICAL DICTIONARY. 2nd Edition. 18mo. 4s. 6d.

HOLLAND (Prof. T. E.).—THE TREATY RELATIONS OF RUSSIA AND TURKEY, FROM 1774 TO 1853. Crown 8vo. 2s.

HOLMES (O. W., Jun.).—THE COMMON LAW. 8vo. 12s.

HOMER.—THE ODYSSEY OF HOMER DONE INTO ENGLISH PROSE. By S. H. BUTCHER, M.A., and A. LANG, M.A. 7th Edition. Crown 8vo. 6s.

—— ODYSSEY. Book I. Edited, with Notes and Vocabulary, by Rev. J. BOND, M.A., and A. S. WALPOLE, M.A. 18mo. 1s. 6d.

—— ODYSSEY. Book IX. Edited by JOHN E. B. MAYOR, M.A. Fcp. 8vo. 2s. 6d.

—— ODYSSEY. THE TRIUMPH OF ODYSSEUS. Books XXI.—XXIV. Edited by S. G. HAMILTON, B.A. Fcp. 8vo. 3s. 6d.

—— THE ODYSSEY OF HOMER. Books I.—XII. Translated into English Verse by the EARL OF CARNARVON. Crown 8vo. 7s. 6d.

—— THE ILIAD. Edited, with English Notes and Introduction, by WALTER LEAF, Litt.D. 2 vols. 8vo. 14s. each.—Vol. I. Books I.—XII; Vol. II. Books XIII.—XXIV.

—— ILIAD. THE STORY OF ACHILLES. Edited by J. H. PRATT, M.A., and WALTER LEAF, Litt.D. Fcap. 8vo. 6s.

—— ILIAD. Book I. Edited by Rev. J. BOND, M.A., and A. S. WALPOLE, M.A. With Notes and Vocabulary. 18mo. 1s. 6d.

—— ILIAD. Book XVIII. THE ARMS OF ACHILLES. Edited by S. R. JAMES, M.A. 18mo. 1s. 6d.

—— ILIAD. Translated into English Prose. By ANDREW LANG, WALTER LEAF, and ERNEST MYERS. Crown 8vo. 12s. 6d.

HON. MISS FERRARD, THE. By the Author of " Hogan, M.P." Globe 8vo. 2s.

HOOKER (Sir J. D.).—THE STUDENT'S FLORA OF THE BRITISH ISLANDS. 3rd Edition. Globe 8vo. 10s. 6d.

—— PRIMER OF BOTANY. 18mo. 1s.

HOOKER (Sir Joseph D.) and BALL (J.).—JOURNAL OF A TOUR IN MAROCCO AND THE GREAT ATLAS. 8vo. 21s.

HOOLE (C. H.).—THE CLASSICAL ELEMENT IN THE NEW TESTAMENT. Considered as a Proof of its Genuineness, with an Appendix on the Oldest Authorities used in the Formation of the Canon. 8vo. 10s. 6d.

HOOPER (G.). — WELLINGTON. Portrait. Crown 8vo. 2s. 6d.

HOOPER (W. H.) and PHILLIPS (W. C.).—A MANUAL OF MARKS ON POTTERY AND PORCELAIN. 16mo. 4s. 6d.

HOPE (Frances J.).—NOTES AND THOUGHTS ON GARDENS AND WOODLANDS. Cr. 8vo. 6s.

HOPKINS (Ellice).—AUTUMN SWALLOWS: A Book of Lyrics. Extra fcp. 8vo. 6s.

HOPPUS (Mary).—A GREAT TREASON: A Story of the War of Independence. 2 vols. Crown 8vo. 9s.

HORACE.—THE WORKS OF HORACE RENDERED INTO ENGLISH PROSE. By J. LONSDALE, M.A., and S. LEE, M.A. 3s. 6d.

—— STUDIES, LITERARY AND HISTORICAL, IN THE ODES OF HORACE. By A. W. VERRALL, Litt.D. 8vo. 8s. 6d.

—— THE ODES OF HORACE IN A METRICAL PARAPHRASE. By R. M. HOVENDEN, B.A. Extra fcap. 8vo. 4s. 6d.

—— LIFE AND CHARACTER: AN EPITOME OF HIS SATIRES AND EPISTLES. By R. M. HOVENDEN, B.A. Extra fcp. 8vo. 4s. 6d.

—— WORD FOR WORD FROM HORACE: The Odes Literally Versified. By W. T. THORNTON, C.B. Crown 8vo. 7s. 6d.

—— ODES. Books I. II. III. and IV. Edited by T. E. PAGE, M.A. With Vocabularies. 18mo. 1s. 6d. each.

—— ODES. Books I.—IV. and CARME SECULARE. Edited by T. E. PAGE. Fcap. 8vo. 6s. ; or separately, 2s. each.

—— THE SATIRES. Edited by ARTHUR PALMER, M.A. Fcap. 8vo. 6s.

—— THE EPISTLES AND ARS POETICA. Edited by A. S. WILKINS, Litt.D. Fcp. 8vo. 6s.

—— SELECTIONS FROM THE EPISTLES AND SATIRES. Edited by Rev. W. J. F. V. BAKER, B.A. 18mo. 1s. 6d.

—— SELECT EPODES AND ARS POETICA. Edited by Rev. H. A. DALTON, M.A. 18mo. 1s. 6d.

HORT.—TWO DISSERTATIONS. I. On ΜΟΝΟΓΕΝΗΣ ΘΕΟΣ in Scripture and Tradition. II. On the "Constantinopolitan" Creed and other Eastern Creeds of the Fourth Century. By FENTON JOHN ANTHONY HORT, D.D. 8vo. 7s. 6d.

HORTON (Hon. S. Dana).—THE SILVER POUND AND ENGLAND'S MONETARY POLICY SINCE THE RESTORATION. With a History of the Guinea. 8vo. 14s.

HOWES (Prof. G. B.).—AN ATLAS OF PRACTICAL ELEMENTARY BIOLOGY. With a Preface by Prof. HUXLEY. 4to. 14s.

HOWSON (Very Rev. J. S.).—BEFORE THE TABLE: AN INQUIRY, HISTORICAL AND THEOLOGICAL, INTO THE MEANING OF THE CONSECRATION RUBRIC IN THE COMMUNION SERVICE OF THE CHURCH OF ENGLAND. 8vo. 7s. 6d.

HOZIER (Lieut.-Colonel H. M.).—THE SEVEN WEEKS' WAR. 3rd Edition. Crown 8vo. 6s.

—— THE INVASIONS OF ENGLAND. 2 vols. 8vo. 28s.

HÜBNER (Baron von).—A RAMBLE ROUND THE WORLD. Crown 8vo. 6s.

HUGHES (Thomas).—ALFRED THE GREAT. Crown 8vo. 6s.

—— THE MANLINESS OF CHRIST. Cr. 8vo. 4s. 6d.

—— MEMOIR OF DANIEL MACMILLAN. With Portrait. Cr. 8vo. 4s. 6d.—Popular Edition. Sewed. Crown 8vo. 1s.

HUGHES (Thomas).—RUGBY, TENNESSEE. Crown 8vo. 4s. 6d.

—— TOM BROWN'S SCHOOL DAYS. By AN OLD BOY. Illustrated Edition. Crown 8vo. 6s.—Golden Treasury Edition. 4s. 6d.—Uniform Edition. 3s. 6d.—People's Edition. 2s.—People's Sixpenny Edition, Illustrated. Med. 8vo. 6d.

—— TOM BROWN AT OXFORD. Crown 8vo. 6s.—Uniform Edition. 3s. 6d.

—— GONE TO TEXAS. Edited by THOMAS HUGHES, Q.C. Crown 8vo. 4s. 6d.

—— JAMES FRASER, Second Bishop of Manchester. A Memoir, 1818—85. Cr. 8vo. 6s.

—— THE SCOURING OF THE WHITE HORSE, AND THE ASHEN FAGGOT. Uniform Ed. 3s. 6d.

—— LIVINGSTONE. With Portrait and Map. Cr. 8vo. 2s. 6d. [English Men of Action.

HULL (E.).—A TREATISE ON ORNAMENTAL AND BUILDING STONES OF GREAT BRITAIN AND FOREIGN COUNTRIES. 8vo. 12s.

HULLAH (John).—THE SONG BOOK. Words and Tunes from the best Poets and Musicians. With Vignette. 18mo. 4s. 6d.

—— MUSIC IN THE HOUSE. 4th Edition. Crown 8vo. 2s. 6d.

HULLAH (M. E.).—HANNAH TARNE. A Story for Girls. Globe 8vo. 2s. 6d.

HUME. By THOMAS H. HUXLEY. Crown 8vo. 1s. 6d.; sewed, 1s.

HUMPHRY (Prof. G. M.).—THE HUMAN SKELETON (INCLUDING THE JOINTS). With 260 Illustrations drawn from Nature. Med. 8vo. 14s.

—— THE HUMAN FOOT AND THE HUMAN HAND. With Illustrations. Fcp. 8vo. 4s. 6d.

—— OBSERVATIONS IN MYOLOGY. 8vo. 6s.

—— OLD AGE. The Results of Information received respecting nearly nine hundred persons who had attained the age of eighty years, including seventy-four centenarians. Crown 8vo. 4s. 6d.

HUNT (Rev. W.).—HISTORY OF ITALY. Maps. 3rd Edition. 18mo. 3s. 6d.

HUNT (W.).—TALKS ABOUT ART. With a Letter from Sir J. E. MILLAIS, Bart., R.A. Crown 8vo. 3s. 6d.

HUSS (Hermann).—A SYSTEM OF ORAL INSTRUCTION IN GERMAN. Crown 8vo. 5s.

HUTTON (R. H.).—ESSAYS ON SOME OF THE MODERN GUIDES OF ENGLISH THOUGHT IN MATTERS OF FAITH. Globe 8vo. 6s.

—— SCOTT. Crown 8vo. 1s. 6d.; sewed, 1s.

—— ESSAYS. 2 vols. Globe 8vo. 6s. each. —Vol. I. Literary Essays; II. Theological Essays.

HUXLEY (Thomas Henry).—LESSONS IN ELEMENTARY PHYSIOLOGY. With numerous Illustrations. New Edit. Fcp. 8vo. 4s. 6d.

—— LAY SERMONS, ADDRESSES, AND REVIEWS. 9th Edition. 8vo. 7s. 6d.

—— ESSAYS SELECTED FROM LAY SERMONS, ADDRESSES, AND REVIEWS. 3rd Edition. Crown 8vo. 1s.

—— CRITIQUES AND ADDRESSES. 8vo. 10s. 6d.

HUXLEY (T. H.).—PHYSIOGRAPHY. AN INTRODUCTION TO THE STUDY OF NATURE. 13th Edition. Crown 8vo. 6s.

—— AMERICAN ADDRESSES, WITH A LECTURE ON THE STUDY OF BIOLOGY. 8vo. 6s. 6d.

—— SCIENCE AND CULTURE, AND OTHER ESSAYS. 8vo. 10s. 6d.

—— INTRODUCTORY PRIMER. 18mo. 1s.
[Science Primers.

—— HUME. Crown 8vo. 1s. 6d.; sewed, 1s.

HUXLEY'S PHYSIOLOGY, QUESTIONS ON, FOR SCHOOLS. By T. ALCOCK, M.D. 5th Edition. 18mo. 1s. 6d.

HUXLEY (T. H.) and MARTIN (H. N.).— A COURSE OF PRACTICAL INSTRUCTION IN ELEMENTARY BIOLOGY. New Edition, Revised and Extended by Prof. G. B. HOWES and D. H SCOTT, M.A., Ph.D. With Preface by T. H. HUXLEY, F.R.S. Cr. 8vo. 10s. 6d.

IBBETSON (W. J.). — AN ELEMENTARY TREATISE ON THE MATHEMATICAL THEORY OF PERFECTLY ELASTIC SOLIDS. 8vo. 21s.

ILLINGWORTH (Rev. J. R.).—SERMONS PREACHED IN A COLLEGE CHAPEL. Crown 8vo. 5s.

IMITATIO CHRISTI, LIBRI IV. Printed in Borders after Holbein, Dürer, and other old Masters, containing Dances of Death, Acts of Mercy, Emblems, &c. Cr. 8vo. 7s. 6d.

INDIAN TEXT-BOOKS.—PRIMER OF ENGLISH GRAMMAR. By R. MORRIS, LL.D. 18mo. 1s.

EASY SELECTIONS FROM MODERN ENGLISH LITERATURE. For the use of the Middle Classes in Indian Schools. With Notes. By Sir ROPER LETHBRIDGE. Cr. 8vo. 1s. 6d.

SELECTIONS FROM MODERN ENGLISH LITERATURE. For the use of the Higher Classes in Indian Schools. By Sir ROPER LETHBRIDGE, M.A. Crown 8vo. 3s. 6d.

SERIES OF SIX ENGLISH READING BOOKS FOR INDIAN CHILDREN. By P. C. SIRCAR. Revised by Sir ROPER LETHBRIDGE. Cr. 8vo. Book I. 5d.; Book II. 6d.; Book III. 8d.; Book IV. 1s.; Book V. 1s. 2d.; Book VI. 1s. 3d.

A GEOGRAPHICAL READER AND COMPANION TO THE ATLAS. By C. B. CLARKE, F.R.S. Crown 8vo. 2s.

A CLASS-BOOK OF GEOGRAPHY. By the same. Fcap. 8vo. 3s. 6d.; sewed, 3s.

THE WORLD'S HISTORY. Compiled under direction of Sir ROPER LETHBRIDGE. Crown 8vo. 1s.

EASY INTRODUCTION TO THE HISTORY OF INDIA. By Sir ROPER LETHBRIDGE. Crown 8vo. 1s. 6d.

HISTORY OF ENGLAND. Compiled under direction of Sir ROPER LETHBRIDGE. Crown 8vo. 1s. 6d.

EASY INTRODUCTION TO THE HISTORY AND GEOGRAPHY OF BENGAL. By Sir ROPER LETHBRIDGE. Crown 8vo. 1s. 6d.

ARITHMETIC. With Answers. By BARNARD SMITH. 18mo. 2s.

ALGEBRA. By I. TODHUNTER, F.R.S. 18mo. 2s. 6d.

INDIAN TEXT-BOOKS—*continued.*
EUCLID. First Four Books. With Notes, &c. By the same Author. 18mo. 2s.

ELEMENTARY MENSURATION AND LAND SURVEYING. By the same Author. 18mo. 2s.

EUCLID. Books I.—IV. By H. S. HALL and F. H. STEVENS. Gl. 8vo. 3s.; sewed, 2s. 6d.

PHYSICAL GEOGRAPHY. By H. F. BLANFORD. Crown 8vo. 2s. 6d.

ELEMENTARY GEOMETRY AND CONIC SECTIONS. By J. M. WILSON. Ex. fcp. 8vo. 6s.

INGRAM (T. Dunbar).—A HISTORY OF THE LEGISLATIVE UNION OF GREAT BRITAIN AND IRELAND. 8vo. 10s. 6d.

—— TWO CHAPTERS OF IRISH HISTORY: 1. The Irish Parliament of James II.; II. The Alleged Violation of the Treaty of Limerick. 8vo. 6s.

IONIA.—ANTIQUITIES OF IONIA. Folio. Vols. I. II. and III. 2l. 2s. each, or 5l. 5s. the set.—Part IV. 3l. 13s. 6d.

IRVING (Joseph).—ANNALS OF OUR TIME. A Diurnal of Events, Social and Political, Home and Foreign. From the Accession of Queen Victoria to Jubilee Day, being the First Fifty Years of Her Majesty's Reign. In 2 vols. 8vo.—Vol. I. June 20th, 1837, to February 28th, 1871. Vol. II. February 24th, 1871, to June 24th, 1887. 18s. each. The Second Volume may also be had in Three Parts: Part I. February 24th, 1871, to March 19th, 1874, 4s. 6d. Part II. March 20th, 1874, to July 22nd, 1878, 4s. 6d. Part III. July 23rd, 1878, to June 24th, 1887, 9s.

IRVING (Washington).—OLD CHRISTMAS. From the Sketch Book. With upwards of 100 Illustrations by RANDOLPH CALDECOTT. Cloth elegant, gilt edges. Crown 8vo. 6s.
Also with uncut edges, paper label. Crown 8vo. 6s.
People's Edition. Medium 4to. 6d.

—— BRACEBRIDGE HALL. With 120 Illustrations by RANDOLPH CALDECOTT. Cloth elegant, gilt edges. Crown 8vo. 6s.
Also with uncut edges, paper label. Crown 8vo. 6s.
People's Edition. Medium 4to. 6d.

—— OLD CHRISTMAS AND BRACEBRIDGE HALL. Illustrations by RANDOLPH CALDECOTT. *Edition de Luxe.* Royal 8vo. 21s.

ISMAY'S CHILDREN. By the Author of "Hogan, M.P." Globe 8vo. 2s.

JACK AND THE BEAN-STALK. English Hexameters by the Honourable HALLAM TENNYSON. With 40 Illustrations by RANDOLPH CALDECOTT. Fcp. 4to. 3s. 6d.

JACKSON (Rev. Blomfield).—FIRST STEPS TO GREEK PROSE COMPOSITION. 12th Edit. 18mo. 1s. 6d.
KEY (supplied to Teachers only). 3s. 6d.

—— SECOND STEPS TO GREEK PROSE COMPOSITION. 18mo. 2s. 6d.
KEY (supplied to Teachers only). 3s. 6d.

JACKSON (Helen).—RAMONA: A Story. Globe 8vo. 2s.

JACOB (Rev. J. A.).—BUILDING IN SILENCE, AND OTHER SERMONS. Extra fcp. 8vo. 6s.

JAMES (Henry).—THE EUROPEANS: A Novel. Crown 8vo. 6s.

JAMES (Henry).—DAISY MILLER, AND OTHER STORIES. Crown 8vo. 6s.—Globe 8vo. 2s.

—— THE AMERICAN. Crown 8vo. 6s.

—— RODERICK HUDSON. Crown 8vo. 6s.—Globe 8vo. 2s.

—— THE MADONNA OF THE FUTURE, AND OTHER TALES. Crown 8vo. 6s.—Globe 8vo. 2s.

—— WASHINGTON SQUARE: THE PENSION BEAUREPAS. Crn. 8vo. 6s.—Globe 8vo. 2s.

—— THE PORTRAIT OF A LADY. Cr. 8vo. 6s.

—— STORIES REVIVED. In Two Series. Crown 8vo. 6s. each.

—— THE BOSTONIANS. Crown 8vo. 6s.

—— NOVELS AND TALES. Pocket Edition. 18mo. 14 vols. 2s. each volume: THE PORTRAIT OF A LADY. 3 vols.—RODERICK HUDSON. 2 vols.—THE AMERICAN. 2 vols.—WASHINGTON SQUARE. 1 vol.—THE EUROPEANS. 1 vol.—CONFIDENCE. 1 vol.—THE SIEGE OF LONDON; MADAME DE MAUVES. 1 vol.—AN INTERNATIONAL EPISODE; THE PENSION BEAUREPAS; THE POINT OF VIEW. 1 vol.—DAISY MILLER, A STUDY; FOUR MEETINGS; LONGSTAFF'S MARRIAGE; BENVOLIO. 1 vol.—THE MADONNA OF THE FUTURE; A BUNDLE OF LETTERS; THE DIARY OF A MAN OF FIFTY; EUGENE PICKERING. 1 vol.

—— HAWTHORNE. Cr. 8vo. 1s. 6d.; swd. 1s.

—— FRENCH POETS AND NOVELISTS. New Edition. Crown 8vo. 4s. 6d.

—— TALES OF THREE CITIES. Cr. 8vo. 4s. 6d.

—— PORTRAITS OF PLACES. Cr. 8vo. 7s. 6d.

—— THE PRINCESS CASAMASSIMA. Crown 8vo. 6s.—Globe 8vo. 2s.

—— PARTIAL PORTRAITS. Crown 8vo. 6s.

—— THE REVERBERATOR. Crown 8vo. 6s.

—— THE ASPERN PAPERS; LOUISA PALLANT; THE MODERN WARNING. 2 vols. Globe 8vo. 12s.

—— A LONDON LIFE. Crown 8vo. 3s. 6d.

JAMES (Right Hon. Sir William Milbourne). —THE BRITISH IN INDIA. 8vo. 12s. 6d.

JARDINE (Rev. Robert).—THE ELEMENTS OF THE PSYCHOLOGY OF COGNITION. Third Edition. Crown 8vo. 6s. 6d.

JEANS (Rev. G. E.).—HAILEYBURY CHAPEL, AND OTHER SERMONS. Fcp. 8vo. 3s. 6d.

—— THE LIFE AND LETTERS OF MARCUS TULLIUS CICERO. Being a Translation of the Letters included in Mr. Watson's Selection. Crown 8vo. 10s. 6d.

JEBB (Prof. R. C.).—THE ATTIC ORATORS, FROM ANTIPHON TO ISAEOS. 2 vols. 8vo. 25s.

—— THE ATTIC ORATORS. Selections from Antiphon, Andocides, Lysias, Isocrates, and Isaeos. Ed., with Notes. 2nd Ed. Fcp. 8vo. 6s.

—— MODERN GREECE. Two Lectures. Crown 8vo. 5s.

—— PRIMER OF GREEK LITERATURE. 18mo. 1s.

—— BENTLEY. Crown 8vo. 1s. 6d.; sewed, 1s.

JELLETT (Rev. Dr.).—THE ELDER SON, AND OTHER SERMONS. Crown 8vo. 6s.

JELLETT (Rev. Dr.).—THE EFFICACY OF PRAYER. 3rd Edition. Crown 8vo. 5s.

JENNINGS (A. C.).—CHRONOLOGICAL TABLES OF ANCIENT HISTORY. With Index. 8vo. 5s.

JENNINGS (A. C.) and LOWE (W. H.).—THE PSALMS, WITH INTRODUCTIONS AND CRITICAL NOTES. 2 vols. 2nd Edition. Crown 8vo. 10s 6d. each.

JEVONS (W. Stanley).—THE PRINCIPLES OF SCIENCE: A TREATISE ON LOGIC AND SCIENTIFIC METHOD. Crown 8vo. 12s. 6d.

—— ELEMENTARY LESSONS IN LOGIC: DEDUCTIVE AND INDUCTIVE. 18mo. 3s. 6d.

—— PRIMER OF LOGIC. 18mo. 1s.

—— THE THEORY OF POLITICAL ECONOMY. 3rd Edition. 8vo. 10s. 6d.

—— PRIMER OF POLITICAL ECONOMY. 18mo. 1s.

—— STUDIES IN DEDUCTIVE LOGIC. 2nd Edition. Crown 8vo. 6s.

—— INVESTIGATIONS IN CURRENCY AND FINANCE. Edited, with an Introduction, by H. S. FOXWELL, M.A. Illustrated by 20 Diagrams. 8vo. 21s.

—— METHODS OF SOCIAL REFORM. 8vo. 10s. 6d.

—— THE STATE IN RELATION TO LABOUR. Crown 8vo. 3s. 6d.

—— LETTERS AND JOURNAL. Edited by His WIFE. 8vo. 14s.

JEX-BLAKE (Dr. Sophia).—THE CARE OF INFANTS: A Manual for Mothers and Nurses. 18mo. 1s.

JOHNSON (W. E.).—A TREATISE ON TRIGONOMETRY. Crown 8vo. 8s. 6d.

JOHNSON (Prof. W. Woolsey).—CURVE TRACING IN CARTESIAN CO-ORDINATES. Crown 8vo. 4s. 6d.

—— A TREATISE ON ORDINARY AND DIFFERENTIAL EQUATIONS. Crown 8vo. 15s.

—— AN ELEMENTARY TREATISE ON THE INTEGRAL CALCULUS. Crown 8vo. 9s.

JOHNSON'S LIVES OF THE POETS. The Six Chief Lives, with Macaulay's "Life of Johnson." Edited by MATTHEW ARNOLD. Crown 8vo. 4s. 6d.

JOHNSON. By LESLIE STEPHEN. Crown 8vo. 1s. 6d.; sewed. 1s.

JONES (D. E.).—EXAMPLES IN PHYSICS. Fcp. 8vo. 3s. 6d.

—— SOUND, LIGHT, AND HEAT. An Elementary Text-Book. Fcp. 8vo.

JONES (F.).—THE OWENS COLLEGE JUNIOR COURSE OF PRACTICAL CHEMISTRY. With Preface by Sir HENRY E. ROSCOE. New Edition. 18mo. 2s. 6d.

—— QUESTIONS ON CHEMISTRY. A Series of Problems and Exercises in Inorganic and Organic Chemistry. 18mo. 3s.

JONES (Rev. C. A.) and CHEYNE (C. H.).—ALGEBRAICAL EXERCISES. Progressively arranged. 18mo. 2s. 6d.

—— SOLUTIONS OF SOME OF THE EXAMPLES IN THE ALGEBRAICAL EXERCISES OF MESSRS. JONES AND CHEYNE. By the Rev. W. FAILES. Crown 8vo. 7s. 6d.

JUVENAL. THIRTEEN SATIRES OF JUVENAL. With a Commentary by Prof. J. E. B. MAYOR, M.A. 4th Edition. Vol. I. Crown 8vo. 10s. 6d.—Vol. II. Crown 8vo. 10s. 6d.

SUPPLEMENT to Third Edition, containing the Principal Changes made in the Fourth Edition. 5s.

—— THIRTEEN SATIRES. Edited, for the Use of Schools, with Notes, Introduction, and Appendices, by E. G. HARDY, M.A. Fcp. 8vo. 5s.

—— SELECT SATIRES. Edited by Prof. JOHN E. B. MAYOR. Satires X. and XI. 3s. 6d.—Satires XII. and XVI. Fcp. 8vo. 4s. 6d.

—— THIRTEEN SATIRES. Translated into English after the Text of J. E. B. MAYOR by ALEX. LEEPER, M.A. Cr. 8vo. 3s. 6d.

KANT.—KANT'S CRITICAL PHILOSOPHY FOR ENGLISH READERS. By JOHN P. MAHAFFY, D.D., and JOHN H. BERNARD, B.D. New Edition. 2 vols. Crown 8vo. Vol. I. THE KRITIK OF PURE REASON EXPLAINED AND DEFENDED. 7s. 6d.—Vol. II. THE "PROLEGOMENA." Translated, with Notes and Appendices. 6s.

KANT—MAX MÜLLER.—CRITIQUE OF PURE REASON BY IMMANUEL KANT. Translated by F. MAX MÜLLER. With Introduction by LUDWIG NOIRÉ. 2 vols. 8vo. 16s. each.—Sold separately. Vol. I. HISTORICAL INTRODUCTION, by LUDWIG NOIRÉ, etc., etc.; Vol. II. CRITIQUE OF PURE REASON.

KAY (Rev. W.).—A COMMENTARY ON ST. PAUL'S TWO EPISTLES TO THE CORINTHIANS. Greek Text, with Commentary. 8vo. 9s.

KEARY (Annie).—JANET'S HOME. Globe 8vo. 2s.

—— CLEMENCY FRANKLYN. Globe 8vo. 2s.

—— OLDBURY. Globe 8vo. 2s.

—— A YORK AND A LANCASTER ROSE. Globe 8vo. 2s.

—— CASTLE DALY: THE STORY OF AN IRISH HOME THIRTY YEARS AGO. Cr. 8vo. 3s. 6d.

—— A DOUBTING HEART. Crown 8vo. 6s.

—— NATIONS AROUND. Crown 8vo. 4s. 6d.

KEARY (Eliza).—THE MAGIC VALLEY; OR, PATIENT ANTOINE. With Illustrations by "E.V.B." Globe 8vo. 4s. 6d.

KEARY (A. and E.).—THE HEROES OF ASGARD. Tales from Scandinavian Mythology. Globe 8vo. 2s. 6d.

KEATS.—THE POETICAL WORKS OF JOHN KEATS. With Notes, by Prof. PALGRAVE. 18mo. 4s. 6d.

KEATS. By SIDNEY COLVIN. Crown 8vo. 1s. 6d.; sewed, 1s.

KELLAND (P.) and TAIT (P. G.).—INTRODUCTION TO QUATERNIONS, WITH NUMEROUS EXAMPLES. 2nd Edition. Cr. 8vo. 7s. 6d.

KELLOGG (Rev. S. H.).—THE LIGHT OF ASIA AND THE LIGHT OF THE WORLD. Cr. 8vo. 7s. 6d.

KEMPE (A. B.).—HOW TO DRAW A STRAIGHT LINE. A Lecture on Linkages. Cr. 8vo. 1s. 6d.

KENNEDY (Prof. Alex. W. B.).—THE MECHANICS OF MACHINERY. With Illustrations. Crown 8vo. 12s. 6d.

KERNEL AND THE HUSK (THE): LETTERS ON SPIRITUAL CHRISTIANITY. By the Author of "Philochristus." Crown 8vo. 5s.

KEYNES (J. N.).—STUDIES AND EXERCISES IN FORMAL LOGIC. 2nd Edition. Crown 8vo. 10s. 6d.

KIEPERT (H.).—MANUAL OF ANCIENT GEOGRAPHY. Crown 8vo. 5s.

KILLEN (W. D.).—ECCLESIASTICAL HISTORY OF IRELAND, FROM THE EARLIEST DATE TO THE PRESENT TIME. 2 vols. 8vo. 25s.

KINGSLEY (Charles).—NOVELS AND POEMS. *Eversley Edition.* 13 vols. Gl. 8vo. 5s. each.
WESTWARD HO! 2 vols.—TWO YEARS AGO. 2 vols.—HYPATIA. 2 vols.—YEAST. 1 vol.—ALTON LOCKE. 2 vols.—HEREWARD THE WAKE. 2 vols.—POEMS. 2 vols.

—— *Complete Edition* OF THE WORKS OF CHARLES KINGSLEY. Cr. 8vo. 3s. 6d. each.
WESTWARD HO! With a Portrait.
HYPATIA.
YEAST.
ALTON LOCKE.
TWO YEARS AGO.
HEREWARD THE WAKE.
POEMS.
THE HEROES; OR, GREEK FAIRY TALES FOR MY CHILDREN.
THE WATER BABIES: A FAIRY TALE FOR A LAND-BABY.
MADAM HOW AND LADY WHY; OR, FIRST LESSONS IN EARTH-LORE FOR CHILDREN.
AT LAST: A CHRISTMAS IN THE WEST INDIES.
PROSE IDYLLS.
PLAYS AND PURITANS.
THE ROMAN AND THE TEUTON. With Preface by Professor MAX MÜLLER.
SANITARY AND SOCIAL LECTURES.
HISTORICAL LECTURES AND ESSAYS.
SCIENTIFIC LECTURES AND ESSAYS.
LITERARY AND GENERAL LECTURES.
THE HERMITS.
GLAUCUS; OR, THE WONDERS OF THE SEA-SHORE. With Coloured Illustrations.
VILLAGE AND TOWN AND COUNTRY SERMONS.
SERMONS ON NATIONAL SUBJECTS, AND THE KING OF THE EARTH.
SERMONS FOR THE TIMES.
GOOD NEWS OF GOD.
THE GOSPEL OF THE PENTATEUCH, AND DAVID.
THE WATER OF LIFE, AND OTHER SERMONS.
DISCIPLINE, AND OTHER SERMONS.
WESTMINSTER SERMONS.

—— A *Sixpenny Edition* OF CHARLES KINGSLEY'S NOVELS. Med. 8vo. 6d. each.
WESTWARD HO!—HYPATIA.—YEAST.—ALTON LOCKE. TWO YEARS AGO.—HEREWARD THE WAKE.

KINGSLEY (Charles).—THE WATER BABIES: A FAIRY TALE FOR A LAND BABY. New Edition, with a Hundred New Pictures by LINLEY SAMBOURNE; engraved by J. SWAIN. Fcp. 4to. 12s. 6d.

—— HEALTH AND EDUCATION. Cr. 8vo. 6s.

—— POEMS. Pocket Edition. 18mo. 1s. 6d.

—— SELECTIONS FROM SOME OF THE WRITINGS OF CHARLES KINGSLEY. Cr. 8vo. 6s.

—— OUT OF THE DEEP: WORDS FOR THE SORROWFUL. From the Writings of CHARLES KINGSLEY. Extra fcp. 8vo. 3s. 6d.

—— DAILY THOUGHTS. Selected from the Writings of CHARLES KINGSLEY. By His WIFE. Crown 8vo. 6s.

—— THE HEROES; OR, GREEK FAIRY TALES FOR MY CHILDREN. Extra cloth, gilt edges. *Presentation Edition.* Crown 8vo. 7s. 6d.

—— GLAUCUS; OR, THE WONDERS OF THE SEA SHORE. With Coloured Illustrations, extra cloth, gilt edges. *Presentation Edition.* Crown 8vo. 7s. 6d.

—— FROM DEATH TO LIFE. Fragments of Teaching to a Village Congregation. With Letters on the "Life after Death." Edited by His WIFE. Fcp. 8vo. 2s. 6d.

—— CHARLES KINGSLEY: HIS LETTERS, AND MEMORIES OF HIS LIFE. Ed. by His WIFE. 2 vols. Crn. 8vo. 12s.—*Cheap Edition,* 6s.

—— ALL SAINTS' DAY, AND OTHER SERMONS. Crown 8vo. 7s. 6d.

—— TRUE WORDS FOR BRAVE MEN. Crown 8vo. 2s. 6d.

KINGSLEY (Henry).—TALES OF OLD TRAVEL. Crown 8vo. 5s.

KITCHENER (F. E.).—GEOMETRICAL NOTE-BOOK. Containing Easy Problems in Geometrical Drawing, preparatory to the Study of Geometry. 4to. 2s.

KLEIN (Dr. E.).—MICRO-ORGANISMS AND DISEASE. An Introduction into the Study of Specific Micro-Organisms. With 121 Engravings. 3rd Edition. Crown 8vo. 6s.

—— THE BACTERIA IN ASIATIC CHOLERA. Crown 8vo. 5s.

KNOX (A.).—DIFFERENTIAL CALCULUS FOR BEGINNERS. Fcp. 8vo. 3s. 6d.

KTESIAS. THE FRAGMENTS OF THE PERSIKA OF KTESIAS. Edited, with Introduction and Notes, by J. GILMORE, M.A. 8vo. 8s. 6d.

KUENEN.—AN HISTORICO-CRITICAL INQUIRY INTO THE ORIGIN AND COMPOSITION OF THE HEXATEUCH (PENTATEUCH AND BOOK OF JOSHUA). By Prof. A. KUENEN, Leiden. Translated by PHILIP H. WICKSTEED, M.A. 8vo. 14s.

KYNASTON (Herbert, D.D.).—SERMONS PREACHED IN THE COLLEGE CHAPEL, CHELTENHAM. Crown 8vo. 6s.

—— PROGRESSIVE EXERCISES IN THE COMPOSITION OF GREEK IAMBIC VERSE. Extra fcp. 8vo. 5s.
KEY (supplied to Teachers only). 4s. 6d.

—— EXEMPLARIA CHELTONIENSIA. Sive quae discipulis suis Carmina identidem Latine reddenda proposuit ipse reddidit ex cathedra dictavit HERBERT KYNASTON, M.A. Extra fcp. 8vo. 5s.

LABBERTON (R. H.).—New Historical Atlas and General History. 4to. 15s.

LAFARGUE (Philip).—The New Judgment of Paris: A Novel. 2 vols. Gl. 8vo. 12s.

LA FONTAINE'S FABLES. A Selection, with Introduction, Notes, and Vocabulary, by L. M. Moriarty, B.A. Illustrations by Randolph Caldecott. Globe 8vo. 2s.6d.

LAMB.—Collected Works. Edited, with Introduction and Notes, by the Rev. Alfred Ainger, M.A. Globe 8vo. 5s. each volume. I. Essays of Elia.—II. Plays, Poems, and Miscellaneous Essays.—III. Mrs. Leicester's School; The Adventures of Ulysses; and other Essays.—IV. Tales from Shakespeare.—V. and VI. Letters. Newly arranged, with additions.

—— The Life of Charles Lamb. By Rev. Alfred Ainger, M.A. Uniform with above. Globe 8vo. 5s.

Tales from Shakspeare. 18mo. 4s. 6d. *Globe Readings Edition.* For Schools. Globe 8vo. 2s.

LAMB. By Rev. Alfred Ainger, M.A. Crown 8vo. 1s. 6d.; sewed, 1s.

LANCIANI (Prof. R.).—Ancient Rome in the Light of Recent Discoveries. 4to. 24s.

LAND OF DARKNESS (THE). Along with some further Chapters in the Experiences of The Little Pilgrim. By the Author of "A Little Pilgrim in the Unseen." Crown 8vo. 5s.

LANDAUER (J.).—Blowpipe Analysis. Authorised English Edition by James Taylor and Wm. E. Kay. Ext. fcp. 8vo. 4s. 6d.

LANDOR.—Selections from the Writings of Walter Savage Landor. Arranged and Edited by Sidney Colvin. 18mo. 4s. 6d.

LANDOR. By Sidney Colvin. Crown 8vo, 1s. 6d.; sewed, 1s.

LANE-POOLE.—Selections from the Speeches and Table-Talk of Mohammad. By S. Lane-Poole. 18mo. 4s. 6d.

LANG (Andrew).—The Library. With a Chapter on Modern Illustrated Books, by Austin Dobson. Crown 8vo. 3s. 6d.

LANKESTER (Prof. E. Ray).—A Chapter in Darwinism, and other Essays and Addresses. 8vo.

LASLETT (Thomas).—Timber and Timber Trees, Native and Foreign. Crown 8vo. 8s. 6d.

LATIN ACCIDENCE AND EXERCISES ARRANGED FOR BEGINNERS. By William Welch, M.A., and C. G. Duffield, M.A. 18mo. 1s. 6d.

LAWRENCE (LORD). By Sir Richard Temple. With Portrait. Crown 8vo. 2s. 6d.

LEAHY (Sergeant).—The Art of Swimming in the Eton Style. With Preface by Mrs. Oliphant. Crown 8vo. 2s.

LECTURES ON ART. By Regd. Stuart Poole, Professor W. B. Richmond, E. J. Poynter, R.A., J. T. Micklethwaite, and William Morris. Crown 8vo. 4s. 6d.

LEE (Margaret).—Faithful and Unfaithful. Crown 8vo. 3s. 6d.

LEGGE (Alfred O.).—The Growth of the Temporal Power of the Papacy. Crown 8vo. 8s. 6d.

LEMON.—The Jest Book. The Choicest Anecdotes and Sayings. Selected by Mark Lemon. 18mo. 4s. 6d.

LETHBRIDGE (Sir Roper).—A Short Manual of the History of India. With Maps. Crown 8vo. 5s.
For other Works by this Author, see *Indian Text-Books Series,* p. 24.

LEVY (Amy).—Reuben Sachs: A Sketch. Crown 8vo. 3s. 6d.

LEWIS (Richard).—History of the Life-boat and its Work. Crown 8vo. 5s.

LIECHTENSTEIN (Princess Marie).—Holland House. With Steel Engravings, Woodcuts, and nearly 40 Illustrations by the Woodburytype Permanent Process. 2 vols. Medium 4to. Half mor., elegant. 4l. 4s.

LIGHTFOOT (The Right Rev. Bishop).—St. Paul's Epistle to the Galatians. A Revised Text, with Introduction, Notes, and Dissertations. 9th Edition. 8vo. 12s.

—— St. Paul's Epistle to the Philippians. A Revised Text, with Introduction, Notes and Dissertations. 9th Edition. 8vo. 12s.

—— St. Clement of Rome. An Appendix, containing the newly-recovered portions. With Introductions, Notes, and Translations. 8vo. 8s. 6d.

—— St. Paul's Epistles to the Colossians and to Philemon. A Revised Text, with Introductions, Notes, and Dissertations. 9th Edition. 8vo. 12s.

—— Primary Charge. Two Addresses delivered to the Clergy of the Diocese of Durham, 1882. 8vo. 2s.

—— The Apostolic Fathers. Part II. S. Ignatius to St. Polycarp. Revised Texts, with Introductions, Notes, Dissertations, and Translations. 3 vols. 2nd Edition. Demy 8vo. 48s.

—— Apostolic Fathers. Abridged Edition. With Short Introductions, Greek Text, and English Translation. 8vo.

—— St. Clement of Rome: The Two Epistles to the Corinthians. A Revised Text, with Introduction and Notes. New Edition. 2 vols. 8vo.

—— A Charge delivered to the Clergy of the Diocese of Durham, Nov. 25th, 1886. Demy 8vo. 2s.

—— Essays on the Work entitled "Supernatural Religion." 8vo. 10s. 6d.

—— Durham Sermons. Crown 8vo.

LIGHTWOOD (J. M.)—The Nature of Positive Law. 8vo. 12s. 6d.

LINDSAY (Dr. J. A.).—The Climatic Treatment of Consumption. Cr. 8vo. 5s.

LITTLE PILGRIM IN THE UNSEEN. 24th Thousand. Crown 8vo. 2s. 6d.

LIVINGSTONE. By Thomas Hughes. With Portrait and Map. Crown 8vo. 2s. 6d.

LIVY. By Rev. W. W. Capes, Fcp. 8vo. 1s. 6d.

LIVY.—HANNIBAL'S FIRST CAMPAIGN IN ITALY. Books XXI. and XXII. Edited by Rev. W. W. CAPES, M.A. Fcp. 8vo. 5s.

—— BOOK I. Edited, with Notes and Vocabulary, by H. M. STEPHENSON, M.A. 18mo. 1s. 6d.

—— BOOKS II. AND III. Edited by H. M. STEPHENSON, M.A. Fcp. 8vo. 5s.

—— THE HANNIBALIAN WAR. Being part of the 21st and 22nd Books of Livy, adapted for the Use of Beginners. By G. C. MACAULAY, M.A. 18mo. 1s. 6d.

—— BOOK XXI. Adapted from Mr. Capes' Edition. With Notes and Vocabulary by W. W. CAPES, M.A., and J. E. MELHUISH, M.A. 18mo. 1s. 6d.

—— BOOKS XXI.—XXV. THE SECOND PUNIC WAR. Translated by A. J. CHURCH, M.A., and W. J. BRODRIBB, M.A. With Maps. Crown 8vo. 7s. 6d.

—— BOOKS XXIII. AND XXIV. Edited by G. C. MACAULAY. Maps. Fcp. 8vo. 5s.

—— THE SIEGE OF SYRACUSE. Being part of Books XXIV. and XXV. of Livy. Adapted for the Use of Beginners, with Notes, Exercises, and Vocabulary, by G. RICHARDS, M.A., and A. S. WALPOLE, M.A. 18mo. 1s. 6d.

—— THE LAST TWO KINGS OF MACEDON. Extracts from the fourth and fifth Decades of Livy. Selected and Edited, with Introduction and Notes, by F. H. RAWLINS, M.A. With Maps. Fcp. 8vo. 3s. 6d.

—— LEGENDS OF ANCIENT ROME, FROM LIVY. Adapted and Edited, with Notes, Exercises, and Vocabularies, by H. WILKINSON, M.A. 18mo. 1s. 6d.

LOCK (Rev. J. B.)—TRIGONOMETRY. Globe 8vo. Part I. ELEMENTARY TRIGONOMETRY. 4s. 6d.—Part II. HIGHER TRIGONOMETRY. 4s. 6d. Complete, 7s. 6d.

—— KEY TO "ELEMENTARY TRIGONOMETRY." By H. CARR, B.A. Crown 8vo. 8s. 6d.

—— TRIGONOMETRY FOR BEGINNERS. As far as the Solution of Triangles. Gl. 8vo. 2s. 6d.

—— KEY TO "TRIGONOMETRY FOR BEGINNERS." Crown 8vo. 6s. 6d.

—— ARITHMETIC FOR SCHOOLS. 4th Edition, revised. Globe 8vo. Complete with Answers, 4s. 6d. Without Answers, 4s. 6d. Part I., with Answers, 2s. Part II., with Answers, 3s.

—— ARITHMETIC FOR BEGINNERS. A School Class-Book of COMMERCIAL ARITHMETIC. Globe 8vo. 2s. 6d.

—— KEY TO "ARITHMETIC FOR BEGINNERS." By Rev. R. G. WATSON. Crown 8vo. 8s. 6d.

—— A SHILLING CLASS-BOOK OF ARITHMETIC ADAPTED FOR USE IN ELEMENTARY SCHOOLS. 18mo.

—— KEY TO "ARITHMETIC FOR SCHOOLS." By the Rev. R. G. WATSON. Cr. 8vo. 10s. 6d.

—— DYNAMICS FOR BEGINNERS. 2nd Edit. Globe 8vo. 4s. 6d.

—— ELEMENTARY STATICS. Gl. 8vo. 4s. 6d.

LOCKE. By Prof. FOWLER. Crown 8vo. 1s. 6d.: sewed, 1s.

LOCKYER (J. Norman, F.R.S.).—ELEMENTARY LESSONS IN ASTRONOMY. With numerous Illustrations and Coloured Diagram. New Edition. 18mo. 5s. 6d.

—— CONTRIBUTIONS TO SOLAR PHYSICS. With Illustrations. Royal 8vo. 31s. 6d.

—— PRIMER OF ASTRONOMY. Illustrated. New Edition. 18mo. 1s.

—— OUTLINES OF PHYSIOGRAPHY: THE MOVEMENTS OF THE EARTH. Crown 8vo. 1s. 6d.

—— THE CHEMISTRY OF THE SUN. 8vo. 14s.

LOCKYER'S ASTRONOMY, QUESTIONS ON. By J. FORBES-ROBERTSON. 18mo. 1s. 6d.

LOCKYER—SEABROKE.—STAR-GAZING PAST AND PRESENT. By J. NORMAN LOCKYER, F.R.S. Expanded from Shorthand Notes with the assistance of G. M. SEABROKE, F.R.A.S. Royal 8vo. 21s.

LODGE (Prof. Oliver J.).—MODERN VIEWS OF ELECTRICITY. Crown 8vo. 6s. 6d.

LOEWY (B.).—QUESTIONS AND EXAMPLES IN EXPERIMENTAL PHYSICS, SOUND, LIGHT, HEAT, ELECTRICITY, AND MAGNETISM. Fcp. 8vo. 2s.

—— A GRADUATED COURSE OF NATURAL SCIENCE, EXPERIMENTAL AND THEORETICAL, FOR SCHOOLS AND COLLEGES. Part I. FIRST YEAR'S COURSE FOR ELEMENTARY SCHOOLS AND THE JUNIOR CLASSES OF TECHNICAL SCHOOLS AND COLLEGES. Globe 8vo. 2s.

LOFTIE (Mrs.).—THE DINING-ROOM. With Illustrations. Crown 8vo. 2s. 6d.

LONGFELLOW.—POEMS OF PLACES: ENGLAND AND WALES. Edited by H. W. LONGFELLOW. 2 vols. 9s.

—— BALLADS, LYRICS, AND SONNETS. From the Poetic Works of HENRY WADSWORTH LONGFELLOW. 18mo. 4s. 6d.

LOWE (W. H.).—THE HEBREW STUDENT'S COMMENTARY ON ZECHARIAH HEBREW AND LXX. 8vo. 10s. 6d.

LOWELL (James Russell).—COMPLETE POETICAL WORKS. 18mo. 4s. 6d.

—— HEARTSEASE AND RUE. Crown 8vo. 5s.

—— POLITICAL ESSAYS. Ext. cr. 8vo. 7s. 6d.

LUBBOCK (Sir John, Bart.).—THE ORIGIN AND METAMORPHOSES OF INSECTS. With Illustrations. Crown 8vo. 3s. 6d.

—— ON BRITISH WILD FLOWERS CONSIDERED IN THEIR RELATION TO INSECTS. With Illustrations. Crown 8vo. 4s. 6d.

—— FLOWERS, FRUITS, AND LEAVES. With Illustrations. Crown 8vo. 4s. 6d.

—— SCIENTIFIC LECTURES. With Illustrations. New Edition, revised. 8vo. 8s. 6d.

—— POLITICAL AND EDUCATIONAL ADDRESSES. 8vo. 8s. 6d.

—— THE PLEASURES OF LIFE. New Edition. Gl. 8vo. 1s. 6d.; swd., 1s. 60th Thousand. *Library Edition.* Globe 8vo. 3s. 6d. Part II. Globe 8vo. 1s. 6d.; sewed, 1s. *Library Edition.* Globe 8vo. 3s. 6d.

LUCAS (F.).—SKETCHES OF RURAL LIFE. Poems. Globe 8vo. 5s.

LUCIAN.—EXTRACTS FROM LUCIAN. Edited, with Introduction, Exercises, Notes, and Vocabulary, by the Rev. J. BOND, M.A., and A. S. WALPOLE, M.A. 18mo. 1s. 6d.

LUCRETIUS.—BOOKS I.—III. Edited by J. H. WARBURTON LEE. Fcp. 8vo. 4s. 6d.

LUPTON (J. H.).—AN INTRODUCTION TO LATIN ELEGIAC VERSE COMPOSITION. Globe 8vo. 2s. 6d.

—— LATIN RENDERING OF THE EXERCISES IN PART II. (XXV.-C.) TO LUPTON'S "INTRODUCTION TO LATIN ELEGIAC VERSE COMPOSITION." Globe 8vo. 3s. 6d.

—— AN INTRODUCTION TO LATIN LYRIC VERSE COMPOSITION. Globe 8vo. 3s.—Key, 4s. 6d.

LUPTON (Sydney).—CHEMICAL ARITHMETIC. With 1200 Examples. Fcp. 8vo. 4s. 6d.

—— NUMERICAL TABLES AND CONSTANTS IN ELEMENTARY SCIENCE. Ex. fcp. 8vo. 2s. 6d.

LYALL (Sir Alfred).—WARREN HASTINGS. With Portrait. 2s. 6d.

LYSIAS.—SELECT ORATIONS. Edited by E. S. SHUCKBURGH, M.A. Fcp. 8vo. 6s.

LYRE FRANÇAISE (LA). Selected and arranged by G. MASSON. 18mo. 4s. 6d.

LYTE (H. C. Maxwell).—ETON COLLEGE, HISTORY OF, 1440—1884. With Illustrations. 2nd Edition. 8vo. 21s.

—— THE UNIVERSITY OF OXFORD, A HISTORY OF, FROM THE EARLIEST TIMES TO THE YEAR 1530. 8vo. 16s.

LYTTON (Rt. Hon. Earl of).—THE RING OF AMASIS: A ROMANCE. Crown 8vo. 3s. 6d.

MACARTHUR (Margaret). — HISTORY OF SCOTLAND. 18mo. 2s.

MACAULAY. By J. C. MORISON. Crown 8vo. 1s. 6d.; sewed, 1s.

M'CLELLAND (W. J.) and PRESTON (T.). —A TREATISE ON SPHERICAL TRIGONOMETRY. With numerous Examples. Crown 8vo. 8s. 6d.—Or Part I. 4s. 6d.; Part II. 5s.

McCOSH (Rev. Dr. James).—THE METHOD OF THE DIVINE GOVERNMENT, PHYSICAL AND MORAL. 8vo. 10s. 6d.

—— THE SUPERNATURAL IN RELATION TO THE NATURAL. Crown 8vo. 7s. 6d.

—— THE INTUITIONS OF THE MIND. New Edition. 8vo. 10s. 6d.

—— AN EXAMINATION OF MR. J. S. MILL'S PHILOSOPHY. 8vo. 10s. 6d.

—— THE LAWS OF DISCURSIVE THOUGHT. A Text-Book of Formal Logic. Crn. 8vo. 5s.

—— CHRISTIANITY AND POSITIVISM. Lectures on Natural Theology and Apologetics. Crown 8vo. 7s. 6d.

—— THE SCOTTISH PHILOSOPHY, FROM HUTCHESON TO HAMILTON, BIOGRAPHICAL, EXPOSITORY, CRITICAL. Royal 8vo. 16s.

—— THE EMOTIONS. 8vo. 9s.

—— REALISTIC PHILOSOPHY DEFENDED IN A PHILOSOPHIC SERIES. 2 vols. Vol. I. EXPOSITORY. Vol. II. HISTORICAL AND CRITICAL. Crown 8vo. 14s.

McCOSH (Rev. Dr.).—PSYCHOLOGY. Crown 8vo. I. THE COGNITIVE POWERS. 6s. 6d.— II. THE MOTIVE POWERS. 6s. 6d.

—— FIRST AND FUNDAMENTAL TRUTHS. Being a Treatise on Metaphysics. 8vo. 9s.

MACDONALD (George).—ENGLAND'S ANTIPHON. Crown 8vo. 4s. 6d.

MACDONELL (John).—THE LAND QUESTION. 8vo. 10s. 6d.

MACFARLANE (Alexander). — PHYSICAL ARITHMETIC. Crown 8vo. 7s. 6d.

MACGREGOR (James Gordon).—AN ELEMENTARY TREATISE ON KINEMATICS AND DYNAMICS. Crown 8vo. 10s. 6d.

MACKENZIE (Sir Morell).—THE HYGIENE OF THE VOCAL ORGANS. 6th Edition. Crn. 8vo. 6s.

MACKIE (Rev. Ellis).—PARALLEL PASSAGES FOR TRANSLATION INTO GREEK AND ENGLISH. Globe 8vo. 4s. 6d.

MACLAGAN (Dr. T.).—THE GERM THEORY. 8vo. 10s. 6d.

MACLAREN (Rev. Alexander). — SERMONS PREACHED AT MANCHESTER. 11th Edition. Fcp. 8vo. 4s. 6d.

—— A SECOND SERIES OF SERMONS. 7th Edition. Fcp. 8vo. 4s. 6d.

—— A THIRD SERIES. 6th Edition. Fcp. 8vo. 4s. 6d.

—— WEEK-DAY EVENING ADDRESSES. 4th Edition. Fcp. 8vo. 2s. 6d.

—— THE SECRET OF POWER, AND OTHER SERMONS. Fcp. 8vo. 4s. 6d.

MACLAREN (Arch.).—THE FAIRY FAMILY. A Series of Ballads and Metrical Tales. Crown 8vo, gilt. 5s.

MACLEAN (Surgeon-General W. C.).— DISEASES OF TROPICAL CLIMATES. Crown 8vo. 10s. 6d.

MACLEAR (Rev. Canon).—A CLASS-BOOK OF OLD TESTAMENT HISTORY. With Four Maps. 18mo. 4s. 6d.

—— A CLASS-BOOK OF NEW TESTAMENT HISTORY. Including the connection of the Old and New Testament. 18mo. 5s. 6d.

—— A CLASS-BOOK OF THE CATECHISM OF THE CHURCH OF ENGLAND. 18mo. 1s. 6d.

—— A SHILLING BOOK OF OLD TESTAMENT HISTORY. 18mo. 1s.

—— A SHILLING BOOK OF NEW TESTAMENT HISTORY. 18mo. 1s.

—— A FIRST CLASS-BOOK OF THE CATECHISM OF THE CHURCH OF ENGLAND, WITH SCRIPTURE PROOFS FOR JUNIOR CLASSES AND SCHOOLS. 18mo. 6d.

—— A MANUAL OF INSTRUCTION FOR CONFIRMATION AND FIRST COMMUNION, WITH PRAYERS AND DEVOTIONS. 32mo. 2s.

—— FIRST COMMUNION, WITH PRAYERS AND DEVOTIONS FOR THE NEWLY CONFIRMED. 32mo. 6d.

—— THE ORDER OF CONFIRMATION, WITH PRAYERS AND DEVOTIONS. 32mo. 6d.

—— THE HOUR OF SORROW; OR, THE OFFICE FOR THE BURIAL OF THE DEAD. 32mo. 2s.

MACLEAR (Rev. Dr.).—APOSTLES OF MEDI-AEVAL EUROPE. Crown 8vo. 4s. 6d.

—— AN INTRODUCTION TO THE CREEDS. 18mo. 2s. 6d.

—— AN INTRODUCTION TO THE THIRTY-NINE ARTICLES. 18mo.

M'LENNAN (J. F.).—THE PATRIARCHAL THEORY. Edited and completed by DONALD M'LENNAN, M.A. 8vo. 14s.

—— STUDIES IN ANCIENT HISTORY. Comprising a Reprint of "Primitive Marriage." New Edition. 8vo. 16s.

MACMILLAN (D.). MEMOIR OF DANIEL MACMILLAN. By THOMAS HUGHES, Q.C. Crown 8vo. 4s. 6d.

Popular Edition. Crown 8vo, sewed. 1s.

MACMILLAN (Rev. Hugh).—BIBLE TEACHINGS IN NATURE. 15th Ed. Gl. 8vo. 6s.

—— HOLIDAYS ON HIGH LANDS; OR, RAMBLES AND INCIDENTS IN SEARCH OF ALPINE PLANTS. 2nd Edition. Globe 8vo. 6s.

—— THE TRUE VINE; OR, THE ANALOGIES OF OUR LORD'S ALLEGORY. 5th Edition. Globe 8vo. 6s.

—— THE MINISTRY OF NATURE. 8th Edition. Globe 8vo. 6s.

—— THE SABBATH OF THE FIELDS. 6th Edition. Globe 8vo. 6s.

—— THE MARRIAGE IN CANA. Globe 8vo. 6s.

—— TWO WORLDS ARE OURS. 3rd Edition. Globe 8vo. 6s.

—— THE OLIVE LEAF. Globe 8vo. 6s.

—— ROMAN MOSAICS; OR, STUDIES IN ROME AND ITS NEIGHBOURHOOD. Globe 8vo. 6s.

MACMILLAN (M. C.) FIRST LATIN GRAMMAR. Extra fcp. 8vo. 1s. 6d.

MACMILLAN'S MAGAZINE. Published Monthly. 1s.—Vols. I.—LXI. 7s. 6d. each.

MACMILLAN'S SIX-SHILLING NOVELS. 6s. each vol. Crown 8vo, cloth.

By the Rev. Charles Kingsley.
WESTWARD HO!
HYPATIA.
HEREWARD THE WAKE.
TWO YEARS AGO.
YEAST.
ALTON LOCKE. With Portrait.

By William Black.
A PRINCESS OF THULE.
STRANGE ADVENTURES OF A PHAETON. Illustrated.
THE MAID OF KILLEENA, AND OTHER TALES.
MADCAP VIOLET.
GREEN PASTURES AND PICCADILLY.
THE BEAUTIFUL WRETCH; THE FOUR MACNICOLS; THE PUPIL OF AURELIUS.
MACLEOD OF DARE. Illustrated.
WHITE WINGS: A YACHTING ROMANCE.
SHANDON BELLS.
YOLANDE.

MACMILLAN'S SIX-SHILLING NOVELS—*continued.*

By William Black.
JUDITH SHAKESPEARE.
THE WISE WOMEN OF INVERNESS, A TALE; AND OTHER MISCELLANIES.
WHITE HEATHER.
SABINA ZEMBRA.

By Mrs. Craik, Author of "John Halifax, Gentleman."
THE OGILVIES. Illustrated.
THE HEAD OF THE FAMILY. Illustrated.
OLIVE. Illustrated.
AGATHA'S HUSBAND. Illustrated.
MY MOTHER AND I. Illustrated.
MISS TOMMY: A MEDIÆVAL ROMANCE. Illustrated.
KING ARTHUR: NOT A LOVE STORY.

By J. H. Shorthouse.
JOHN INGLESANT.
SIR PERCIVAL.
A TEACHER OF THE VIOLIN, AND OTHER TALES.
THE COUNTESS EVE.

By Annie Keary.
A DOUBTING HEART.

By Henry James.
THE AMERICAN.
THE EUROPEANS.
DAISY MILLER; AN INTERNATIONAL EPISODE; FOUR MEETINGS.
THE MADONNA OF THE FUTURE, AND OTHER TALES.
RODERICK HUDSON.
WASHINGTON SQUARE; THE PENSION BEAUREPAS; A BUNDLE OF LETTERS.
THE PORTRAIT OF A LADY.
STORIES REVIVED. Two Series. 6s. each.
THE BOSTONIANS.
THE REVERBERATOR.

By F. Marion Crawford.
SANT' ILARIO.
GREIFENSTEIN.

———

REALMAH. By the Author of "Friends in Council."
OLD SIR DOUGLAS. By the Hon. Mrs. NORTON.
VIRGIN SOIL. By TOURGENIEF.
THE HARBOUR BAR.
BENGAL PEASANT LIFE. By LAL BEHARI DAY.
VIDA: STUDY OF A GIRL. By AMY DUNSMUIR.
JILL. By E. A. DILLWYN.
NEÆRA: A TALE OF ANCIENT ROME. By J. W. GRAHAM.
THE NEW ANTIGONE: A ROMANCE.

MACMILLAN'S THREE - AND - SIX-PENNY NOVELS. Crown 8vo. 3s. 6d.

ROBBERY UNDER ARMS: A Story of Life and Adventure in the Bush and in the Goldfields of Australia. By ROLF BOLDREWOOD.

SCHWARTZ. By D. CHRISTIE MURRAY.

NEIGHBOURS ON THE GREEN. By Mrs. OLIPHANT.

THE WEAKER VESSEL. By D. CHRISTIE MURRAY.

JOYCE. By Mrs. OLIPHANT.

CRESSY. By BRET HARTE.

FAITHFUL AND UNFAITHFUL. By MARGARET LEE.

REUBEN SACHS. By AMY LEVY.

WESSEX TALES: STRANGE, LIVELY, AND COMMONPLACE. By THOMAS HARDY.

MISS BRETHERTON. By Mrs. HUMPHRY WARD.

A LONDON LIFE. By HENRY JAMES.

A BELEAGUERED CITY. By Mrs. OLIPHANT.

CASTLE DALY. By ANNIE KEARY.

THE WOODLANDERS. By THOMAS HARDY.

AUNT RACHEL. By D. CHRISTIE MURRAY.

LOUISIANA, AND THAT LASS O' LOWRIE'S. By FRANCES HODGSON BURNETT.

THE CŒRULEANS. By Sir H. CUNNINGHAM.

THE RING OF AMASIS. By Lord LYTTON.

Uniform with the above.

STORM WARRIORS; OR, LIFEBOAT WORK ON THE GOODWIN SANDS. By the Rev. JOHN GILMORE.

TALES OF OLD JAPAN. By A. B. MITFORD.

A YEAR WITH THE BIRDS. By W. WARDE FOWLER. Illustrated by BRYAN HOOK.

TALES OF THE BIRDS. By the same. Illustrated by BRYAN HOOK.

MACMILLAN'S TWO SHILLING NOVELS. Globe 8vo. 2s. each.

By Mrs. Craik, Author of "John Halifax, Gentleman."

TWO MARRIAGES.

AGATHA'S HUSBAND.

THE OGILVIES.

By Mrs. Oliphant.

THE CURATE IN CHARGE.

A SON OF THE SOIL.

YOUNG MUSGRAVE.

HE THAT WILL NOT WHEN HE MAY.

A COUNTRY GENTLEMAN.

HESTER. | SIR TOM.

THE SECOND SON.

THE WIZARD'S SON.

By the Author of "Hogan, M.P."

HOGAN, M.P.

THE HONOURABLE MISS FERRARD.

FLITTERS, TATTERS, AND THE COUNSELLOR, WEEDS, AND OTHER SKETCHES.

CHRISTY CAREW. | ISMAY'S CHILDREN.

MACMILLAN'S TWO-SHILLING NOVELS—*continued*.

By George Fleming.

A NILE NOVEL.

MIRAGE.

THE HEAD OF MEDUSA.

VESTIGIA.

By Mrs. Macquoid.

PATTY.

By Annie Keary.

JANET'S HOME.

OLDBURY.

CLEMENCY FRANKLYN.

A YORK AND A LANCASTER ROSE.

By W. E. Norris.

MY FRIEND JIM. | CHRIS.

By Henry James.

DAISY MILLER; AN INTERNATIONAL EPISODE; FOUR MEETINGS.

RODERICK HUDSON.

THE MADONNA OF THE FUTURE, AND OTHER TALES.

WASHINGTON SQUARE.

PRINCESS CASAMASSIMA.

By Frances Hodgson Burnett.

LOUISIANA, AND THAT LASS O' LOWRIE'S. Two Stories.

HAWORTH'S.

By Hugh Conway.

A FAMILY AFFAIR.

LIVING OR DEAD.

By D. Christie Murray.

AUNT RACHEL.

By Helen Jackson.

RAMONA: A STORY.

A SLIP IN THE FENS.

MACMILLAN'S HALF-CROWN SERIES OF JUVENILE BOOKS. Globe 8vo, cloth, extra. 2s. 6d.

OUR YEAR. By the Author of "John Halifax, Gentleman."

LITTLE SUNSHINE'S HOLIDAY. By the Author of "John Halifax, Gentleman."

WHEN I WAS A LITTLE GIRL. By the Author of "St. Olave's."

NINE YEARS OLD. By the Author of "When I was a Little Girl," etc.

A STOREHOUSE OF STORIES. Edited by CHARLOTTE M. YONGE. 2 vols.

AGNES HOPETOUN'S SCHOOLS AND HOLIDAYS. By Mrs. OLIPHANT.

THE STORY OF A FELLOW SOLDIER. By FRANCES AWDRY. (A Life of Bishop Patteson for the Young.)

RUTH AND HER FRIENDS: A STORY FOR GIRLS.

THE HEROES OF ASGARD: TALES FROM SCANDINAVIAN MYTHOLOGY. By A. and E. KEARY.

MACMILLAN'S HALF-CROWN SERIES OF JUVENILE BOOKS—*continued*.

THE RUNAWAY. By the Author of "Mrs. Jerningham's Journal."

WANDERING WILLIE. By the Author of "Conrad the Squirrel."

PANSIE'S FLOUR BIN. Illustrated by ADRIAN STOKES.

MILLY AND OLLY. By Mrs. T. H. WARD. Illustrated by Mrs. ALMA TADEMA.

HANNAH TARNE. By MARY E. HULLAH. Illustrated by W. J. HENNESSY.

"CARROTS," JUST A LITTLE BOY. By Mrs. MOLESWORTH. Illust. by WALTER CRANE.

TELL ME A STORY. By Mrs. MOLESWORTH. Illustrated by WALTER CRANE.

THE CUCKOO CLOCK. By Mrs. MOLESWORTH. Illustrated by WALTER CRANE.

A CHRISTMAS CHILD. By Mrs. MOLESWORTH. Illustrated by WALTER CRANE.

ROSY. By Mrs. MOLESWORTH. Illustrated by WALTER CRANE.

THE TAPESTRY ROOM. by Mrs. MOLESWORTH. Illustrated by WALTER CRANE.

GRANDMOTHER DEAR. By Mrs. MOLESWORTH. Illustrated by WALTER CRANE.

HERR BABY. By Mrs. MOLESWORTH. Illustrated by WALTER CRANE.

"US": AN OLD-FASHIONED STORY. By Mrs. MOLESWORTH. Illust. by W. CRANE.

THE POPULATION OF AN OLD PEAR TREE; OR, STORIES OF INSECT LIFE. From the French of E. VAN BRUYSSEL. Edited by CHARLOTTE M. YONGE. Illustrated.

LITTLE MISS PEGGY. By Mrs. MOLESWORTH. Illustrated by WALTER CRANE.

TWO LITTLE WAIFS. By Mrs. MOLESWORTH. Illustrated by WALTER CRANE.

CHRISTMAS-TREE LAND. By Mrs. MOLESWORTH. Illustrated by WALTER CRANE.

MACMILLAN'S READING BOOKS.

Adapted to the English and Scotch Codes.

Primer . . . . (48 pp.) 18mo, 2*d*.
Book I. for Standard I. (96 pp.) 18mo, 4*d*.
Book II. for Standard II. (144 pp.) 18mo, 5*d*.
Book III. for Standard III. (160 pp.) 18mo, 6*d*.
Book IV. for Standard IV. (176 pp.) 18mo, 8*d*.
Book V. for Standard V. (380 pp.) 18mo, 1s.
Book VI. for Standard VI. (430 pp.) Cr. 8vo, 2s.

MACMILLAN'S COPY-BOOKS.

*1. Initiatory Exercises and Short Letters.
*2. Words consisting of Short Letters.
*3. Long Letters, with words containing Long Letters. Figures.
*4. Words containing Long Letters.
4A. Practising and Revising Copybook for Nos. 1 to 4.
*5. Capitals, and Short Half-text Words beginning with a Capital.
*6. Half-text Words beginning with a Capital. Figures.
*7. Small-hand and Half-text, with Capitals and Figures.
*8. Small-hand and Half-text, with Capitals and Figures.

MACMILLAN'S COPY-BOOKS—*contd*.

8A. Practising and Revising Copybook for Nos. 5 to 8.
*9. Small-hand Single Head Lines. Figures.
10. Small-hand Single Head Lines. Figures.
*11. Small-hand Double Head Lines. Figures.
12. Commercial and Arithmetical Examples, etc.
12A. Practising and Revising Copybook for Nos. 8 to 12.

The Copybooks may be had in two sizes:
(1) Large Post 4to, 4*d*. each;
(2) Post oblong, 2*d*. each.

The numbers marked * may also be had in Large Post 4to, with GOODMAN'S PATENT SLIDING COPIES. 6*d*. each.

MACMILLAN'S LATIN COURSE. Part I. By A. M. COOK, M.A. 2nd Edition, enlarged. Globe 8vo. 3s. 6*d*.

Part II. By the same. Gl. 8vo. 2s. 6*d*.

MACMILLAN'S SHORTER LATIN COURSE. By A. M. COOK, M.A. Being an Abridgment of "Macmillan's Latin Course, Part I." Globe 8vo. 1s. 6*d*.

MACMILLAN'S LATIN READER. A Latin Reader for the Lower Forms in Schools. By H. J. HARDY. Gl. 8vo. 2s. 6*d*.

MACMILLAN'S GREEK COURSE. Edit. by Rev. W. G. RUTHERFORD, M.A. Gl. 8vo.

I. FIRST GREEK GRAMMAR. By the Rev. W. G. RUTHERFORD, M.A., LL.D. Part I. Accidence, 2s.; Part II. Syntax, 2s.; or in 1 vol. 3s. 6*d*.

II. EASY EXERCISES IN GREEK ACCIDENCE. By H. G. UNDERHILL, M.A. 2s.

III. SECOND GREEK EXERCISE BOOK. By Rev. W. A. HEARD, M.A.

MACMILLAN'S GREEK READER. Stories and Legends. A First Greek Reader. With Notes, Vocabulary, and Exercises, by F. H. COLSON, M.A. Globe 8vo. 3s.

MACMILLAN'S ELEMENTARY CLASSICS. 18mo. 1s. 6*d*. each.

This Series falls into two classes:—

(1) First Reading Books for Beginners, provided not only with *Introductions and Notes*, but with *Vocabularies*, and in some cases with *Exercises* based upon the Text.

(2) Stepping-stones to the study of particular authors, intended for more advanced students, who are beginning to read such authors as Terence, Plato, the Attic Dramatists, and the harder parts of Cicero, Horace, Virgil, and Thucydides.

These are provided with Introductions and Notes, but no *Vocabulary*. The Publishers have been led to provide the more strictly Elementary Books with Vocabularies by the representations of many teachers, who hold that beginners do not understand the use of a Dictionary, and of others who, in the case of middle-class schools where the cost of books is a serious consideration, advocate the Vocabulary system on grounds of economy. It is hoped that the two parts of the Series, fitting into one another, may together fulfil all the requirements of Elementary and Preparatory Schools, and the Lower Forms of Public Schools.

MACMILLAN'S ELEMENTARY CLAS-SICS—*continued.*

The following Elementary Books, *with Introductions, Notes, and Vocabularies,* and in some cases with *Exercises,* are either ready or in preparation:

LATIN ACCIDENCE AND EXERCISES ARRANGED FOR BEGINNERS. By WILLIAM WELCH, M.A., and C. G. DUFFIELD, M.A.

ÆSCHYLUS.—PROMETHEUS VINCTUS. Edit. by Rev. H. M. STEPHENSON, M.A.

ARRIAN.—SELECTIONS. Edited by JOHN BOND, M.A., and A. S. WALPOLE, M.A.

AULUS GELLIUS, STORIES FROM. By Rev. G. H. NALL, M.A.

CÆSAR.—THE GALLIC WAR. Book I. Edit. by A. S. WALPOLE, M.A.

— THE INVASION OF BRITAIN. Being Selections from Books IV. and V. of the "De Bello Gallico." Adapted for Beginners by W. WELCH, and C. G. DUFFIELD.

— THE HELVETIAN WAR. Selected from Book I. of "The Gallic War," arranged for the use of Beginners by W. WELCH, M.A., and C. G. DUFFIELD, M.A.

— THE GALLIC WAR. Books II. and III. Ed. by Rev. W. G. RUTHERFORD, M.A.

— THE GALLIC WAR. Book IV. Edited by C. BRYANS, M.A.

— THE GALLIC WAR. Scenes from Books V. and VI. Edited by C. COLBECK, M.A.

— THE GALLIC WAR. Books V. and VI. (separately). By the same Editor.

— THE GALLIC WAR. Book VII. Ed. by J. BOND, M.A., and A. S. WALPOLE, M.A.

CICERO.—DE SENECTUTE. Edited by E. S. SHUCKBURGH, M.A.

— DE AMICITIA. Edited by E. S. SHUCKBURGH, M.A.

— STORIES OF ROMAN HISTORY. Edited by Rev. G. E. JEANS, M.A., and A. V. JONES, M.A.

EURIPIDES.—ALCESTIS. By the Rev. M. A. BAYFIELD, M.A.

— HECUBA. Edited by Rev. J. BOND, M.A., and A. S. WALPOLE, M.A.

EUTROPIUS. Adapted for the use of Beginners by W. WELCH, M.A., and C. G. DUFFIELD, M.A.

HOMER.—ILIAD. Book I. Ed. by Rev. J. BOND, M.A., and A. S. WALPOLE, M.A.

— ILIAD. Book XVIII. THE ARMS OF ACHILLES. Edited by S. R. JAMES, M.A.

— ODYSSEY. Book I. Edited by Rev. J. BOND, M.A., and A. S. WALPOLE, M.A.

HORACE.—ODES. Books I.—IV. Edited by T. E. PAGE, M.A. 1s. 6d. each.

LIVY. Book I. Edited by H. M. STEPHENSON, M.A.

— THE HANNIBALIAN WAR. Being part of the 21st and 22nd Books of Livy. Adapted for Beginners by G. C. MACAULAY, M.A.

— THE SIEGE OF SYRACUSE. Being part of the 24th and 25th Books of Livy. Adapted for the use of Beginners by G. RICHARDS, M.A., and A. S. WALPOLE, M.A.

MACMILLAN'S ELEMENTARY CLAS-SICS—*continued.*

LIVY, Book XXI. With Notes adapted from Mr. Capes' Edition for the Use of Junior Students, by W. W. CAPES, M.A., and J. E. MELHUISH, M.A.

— LEGENDS OF ANCIENT ROME, FROM LIVY. Adapted for the Use of Beginners. With Notes, Exercises, and Vocabulary, by H. WILKINSON, M.A.

LUCIAN, EXTRACTS FROM. Edited by J. BOND, M.A., and A. S. WALPOLE, M.A.

NEPOS.—SELECTIONS ILLUSTRATIVE OF GREEK AND ROMAN HISTORY. Edited by G. S. FARNELL, B.A.

OVID.—SELECTIONS. Edited by E. S. SHUCKBURGH, M.A.

— EASY SELECTIONS FROM OVID IN ELEGIAC VERSE. Arranged for the use of Beginners by H. WILKINSON, M.A.

— STORIES FROM THE METAMORPHOSES. Arranged for the use of Beginners by J. BOND, M.A., and A. S. WALPOLE, M.A.

PHÆDRUS.—SELECT FABLES. Adapted for use of Beginners by A. S. WALPOLE, M.A.

THUCYDIDES.—THE RISE OF THE ATHENIAN EMPIRE. Book I. Chaps. lxxxix.—cxvii. and cxxviii.—cxxxviii. Edited by F. H. COLSON, M.A.

VIRGIL.—GEORGICS. Book I. Edited by T. E. PAGE, M.A.

— ÆNEID. Book I. Edited by A. S. WALPOLE, M.A.

— ÆNEID. Book II. Ed. by T. E. PAGE.

— ÆNEID. Book III. Edited by T. E. PAGE, M.A.

— ÆNEID. Book IV. Edit. by Rev. H. M. STEPHENSON, M.A.

— ÆNEID. Book V. Edited by Rev. A. CALVERT, M.A.

— ÆNEID. Book VI. Ed. by T. E. PAGE, M.A.

— ÆNEID. Book VII. THE WRATH OF TURNUS. Edited by A. CALVERT, M.A.

— ÆNEID. Book IX. Edited by Rev. H. M. STEPHENSON, M.A.

— SELECTIONS. Edited by E. S. SHUCKBURGH, M.A.

XENOPHON.—ANABASIS. Book I. Edited by A. S. WALPOLE, M.A.

— ANABASIS. Book I., Chaps. i.—viii. Edit. by E. A. WELLS, M.A.

— ANABASIS. Book II. Edited by A. S. WALPOLE, M.A.

— SELECTIONS FROM BOOK IV. OF "THE ANABASIS." Edit. by Rev. E. D. STONE.

— SELECTIONS FROM THE CYROPAEDIA. Edited by Rev. A. H. COOKE, M.A.

The following more advanced books have *Introductions, Notes,* but no *Vocabularies:*

CICERO.—SELECT LETTERS. Edit. by Rev. G. E. JEANS, M.A.

HERODOTUS.—SELECTIONS FROM BOOKS VII. AND VIII. THE EXPEDITION OF XERXES. Edited by A. H. COOKE, M.A.

MACMILLAN'S ELEMENTARY CLAS-SICS—*continued.*

HORACE.—SELECTIONS FROM THE SATIRES AND EPISTLES. Edited by Rev. W. J. V. BAKER, M.A.

— SELECT EPODES AND ARS POETICA. Edited by H. A. DALTON, M.A.

PLATO.—EUTHYPHRO AND MENEXENUS. Edited by C. E. GRAVES, M.A.

TERENCE.—SCENES FROM THE ANDRIA. Edited by F. W. CORNISH, M.A.

THE GREEK ELEGIAC POETS, FROM CAL-LINUS TO CALLIMACHUS. Selected and Edited by Rev. H. KYNASTON.

THUCYDIDES. Book IV., Chaps. i.—lxi. THE CAPTURE OF SPHACTERIA. Edited by C. E. GRAVES, M.A.

VIRGIL.—GEORGICS. Book II. Edited by Rev. J. H. SKRINE, M.A.

Other Volumes to follow.

MACMILLAN'S CLASSICAL SERIES FOR COLLEGES AND SCHOOLS. Fcp. 8vo. Being select portions of Greek and Latin authors, edited, with Introductions and Notes, for the use of Middle and Upper Forms of Schools, or of Candidates for Public Examinations at the Universities and else-where.

ÆSCHINES.—IN CTESIPHONTEM. Edited by Rev. T. GWATKIN, M.A., and E. S. SHUCKBURGH, M.A. *[In the Press.*

ÆSCHYLUS.—PERSÆ. Edited by A. O. PRICKARD, M.A. With Map. 3s. 6d.

— THE "SEVEN AGAINST THEBES." Edit. by A. W. VERRALL, Litt.D., and M. A. BAYFIELD, M.A. 3s. 6d.

ANDOCIDES.—DE MYSTERIIS. Edited by W. J. HICKIE, M.A. 2s. 6d.

ATTIC ORATORS, SELECTIONS FROM THE. Antiphon, Andocides, Lysias, Isocrates, and Isæus. Ed. by R. C. JEBB, Litt.D. 6s.

CÆSAR.—THE GALLIC WAR. Edited after Kraner by Rev. J. BOND, M.A., and A. S. WALPOLE, M.A. With Maps. 6s.

CATULLUS.—SELECT POEMS. Edited by F. P. SIMPSON, B.A. 5s. [The Text of this Edition is carefully adapted to School use.]

CICERO.—THE CATILINE ORATIONS. From the German of Karl Halm. Edited by A. S. WILKINS, Litt.D. 3s. 6d.

— PRO LEGE MANILIA. Edited, after Halm, by Prof. A. S. WILKINS, Litt.D. 2s. 6d.

— THE SECOND PHILIPPIC ORATION. From the German of Karl Halm. Edited, with Corrections and Additions, by Prof. J. E. B. MAYOR. 5s.

— PRO ROSCIO AMERINO. Edited, after Halm, by E. H. DONKIN, M.A. 4s. 6d.

— PRO P. SESTIO. Edited by Rev. H. A. HOLDEN, M.A. 5s.

DEMOSTHENES.—DE CORONA. Edited by B. DRAKE, M.A. New and revised edit. 4s. 6d.

— ADVERSUS LEPTINEM. Edited by Rev. J. R. KING, M.A. 4s. 6d.

— THE FIRST PHILIPPIC. Edited, after C. Rehdantz, by Rev. T. GWATKIN. 2s. 6d.

MACMILLAN'S CLASSICAL SERIES—*continued.*

EURIPIDES.—HIPPOLYTUS. Edited by Prof. J. P. MAHAFFY and J. B. BURY. 3s. 6d.

— MEDEA. Edited by A. W. VERRALL, Litt.D. 3s. 6d.

— IPHIGENIA IN TAURIS. Edited by E. B. ENGLAND, M.A. 4s. 6d.

— ION. Ed. by M. A. BAYFIELD, M.A. 3s. 6d.

HERODOTUS. Books VII. and VIII. Edit. by Mrs. MONTAGU BUTLER.

HOMER.—ILIAD. Books I. IX. XI. XVI.-XXIV. THE STORY OF ACHILLES. Ed. by J. H. PRATT, M.A., and W. LEAF, Litt.D. 6s.

— ODYSSEY. Book IX. Edited by Prof. J. E. B. MAYOR, M.A. 2s. 6d.

— ODYSSEY. Books XXI.—XXIV. THE TRIUMPH OF ODYSSEUS. Edited by S. G. HAMILTON, B.A. 3s. 6d.

HORACE.—THE ODES. Edited by T. E. PAGE, M.A. 6s. (Books I. II. III. and IV. separately, 2s. each.)

— THE SATIRES. Edited by Prof. A. PALMER, M.A. 6s.

— THE EPISTLES AND ARS POETICA. Edit. by Prof. A. S. WILKINS, Litt.D. 6s.

JUVENAL.—THIRTEEN SATIRES. Edited, for the use of Schools, by E. G. HARDY, M.A. 5s. [The Text of this Edition is carefully adapted to School use.]

— SELECT SATIRES. Edited by Prof. JOHN E. B. MAYOR. X. and XI. 3s. 6d.; XII.—XVI. 4s. 6d.

LIVY. Books II. and III. Edited by Rev. H. M. STEPHENSON, M.A. 5s.

— Books XXI. and XXII. Edited by Rev. W. W. CAPES, M.A. 5s.

— Books XXIII. and XXIV. Ed. by G. C. MACAULAY. With Maps. 5s.

— THE LAST TWO KINGS OF MACEDON. Extracts from the Fourth and Fifth De-cades of Livy. Selected and Edit. by F. H. RAWLINS, M.A. With Maps. 3s. 6d.

LUCRETIUS. Books I.—III. Edited by J. H. WARBURTON LEE, M.A. 4s. 6d.

LYSIAS.—SELECT ORATIONS. Edited by E. S. SHUCKBURGH, M.A. 6s.

MARTIAL.—SELECT EPIGRAMS. Edited by Rev. H. M. STEPHENSON, M.A. 6s. 6d.

OVID.—FASTI. Edited by G. H. HALLAM, M.A. With Maps. 5s.

— HEROIDUM EPISTULÆ XIII. Edited by E. S. SHUCKBURGH, M.A. 4s. 6d.

— METAMORPHOSES. Books XIII. and XIV. Edited by C. SIMMONS, M.A. 4s. 6d.

PLATO.—THE REPUBLIC. Books I.—V. Edited by T. H. WARREN, M.A. 6s.

— LACHES. Edited by M. T. TATHAM, M.A. 2s. 6d.

PLAUTUS.—MILES GLORIOSUS. Edited by Prof. R. Y. TYRRELL, M.A. 5s.

— AMPHITRUO. Ed. by A. PALMER, M.A. 5s.

PLINY.—LETTERS. Books I. and II. Edited by J. COWAN, M.A. 5s.

MACMILLAN'S CLASSICAL SERIES—
continued.

PLINY.—LETTERS. Book III. Edited by Prof. J. E. B. MAYOR. With Life of Pliny by G. H. RENDALL. 5*s.*

PLUTARCH.—LIFE OF THEMISTOKLES. Ed. by Rev. H. A. HOLDEN, M.A., L.L.D. 5*s.*

— LIVES OF GALBA AND OTHO. Edited by E. G. HARDY, M.A. 6*s.*

POLYBIUS. The History of the Achæan League as contained in the remains of Polybius. Edited by W. W. CAPES. 6*s.* 6*d.*

PROPERTIUS.—SELECT POEMS. Edited by Prof. J. P. POSTGATE, M.A. 6*s.*

SALLUST.—CATILINE AND JUGURTHA. Ed. by C. MERIVALE, D.D. 4*s.* 6*d.*—Or separately, 2*s.* 6*d.* each.

— BELLUM CATULINAE. Edited by A. M. COOK, M.A. 4*s.* 6*d.*

TACITUS.—AGRICOLA AND GERMANIA. Ed. by A. J. CHURCH, M.A., and W. J. BRODRIBB, M.A. 3*s.* 6*d.*—Or separately, 2*s.* each.

— THE ANNALS. Book VI. By the same Editors. 2*s.* 6*d.*

— THE HISTORIES. Books I. and II. Edited by A. D. GODLEY, M.A. 5*s.*

— THE HISTORIES. Books III.—V. By the same Editor. 5*s.*

TERENCE.—HAUTON TIMORUMENOS. Edit. by E. S. SHUCKBURGH, M.A. 3*s.*—With Translation, 4*s.* 6*d.*

— PHORMIO. Ed. by Rev. J. BOND, M.A., and A. S. WALPOLE, M.A. 4*s.* 6*d.*

THUCYDIDES. Book IV. Edited by C. E. GRAVES, M.A. 5*s.*

— Book V. By the same Editor.

— Books VI. and VII. THE SICILIAN EXPEDITION. Edited by Rev. P. FROST, M.A. With Map. 5*s.*

VIRGIL.—ÆNEID. Books I. and II. THE NARRATIVE OF ÆNEAS. Edited by E. W. HOWSON, M.A. 3*s.*

XENOPHON.—HELLENICA. Books I. and II. Edited by H. HAILSTONE, M.A. 4*s.* 6*d.*

— CYROPÆDIA. Books VII. and VIII. Ed. by Prof. A. GOODWIN, M.A. 5*s.*

— MEMORABILIA SOCRATIS. Edited by A. R. CLUER, B.A. 6*s.*

— THE ANABASIS. Books I.—IV. Edited by Professors W. W. GOODWIN and J. W. WHITE. Adapted to Goodwin's Greek Grammar. With a Map. 5*s.*

— HIERO. Edited by Rev. H. A. HOLDEN, M.A., L.L.D. 3*s.* 6*d.*

— OECONOMICUS. By the same Editor. With Introduction, Explanatory Notes, Critical Appendix, and Lexicon. 6*s.*

The following are in preparation:

DEMOSTHENES.—IN MIDIAM. Edited by Prof. A. S. WILKINS, Litt.D., and HERMAN HAGER, Ph.D.

HERODOTUS. Books V. and VI. Edited by Prof. J. STRACHAN, M.A.

ISÆOS.—THE ORATIONS. Edited by Prof. WM. RIDGEWAY, M.A.

MACMILLAN'S CLASSICAL SERIES—
continued.

OVID.—METAMORPHOSES. Books I.—III. Edited by C. SIMMONS, M.A.

SALLUST.—JUGURTHA. Edited by A. M. COOK, M.A.

TACITUS.—THE ANNALS. Books I. and II. Edited by J. S. REID, Litt.D.

Other Volumes will follow.

MACMILLAN'S GEOGRAPHICAL SERIES. Edited by ARCHIBALD GEIKIE, F.R.S., Director-General of the Geological Survey of the United Kingdom.

THE TEACHING OF GEOGRAPHY. A Practical Handbook for the use of Teachers. Cr. 8vo. 2*s.*

GEOGRAPHY OF THE BRITISH ISLES. By ARCHIBALD GEIKIE, F.R.S. 18mo. 1*s.*

THE ELEMENTARY SCHOOL ATLAS. 24 Maps in Colours. By JOHN BARTHOLOMEW, F.R.G.S. 4to. 1*s.*

AN ELEMENTARY CLASS-BOOK OF GENERAL GEOGRAPHY. By HUGH ROBERT MILL, D.Sc. Edin. Illustrated. Cr. 8vo. 3*s.* 6*d.*

MAP DRAWING AND MAP MAKING. By W. A. ELDERTON.

GEOGRAPHY OF THE BRITISH COLONIES. By G. M. DAWSON and ALEX. SUTHERLAND.

GEOGRAPHY OF EUROPE. By JAMES SIME, M.A. With Illustrations. Globe 8vo.

GEOGRAPHY OF NORTH AMERICA. By Prof. N. S. SHALER.

GEOGRAPHY OF INDIA. By H. F. BLANFORD, F.G.S.

MACMILLAN'S SCIENTIFIC CLASS-BOOKS. Fcp. 8vo.

ELEMENTARY LESSONS IN THE SCIENCE OF AGRICULTURAL PRACTICE. By Prof. H. TANNER. 3*s.* 6*d.*

POPULAR ASTRONOMY. By Sir G. B. AIRY, K.C.B., late Astronomer-Royal. 4*s.* 6*d.*

ELEMENTARY LESSONS IN PHYSIOLOGY. By T. H. HUXLEY, F.R.S. 4*s.* 6*d.* (Questions on, 1*s.* 6*d.*)

LESSONS IN LOGIC, INDUCTIVE AND DEDUCTIVE. By W. S. JEVONS, LL.D. 3*s.* 6*d.*

LESSONS IN ELEMENTARY CHEMISTRY. By Sir H. ROSCOE, F.R.S. 4*s.* 6*d.*—Problems adapted to the same, by Prof. THORPE. With Key. 2*s.*

OWENS COLLEGE JUNIOR COURSE OF PRACTICAL CHEMISTRY. By F. JONES. With Preface by Sir H. ROSCOE, F.R.S. 2*s.* 6*d.*

EXPERIMENTAL PROOFS OF CHEMICAL THEORY FOR BEGINNERS. By WILLIAM RAMSAY, Ph.D. 2*s.* 6*d.*

NUMERICAL TABLES AND CONSTANTS IN ELEMENTARY SCIENCE. By SYDNEY LUPTON, M.A. 2*s.* 6*d.*

LESSONS IN ELEMENTARY ANATOMY. By ST. G. MIVART, F.R.S. 6*s.* 6*d.*

POLITICAL ECONOMY FOR BEGINNERS. By Mrs. FAWCETT. With Questions. 2*s.* 6*d.*

DISEASES OF FIELD AND GARDEN CROPS. By W. G. SMITH. 4*s.* 6*d.*

MACMILLAN'S SCIENTIFIC CLASS-BOOKS—*continued.*

LESSONS IN ELEMENTARY BOTANY. By Prof. OLIVER, F.R.S. 4s. 6d.

LESSONS IN ELEMENTARY PHYSICS. By Prof. BALFOUR STEWART, F.R.S. New Edition. 4s. 6d. (Questions on, 2s.)

ELEMENTARY LESSONS ON ASTRONOMY. By J. N. LOCKYER, F.R.S. New Edition. 5s. 6d. (Questions on, 1s. 6d.)

AN ELEMENTARY TREATISE ON STEAM. By Prof. J. PERRY, C.E. 4s. 6d.

QUESTIONS AND EXAMPLES ON EXPERIMENTAL PHYSICS: Sound, Light, Heat, Electricity, and Magnetism. By B. LOEWY, F.R.A.S. Fcp. 8vo. 2s.

A GRADUATED COURSE OF NATURAL SCIENCE FOR ELEMENTARY AND TECHNICAL SCHOOLS AND COLLEGES. Part I. First Year's Course. By the same. Gl. 8vo. 2s.

PHYSICAL GEOGRAPHY, ELEMENTARY LESSONS IN. By ARCHIBALD GEIKIE, F.R.S. 4s. 6d. (Questions, 1s. 6d.)

SOUND, ELEMENTARY LESSONS ON. By Dr. W. H. STONE. 3s. 6d.

CLASS-BOOK OF GEOGRAPHY. By C. B. CLARKE, F.R.S. 3s. 6d.; sewed, 3s.

QUESTIONS ON CHEMISTRY. A Series of Problems and Exercises in Inorganic and Organic Chemistry. By F. JONES. 3s.

ELECTRICITY AND MAGNETISM. By Prof. SILVANUS THOMPSON. 4s. 6d.

ELECTRIC LIGHT ARITHMETIC. By R. E. DAY, M.A. 2s.

THE ECONOMICS OF INDUSTRY. By Prof. A. MARSHALL and M. P. MARSHALL. 2s. 6d.

SHORT GEOGRAPHY OF THE BRITISH ISLANDS. By J. R. GREEN and ALICE S. GREEN. With Maps. 3s. 6d.

A COLLECTION OF EXAMPLES ON HEAT AND ELECTRICITY. By H. H. TURNER. 2s. 6d.

OWENS COLLEGE COURSE OF PRACTICAL ORGANIC CHEMISTRY. By JULIUS B. COHEN, Ph.D. With Preface by Sir H. ROSCOE and Prof. SCHORLEMMER. 2s. 6d.

ELEMENTS OF CHEMISTRY. By Prof. IRA REMSEN. 2s. 6d.

EXAMPLES IN PHYSICS. By Prof. D. E. JONES, B.Sc. 3s. 6d.

MACMILLAN'S PROGRESSIVE FRENCH COURSE. By G. EUGÈNE FASNACHT. Extra fcp. 8vo.

I. FIRST YEAR, CONTAINING EASY LESSONS IN THE REGULAR ACCIDENCE. Thoroughly revised Edition. 1s.

II. SECOND YEAR, CONTAINING AN ELEMENTARY GRAMMAR. With copious Exercises, Notes, and Vocabularies. New Edition, enlarged. 2s.

III. THIRD YEAR, CONTAINING A SYSTEMATIC SYNTAX AND LESSONS IN COMPOSITION. 2s. 6d.

THE TEACHER'S COMPANION TO THE SAME. With copious Notes, Hints for different renderings, Synonyms, Philological Remarks, etc. 1st Year, 4s. 6d. 2nd Year, 4s. 6d. 3rd Year, 4s. 6d.

MACMILLAN'S PROGRESSIVE FRENCH READERS. By G. EUGÈNE FASNACHT. Extra fcp. 8vo.

I. FIRST YEAR, CONTAINING TALES, HISTORICAL EXTRACTS, LETTERS, DIALOGUES, FABLES, BALLADS, NURSERY SONGS, etc. With Two Vocabularies: (1) In the Order of Subjects; (2) In Alphabetical Order. 2s. 6d.

II. SECOND YEAR, CONTAINING FICTION IN PROSE AND VERSE, HISTORICAL AND DESCRIPTIVE EXTRACTS, ESSAYS, LETTERS, etc. 2s. 6d.

MACMILLAN'S FRENCH COMPOSITION. By G. EUGÈNE FASNACHT. Extra fcp. 8vo.

Part I. ELEMENTARY. 2s. 6d. — Part II. ADVANCED.

THE TEACHER'S COMPANION TO THE SAME. Part I. 4s. 6d.

MACMILLAN'S PROGRESSIVE GERMAN COURSE. By G. EUGÈNE FASNACHT. Extra fcp. 8vo.

I. FIRST YEAR, CONTAINING EASY LESSONS ON THE REGULAR ACCIDENCE. 1s. 6d.

II. SECOND YEAR, CONTAINING CONVERSATIONAL LESSONS ON SYSTEMATIC ACCIDENCE AND ELEMENTARY SYNTAX, WITH PHILOLOGICAL ILLUSTRATIONS AND ETYMOLOGICAL VOCABULARY. New Edition, enlarged. 3s. 6d.

THE TEACHER'S COMPANION TO THE SAME. 1st Year, 4s. 6d. 2nd Year, 4s. 6d.

MACMILLAN'S PROGRESSIVE GERMAN READERS. By G. EUGÈNE FASNACHT. Extra fcap. 8vo.

I. FIRST YEAR, CONTAINING AN INTRODUCTION TO THE GERMAN ORDER OF WORDS, WITH COPIOUS EXAMPLES, EXTRACTS FROM GERMAN AUTHORS IN PROSE AND POETRY, NOTES, VOCABULARIES. 2s. 6d.

MACMILLAN'S SERIES OF FOREIGN SCHOOL CLASSICS. Edited by G. E. FASNACHT. 18mo.

Select works of the best foreign Authors, with suitable Notes and Introductions based on the latest researches of French and German Scholars by practical masters and teachers.

FRENCH.

CORNEILLE.—LE CID. Edited by G. E. FASNACHT. 1s.

DUMAS.—LES DEMOISELLES DE ST. CYR. Edited by VICTOR OGER. 1s. 6d.

LA FONTAINE'S FABLES. Books I.—VI. Edit. by L. M. MORIARTY. [*In the Press.*

MOLIÈRE.—LES FEMMES SAVANTES. By G. E. FASNACHT. 1s.

— LE MISANTHROPE. By the same. 1s.

— LE MÉDECIN MALGRÉ LUI. By the same. 1s.

— L'AVARE. Ed. by L. M. MORIARTY. 1s.

— LE BOURGEOIS GENTILHOMME. By the same. 1s. 6d.

RACINE.—BRITANNICUS. Edited by EUGÈNE PELLISSIER. 2s.

MACMILLAN'S FOREIGN SCHOOL CLASSICS—*continued.*

FRENCH.

FRENCH READINGS FROM ROMAN HISTORY. Selected from various Authors. Edited by C. COLBECK, M.A. 4s. 6d.

SAND (George).—LA MARE AU DIABLE. Edited by W. E. RUSSELL, M.A. 1s.

SANDEAU (Jules).—MADEMOISELLE DE LA SEIGLIÈRE. Edit. by H. C. STEEL. 1s. 6d.

THIERS'S HISTORY OF THE EGYPTIAN EXPEDITION. Edit. by Rev. H. A. BULL, M.A.

VOLTAIRE.—CHARLES XII. Edited by G. E. FASNACHT. 3s. 6d.

GERMAN.

FREYTAG.—DOKTOR LUTHER. Edited by FRANCIS STORR, M.A.   [*In the Press.*

GOETHE.—GÖTZ VON BERLICHINGEN. Edit. by H. A. BULL, M.A. 2s.

— FAUST. Part I. Ed. by Miss J. LEE. 4s. 6d.

HEINE.—SELECTIONS FROM THE REISEBILDER AND OTHER PROSE WORKS. Edit. by C. COLBECK, M.A. 2s. 6d.

LESSING.—MINNA VON BARNHELM. Edited by J. SIME, M.A.

SCHILLER.—DIE JUNGFRAU VON ORLEANS. Edited by JOSEPH GOSTWICK. 2s. 6d.

— MARIA STUART. Edited by C. SHELDON, M.A., D.Lit. 2s. 6d.

— WALLENSTEIN. Part I. DAS LÄGER. Edited by H. B. COTTERILL, M.A. 2s.

— WILHELM TELL. Edited by G. E. FASNACHT. 2s. 6d.

— SELECTIONS FROM SCHILLER'S LYRICAL POEMS. Edited by E. J. TURNER, M.A., and E. D. A. MORSHEAD, M.A. 2s. 6d.

UHLAND.—SELECT BALLADS. Adapted as a First Easy Reading Book for Beginners. Edited by G. E. FASNACHT. 1s.

MACMILLAN'S PRIMARY SERIES OF FRENCH AND GERMAN READING BOOKS. Edited by G. EUGÈNE FASNACHT. With Illustrations. Globe 8vo.

CORNAZ.—NOS ENFANTS ET LEURS AMIS. Edited by EDITH HARVEY. 1s. 6d.

DE MAISTRE.—LA JEUNE SIBÉRIENNE ET LE LÉPREUX DE LA CITÉ D'AOSTE. Edit. by S. BARLET, B.Sc. 1s. 6d.

FLORIAN.—SELECT FABLES. Edited by CHARLES YELD, M.A. 1s. 6d.

GRIMM.—KINDER- UND HAUSMÄRCHEN. Selected and Edited by G. E. FASNACHT. Illustrated. 2s. 6d.

HAUFF.—DIE KARAVANE. Edited by HERMAN HAGER, Ph.D. With Exercises by G. E. FASNACHT. 3s.

LA FONTAINE.—FABLES. A Selection, by L. M. MORIARTY, M.A. With Illustrations by RANDOLPH CALDECOTT. 2s. 6d.

MOLESWORTH.— FRENCH LIFE IN LETTERS. By Mrs. MOLESWORTH. 1s. 6d.

PERRAULT.—CONTES DE FÉES. Edited by G. E. FASNACHT. 1s. 6d.

SCHMID.—HEINRICH VON EICHENFELS. Ed. by G. E. FASNACHT. 2s. 6d.

SCHWAB (G.).—ODYSSEUS. By same Editor.

MACNAMARA (C.).—A HISTORY OF ASIATIC CHOLERA. Crown 8vo. 10s. 6d.

MACQUOID (K. S.).—PATTY. Globe 8vo. 2s.

MADAGASCAR: AN HISTORICAL AND DESCRIPTIVE ACCOUNT OF THE ISLAND AND ITS FORMER DEPENDENCIES. By Captain S. OLIVER, F.S.A. 2 vols. Med. 8vo. 2l. 12s. 6d.

MADAME TABBY'S ESTABLISHMENT. By KARI. Illustrated by L. WAIN. Crown 8vo. 4s. 6d.

MADOC (Fayr).—THE STORY OF MELICENT. Crown 8vo. 4s. 6d.

—— MARGARET JERMINE. 3 vols. Crown 8vo. 31s. 6d.

MAGUIRE (J. F.).—YOUNG PRINCE MARIGOLD. Illustrated. Globe 8vo. 4s. 6d.

MAHAFFY (Rev. Prof. J. P.).—SOCIAL LIFE IN GREECE, FROM HOMER TO MENANDER. 6th Edition. Crown 8vo. 9s.

—— GREEK LIFE AND THOUGHT FROM THE AGE OF ALEXANDER TO THE ROMAN CONQUEST. Crown 8vo. 12s. 6d.

—— RAMBLES AND STUDIES IN GREECE. Illustrated. 3rd Edition. Crown 8vo. 10s. 6d.

—— A HISTORY OF CLASSICAL GREEK LITERATURE. 2 vols. Cr. 8vo. 9s. each.—Vol. I. The Poets. With an Appendix on Homer by Prof. SAYCE.—Vol. II. The Prose Writers.

—— GREEK ANTIQUITIES. Illust. 18mo. 1s.

—— EURIPIDES. 18mo. 1s. 6d.

—— THE DECAY OF MODERN PREACHING: AN ESSAY. Crown 8vo. 3s. 6d.

—— THE PRINCIPLES OF THE ART OF CONVERSATION. 2nd Ed. Crown 8vo. 4s. 6d.

MAHAFFY (Rev. Prof. J. P.) and ROGERS (J. E.).—SKETCHES FROM A TOUR THROUGH HOLLAND AND GERMANY. Illustrated by J. E. ROGERS. Extra crown 8vo. 10s. 6d.

MAHAFFY (Prof. J. P.) and BERNARD (J. H.).—KANT'S CRITICAL PHILOSOPHY FOR ENGLISH READERS. A new and completed Edition in 2 vols. Crown 8vo.—Vol. I. THE KRITIK OF PURE REASON EXPLAINED AND DEFENDED. 7s. 6d.—Vol. II. THE "PROLEGOMENA." Translated, with Notes and Appendices. 6s.

MAITLAND (F. W.).—PLEAS OF THE CROWN FOR THE COUNTY OF GLOUCESTER, A.D. 1221. Edited by F. W. MAITLAND. 8vo. 7s. 6d.

—— JUSTICE AND POLICE. Cr. 8vo. 3s. 6d.

MALET (Lucas).—MRS. LORIMER: A SKETCH IN BLACK AND WHITE. Cr. 8vo. 4s. 6d.

MANCHESTER SCIENCE LECTURES FOR THE PEOPLE. Eighth Series, 1876—77. With Illustrations. Cr. 8vo. 2s.

MANSFIELD (C. B.).—A THEORY OF SALTS. Crown 8vo. 14s.

—— AERIAL NAVIGATION. Cr. 8vo. 10s. 6d.

MARKHAM (C. R.).—LIFE OF ROBERT FAIRFAX, OF STEETON. 8vo. 12s. 6d.

MARRIOTT (J. A. R.).—THE MAKERS OF MODERN ITALY: MAZZINI, CAVOUR, GARIBALDI. Three Oxford Lectures. Crown 8vo. 1s. 6d.

MARSHALL (Prof. Alfred).—THE PRINCIPLES OF ECONOMICS. 2 vols. 8vo. [*Vol. I. shortly.*

MARSHALL (Prof. A. and Mary P.).—THE ECONOMICS OF INDUSTRY. Ex. fcp. 8vo. 2s. 6d.

MARSHALL (J. M.).—A TABLE OF IRREGULAR GREEK VERBS. 8vo. 1s.

MARTEL (Chas.).—MILITARY ITALY. With Map. 8vo. 12s. 6d.

MARTIAL.—SELECT EPIGRAMS FOR ENGLISH READERS. Translated by W. T. WEBB, M.A. Extra fcp. 8vo. 4s. 6d.

—— SELECT EPIGRAMS. Edit. by Rev. H. M. STEPHENSON, M.A. Fcp. 8vo. 6s. 6d.

MARTIN (Frances).—THE POET'S HOUR. Poetry Selected and Arranged for Children. 12mo. 2s. 6d.

—— SPRING-TIME WITH THE POETS. 18mo. 3s. 6d.

—— ANGÉLIQUE ARNAULD, Abbess of Port Royal. Crown 8vo. 4s. 6d.

MARTIN (Frederick).—THE HISTORY OF LLOYD'S, AND OF MARINE INSURANCE IN GREAT BRITAIN. 8vo. 14s.

MARTINEAU (Harriet). — BIOGRAPHICAL SKETCHES, 1852—75. Crown 8vo. 6s.

MARTINEAU (Dr. James).—SPINOZA. 2nd Edition. Crown 8vo. 6s.

MARTINEAU (Miss C. A.).—EASY LESSONS ON HEAT. Globe 8vo. 2s. 6d.

MASSON (Prof. David).—RECENT BRITISH PHILOSOPHY. 3rd Edition. Cr. 8vo. 6s.

—— DRUMMOND OF HAWTHORNDEN. Crown 8vo. 10s. 6d.

—— WORDSWORTH, SHELLEY, KEATS, AND OTHER ESSAYS. Crown 8vo. 5s.

—— CHATTERTON: A STORY OF THE YEAR 1770. Crown 8vo. 5s.

—— LIFE OF MILTON. See "Milton."

—— MILTON'S POEMS. See "Milton."

—— DE QUINCEY. Cr. 8vo. 1s. 6d.; sewed, 1s.

MASSON (Gustave).—A COMPENDIOUS DICTIONARY OF THE FRENCH LANGUAGE (FRENCH-ENGLISH AND ENGLISH-FRENCH). Crown 8vo. 6s.

—— LA LYRE FRANÇAISE. Selected and arranged, with Notes. Vignette. 18mo. 4s. 6d.

MASSON (Mrs.).—THREE CENTURIES OF ENGLISH POETRY. Being Selections from Chaucer to Herrick. Globe 8vo. 3s. 6d.

MATHEWS.—THE LIFE OF CHARLES J. MATHEWS. Edited by CHARLES DICKENS. With Portraits. 2 vols. 8vo. 25s.

MATURIN (Rev. W.).—THE BLESSEDNESS OF THE DEAD IN CHRIST. Cr. 8vo. 7s. 6d.

MAUDSLEY (Dr. Henry).—THE PHYSIOLOGY OF MIND. Crown 8vo. 10s. 6d.

—— THE PATHOLOGY OF MIND. 8vo. 18s.

—— BODY AND MIND. Crown 8vo. 6s. 6d.

MAURICE.—LIFE OF FREDERICK DENISON MAURICE. By his Son, FREDERICK MAURICE. Two Portraits. 3rd Ed. 2 vols. Demy 8vo. 36s. Popular Edition (4th Thousand) 2 vols. Crown 8vo. 16s.

MAURICE (Frederick Denison).—THE KINGDOM OF CHRIST. 3rd Ed. 2 vols. Cr. 8vo. 12s.

MAURICE (F. D.).—LECTURES ON THE APOCALYPSE. 2nd Edition. Cr. 8vo. 6s.

—— SOCIAL MORALITY. 3rd Ed. Cr. 8vo. 6s.

—— THE CONSCIENCE. Lectures on Casuistry. 3rd Edition. Crown 8vo. 4s. 6d.

—— DIALOGUES ON FAMILY WORSHIP. Crown 8vo. 4s. 6d.

—— THE PATRIARCHS AND LAWGIVERS OF THE OLD TESTAMENT. 7th Ed. Cr. 8vo. 4s. 6d.

—— THE PROPHETS AND KINGS OF THE OLD TESTAMENT. 5th Edition. Cr. 8vo. 6s.

—— THE GOSPEL OF THE KINGDOM OF HEAVEN. 3rd Edition. Crown 8vo. 6s.

—— THE GOSPEL OF ST. JOHN. 8th Edition. Crown 8vo. 6s.

—— THE EPISTLES OF ST. JOHN. 4th Edition. Crown 8vo. 6s.

—— EXPOSITORY SERMONS ON THE PRAYER-BOOK; AND ON THE LORD'S PRAYER. New Edition. Crown 8vo. 6s.

—— THEOLOGICAL ESSAYS. 4th Ed. Cr. 8vo. 6s.

—— THE DOCTRINE OF SACRIFICE DEDUCED FROM THE SCRIPTURES. 2nd Ed. Cr. 8vo. 6s.

—— MORAL AND METAPHYSICAL PHILOSOPHY. 4th Edition. 2 vols. 8vo. 16s.

—— THE RELIGIONS OF THE WORLD. 6th Edition. Crown 8vo. 4s. 6d.

—— ON THE SABBATH DAY; THE CHARACTER OF THE WARRIOR; AND ON THE INTERPRETATION OF HISTORY. Fcp. 8vo. 2s. 6d.

—— LEARNING AND WORKING. Cr. 8vo. 4s. 6d.

—— THE LORD'S PRAYER, THE CREED, AND THE COMMANDMENTS. 18mo. 1s.

—— SERMONS PREACHED IN COUNTRY CHURCHES. 2nd Edition. Crown 8vo. 6s.

—— THE FRIENDSHIP OF BOOKS, AND OTHER LECTURES. 3rd Edition. Cr. 8vo. 4s. 6d.

—— THE UNITY OF THE NEW TESTAMENT. 2nd Edition. 2 vols. Crown 8vo. 12s.

—— LESSONS OF HOPE. Readings from the Works of F. D. MAURICE. Selected by Rev. J. Ll. DAVIES, M.A. Crown 8vo. 5s.

—— THE COMMUNION SERVICE FROM THE BOOK OF COMMON PRAYER, WITH SELECT READINGS FROM THE WRITINGS OF THE REV. F. D. MAURICE. Edited by the Right Rev. Bishop COLENSO. 16mo. 2s. 6d.

MAXWELL.—PROFESSOR CLERK MAXWELL, A LIFE OF. By Prof. L. CAMPBELL, M.A., and W. GARNETT, M.A. 2nd Edition. Crown 8vo. 7s. 6d.

MAYER (Prof. A. M.).—SOUND. A Series of Simple, Entertaining, and Inexpensive Experiments in the Phenomena of Sound. With Illustrations. Crown 8vo. 3s. 6d.

MAYER (Prof. A. M.) and BARNARD (C.)—LIGHT. A Series of Simple, Entertaining, and Useful Experiments in the Phenomena of Light. Illustrated. Crown 8vo. 2s. 6d.

MAYOR (Prof. John E. B.).—A FIRST GREEK READER. New Edition. Fcp. 8vo. 4s. 6d.

—— AUTOBIOGRAPHY OF MATTHEW ROBINSON. Fcp. 8vo. 5s.

—— A BIBLIOGRAPHICAL CLUE TO LATIN LITERATURE. Crown 8vo. 10s. 6d. [See also under "Juvenal."]

MAYOR (Prof. Joseph B.).—GREEK FOR BE-
GINNERS. Fcp. 8vo. Part I. 1s. 6d.—Parts
II. and III. 3s. 6d.—Complete, 4s. 6d.

MAZINI (Linda).—IN THE GOLDEN SHELL.
With Illustrations. Globe 8vo. 4s. 6d.

MELBOURNE.—MEMOIRS OF VISCOUNT
MELBOURNE. By W. M. TORRENS. With
Portrait. 2nd Edition. 2 vols. 8vo. 32s.

MELDOLA (Prof. R.)—THE CHEMISTRY OF
PHOTOGRAPHY. Crown 8vo. 6s.

MELDOLA (Prof. R.) and WHITE (Wm.).—
REPORT ON THE EAST ANGLIAN EARTH-
QUAKE OF 22ND APRIL, 1884. 8vo. 3s. 6d.

MENDENHALL (T. C.).—A CENTURY OF
ELECTRICITY. Crown 8vo. 4s. 6d.

MERCIER (Dr. C.).—THE NERVOUS SYSTEM
AND THE MIND. 8vo. 12s. 6d.

MERCUR (Prof. J.).—ELEMENTS OF THE
ART OF WAR. 8vo. 17s.

MEREDITH (George).—A READING OF
EARTH. Extra fcp. 8vo. 5s.

—— POEMS AND LYRICS OF THE JOY OF
EARTH. Extra fcp. 8vo. 6s.

—— BALLADS AND POEMS OF TRAGIC LIFE.
Crown 8vo. 6s.

MIALL.—LIFE OF EDWARD MIALL. By his
Son, ARTHUR MIALL. 8vo. 10s. 6d.

MILL (H. R.).—AN ELEMENTARY CLASS-
BOOK OF GENERAL GEOGRAPHY. Crown
8vo. 3s. 6d.

MILLAR (J. B.)—ELEMENTS OF DESCRIPTIVE
GEOMETRY. 2nd Edition. Crown 8vo. 6s.

MILLER (R. Kalley).—THE ROMANCE OF
ASTRONOMY. 2nd Ed. Cr. 8vo. 4s. 6d.

MILLIGAN (Rev. Prof. W.).—THE RESUR-
RECTION OF OUR LORD. 2nd Ed. Cr. 8vo. 5s.

—— THE REVELATION OF ST. JOHN. 2nd
Edition. Crown 8vo. 7s. 6d.

MILNE (Rev. John J.).—WEEKLY PROBLEM
PAPERS. Fcp. 8vo. 4s. 6d.

—— COMPANION TO WEEKLY PROBLEMS. Cr.
8vo. 10s. 6d.

—— SOLUTIONS OF WEEKLY PROBLEM PAPERS.
Crown 8vo. 10s. 6d.

MILNE (Rev. J. J.) and DAVIS (R. F.).—
GEOMETRICAL CONICS. Part I. THE PARA-
BOLA. Crown 8vo.

MILTON.—THE LIFE OF JOHN MILTON.
By Prof. DAVID MASSON. Vol. I., 21s.;
Vol. III., 18s.; Vols. IV. and V., 32s.; Vol.
VI., with Portrait, 21s.

—— POETICAL WORKS. Edited, with Introductions and Notes, by Prof. DAVID MASSON,
M.A. 3 vols. 8vo. (Uniform with the Cambridge Shakespeare.)

—— POETICAL WORKS. Ed. by Prof. MASSON.
3 vols. Fcp. 8vo. 15s.

—— POETICAL WORKS. (*Globe Edition.*) Ed.
by Prof. MASSON. Globe 8vo. 3s. 6d.

—— PARADISE LOST. Books I. and II. Ed.,
with Introduction and Notes, by Prof. M.
MACMILLAN. Globe 8vo. 2s. 6d. (Or separately, 1s. 6d. each Book.)

—— L'ALLEGRO, IL PENSEROSO, LYCIDAS,
ARCADES, SONNETS, ETC. Edited by Prof.
WM. BELL, M.A. Globe 8vo. 2s.

MILTON.—COMUS. Edited by Prof. WM.
BELL, M.A. Globe 8vo. 1s. 6d.

—— SAMSON AGONISTES. By H. M. PER-
CIVAL, M.A. Globe 8vo. 2s. 6d.

MILTON. By MARK PATTISON. Cr. 8vo.
1s. 6d.; sewed, 1s.

MILTON. By Rev. STOPFORD A. BROOKE,
M.A. Fcp. 8vo. 1s. 6d.
Large Paper Edition. 21s.

MINCHIN (Rev. Prof. G. M.).—NATURÆ
VERITAS. Fcp. 8vo. 2s. 6d.

MINTO (W.).—THE MEDIATION OF RALPH
HARDELOT. 3 vols. Crown 8vo. 31s. 6d.

—— DEFOE. Crown 8vo. 1s. 6d.; sewed, 1s.

MITFORD (A. B.).—TALES OF OLD JAPAN.
With Illustrations. Crown 8vo. 3s. 6d.

MIVART (St. George).—LESSONS IN ELE-
MENTARY ANATOMY. 18mo. 6s. 6d.

MIXTER (Prof. W. G.).—AN ELEMENTARY
TEXT-BOOK OF CHEMISTRY. 2nd Edition.
Crown 8vo. 7s. 6d.

MIZ MAZE (THE); OR, THE WINKWORTH
PUZZLE. A Story in Letters by Nine
Authors. Crown 8vo. 4s. 6d.

MOHAMMAD. THE SPEECHES AND TABLE-
TALK OF THE PROPHET. Translated by
STANLEY LANE-POOLE. 18mo. 4s. 6d.

MOLESWORTH (Mrs.).—HERR BABY. Illustrated by WALTER CRANE. Gl. 8vo. 2s. 6d.

—— GRANDMOTHER DEAR. Illustrated by
WALTER CRANE. Globe 8vo. 2s. 6d.

—— THE TAPESTRY ROOM. Illustrated by
WALTER CRANE. Globe 8vo. 2s. 6d.

—— A CHRISTMAS CHILD. Illustrated by
WALTER CRANE. Globe 8vo. 2s. 6d.

—— SUMMER STORIES. Crown 8vo. 4s. 6d.

—— ROSY. Illustrated by WALTER CRANE.
Globe 8vo. 2s. 6d.

—— TWO LITTLE WAIFS. Illustrated by
WALTER CRANE. Globe 8vo. 2s. 6d.

—— CHRISTMAS TREE LAND. Illustrated by
WALTER CRANE. Globe 8vo. 2s. 6d.

—— "US": AN OLD-FASHIONED STORY. Illustrated by WALTER CRANE. Gl. 8vo. 2s. 6d.

—— "CARROTS," JUST A LITTLE BOY. Illustrated by WALTER CRANE. Gl. 8vo. 2s. 6d.

—— TELL ME A STORY. Illustrated by
WALTER CRANE. Globe 8vo. 2s. 6d.

—— THE CUCKOO CLOCK. Illustrated by
WALTER CRANE. Globe 8vo. 2s. 6d.

—— FOUR WINDS FARM. Illustrated by
WALTER CRANE. Globe 8vo. 2s. 6d.

—— LITTLE MISS PEGGY. Illustrated by
WALTER CRANE. Globe 8vo. 2s. 6d.

—— FOUR GHOST STORIES. Crown 8vo. 6s.

—— A CHRISTMAS POSY. Illustrated by
WALTER CRANE. Crown 8vo. 4s. 6d.

—— FRENCH LIFE IN LETTERS. With Notes
on Idioms, etc. Globe 8vo. 1s. 6d.

—— THE RECTORY CHILDREN. Illustrated by
WALTER CRANE. Crown 8vo. 4s. 6d.

MOLIÈRE.—LE MALADE IMAGINAIRE.
Edit. by F. TARVER, M.A. Fcp. 8vo. 2s. 6d.

MOLIÈRE.—LES FEMMES SAVANTES. Edit. by G. E. FASNACHT. 18mo. 1s.

—— LE MÉDECIN MALGRÉ LUI. By the same Editor. 18mo. 1s.

—— LE MISANTHROPE. By the same Editor. 18mo. 1s.

—— L'AVARE. Edited by L. M. MORIARTY, M.A. 18mo. 1s.

—— LE BOURGEOIS GENTILHOMME. By the same Editor. 1s. 6d.

MOLLOY (Rev. G.).—GLEANINGS IN SCIENCE: A SERIES OF POPULAR LECTURES ON SCIENTIFIC SUBJECTS. 8vo. 7s. 6d.

MONAHAN (James H.).—THE METHOD OF LAW. Crown 8vo. 6s.

MONK. By JULIAN CORBETT. With Portrait. Crown 8vo. 2s. 6d.

MONTELIUS—WOODS.—THE CIVILISATION OF SWEDEN IN HEATHEN TIMES. By Prof. OSCAR MONTELIUS. Translated by Rev. F. H. WOODS, B.D. With Illustrations. 8vo. 14s.

MOORE (Prof. C. H.).—THE DEVELOPMENT AND CHARACTER OF GOTHIC ARCHITECTURE. Illustrated. Medium 8vo. 18s.

MOORHOUSE (Rt. Rev. Bishop).—JACOB: THREE SERMONS. Extra fcp. 8vo. 3s. 6d.

MORISON (J. C.).—THE LIFE AND TIMES OF SAINT BERNARD. 4th Ed. Cr. 8vo. 6s.

—— GIBBON. Cr. 8vo. 1s. 6d. ; sewed, 1s.

—— MACAULAY. Cr. 8vo. 1s. 6d. ; sewed, 1s.

MORISON (Jeanie).—THE PURPOSE OF THE AGES. Crown 8vo. 9s.

MORLEY (John).—WORKS. Collected Edit. In 10 vols. Globe 8vo. 5s. each. VOLTAIRE. 1 vol.—ROUSSEAU. 2 vols.—DIDEROT AND THE ENCYCLOPÆDISTS. 2 vols.—ON COMPROMISE. 1 vol.—MISCELLANIES. 3 vols.—BURKE. 1 vol.

—— ON THE STUDY OF LITERATURE. Crown 8vo. 1s. 6d. Also a Popular Edition for distribution, 2d.

—— BURKE. Crown 8vo. 1s. 6d. ; sewed, 1s.

—— WALPOLE. Crown 8vo. 2s. 6d.

—— APHORISMS. An Address before the Philosophical Society of Edinburgh. Globe 8vo. 1s. 6d.

MORRIS (Rev. Richard, LL.D.).—HISTORICAL OUTLINES OF ENGLISH ACCIDENCE. Fcp. 8vo. 6s.

—— ELEMENTARY LESSONS IN HISTORICAL ENGLISH GRAMMAR. 18mo. 2s. 6d.

—— PRIMER OF ENGLISH GRAMMAR. 18mo, cloth. 1s.

MORRIS (R.) and BOWEN (H. C.)—ENGLISH GRAMMAR EXERCISES. 18mo. 1s.

MORTE D'ARTHUR. THE EDITION OF CAXTON REVISED FOR MODERN USE. By Sir EDWARD STRACHEY. Gl. 8vo. 3s. 6d.

MOULTON (Louise Chandler).—SWALLOWFLIGHTS. Extra fcp. 8vo. 4s. 6d.

MOULTON (Louise Chandler).—IN THE GARDEN OF DREAMS: LYRICS AND SONNETS. Crown 8vo. 6s.

MOULTRIE (J.).—POEMS. Complete Edition. 2 vols. Crown 8vo. 7s. each.

MUDIE (C. E.).—STRAY LEAVES: POEMS. 4th Edition. Extra fcp. 8vo. 3s. 6d.

MUIR (Thomas).—A TREATISE ON THE THEORY OF DETERMINANTS. Cr. 8vo. 7s. 6d.

—— THE THEORY OF DETERMINANTS IN THE HISTORICAL ORDER OF ITS DEVELOPMENT. Part I. DETERMINANTS IN GENERAL. Leibnitz (1693) to Cayley (1841). 8vo. 10s. 6d.

MUIR (M. M. Pattison).—PRACTICAL CHEMISTRY FOR MEDICAL STUDENTS. Fcp. 8vo. 1s. 6d.

MUIR (M. M. P.) and WILSON (D. M.).—THE ELEMENTS OF THERMAL CHEMISTRY. 8vo. 12s. 6d.

MÜLLER—THOMPSON.—THE FERTILISATION OF FLOWERS. By Prof. HERMANN MÜLLER. Translated by D'ARCY W. THOMPSON. With a Preface by CHARLES DARWIN, F.R.S. Medium 8vo. 21s.

MULLINGER (J. B.).—CAMBRIDGE CHARACTERISTICS IN THE SEVENTEENTH CENTURY. Crown 8vo. 4s. 6d.

MURPHY (J. J.).—HABIT AND INTELLIGENCE. 2nd Ed. Illustrated. 8vo. 16s.

MURRAY (E. C. Grenville).—ROUND ABOUT FRANCE. Crown 8vo. 7s. 6d.

MURRAY (D. Christie).—AUNT RACHEL. Crown 8vo. 3s. 6d.

—— SCHWARTZ. Crown 8vo. 3s. 6d.

—— THE WEAKER VESSEL. Cr. 8vo. 3s. 6d.

—— JOHN VALE'S GUARDIAN. 3 vols. Crown 8vo. 31s. 6d.

MUSIC.—A DICTIONARY OF MUSIC AND MUSICIANS, A.D. 1450—1889. Edited by Sir GEORGE GROVE, D.C.L. In 4 vols. 8vo. 21s. each.—Parts I.—XIV., XIX.—XXII. 3s. 6d. each.—Parts XV. XVI. 7s.—Parts XVII. XVIII. 7s.—Parts XXIII.—XXV. APPENDIX. Edited by J. A. FULLER MAITLAND, M.A. 9s. [Cloth cases for binding, 1s. each.]

MYERS (F. W. H.).—THE RENEWAL OF YOUTH, AND OTHER POEMS. Crown 8vo. 7s. 6d.

—— ST. PAUL: A POEM. Ex. fcp. 8vo. 2s. 6d.

—— WORDSWORTH. Cr. 8vo. 1s. 6d. ; sewed, 1s.

—— ESSAYS. 2 vols.—I. Classical. II. Modern. Crown 8vo. 4s. 6d. each.

MYERS (E.).—THE PURITANS: A POEM. Extra fcap. 8vo. 2s. 6d.

—— PINDAR'S ODES. Translated, with Introduction and Notes. Crown 8vo. 5s.

—— POEMS. Extra fcp. 8vo. 4s. 6d.

—— THE DEFENCE OF ROME, AND OTHER POEMS. Extra fcp. 8vo. 5s.

—— THE JUDGMENT OF PROMETHEUS, AND OTHER POEMS. Extra fcp. 8vo. 3s. 6d.

MYLNE (The Rt. Rev. Bishop).—SERMONS PREACHED IN ST. THOMAS'S CATHEDRAL, BOMBAY. Crown 8vo. 6s.

NADAL (E. S.).—ESSAYS AT HOME AND ELSEWHERE. Crown 8vo. 6s.

NAPOLEON I., HISTORY OF. By P. LANFREY. 4 vols. Crown 8vo. 30s.

NATURAL RELIGION. By the Author of "Ecce Homo." 2nd Edition. 8vo. 9s.

NATURE : A WEEKLY ILLUSTRATED JOURNAL OF SCIENCE. Published every Thursday. Price 6d. Monthly Parts, 2s. and 2s. 6d. ; Current Half-yearly vols., 15s. each. Vols. I.—XL. [Cases for binding vols. 1s. 6d. each.]

NATURE PORTRAITS. A Series of Portraits of Scientific Worthies engraved by JEENS and others in Portfolio. India Proofs, 5s. each. [Portfolio separately, 6s.]

NATURE SERIES. Crown 8vo :

THE ORIGIN AND METAMORPHOSES OF INSECTS. By Sir JOHN LUBBOCK, M.P., F.R.S. With Illustrations. 3s. 6d.

THE TRANSIT OF VENUS. By Prof. G. FORBES. With Illustrations. 3s. 6d.

POLARISATION OF LIGHT. By W. SPOTTISWOODE, LL.D. Illustrated. 3s. 6d.

ON BRITISH WILD FLOWERS CONSIDERED IN RELATION TO INSECTS. By Sir JOHN LUBBOCK, M.P., F.R.S. Illustrated. 4s.6d.

FLOWERS, FRUITS, AND LEAVES. By Sir JOHN LUBBOCK. Illustrated. 4s. 6d.

HOW TO DRAW A STRAIGHT LINE : A LECTURE ON LINKAGES. By A. B. KEMPE, B.A. Illustrated. 1s. 6d.

LIGHT : A SERIES OF SIMPLE, ENTERTAINING, AND USEFUL EXPERIMENTS. By A. M. MAYER and C. BARNARD. Illustrated. 2s. 6d.

SOUND : A SERIES OF SIMPLE, ENTERTAINING, AND INEXPENSIVE EXPERIMENTS. By A. M. MAYER. 3s. 6d.

SEEING AND THINKING. By Prof. W. K. CLIFFORD, F.R.S. Diagrams. 3s. 6d.

CHARLES DARWIN. Memorial Notices reprinted from "Nature." By THOMAS H. HUXLEY, F.R.S., G. J. ROMANES, F.R.S., ARCHIBALD GEIKIE, F.R.S., and W. T. DYER, F.R.S. 2s. 6d.

ON THE COLOURS OF FLOWERS. By GRANT ALLEN. Illustrated. 3s. 6d.

THE CHEMISTRY OF THE SECONDARY BATTERIES OF PLANTÉ AND FAURE. By J. H. GLADSTONE and A. TRIBE. 2s. 6d.

A CENTURY OF ELECTRICITY. By T. C. MENDENHALL. 4s. 6d.

ON LIGHT. The Burnett Lectures. By Sir GEORGE GABRIEL STOKES, M.P., P.R.S. Three Courses : I. On the Nature of Light. II. On Light as a Means of Investigation. III. On Beneficial Effects of Light. 7s. 6d.

THE SCIENTIFIC EVIDENCES OF ORGANIC EVOLUTION. By GEORGE J. ROMANES, M.A., LL.D. 2s. 6d.

POPULAR LECTURES AND ADDRESSES. By Sir WM. THOMSON. In 3 vols. Vol. I. Constitution of Matter. Illustrated. 6s.

THE CHEMISTRY OF PHOTOGRAPHY. By Prof. R. MELDOLA, F.R.S. Illustrated. 6s.

NATURE SERIES—continued.

MODERN VIEWS OF ELECTRICITY. By Prof. O. J. LODGE, LL.D. Illustrated. 6s. 6d.

TIMBER AND SOME OF ITS DISEASES. By Prof. H. M. WARD, M.A. Illustrated. 6s.

NEPOS. SELECTIONS ILLUSTRATIVE OF GREEK AND ROMAN HISTORY, FROM CORNELIUS NEPOS. Edited by G. S. FARNELL, M.A. 18mo. 1s. 6d.

NETTLESHIP.—VIRGIL. By Prof. NETTLESHIP, M.A. Fcap. 8vo. 1s. 6d.

NEW ANTIGONE, THE : A ROMANCE. Crown 8vo. 6s.

NEWCOMB (Prof. Simon).—POPULAR ASTRONOMY. With 112 Engravings and Maps of the Stars. 2nd Edition. 8vo. 18s.

NEWMAN (F. W.). — MATHEMATICAL TRACTS. Part I. 8vo. 5s.—Part II. 4s.

—— ELLIPTIC INTEGRALS. 8vo. 9s.

NEWTON (Sir C. T.).—ESSAYS ON ART AND ARCHÆOLOGY. 8vo. 12s. 6d.

NEWTON'S PRINCIPIA. Edited by Prof. Sir W. THOMSON and Prof. BLACKBURN. 4to. 31s. 6d.

—— FIRST BOOK. Sections I. II. III. With Notes, Illustrations, and Problems. By P. FROST, M.A. 3rd Edition. 8vo. 12s.

NICHOL (Prof. John).—PRIMER OF ENGLISH COMPOSITION. 18mo. 1s.

—— EXERCISES IN ENGLISH COMPOSITION. 18mo. 1s.

—— BYRON. Crown 8vo. 1s. 6d. ; sewed, 1s.

NINE YEARS OLD. By the Author of "St. Olave's." Illustrated by FRÖLICH. New Edition. Globe 8vo. 2s. 6d.

NIXON (J. E.).—PARALLEL EXTRACTS. Arranged for Translation into English and Latin, with Notes on Idioms. Part I. Historical and Epistolary. 2nd Edition. Crown 8vo. 3s. 6d.

—— PROSE EXTRACTS. Arranged for Translation into English and Latin, with General and Special Prefaces on Style and Idiom. I. Oratorical. II. Historical. III. Philosophical. IV. Anecdotes and Letters. 2nd Edition, enlarged to 280 pages. Crown 8vo. 4s. 6d.

—— SELECTIONS FROM PROSE EXTRACTS. Including Anecdotes and Letters, with Notes and Hints, pp. 120. Globe 8vo. 3s.

NOEL (Lady Augusta).—WANDERING WILLIE. Globe 8vo. 2s. 6d.

—— HITHERSEA MERE. 3 vols. Cr.8vo. 31s.6d.

NORDENSKIÖLD. — VOYAGE OF THE "VEGA" ROUND ASIA AND EUROPE. By Baron A. E. VON NORDENSKIÖLD. Translated by ALEXANDER LESLIE. 400 Illustrations, Maps, etc. 2 vols. Medium 8vo. 45s. *Popular Edition.* With Portrait, Maps, and Illustrations. Crown 8vo. 6s.

—— THE ARCTIC VOYAGES OF ADOLPH ERIC NORDENSKIÖLD, 1858—79. By ALEXANDER LESLIE. 8vo. 16s.

NORGATE (Kate).—ENGLAND UNDER THE ANGEVIN KINGS. In 2 vols. With Maps and Plans. 8vo. 32s.

NORRIS (W. E.).—MY FRIEND JIM. Globe 8vo. 2s.

—— CHRIS. Globe 8vo. 2s.

NORTON (the Hon. Mrs.).—THE LADY OF LA GARAYE. 9th Ed. Fcp. 8vo. 4s. 6d.

—— OLD SIR DOUGLAS. Crown 8vo. 6s.

O'BRIEN (Bishop J. T.).—PRAYER. Five Sermons. 8vo. 6s.

OLD SONGS. With Drawings by E. A. ABBEY and A. PARSONS. 4to. Morocco gilt. 1l. 11s. 6d.

OLIPHANT (Mrs. M. O. W.).—A SON OF THE SOIL. Globe 8vo. 2s.

—— THE CURATE IN CHARGE. Globe 8vo. 2s.

—— FRANCIS OF ASSISI. Crown 8vo. 6s.

—— YOUNG MUSGRAVE. Globe 8vo. 2s.

—— HE THAT WILL NOT WHEN HE MAY. Globe 8vo. 2s.

—— SIR TOM. Globe 8vo. 2s.

—— HESTER. Globe 8vo. 2s.

—— THE WIZARD'S SON. Globe 8vo. 2s.

—— A COUNTRY GENTLEMAN AND HIS FAMILY. Globe 8vo. 2s.

—— THE SECOND SON. Globe 8vo. 2s.

—— NEIGHBOURS ON THE GREEN. Crown 8vo. 3s. 6d.

—— JOYCE. Crown 8vo. 3s. 6d.

—— A BELEAGUERED CITY. Cr. 8vo. 3s. 6d.

—— THE MAKERS OF VENICE. With numerous Illustrations. Crown 8vo. 10s. 6d.

—— THE MAKERS OF FLORENCE: DANTE, GIOTTO, SAVONAROLA, AND THEIR CITY. With Illustrations. Cr. 8vo, cloth. 10s. 6d.

—— AGNES HOPETOUN'S SCHOOLS AND HOLIDAYS. Illustrated. Globe 8vo. 2s. 6d.

—— THE LITERARY HISTORY OF ENGLAND IN THE END OF THE EIGHTEENTH AND BEGINNING OF THE NINETEENTH CENTURY. 3 vols. 8vo. 21s.

—— SHERIDAN. Cr. 8vo. 1s. 6d.; sewed, 1s.

—— SELECTIONS FROM COWPER'S POEMS. 18mo. 4s. 6d.

OLIPHANT (T. L. Kington).—THE OLD AND MIDDLE ENGLISH. Globe 8vo. 9s.

—— THE DUKE AND THE SCHOLAR, AND OTHER ESSAYS. 8vo. 7s. 6d.

—— THE NEW ENGLISH. 2 vols. Cr. 8vo. 21s.

OLIVER (Prof. Daniel).—LESSONS IN ELEMENTARY BOTANY. Illustrated. Fcp. 8vo. 4s. 6d.

—— FIRST BOOK OF INDIAN BOTANY. Illustrated. Extra fcp. 8vo. 6s. 6d.

OLIVER (Capt. S. P.).—MADAGASCAR: AN HISTORICAL AND DESCRIPTIVE ACCOUNT OF THE ISLAND AND ITS FORMER DEPENDENCIES. 2 vols. Medium 8vo. 2l. 12s. 6d.

ORCHIDS: BEING THE REPORT ON THE ORCHID CONFERENCE HELD AT SOUTH KENSINGTON, 1885. 8vo. 2s. 6d.

OTTÉ (E. C.).—SCANDINAVIAN HISTORY. With Maps. Globe 8vo. 6s.

OVID.—SELECTIONS. Edited by E. S. SHUCKBURGH, M.A. 18mo. 1s. 6d.

OVID.—FASTI. Edited by G. H. HALLAM, M.A. Fcp. 8vo. 5s.

—— HEROIDUM EPISTULÆ XIII. Edited by E. S. SHUCKBURGH, M.A. Fcp. 8vo. 4s. 6d.

—— METAMORPHOSES. Books I.–III. Edited by C. SIMMONS, M.A.

—— STORIES FROM THE METAMORPHOSES. Edited by the Rev. J. BOND, M.A., and A. S. WALPOLE, M.A. With Notes, Exercises, and Vocabulary. 18mo. 1s. 6d.

—— METAMORPHOSES. Books XIII. and XIV. Ed. by C. SIMMONS. Fcp. 8vo. 4s. 6d.

—— EASY SELECTIONS FROM OVID IN ELEGIAC VERSE. Arranged and Edited by H. WILKINSON, M.A. 18mo. 1s. 6d.

OWENS COLLEGE CALENDAR, 1889–90. Crown 8vo. 3s.

OWENS COLLEGE ESSAYS AND ADDRESSES. By Professors and Lecturers of the College. 8vo. 14s.

OXFORD, A HISTORY OF THE UNIVERSITY OF. From the Earliest Times to the Year 1530. By H. C. MAXWELL LYTE, M.A. 8vo. 16s.

PALGRAVE (Sir Francis). — HISTORY OF NORMANDY AND OF ENGLAND. 4 vols. 8vo. 4l. 4s.

PALGRAVE (William Gifford).—A NARRATIVE OF A YEAR'S JOURNEY THROUGH CENTRAL AND EASTERN ARABIA, 1862—63. 9th Edition. Crown 8vo. 6s.

—— ESSAYS ON EASTERN QUESTIONS. 8vo. 10s. 6d.

—— DUTCH GUIANA. 8vo. 9s.

—— ULYSSES; OR, SCENES AND STUDIES IN MANY LANDS. 8vo. 12s. 6d.

PALGRAVE (Prof. Francis Turner).—THE FIVE DAYS' ENTERTAINMENTS AT WENTWORTH GRANGE. A Book for Children. Small 4to, cloth extra. 6s.

—— ESSAYS ON ART. Extra fcp. 8vo. 6s.

—— ORIGINAL HYMNS. 3rd Ed. 18mo. 1s. 6d.

—— LYRICAL POEMS. Extra fcp. 8vo. 6s.

—— VISIONS OF ENGLAND: A SERIES OF LYRICAL POEMS ON LEADING EVENTS AND PERSONS IN ENGLISH HISTORY. Crown 8vo. 7s. 6d.

—— THE GOLDEN TREASURY OF THE BEST SONGS AND LYRICAL POEMS IN THE ENGLISH LANGUAGE. 18mo. 4s. 6d.

—— SONNETS AND SONGS OF SHAKESPEARE. Edited by F. T. PALGRAVE. 18mo. 4s. 6d.

—— THE CHILDREN'S TREASURY OF LYRICAL POETRY. 18mo. 2s. 6d.—Or in Two Parts, 1s. each.

—— HERRICK: SELECTIONS FROM THE LYRICAL POEMS. 18mo. 4s. 6d.

—— THE POETICAL WORKS OF JOHN KEATS. With Notes. 18mo. 4s. 6d.

—— LYRICAL POEMS OF LORD TENNYSON. Selected and Annotated. 18mo. 4s. 6d. Large Paper Edition. 8vo. 9s.

PALGRAVE (Reginald F. D.).—THE HOUSE OF COMMONS: ILLUSTRATIONS OF ITS HISTORY AND PRACTICE. Crown 8vo. 2s. 6d.

PALMER (Lady Sophia).—MRS. PENICOTT'S LODGER, AND OTHER STORIES. Cr. 8vo. 2s. 6d.

PALMER (J. H.).—Text-Book of Practical Logarithms and Trigonometry. Crown 8vo. 4s. 6d.

PANSIE'S FLOUR BIN. By the Author of "When I was a Little Girl," etc. Illustrated. Globe 8vo. 2s. 6d.

PANTIN (W. E. P.).—A First Latin Verse Book. Globe 8vo. 1s. 6d.

PARADOXICAL PHILOSOPHY: A Sequel to "The Unseen Universe." Cr. 8vo. 7s. 6d.

PARKER (H.).—The Nature of the Fine Arts. Crown 8vo. 10s. 6d.

PARKER (Prof. W. K.) and BETTANY (G. T.).—The Morphology of the Skull. Crown 8vo. 10s. 6d.

PARKER (Prof. T. Jeffrey).—A Course of Instruction in Zootomy (Vertebrata). With 74 Illustrations. Crown 8vo. 8s. 6d.

PARKINSON (S.).—A Treatise on Elementary Mechanics. Crown 8vo. 9s. 6d.

—— A Treatise on Optics. 4th Edition, revised. Crown 8vo. 10s. 6d.

PARKMAN (Francis). — Montcalm and Wolfe. Library Edition. Illustrated with Portraits and Maps. 2 vols. 8vo. 12s. 6d. each.

—— The Collected Works of Francis Parkman. Popular Edition. In 10 vols. Crown 8vo. 7s. 6d. each; or complete, 3l. 13s. 6d.—Pioneers of France in the New World. 1 vol.—The Jesuits in North America. 1 vol.—La Salle and the Discovery of the Great West. 1 vol.—The Oregon Trail. 1 vol.—The Old Régime in Canada under Louis XIV. 1 vol.—Count Frontenac and New France under Louis XIV. 1 vol.—Montcalm and Wolfe. 2 vols.—The Conspiracy of Pontiac. 2 vols.

PASTEUR — FAULKNER. — Studies on Fermentation: The Diseases of Beer, their Causes, and the Means of preventing them. By L. Pasteur. Translated by Frank Faulkner. 8vo. 21s.

PATER (W.).—The Renaissance: Studies in Art and Poetry. 4th Ed. Cr.8vo. 10s.6d.

—— Marius the Epicurean: His Sensations and Ideas. 3rd Edition. 2 vols. 8vo. 12s.

—— Imaginary Portraits. Crown 8vo. 6s.

—— Appreciations. With an Essay on Style. 2nd Edition. Crown 8vo. 8s. 6d.

PATERSON (James).—Commentaries on the Liberty of the Subject, and the Laws of England relating to the Security of the Person. 2 vols. Cr.8vo. 21s.

—— The Liberty of the Press, Speech, and Public Worship. Crown 8vo. 12s.

PATMORE (C.).—The Children's Garland from the Best Poets. With a Vignette. 18mo. 4s. 6d.
Globe Readings Edition. For Schools. Globe 8vo. 2s.

PATTESON.—Life and Letters of John Coleridge Patteson, D.D., Missionary Bishop. By Charlotte M. Yonge. 8th Edition. 2 vols. Crown 8vo. 12s.

PATTISON (Mark).—Milton. Crown 8vo. 1s. 6d.; sewed, 1s.

—— Memoirs. Crown 8vo. 8s. 6d.

—— Sermons. Crown 8vo. 6s.

PAUL OF TARSUS. 8vo. 10s. 6d.

PAYNE (E. J.).—History of European Colonies. 18mo. 4s. 6d.

PEABODY (Prof. C. H.).—Thermodynamics of the Steam Engine and other Heat-Engines. 8vo. 21s.

PEDLEY (S.).—Exercises in Arithmetic. With upwards of 7000 Examples and Answers. Crown 8vo. 5s.—Also in Two Parts. 2s. 6d. each.

PEEL (Edmund).—Echoes from Horeb, and other Poems. Crown 8vo. 3s. 6d.

PEILE (John).—Philology. 18mo. 1s.

PELLISSIER (Eugène).—French Roots and their Families. Globe 8vo. 6s.

PENNELL (Joseph).—Pen Drawing and Pen Draughtsmen: Their Work and Methods, a Study of the Art to-day, with Technical Suggestions. With 158 Illustrations. 4to. 3l. 13s. 6d. net.

PENNINGTON (Rooke).—Notes on the Barrows and Bone Caves of Derbyshire. 8vo. 6s.

PENROSE (Francis).—On a Method of Predicting, by Graphical Construction, Occultations of Stars by the Moon and Solar Eclipses for any given place. 4to. 12s.

—— An Investigation of the Principles of Athenian Architecture. Illustrated. Folio. 7l. 7s.

PERRAULT.—Contes de Fées. Edited by G. Eugène Fasnacht. Globe 8vo. 1s. 6d.

PERRY (Prof. John).—An Elementary Treatise on Steam. 18mo. 4s. 6d.

PERSIA, EASTERN. An Account of the Journeys of the Persian Boundary Commission, 1870—71—72. 2 vols. 8vo. 42s.

PETERBOROUGH. By W. Stebbing. With Portrait. Crown 8vo. 2s. 6d.

PETTIGREW (J. Bell).—The Physiology of the Circulation. 8vo. 12s.

PHAEDRUS.—Select Fables. Edited by A. S. Walpole, M.A. With Notes, Exercises, and Vocabularies. 18mo. 1s. 6d.

PHILLIMORE (John G.).—Private Law among the Romans. 8vo. 16s.

PHILLIPS (J. A.).—A Treatise on Ore Deposits. Illustrated. Medium 8vo. 25s.

PHILOCHRISTUS.—Memoirs of a Disciple of the Lord. 3rd Ed. 8vo. 12s.

PHILOLOGY.—The Journal of Sacred and Classical Philology. 4 vols. 8vo. 12s. 6d. each.

—— The Journal of Philology. New Series. Edited by W. A. Wright, M.A., I. Bywater, M.A., and H. Jackson, M.A. 4s. 6d. each number (half-yearly).

—— The American Journal of Philology. Edited by Prof. Basil L. Gildersleeve. 4s. 6d. each (quarterly).

PHRYNICHUS. The New Phrynichus. A revised text of "The Ecloga" of the Grammarian Phrynichus. With Introductions and Commentary. By W. Gunion Rutherford, M.A. 8vo. 18s.

PICKERING (Prof. Edward C.).—Elements of Physical Manipulation. Medium 8vo. Part I., 12s. 6d.; Part II., 14s.

PICTON (J. A.).—The Mystery of Matter, and other Essays. Crown 8vo. 6s.

PIFFARD (H. G.).—An Elementary Treatise on Diseases of the Skin. 8vo. 16s.

PINDAR'S EXTANT ODES. Translated by Ernest Myers. Crown 8vo. 5s.

PIRIE (Prof. G.).—Lessons on Rigid Dynamics. Crown 8vo. 6s.

PLATO.—Phædo. Edited by R. D. Archer-Hind, M.A. 8vo. 8s. 6d.

—— Timæus. With Introduction, Notes, and Translation, by the same Editor. 8vo. 16s.

—— Phædo. Ed. by Principal W. D. Geddes, LL.D. 2nd Edition. 8vo. 8s. 6d.

—— The Trial and Death of Socrates: Being the Euthyphron, Apology, Crito, and Phædo of Plato. Translated by F. J. Church. 18mo. 4s. 6d.

—— Euthyphro and Menexenus. Ed. by C. E. Graves, M.A. 18mo. 1s. 6d.

—— The Republic. Books I.—V. Edited by T. H. Warren, M.A. Fcp. 8vo. 6s.

—— The Republic of Plato. Translated by J. Ll. Davies, M.A., and D. J. Vaughan, M.A. 18mo. 4s. 6d.

—— Laches. Edited by M. T. Tatham, M.A. Fcap. 8vo. 2s. 6d.

—— Phaedrus, Lysis, and Protagoras. A New Translation, by J. Wright, M.A. 18mo. 4s. 6d.

PLAUTUS.—The Mostellaria. With Notes, Prolegomena, and Excursus. By the late Prof. Ramsay. Ed. by G. G. Ramsay, M.A. 8vo. 14s.

—— Miles Gloriosus. Edit. by Prof. R. Y. Tyrrell, M.A. 2nd Ed. Fcp. 8vo. 5s.

—— Amphitruo. Edited by Prof. A. Palmer, M.A. Fcp. 8vo. 5s.

PLINY.—Letters. Books I. and II. Edit. by James Cowan, M.A. Fcp. 8vo. 5s.

—— Letters. Book III. Edited by Prof. John E. B. Mayor. Fcp. 8vo. 5s.

—— Correspondence with Trajan. Ed., with Notes and Introductory Essays, by E. G. Hardy, M.A. 8vo. 10s. 6d.

PLUMPTRE (Prof. E. H.).—Movements in Religious Thought. Fcp. 8vo. 3s. 6d.

PLUTARCH. Being a Selection from the Lives in North's Plutarch which illustrate Shakespeare's Plays. Edited by Rev. W. W. Skeat, M.A. Crown 8vo. 6s.

—— Life of Themistokles. Edited by Rev. H. A. Holden, M.A. Fcp. 8vo. 5s.

—— Lives of Galba and Otho. Edited by E. G. Hardy, M.A. Fcp. 8vo. 6s.

POLLOCK (Prof. Sir F., Bart.).—Essays in Jurisprudence and Ethics. 8vo. 10s. 6d.

—— The Land Laws. 2nd Edition. Crown 8vo. 3s. 6d.

POLLOCK (W. H. and Lady).—Amateur Theatricals. Crown 8vo. 2s. 6d.

POLLOCK (Sir Frederick).—Personal Remembrances. 2 vols. Crown 8vo. 16s.

POLYBIUS.—The History of the Achæan League. As contained in the "Remains of Polybius." Edited by Rev. W. W. Capes. Fcp. 8vo. 6s. 6d.

—— The Histories of Polybius. Transl. by E. S. Shuckburgh. 2 vols. Cr. 8vo. 24s.

POOLE (M. E.).—Pictures of Cottage Life in the West of England. 2nd Ed. Crown 8vo. 3s. 6d.

POOLE (Reginald Lane).—A History of the Huguenots of the Dispersion at the Recall of the Edict of Nantes. Crown 8vo. 6s.

POOLE, THOMAS, AND HIS FRIENDS. By Mrs. Sandford. 2 vols. Crn. 8vo. 15s.

POPE.—The Poetical Works of Alex. Pope. Edited by Prof. Ward. Globe 8vo. 3s. 6d.

—— Pope. By Leslie Stephen. Crown 8vo. 1s. 6d.; sewed, 1s.

POPULATION OF AN OLD PEAR TREE; or, Stories of Insect Life. From the French of E. Van Bruyssel. Ed. by C. M. Yonge. Illustrated. Globe 8vo. 2s. 6d.

POSTGATE (Prof. J. P.).—Sermo Latinus. A Short Guide to Latin Prose Composition. Part I. Introduction. Part II. Selected Passages for Translation. Gl. 8vo. 2s. 6d.— Key to "Selected Passages." Cr. 8vo. 3s. 6d.

POTTER (Louisa).—Lancashire Memories. Crown 8vo. 6s.

POTTER (R.).—The Relation of Ethics to Religion. Crown 8vo. 2s. 6d.

POTTS (A. W.).—Hints towards Latin Prose Composition. Globe 8vo. 3s.

—— Passages for Translation into Latin Prose. 4th Ed. Extra fcp. 8vo. 2s. 6d.

—— Latin Versions of Passages for Translation into Latin Prose. Extra fcp. 8vo. 2s. 6d. (For Teachers only.)

PRACTICAL POLITICS. Published under the auspices of the National Liberal Federation. 8vo. 6s.

PRACTITIONER (THE): A Monthly Journal of Therapeutics and Public Health. Edited by T. Lauder Brunton, M.D., F.R.C.P., F.R.S., Assistant Physician to St. Bartholomew's Hospital, etc., etc.; Donald MacAlister, M.A., M.D., B.Sc., F.R.C.P., Fellow and Medical Lecturer, St. John's College, Cambridge, Physician to Addenbrooke's Hospital and University Lecturer in Medicine; and J. Mitchell Bruce, M.A., M.D., F.R.C.P., Physician and Lecturer on Therapeutics at Charing Cross Hospital. 1s. 6d. monthly. Vols. I.—XLIII. Half-yearly vols. 10s. 6d.

PRESTON (Rev. G.).—Exercises in Latin Verse of Various Kinds. Globe 8vo. 2s. 6d.—Key. Globe 8vo. 5s.

PRESTON (T.).— A Treatise on the Theory of Light. Illustrated. 8vo.

PRICE (L. L. F. R.).—Industrial Peace: Its Advantages, Methods, and Difficulties. Medium 8vo. 6s.

PRIMERS.—History. Edited by John R. Green, Author of "A Short History of the English People," etc. 18mo. 1s. each:
Europe. By E. A. Freeman, M.A.
Greece. By C. A. Fyffe, M.A.
Rome. By Prof. Creighton.
Greek Antiquities. By Prof. Mahaffy.
Roman Antiquities. By Prof. Wilkins.
Classical Geography. By H. F. Tozer.
France. By Charlotte M. Yonge.
Geography. By Sir Geo. Grove, D.C.L.

PRIMERS.—Literature. Edited by John R. Green, M.A., LL.D. 18mo. 1s. each:
English Grammar. By Rev. R. Morris.
English Grammar Exercises. By Rev. R. Morris and H. C. Bowen.
Exercises on Morris's Primer of English Grammar. By J. Wetherell, M.A.
English Composition. By Prof. Nichol.
Exercises in English Composition. By Prof. Nichol.
Philology. By J. Peile, M.A.
English Literature. By Rev. Stopford Brooke, M.A.
Children's Treasury of Lyrical Poetry. Selected by Prof. F. T. Palgrave. In 2 parts. 1s. each.
Shakspere. By Prof. Dowden.
Greek Literature. By Prof. Jebb.
Homer. By Right Hon. W. E. Gladstone.
Roman Literature. By A. S. Wilkins.

PRIMERS.—Science. Under the joint Editorship of Prof. Huxley, Sir H. E. Roscoe, and Prof. Balfour Stewart. 18mo. 1s. each:
Introductory. By Prof. Huxley.
Chemistry. By Sir Henry Roscoe, F.R.S. With Illustrations, and Questions.
Physics. By Balfour Stewart, F.R.S. With Illustrations, and Questions.
Physical Geography. By A. Geikie, F.R.S. With Illustrations, and Questions.
Geology. By Archibald Geikie, F.R.S.
Physiology. By Michael Foster, F.R.S.
Astronomy. By J. N. Lockyer, F.R.S.
Botany. By Sir J. D. Hooker, C.B.
Logic. By W. Stanley Jevons, F.R.S.
Political Economy. By W. Stanley Jevons, LL.D., M.A., F.R.S.

PROCTER (Rev. F.).—A History of the Book of Common Prayer. 18th Edition. Crown 8vo. 10s. 6d.

PROCTER (Rev. F.) and MACLEAR (Rev. Canon).—An Elementary Introduction to the Book of Common Prayer. 18mo. 2s. 6d.

PROPERT (J. Lumsden).—A History of Miniature Art. With Illustrations. Super royal 4to. 3l. 13s. 6d.
Also bound in vellum. 4l. 14s. 6d.

PROPERTIUS.—Select Poems. Edited by J. P. Postgate, M.A. Fcp. 8vo. 6s.

PSALMS (THE). With Introductions and Critical Notes. By A. C. Jennings, M.A., and W. H. Lowe, M.A. In 2 vols. 2nd Edition. Crown 8vo. 10s. 6d. each.

PUCKLE (G. H.).—An Elementary Treatise on Conic Sections and Algebraic Geometry. 6th Edit. Crn. 8vo. 7s. 6d.

PYLODET (L.).—New Guide to German Conversation. 18mo. 2s. 6d.

RACINE.—Britannicus. Ed. by Eugène Pellissier, M.A. 18mo. 2s.

RADCLIFFE (Charles B.).—Behind the Tides. 8vo. 6s.

RAMSAY (Prof. William).—Experimental Proofs of Chemical Theory. 18mo. 2s. 6d.

RAY (Prof. P. K.).—A Text-Book of Deductive Logic. 4th Ed. Globe 8vo. 4s. 6d.

RAYLEIGH (Lord).—Theory of Sound. 8vo. Vol. I. 12s. 6d.—Vol. II. 12s. 6d.—Vol. III. (in preparation.)

RAYS OF SUNLIGHT FOR DARK DAYS. With a Preface by C. J. Vaughan, D.D. New Edition. 18mo. 3s. 6d.

REALMAH. By the Author of "Friends in Council." Crown 8vo. 6s.

REASONABLE FAITH: A Short Religious Essay for the Times. By "Three Friends." Crown 8vo. 1s.

RECOLLECTIONS OF A NURSE. By E. D. Crown 8vo. 2s.

REED.—Memoir of Sir Charles Reed. By his Son, Charles E. B. Reed, M.A. With Portrait. Crown 8vo. 4s. 6d.

REMSEN (Prof. Ira).—An Introduction to the Study of Organic Chemistry. Crown 8vo. 6s. 6d.

—— An Introduction to the Study of Chemistry (Inorganic Chemistry). Cr. 8vo. 6s. 6d.

—— The Elements of Chemistry. A Text-Book for Beginners. Fcp. 8vo. 2s. 6d.

—— Text-Book of Inorganic Chemistry. 8vo. 16s.

RENDALL (Rev. Frederic).—The Epistle to the Hebrews in Greek and English. With Notes. Crown 8vo. 6s.

—— The Theology of the Hebrew Christians. Crown 8vo. 5s.

—— The Epistle to the Hebrews. English Text, with Commentary. Cr. 8vo. 7s. 6d.

RENDALL (Prof. G. H.).—The Cradle of the Aryans. 8vo. 3s.

RENDU—WILLS.—The Theory of the Glaciers of Savoy. By M. Le Chanoine Rendu. Translated by A. Wills, Q.C. 8vo. 7s. 6d.

REULEAUX—KENNEDY.—THE KINE-MATICS OF MACHINERY. By Prof. F. REULEAUX. Translated by Prof. A. B. W. KENNEDY, F.R.S., C.E. Medium 8vo. 21s.

REYNOLDS (J. R.).—A SYSTEM OF MEDICINE. Edited by J. RUSSELL REYNOLDS, M.D., F.R.C.P. London. In 5 vols. Vols. I. II. III. and V. 8vo. 25s. each.—Vol. IV. 21s.

REYNOLDS (H. R.).—NOTES OF THE CHRISTIAN LIFE. Crown 8vo. 7s. 6d.

REYNOLDS (Prof. Osborne).—SEWER GAS, AND HOW TO KEEP IT OUT OF HOUSES. 3rd Edition. Crown 8vo. 1s. 6d.

RICE (Prof. J. M.) and JOHNSON (W. W.).—AN ELEMENTARY TREATISE ON THE DIFFERENTIAL CALCULUS. New Edition. 8vo. 18s. Abridged Edition. 9s.

RICHARDSON (Dr. B. W.).—ON ALCOHOL. Crown 8vo. 1s.

—— DISEASES OF MODERN LIFE. Crown 8vo. 6s.

—— HYGEIA: A CITY OF HEALTH. Crown 8vo. 1s.

—— THE FUTURE OF SANITARY SCIENCE. Crown 8vo. 1s.

RICHEY (Alex. G.).—THE IRISH LAND LAWS. Crown 8vo. 3s. 6d.

ROBINSON CRUSOE. Edited by HENRY KINGSLEY. Globe Edition. 3s. 6d.—Golden Treasury Edition. Edit. by J. W. CLARK, M.A. 18mo. 4s. 6d.

ROBINSON (Prebendary H. G.).—MAN IN THE IMAGE OF GOD, AND OTHER SERMONS. Crown 8vo. 7s. 6d.

ROBINSON (Rev. J. L.).—MARINE SURVEYING: AN ELEMENTARY TREATISE ON. Prepared for the Use of Younger Naval Officers. With Illustrations. Crown 8vo. 7s. 6d.

ROBY (H. J.).—A GRAMMAR OF THE LATIN LANGUAGE FROM PLAUTUS TO SUETONIUS. In Two Parts.—Part I. containing Sounds, Inflexions, Word Formation, Appendices, etc. 5th Edition. Crown 8vo. 9s.—Part II. Syntax, Prepositions, etc. 6th Edition. Crown 8vo. 10s. 6d.

—— A LATIN GRAMMAR FOR SCHOOLS. Cr. 8vo. 5s.

—— AN ELEMENTARY LATIN GRAMMAR. Globe 8vo.

—— EXERCISES IN LATIN SYNTAX AND IDIOM. Arranged with reference to Roby's School Latin Grammar. By E. B. ENGLAND, M.A. Crown 8vo. 2s. 6d. Key, 2s. 6d.

ROCKSTRO (W. S.).—LIFE OF GEORGE FREDERICK HANDEL. Crown 8vo. 10s. 6d.

ROGERS (Prof. J. E. T.).—HISTORICAL GLEANINGS.—First Series. Cr. 8vo. 4s. 6d. — Second Series. Crown 8vo. 6s.

—— COBDEN AND POLITICAL OPINION. 8vo. 10s. 6d.

ROMANES (George J.).—THE SCIENTIFIC EVIDENCES OF ORGANIC EVOLUTION. Cr. 8vo. 2s. 6d.

ROSCOE (Sir Henry E., M.P., F.R.S.).—LESSONS IN ELEMENTARY CHEMISTRY. With Illustrations. Fcp. 8vo. 4s. 6d.

—— PRIMER OF CHEMISTRY. With Illustrations. 18mo, cloth. With Questions. 1s.

ROSCOE (Sir H. E.) and SCHORLEMMER (C.).—A TREATISE ON CHEMISTRY. With Illustrations. 8vo.—Vols. I. and II. INORGANIC CHEMISTRY: Vol. I. THE NON-METALLIC ELEMENTS. With a Portrait of DALTON. 21s.—Vol. II. Part I. METALS. 18s.; Part II. METALS. 18s.—Vol. III. ORGANIC CHEMISTRY: Parts I. II. and IV. 21s. each; Parts III. and V. 18s. each.

ROSCOE—SCHUSTER. SPECTRUM ANALYSIS. By Sir HENRY E. ROSCOE, LL.D., F.R.S. 4th Edition, revised by the Author and A. SCHUSTER, Ph.D., F.R.S. Medium 8vo. 21s.

ROSENBUSCH—IDDINGS. MICROSCOPICAL PHYSIOGRAPHY OF THE ROCK-MAKING MINERALS. By Prof. H. ROSENBUSCH. Translated by J. P. IDDINGS. Illustrated. 8vo. 24s.

ROSS (Percy).—A MISGUIDIT LASSIE. Crown 8vo. 4s. 6d.

ROSSETTI (Dante Gabriel). — A RECORD AND A STUDY. By W. SHARP. Crown 8vo. 10s. 6d.

ROSSETTI (Christina).—POEMS. Complete Edition. Extra fcp. 8vo. 6s.

—— A PAGEANT, AND OTHER POEMS. Extra fcp. 8vo. 6s.

—— SPEAKING LIKENESSES. Illustrated by ARTHUR HUGHES. Crown 8vo. 4s. 6d.

ROUSSEAU. By JOHN MORLEY. 2 vols. Globe 8vo. 10s.

ROUTH (E. J.).—A TREATISE ON THE DYNAMICS OF A SYSTEM OF RIGID BODIES. 4th Edition, revised and enlarged. 8vo. In Two Parts.—Part I. ELEMENTARY. 14s.—Part II. ADVANCED. 14s.

—— STABILITY OF A GIVEN STATE OF MOTION, PARTICULARLY STEADY MOTION. 8vo. 8s. 6d.

ROUTLEDGE (James).—POPULAR PROGRESS IN ENGLAND. 8vo. 16s.

RUMFORD (Count).—COMPLETE WORKS OF COUNT RUMFORD. With Memoir by GEORGE ELLIS, and Portrait. 5 vols. 8vo. 4l. 14s. 6d.

RUNAWAY (THE). By the Author of "Mrs. Jerningham's Journal." Gl. 8vo. 2s. 6d.

RUSH (Edward).—THE SYNTHETIC LATIN DELECTUS. A First Latin Construing Book. Extra fcp. 8vo. 2s. 6d.

RUSHBROOKE (W. G.).—SYNOPTICON: AN EXPOSITION OF THE COMMON MATTER OF THE SYNOPTIC GOSPELS. Printed in Colours. In Six Parts, and Appendix. 4to.—Part I. 3s. 6d.—Parts II. and III. 7s.—Parts IV. V. and VI., with Indices. 10s. 6d.—Appendices. 10s. 6d.—Complete in 1 vol. 35s.

RUSSELL (W. Clark).—MAROONED. 3 vols. Crown 8vo. 31s. 6d.

—— DAMPIER. Portrait. Cr. 8vo. 2s. 6d.

RUSSELL (Sir Charles).—New Views on Ireland. Crown 8vo. 2s. 6d.

—— The Parnell Commission: The Opening Speech for the Defence. 8vo. 10s.6d. *Popular Edition.* Sewed. 2s.

RUST (Rev. George).—First Steps to Latin Prose Composition. 18mo. 1s. 6d.

—— A Key to Rust's First Steps to Latin Prose Composition. By W. Yates. 18mo. 3s. 6d.

RUTH AND HER FRIENDS: A Story for Girls. Illustrated. Gl. 8vo. 2s. 6d.

RUTHERFORD (W. Gunion, M.A., LL.D.).—First Greek Grammar. Part I. Accidence, 2s.; Part II. Syntax, 2s.; or in 1 vol. 3s. 6d.

—— The New Phrynichus. Being a revised Text of the Ecloga of the Grammarian Phrynichus, with Introduction and Commentary. 8vo. 18s.

—— Babrius. With Introductory Dissertations, Critical Notes, Commentary, and Lexicon. 8vo. 12s. 6d.

—— Thucydides. Book IV. A Revision of the Text, illustrating the Principal Causes of Corruption in the Manuscripts of this Author. 8vo. 7s. 6d.

RYLAND (F.).—Chronological Outlines of English Literature. Cr. 8vo.

ST. JOHNSTON (A.).—Camping among Cannibals. Crown 8vo. 4s. 6d.

—— Charlie Asgarde: The Story of a Friendship. Crown 8vo. 5s.

SAINTSBURY (George).—A History of Elizabethan Literature. Cr. 8vo. 7s.6d.

—— Dryden. Crown 8vo. 1s. 6d.; sewed, 1s.

SALLUST.—Caii Sallustii Crispi Catilina et Jugurtha. For Use in Schools. By C. Merivale, D.D. Fcp. 8vo. 4s. 6d.

    The Jugurtha and the Catiline may be had separately, 2s. 6d. each.

—— The Conspiracy of Catiline and the Jugurthine War. Translated into English by A. W. Pollard, B.A. Crown 8vo. 6s.

    Catiline separately. Crown 8vo. 3s.

—— Bellum Catulinae. Edited, with Introduction and Notes, by A. M. Cook, M.A. Fcp. 8vo. 4s. 6d.

SALMON (Rev. Prof. George).—Non-Miraculous Christianity, and other Sermons. 2nd Edition. Crown 8vo. 6s.

—— Gnosticism and Agnosticism, and other Sermons. Crown 8vo. 7s. 6d.

SAND (G.).—La Mare au Diable. Edited by W. E. Russell, M.A. 18mo. 1s.

SANDEAU (Jules).—Mademoiselle de la Seiglière. Ed. H. C. Steel. 18mo. 1s. 6d.

SANDERSON (F. W.).—Hydrostatics for Beginners. Globe 8vo. 4s. 6d.

SANDYS (J. E.).—An Easter Vacation in Greece. Crown 8vo. 3s. 6d.

SAYCE (Prof. A. H.).—The Ancient Empires of the East. Crown 8vo. 6s.

—— Herodotos. Books I.—III. The Ancient Empires of the East. Edited, with Notes, and Introduction. 8vo. 16s.

SCHILLER.—Die Jungfrau von Orleans. Edited by Joseph Gostwick. 18mo. 2s. 6d.

—— Maria Stuart. Edited, with Introduction and Notes, by C. Sheldon. 18mo. 2s.6d.

—— Selections from Schiller's Lyrical Poems. Edit. E. J. Turner and E. D. A. Morshead. 18mo. 2s. 6d.

—— Wallenstein. Part I. Das Läger. Edit. by H. B. Cotterill, M.A. 18mo. 2s.

—— Wilhelm Tell. Edited by G. E. Fasnacht. 18mo. 2s. 6d.

SCHILLER'S LIFE. By Prof. Heinrich Düntzer. Translated by Percy E. Pinkerton. Crown 8vo. 10s. 6d.

SCHMID.—Heinrich von Eichenfels. Edited by G. E. Fasnacht. 2s. 6d.

SCHMIDT—WHITE.—An Introduction to the Rhythmic and Metric of the Classical Languages. By Dr. J. H. Heinrich Schmidt. Translated by John Williams White, Ph.D. 8vo. 10s. 6d.

SCIENCE LECTURES AT SOUTH KENSINGTON. With Illustrations.—Vol. I. Containing Lectures by Capt. Abney, R.E., F.R.S.; Prof. Stokes; Prof. A. B. W. Kennedy, F.R.S., C.E.; F. J. Bramwell, C.E., F.R.S.; Prof. F. Forbes; H. C. Sorby, F.R.S.; J. T. Bottomley, F.R.S.E.; S. H. Vines, D.Sc.; Prof. Carey Forster. Crown 8vo. 6s.
    Vol. II. Containing Lectures by W. Spottiswoode, F.R.S.; Prof. Forbes; H. W. Chisholm; Prof. T. F. Pigot; W. Froude, LL.D., F.R.S.; Dr. Siemens; Prof. Barrett; Dr. Burdon-Sanderson; Dr. Lauder Brunton, F.R.S.; Prof. McLeod; Sir H. E. Roscoe, F.R.S. Illust. Cr.8vo. 6s.

SCOTCH SERMONS, 1880. By Principal Caird and others. 3rd Edit. 8vo. 10s. 6d.

SCOTT.—The Poetical Works of Sir Walter Scott. Edited by Prof. F. T. Palgrave. Globe 8vo. 3s. 6d.

—— The Lay of the Last Minstrel, and The Lady of the Lake. Edited, with Introductions and Notes, by Prof. F. T. Palgrave. Globe 8vo. 1s.

—— Marmion, and The Lord of the Isles. By the same Editor. Globe 8vo. 1s.

—— Marmion. A Tale of Flodden Field in Six Cantos. Edited, with Introduction and Notes, by Prof. M. Macmillan, B.A. Globe 8vo. 3s. 6d.

—— Rokeby. By the same. Gl. 8vo. 3s. 6d.

—— The Lay of the Last Minstrel. Cantos I.—III. Edited, with Introduction and Notes, by Prof. G. H. Stuart, M.A. Globe 8vo. 1s. 6d.—Canto I. (separately), 9d.

—— The Lady of the Lake. By the same Editor. Globe 8vo.

SCOTT (Sir Walter). By R. H. Hutton. Crown 8vo. 1s. 6d.; sewed, 1s.

SCOTTISH SONG: A Selection of the Lyrics of Scotland. Compiled by Mary Carlyle Aitken. 18mo. 4s. 6d.

SCRATCHLEY—KINLOCH COOKE.— Australian Defences and New Guinea. Compiled from the Papers of the late Major-General Sir Peter Scratchley, R.E., K.C.M.G., by C. Kinloch Cooke, B.A. 8vo. 14s.

SCULPTURE, SPECIMENS OF ANCIENT. Egyptian, Etruscan, Greek, and Roman. Selected from different Collections in Great Britain by the Society of Dilettanti. Vol. II. 5l. 5s.

SEATON (Dr. Edward C.).—A Hand-Book of Vaccination. Extra fcp. 8vo. 8s. 6d.

SEELEY (Prof. J. R.).—Lectures and Essays. 8vo. 10s. 6d.

—— The Expansion of England. Two Courses of Lectures. Crown 8vo. 4s. 6d.

—— Our Colonial Expansion. Extracts from "The Expansion of England." Crown 8vo. 1s.

SEILER.—Micro-Photographs in Histology, Normal and Pathological. By Carl Seiler, M.D. 4to. 31s. 6d.

SELBORNE (Roundell, Earl of).—A Defence of the Church of England against Disestablishment. Cr. 8vo. 2s. 6d.

—— Ancient Facts and Fictions concerning Churches and Tithes. Cr. 8vo. 7s. 6d.

—— The Book of Praise. From the Best English Hymn Writers. 18mo. 4s. 6d.

——A Hymnal. Chiefly from "The Book of Praise." In various sizes.—A. In Royal 32mo, cloth limp. 6d.—B. Small 18mo, larger type, cloth limp. 1s.—C. Same Edition, fine paper, cloth. 1s. 6d.—An Edition with Music, Selected, Harmonised, and Composed by John Hullah. Square 18mo. 3s. 6d.

SERVICE (Rev. John).—Sermons. With Portrait. Crown 8vo. 6s.

—— Prayers for Public Worship. Crown 8vo. 4s. 6d.

SHAIRP (John Campbell).—Glen Desseray, and other Poems, Lyrical and Elegiac. Ed. by F. T. Palgrave. Crown 8vo. 6s.

—— Burns. Crown 8vo. 1s. 6d. ; sewed, 1s.

SHAKESPEARE.—The Works of William Shakespeare. Cambridge Edition. Edit. by Wm. George Clark, M.A., and W. Aldis Wright, M.A. 9 vols. 8vo. 10s. 6d. each.

—— Shakespeare. By the same Editors. Globe 8vo. 3s. 6d.

—— The Works of William Shakespeare. Victoria Edition.—Vol. I. Comedies.—Vol. II. Histories.—Vol. III. Tragedies. In Three Vols. Crown 8vo. 6s. each.

—— Shakespeare's Songs and Sonnets. Edited, with Notes, by F. T. Palgrave. 18mo. 4s. 6d.

—— Charles Lamb's Tales from Shakspeare. Edited, with Preface, by the Rev. A. Ainger, M.A. 18mo. 4s. 6d.
Globe Readings Edition. For Schools. Globe 8vo. 2s.—*Library Edition.* Globe 8vo. 5s.

—— Shakspere. By Prof. Dowden. 18mo. 1s.

SHAKESPEARE.—Much Ado about Nothing. Edited by K. Deighton. Globe 8vo. 2s.

—— Richard III. Edited by Prof. C. H. Tawney, M.A. Globe 8vo. 2s. 6d.

—— The Winter's Tale. Edited by K. Deighton. Globe 8vo. 2s. 6d.

—— Henry V. By the same Editor. Globe 8vo. 2s.

—— Othello. By the same Editor. Globe 8vo. 2s. 6d.

—— Cymbeline. By the same Editor. Globe 8vo. 2s. 6d.

—— The Tempest. By the same Editor. Globe 8vo. 1s. 6d.

—— Twelfth Night ; or, What You Will. By the same Editor. Globe 8vo. 1s. 6d.

—— Macbeth. By same Editor. Gl. 8vo. 1s. 6d.

SHANN (G.).—An Elementary Treatise on Heat in Relation to Steam and the Steam-Engine. Illustr. Cr. 8vo. 4s. 6d.

SHARP (W.).—Dante Gabriel Rossetti. Crown 8vo. 10s. 6d.

SHELBURNE.—Life of William, Earl of Shelburne. By Lord Edmond Fitzmaurice. In 3 vols.—Vol. I. 8vo. 12s.—Vol. II. 8vo. 12s.—Vol. III. 8vo. 16s.

SHELLEY. Selections. Edited by Stopford A. Brooke. 18mo. 4s. 6d.
Large Paper Edition. Crown 8vo. 12s. 6d.

SHELLEY. By J. A. Symonds, M.A. Crown 8vo. 1s. 6d. ; sewed, 1s.

SHERIDAN. By Mrs. Oliphant. Crown 8vo. 1s. 6d. ; sewed, 1s.

SHIRLEY (W. N.).—Elijah : Four University Sermons. Fcp. 8vo. 2s. 6d.

SHORTHOUSE (J. H.).—John Inglesant : A Romance. Crown 8vo. 6s.

—— The Little Schoolmaster Mark : A Spiritual Romance. Two Parts. Crown 8vo. 2s. 6d. each : or complete, in one volume, 4s. 6d.

—— Sir Percival : A Story of the Past and of the Present. Crown 8vo. 6s.

—— A Teacher of the Violin, and other Tales. Crown 8vo. 6s.

—— The Countess Eve. Crown 8vo. 6s.

SHORTLAND (Admiral).—Nautical Surveying. 8vo.

SHUCKBURGH (E. S.).—Passages from Latin Authors for Translation into English. Crown 8vo. 2s.

SIBSON.—Dr. Francis Sibson's Collected Works. Edited by W. M. Ord, M.D. Illustrated. 4 vols. 8vo. 3l. 3s.

SIDGWICK (Prof. Henry).—The Methods of Ethics. 3rd Edit., revised. 8vo. 14s.

—— A Supplement to the Second Edition. Containing all the important Additions and Alterations in the 3rd Edit. 8vo. 6s.

—— The Principles of Political Economy. 2nd Edition. 8vo. 16s.

—— Outlines of the History of Ethics for English Readers. Cr. 8vo. 3s. 6d.

—— The Elements of Politics. 8vo.

SIDNEY, SIR PHILIP. By John Addington Symonds. Cr. 8vo. 1s.6d. ; sewed, 1s

SIME (James).—History of Germany. 2nd Edition. Maps. 18mo. 3s.

—— Geography of Europe. Globe 8vo.

SIMPSON (F. P.).—Latin Prose after the Best Authors.—Part I. Cæsarian Prose. Extra fcp. 8vo. 2s. 6d.

     Key (for Teachers only). Ex. fcp. 8vo. 5s.

SIMPSON (W.).—An Epitome of the History of the Christian Church. Fcp. 8vo. 3s. 6d.

SKRINE (J. H.).—Under two Queens. Crown 8vo. 3s.

—— A Memory of Edward Thring. Crown 8vo. 6s.

SLIP IN THE FENS (A). Globe 8vo. 2s.

SMITH (Barnard).—Arithmetic and Algebra. New Edition. Crown 8vo. 10s. 6d.

—— Arithmetic for the Use of Schools. New Edition. Crown 8vo. 4s. 6d.

—— Key to Arithmetic for Schools. New Edition. Crown 8vo. 8s. 6d.

—— Exercises in Arithmetic. Crown 8vo, 2 Parts, 1s. each, or complete, 2s.—With Answers, 2s. 6d.—Answers separately, 6d.

—— School Class-Book of Arithmetic. 18mo. 3s.—Or, sold separately, in Three Parts. 1s. each.

—— Key to School Class-Book of Arithmetic. In Parts I. II. and III. 2s. 6d. each.

—— Shilling Book of Arithmetic for National and Elementary Schools. 18mo, cloth.—Or separately, Part I. 2d. ; II. 3d. ; III. 7d.—With Answers, 1s. 6d.

—— Answers to the Shilling Book of Arithmetic. 18mo. 6d.

—— Key to the Shilling Book of Arithmetic. 18mo. 4s. 6d.

—— Examination Papers in Arithmetic. In Four Parts. 18mo. 1s. 6d.—With Answers, 2s.—Answers, 6d.

—— Key to Examination Papers in Arithmetic. 18mo. 4s. 6d.

—— The Metric System of Arithmetic. 3d.

—— A Chart of the Metric System of Arithmetic. On a Sheet size, 42 by 34 in., on Roller mounted and varnished. 3s. 6d.

—— Easy Lessons in Arithmetic. Combining Exercises in Reading, Writing, Spelling, and Dictation. Part I. for Standard I. in National Schools. Crown 8vo. 9d.

—— Examination Cards in Arithmetic. With Answers and Hints. Standards I. and II. In box. 1s.—Standards III. IV. and V. In boxes. 1s. each.—Standard VI. in Two Parts. In boxes. 1s. each.

SMITH (Catherine Barnard).—Poems. Fcp. 8vo. 5s.

SMITH (Charles).—An Elementary Treatise on Conic Sections. 7th Edition. Crown 8vo. 7s. 6d.

—— Solutions of the Examples in "An Elementary Treatise on Conic Sections." Crown 8vo. 10s. 6d.

SMITH (Charles).—An Elementary Treatise on Solid Geometry. 2nd Edition. Crown 8vo. 9s. 6d.

—— Elementary Algebra. Gl. 8vo. 4s. 6d.

—— A Treatise on Algebra. Cr. 8vo. 7s. 6d.

—— Solutions of the Examples in "A Treatise on Algebra." Cr. 8vo. 10s. 6d.

SMITH (Goldwin).—Three English Statesmen. New Edition. Crown 8vo. 5s.

—— Cowper. Crown 8vo. 1s. 6d. ; sewed, 1s.

—— Prohibitionism in Canada and the United States. 8vo, sewed. 6d.

SMITH (Horace).—Poems. Globe 8vo. 5s.

SMITH (J.).—Economic Plants, Dictionary of Popular Names of : Their History, Products, and Uses. 8vo. 14s.

SMITH (W. Saumarez).—The Blood of the New Covenant : A Theological Essay. Crown 8vo. 2s. 6d.

SMITH (Rev. Travers).—Man's Knowledge of Man and of God. Crown 8vo. 6s.

SMITH (W. G.).—Diseases of Field and Garden Crops, chiefly such as are caused by Fungi. With 143 new Illustrations. Fcp. 8vo. 4s. 6d.

SNOWBALL (J. C.).—The Elements of Plane and Spherical Trigonometry. 14th Edition. Crown 8vo. 7s. 6d.

SONNENSCHEIN (A.) and MEIKLEJOHN (J. M. D.).—The English Method of Teaching to Read. Fcp. 8vo. Comprising—

The Nursery Book, containing all the Two Letter Words in the Language. 1d.—Also in Large Type on Four Sheets, with Roller. 5s.

The First Course, consisting of Short Vowels with Single Consonants. 7d.

The Second Course, with Combinations and Bridges, consisting of Short Vowels with Double Consonants. 7d.

The Third and Fourth Courses, consisting of Long Vowels and all the Double Vowels in the Language. 7d.

SOPHOCLES.—Œdipus the King. Translated into Greek from the English Verse by E. D. A. Morshead, M.A. Fcp. 8vo. 3s. 6d.

—— Œdipus Tyrannus. A Record by L. Speed and F. R. Pryor of the performance at Cambridge. Illustr. Small folio. 12s. 6d.

—— By Prof. L. Campbell. Fcp. 8vo. 1s. 6d.

SOUTHEY. By Prof. Dowden. Crown 8vo. 1s. 6d. ; sewed, 1s.

SPENDER (J. Kent).—Therapeutic Means for the Relief of Pain. 8vo. 8s. 6d.

SPENSER.—Complete Works of Edmund Spenser. Ed. by R. Morris, with Memoir by J. W. Hales. Globe 8vo. 3s. 6d.

SPENSER. By the Very Rev. Dean Church. Cr. 8vo. 1s. 6d. ; swd., 1s.—Library Ed., 5s.

SPINOZA : A Study of. By James Martineau, LL.D. 2nd Ed. Cr. 8vo. 6s.

SPOTTISWOODE (W.).—Polarisation of Light. Illustrated. Crown 8vo. 3s. 6d.

STANLEY (Very Rev. A. P.).—THE ATHANASIAN CREED. Crown 8vo. 2s.

—— THE NATIONAL THANKSGIVING. Sermons preached in Westminster Abbey. 2nd Ed. Crown 8vo. 2s. 6d.

—— ADDRESSES AND SERMONS DELIVERED AT ST. ANDREWS IN 1872—75 and 1877. Crown 8vo. 5s.

—— ADDRESSES AND SERMONS DELIVERED DURING A VISIT TO THE UNITED STATES AND CANADA IN 1878. Crown 8vo. 6s.

STANLEY (Hon. Maude).—CLUBS FOR WORKING GIRLS. Crown 8vo. 6s.

STATESMAN'S YEAR-BOOK (THE). A Statistical and Historical Annual of the States of the Civilised World for the year 1890. Twenty-seventh Annual Publication. Revised after Official Returns. Edited by J. SCOTT KELTIE. Crown 8vo. 10s. 6d.

STATHAM (R.).—BLACKS, BOERS, AND BRITISH. Crown 8vo. 6s.

STEPHEN (Sir J. Fitzjames, Q.C., K.C.S.I.). —A DIGEST OF THE LAW OF EVIDENCE. 5th Edition. Crown 8vo. 6s.

—— A DIGEST OF THE CRIMINAL LAW: CRIMES AND PUNISHMENTS. 4th Edition. 8vo. 16s.

—— A DIGEST OF THE LAW OF CRIMINAL PROCEDURE IN INDICTABLE OFFENCES. By Sir JAMES F. STEPHEN, K.C.S.I., etc., and HERBERT STEPHEN, LL.M. 8vo. 12s. 6d.

—— A HISTORY OF THE CRIMINAL LAW OF ENGLAND. 3 vols. 8vo. 48s.

—— THE STORY OF NUNCOMAR AND THE IMPEACHMENT OF SIR ELIJAH IMPEY. 2 vols. Crown 8vo. 15s.

—— A GENERAL VIEW OF THE CRIMINAL LAW OF ENGLAND. 2nd Edition. 8vo.

STEPHEN (J. K.).—INTERNATIONAL LAW AND INTERNATIONAL RELATIONS. Crown 8vo. 6s.

STEPHEN (Leslie).—JOHNSON. Crown 8vo. 1s. 6d. ; sewed, 1s.

—— SWIFT. Crown 8vo. 1s. 6d. ; sewed, 1s.

—— POPE. Crown 8vo. 1s. 6d. ; sewed, 1s.

STEPHEN (Caroline E.).—THE SERVICE OF THE POOR. Crown 8vo. 6s. 6d.

STEPHENS (J. B.).—CONVICT ONCE, AND OTHER POEMS. Crown 8vo. 7s. 6d.

STERNE. By H. D. TRAILL. Crown 8vo. 1s. 6d. ; sewed, 1s.

STEVENS (F. H.).—ELEMENTARY MENSURATION. With Exercises in the Mensuration of Plane and Solid Figures. Globe 8vo.

STEVENSON (J. J.).—HOUSE ARCHITECTURE. With Illustrations. 2 vols. Royal 8vo. 18s. each. Vol. I. ARCHITECTURE. Vol. II. HOUSE PLANNING.

STEWART (Aubrey).—THE TALE OF TROY. Done into English. Globe 8vo. 3s. 6d.

STEWART (Prof. Balfour).—LESSONS IN ELEMENTARY PHYSICS. With Illustrations and Coloured Diagram. New Edition. Fcp. 8vo. 4s. 6d.

—— PRIMER OF PHYSICS. Illustrated. New Edition, with Questions. 18mo. 1s.

STEWART (Prof. Balfour).—QUESTIONS ON STEWART'S LESSONS ON ELEMENTARY PHYSICS. By T. H. CORE. 12mo. 2s.

STEWART (Prof. Balfour) and GEE (W. W. Haldane).—LESSONS IN ELEMENTARY PRACTICAL PHYSICS. Crown 8vo. Illustrated. Vol. I. GENERAL PHYSICAL PROCESSES. 6s. —Vol. II. ELECTRICITY AND MAGNETISM. Cr. 8vo. 7s. 6d.—Vol. III. OPTICS, HEAT, AND SOUND.

—— PRACTICAL PHYSICS FOR SCHOOLS AND THE JUNIOR STUDENTS OF COLLEGES. Globe 8vo. Vol. I. ELECTRICITY AND MAGNETISM. 2s. 6d.—Vol. II. HEAT, LIGHT, AND SOUND.

STEWART (Prof. Balfour) and TAIT (P. G.). —THE UNSEEN UNIVERSE ; OR, PHYSICAL SPECULATIONS ON A FUTURE STATE. 15th Edition. Crown 8vo. 6s.

STEWART (S. A.) and CORRY (T. H.).— A FLORA OF THE NORTH-EAST OF IRELAND. Crown 8vo. 5s. 6d.

STOKES (Sir George G.).—ON LIGHT. The Burnett Lectures. Crown 8vo. 7s. 6d.

STONE (W. H.).—ELEMENTARY LESSONS ON SOUND. Illustrated. Fcap. 8vo. 3s. 6d.

STRACHAN (J. S.) and WILKINS (A. S.).— ANALECTA. Passages for Translation. Cr. 8vo. 5s.

STRACHEY (Lieut.-Gen. R.).—LECTURES ON GEOGRAPHY. Crown 8vo. 4s. 6d.

STRAFFORD. By H. D. TRAILL. With Portrait. Crown 8vo. 2s. 6d.

STRANGFORD (Viscountess).—EGYPTIAN SEPULCHRES AND SYRIAN SHRINES. New Edition. Crown 8vo. 7s. 6d.

STRETTELL (Alma).—SPANISH AND ITALIAN FOLK SONGS. Illust. Roy. 16mo. 12s. 6d.

STUBBS (Rev. C. W.).—FOR CHRIST AND CITY. Sermons and Addresses. Cr. 8vo.

SURGERY, THE INTERNATIONAL ENCYCLOPAEDIA OF. A Systematic Treatise on the Theory and Practice of Surgery by Authors of Various Nations. Edited by JOHN ASHHURST, Jun., M.D., Professor of Clinical Surgery in the University of Pennsylvania. 6 vols. Royal 8vo. 31s. 6d. each.

SWIFT. By LESLIE STEPHEN. Crown 8vo. 1s. 6d. ; sewed, 1s.

SYLLABUS OF PLANE GEOMETRY, A. Corresponding to Euclid, Books I. to VI. Prepared by the Association for the Improvement of Geometrical Teaching. 9th Edition, revised. 12mo. 1s.

SYLLABUS OF MODERN PLANE GEOMETRY. Association for the Improvement of Geometrical Teaching. Crown 8vo. 1s.

SYLLABUS OF ELEMENTARY DYNAMICS. With an Appendix on the Alternative Mode of regarding symbols in Physical Equations. 4to. 1s.

SYMONS (Arthur).—DAYS AND NIGHTS: POEMS. Globe 8vo. 6s.

SYMONDS (J. A.).—SHELLEY. Crown 8vo. 1s. 6d. ; sewed, 1s.

—— SIR PHILIP SIDNEY. 1s. 6d. ; sewed, 1s.

TACITUS, THE WORKS OF. Transl. by A. J. CHURCH, M.A., and W. J. BRODRIBB, M.A.

THE HISTORY OF TACITUS. 4th Edition. Crown 8vo. 6s.

THE AGRICOLA AND GERMANIA. A Revised Text. With Notes. Fcp. 8vo. 3s. 6d. The AGRICOLA and GERMANIA may be had separately. 2s. each.

THE ANNALS. Book VI. With Introduction and Notes. Fcp. 8vo. 2s. 6d.

THE AGRICOLA AND GERMANIA. With the Dialogue on Oratory. Translated. Crown 8vo. 4s. 6d.

ANNALS OF TACITUS. Translated. 5th Ed. Crown 8vo. 7s. 6d.

—— THE ANNALS. Edited by Prof. G. O. HOLBROOKE, M.A. 8vo. 16s.

—— THE HISTORIES. Books I. and II. Ed. by A. D. GODLEY, M.A. Fcp. 8vo. 5s.

—— THE HISTORIES. Books III.—V. Edited by A. D. GODLEY, M.A. Fcp. 8vo. 5s.

TACITUS. By A. J. CHURCH, M.A., and W. J. BRODRIBB, M.A. Fcp. 8vo. 1s. 6d.

TAIT (Archbishop).—THE PRESENT POSITION OF THE CHURCH OF ENGLAND. Being the Charge delivered at his Primary Visitation. 3rd Edition. 8vo. 3s. 6d.

—— DUTIES OF THE CHURCH OF ENGLAND. Being Seven Addresses delivered at his Second Visitation. 8vo. 4s. 6d.

—— THE CHURCH OF THE FUTURE. Charges delivered at his Third Quadrennial Visitation. 2nd Edition. Crown 8vo. 3s. 6d.

TAIT.—THE LIFE OF ARCHIBALD CAMPBELL TAIT, ARCHBISHOP OF CANTERBURY. By the Very Rev. the DEAN OF WINDSOR and Rev. W. BENHAM, B.D. 2 vols. 8vo.

TAIT.—CATHARINE AND CRAWFURD TAIT, WIFE AND SON OF ARCHIBALD CAMPBELL, ARCHBISHOP OF CANTERBURY: A MEMOIR. Edited by the Rev. W. BENHAM, B.D. Crown 8vo. 6s.
Popular Edition, abridged. Cr. 8vo. 2s. 6d.

TAIT (C. W. A.).—ANALYSIS OF ENGLISH HISTORY, BASED ON GREEN'S "SHORT HISTORY OF THE ENGLISH PEOPLE." Crown 8vo. 3s. 6d.

TAIT (Prof. P. G.).—LECTURES ON SOME RECENT ADVANCES IN PHYSICAL SCIENCE. 3rd Edition. Crown 8vo. 9s.

—— HEAT. With Illustrations. Cr. 8vo. 6s.

TAIT (P. G.) and STEELE (W. J.).—A TREATISE ON DYNAMICS OF A PARTICLE. 6th Edition. Crown 8vo. 12s.

TANNER (Prof. Henry).—FIRST PRINCIPLES OF AGRICULTURE. 18mo. 1s.

—— THE ABBOTT'S FARM; OR, PRACTICE WITH SCIENCE. Crown 8vo. 3s. 6d.

—— THE ALPHABET OF THE PRINCIPLES OF AGRICULTURE. Extra fcp. 8vo. 6d.

—— FURTHER STEPS IN THE PRINCIPLES OF AGRICULTURE. Extra fcp. 8vo. 1s.

—— ELEMENTARY SCHOOL READINGS IN THE PRINCIPLES OF AGRICULTURE FOR THE THIRD STAGE. Extra fcp. 8vo. 1s.

—— ELEMENTARY LESSONS IN THE SCIENCE OF AGRICULTURAL PRACTICE. Fcp. 8vo. 3s. 6d.

TAYLOR (Franklin).—PRIMER OF PIANOFORTE PLAYING. 18mo. 1s.

TAYLOR (Isaac).—THE RESTORATION OF BELIEF. Crown 8vo. 8s. 6d.

TAYLOR (Isaac).—WORDS AND PLACES. 9th Edition. Maps. Globe 8vo. 6s.

—— ETRUSCAN RESEARCHES. With Woodcuts. 8vo. 14s.

—— GREEKS AND GOTHS: A STUDY OF THE RUNES. 8vo. 9s.

TAYLOR (Sedley).—SOUND AND MUSIC. 2nd Edition. Extra Crown 8vo. 8s. 6d.

—— A SYSTEM OF SIGHT-SINGING FROM THE ESTABLISHED MUSICAL NOTATION. 8vo.

TEBAY (S.).—ELEMENTARY MENSURATION FOR SCHOOLS. Extra fcp. 8vo. 3s. 6d.

TEGETMEIER (W. B.).—HOUSEHOLD MANAGEMENT AND COOKERY. 18mo. 1s.

TEMPLE (Right Rev. Frederick, D.D., Bishop of London).—SERMONS PREACHED IN THE CHAPEL OF RUGBY SCHOOL. 3rd and Cheaper Edition. Extra fcp. 8vo. 4s. 6d.

—— SECOND SERIES. 3rd Ed. Ex. fcp. 8vo. 6s.

—— THIRD SERIES. 4th Ed. Ex. fcp. 8vo. 6s.

—— THE RELATIONS BETWEEN RELIGION AND SCIENCE. Bampton Lectures, 1884. 7th and Cheaper Edition. Crown 8vo. 6s.

TENNYSON (Lord).—COMPLETE WORKS. New and enlarged Edition, with Portrait. Crown 8vo. 7s. 6d.
School Edition. In Four Parts. Crown 8vo. 2s. 6d. each.

—— WORKS. *Library Edition.* In 8 vols. Globe 8vo. 5s. each. Each volume may be had separately.—POEMS. 2 vols.—IDYLLS OF THE KING.—THE PRINCESS, AND MAUD. —ENOCH ARDEN, AND IN MEMORIAM.— BALLADS, AND OTHER POEMS. — QUEEN MARY, AND HAROLD.—BECKET, AND OTHER PLAYS.

—— WORKS. *Extra Fcp. 8vo. Edition*, on Hand-made Paper. In 7 volumes (supplied in sets only). 3l. 13s. 6d. — Vol. I. EARLY POEMS; II. LUCRETIUS, AND OTHER POEMS; III. IDYLLS OF THE KING; IV. THE PRINCESS, AND MAUD; V. ENOCH ARDEN, AND IN MEMORIAM; VI. QUEEN MARY, AND HAROLD; VII. BALLADS, AND OTHER POEMS.

—— THE COLLECTED WORKS. Miniature Edition, in 14 volumes, namely, "THE POETICAL WORKS," 10 vols. in a box. 21s. —"THE DRAMATIC WORKS," 4 vols. in a box. 10s. 6d.

—— LYRICAL POEMS. Selected and Annotated by Prof. F. T. PALGRAVE. 18mo. 4s. 6d.
Large Paper Edition. 8vo. 9s.

—— IN MEMORIAM. 18mo. 4s. 6d.
Large Paper Edition. 8vo. 9s.

—— THE TENNYSON BIRTHDAY BOOK. Edit. by EMILY SHAKESPEAR. 18mo. 2s. 6d.

—— THE BROOK. With 20 Illustrations by A. WOODRUFF. 32mo. 2s. 6d.

—— SELECTIONS FROM TENNYSON. With Introduction and Notes, by F. J. ROWE, M.A., and W. T. WEBB, M.A. Globe 8vo. 3s. 6d.

TENNYSON.—A Companion to "In Memoriam." By Elizabeth R. Chapman. Globe 8vo. 2s.

—— *The Original Editions.* Fcp. 8vo.
Poems. 6s.
Maud, and other Poems. 3s. 6d.
The Princess. 3s. 6d.
Idylls of the King. (Collected.) 6s.
Enoch Arden, etc. 3s. 6d.
The Holy Grail, and other Poems. 4s. 6d.
In Memoriam. 4s.
Ballads, and other Poems. 5s.
Harold: A Drama. 6s.
Queen Mary: A Drama. 6s.
The Cup, and the Falcon. 6s.
Becket. 6s.
Tiresias, and other Poems. 6s.
Locksley Hall, Sixty Years After, etc. 6s.
Demeter, and other Poems. 6s.

—— The Royal Edition. 1 vol. 8vo. 16s.
—— Selections from Tennyson's Works. Square 8vo. 3s. 6d.; gilt, square 8vo, 4s.
—— Songs from Tennyson's Writings. Square 8vo. 2s. 6d.

TENNYSON (Hallam). — Jack and the Bean-stalk. With 40 Illustrations by Randolph Caldecott. Fcp. 4to. 3s. 6d.

TERENCE.—Hauton Timorumenos. Edit. by E. S. Shuckburgh, M.A. Fcp. 8vo. 3s.—With Translation, 4s. 6d.

—— Phormio. Edited by Rev. John Bond, and A. S. Walpole. Fcp. 8vo. 4s. 6d.

—— Scenes from the Andria. Edited by F. W. Cornish, M.A. 18mo. 1s. 6d.

TERESA (ST.), LIFE OF. By the Author of "Devotions before and after Holy Communion." Crown 8vo. 8s. 6d.

THACKERAY. By Anthony Trollope. Crown 8vo. 1s. 6d.; sewed, 1s.

THEOCRITUS, BION, and MOSCHUS. Rendered into English Prose, with Introductory Essay, by A. Lang, M.A. 18mo. 4s. 6d.
Large Paper Edition. 8vo. 9s.

THOMPSON (Edith).—History of England. New Edit., with Maps. 18mo. 2s. 6d.

THOMPSON (Prof. Silvanus P.).—Electricity and Magnetism, Elementary. Illustrated. New Edition. Fcp. 8vo. 4s. 6d.

THOMPSON (G. Carslake).—Public Opinion and Lord Beaconsfield, 1875—80. 2 vols. 8vo. 36s.

THOMSON (J. J.).—A Treatise on the Motion of Vortex Rings. 8vo. 6s.

—— Applications of Dynamics to Physics and Chemistry. Crown 8vo. 7s. 6d.

THOMSON (Sir Wm.).—Reprint of Papers on Electrostatics and Magnetism. 2nd Edition. 8vo. 18s.

—— Popular Lectures and Addresses. In 3 vols.—Vol. I. Constitution of Matter. Illustrated. Crown 8vo. 6s.

THOMSON (Sir C. Wyville).—The Depths of the Sea. An Account of the General Results of the Dredging Cruises of H.M.SS. "Lightning" and "Porcupine" during the Summers of 1868-69-70. With Illustrations, Maps, and Plans. 2nd Edit. 8vo. 31s. 6d.

—— The Voyage of the "Challenger": The Atlantic. With Illustrations, Coloured Maps, Charts, etc. 2 vols. 8vo. 45s.

THORNTON (W. T.).--A Plea for Peasant Proprietors. New Edit. Cr. 8vo. 7s. 6d.

—— Old-Fashioned Ethics and Common-Sense Metaphysics. 8vo. 10s. 6d.

—— Indian Public Works, and Cognate Indian Topics. Crown 8vo. 8s. 6d.

—— Word for Word from Horace: The Odes Literally Versified. Cr. 8vo. 7s. 6d.

THORNTON (J.).—First Lessons in Book-keeping. New Edition. Crown 8vo. 2s. 6d.

—— Key to "First Lessons in Book-keeping." Containing all the Exercises fully worked out, with brief Notes. Oblong 4to. 10s. 6d.

THORPE (Prof. T. E.).—A Series of Problems, for Use in Colleges and Schools. New Edition, with Key. 18mo. 2s.

THRING (Rev. Edward).—A Construing Book. Fcp. 8vo. 2s. 6d.

—— A Latin Gradual. 2nd Ed. 18mo. 2s. 6d.

—— The Elements of Grammar taught in English. 5th Edition. 18mo. 2s.

—— Education and School. 2nd Edition. Crown 8vo. 6s.

—— A Manual of Mood Constructions. Extra fcp. 8vo. 1s. 6d.

—— Thoughts on Life Science. 2nd Edit. Crown 8vo. 7s. 6d.

—— A Memory of Edward Thring. By J. H. Skrine. Portrait. Crown 8vo. 6s.

THROUGH THE RANKS TO A COMMISSION. New Edit. Cr. 8vo. 2s. 6d.

THRUPP (Rev. J. F.).—Introduction to the Study and Use of the Psalms. 2nd Edition. 2 vols. 8vo. 25s.

THUCYDIDES.--The Sicilian Expedition. Books VI. and VII. Edited by the Rev. Percival Frost, M.A. Fcp. 8vo. 5s.

—— The Capture of Sphacteria. Book IV. Chaps. 1—41. Edit. by C. E. Graves, M.A. 18mo. 1s. 6d.

—— Book IV. By the same. Fcp. 8vo. 5s.

—— The Rise of the Athenian Empire. Being Selections from Book I. Edited by F. H. Colson, M.A. 18mo. 1s. 6d.

—— Book IV. A Revision of the Text, illustrating the Principal Causes of Corruption in the Manuscripts of this Author. By William G. Rutherford, M.A., LL.D. 8vo. 7s. 6d.

THUDICHUM (J. L. W.) and DUPRÉ (A.). —Treatise on the Origin, Nature, and Varieties of Wine. Medium 8vo. 25s.

TODHUNTER (Isaac).—Euclid for Colleges and Schools. 18mo. 3s. 6d.

—— Key to Exercises in Euclid. Crown 8vo. 6s. 6d.

TODHUNTER (I.).—MENSURATION FOR BEGINNERS. With Examples. 18mo. 2s. 6d.

—— KEY TO MENSURATION FOR BEGINNERS. By Rev. FR. L. McCARTHY. Cr. 8vo. 7s. 6d.

—— ALGEBRA FOR BEGINNERS. With numerous Examples. 18mo. 2s. 6d.

—— KEY TO ALGEBRA FOR BEGINNERS. Cr. 8vo. 6s. 6d.

—— TRIGONOMETRY FOR BEGINNERS. With numerous Examples. 18mo. 2s. 6d.

—— KEY TO TRIGONOMETRY FOR BEGINNERS. Crown 8vo. 8s. 6d.

—— MECHANICS FOR BEGINNERS. With numerous Examples. 18mo. 4s.

—— KEY TO MECHANICS FOR BEGINNERS. 6s. 6d.

—— ALGEBRA FOR THE USE OF COLLEGES AND SCHOOLS. Crown 8vo. 7s. 6d.

—— KEY TO ALGEBRA FOR COLLEGES AND SCHOOLS. Crown 8vo. 10s. 6d.

—— A TREATISE ON THE THEORY OF EQUATIONS. Crown 8vo. 7s. 6d.

—— PLANE TRIGONOMETRY FOR COLLEGES AND SCHOOLS. Crown 8vo. 5s.

—— KEY TO PLANE TRIGONOMETRY. Crown 8vo. 10s. 6d.

—— A TREATISE ON SPHERICAL TRIGONOMETRY FOR THE USE OF COLLEGES AND SCHOOLS. Crown 8vo. 4s. 6d.

—— A TREATISE ON PLANE CO-ORDINATE GEOMETRY. Crown 8vo. 7s. 6d.

—— SOLUTIONS AND PROBLEMS CONTAINED IN A TREATISE ON PLANE CO-ORDINATE GEOMETRY. By C. W. BOURNE, M.A. Crown 8vo. 10s. 6d.

—— A TREATISE ON THE DIFFERENTIAL CALCULUS. Crown 8vo. 10s. 6d.

—— KEY TO TREATISE ON THE DIFFERENTIAL CALCULUS. By H. ST. J. HUNTER, M.A. Crown 8vo. 10s. 6d.

—— A TREATISE ON THE INTEGRAL CALCULUS. Crown 8vo. 10s. 6d.

—— KEY TO TREATISE ON THE INTEGRAL CALCULUS AND ITS APPLICATIONS. By H. ST. J. HUNTER, M.A. Cr. 8vo. 10s. 6d.

—— EXAMPLES OF ANALYTICAL GEOMETRY OF THREE DIMENSIONS. Crown 8vo. 4s.

—— THE CONFLICT OF STUDIES. 8vo. 10s. 6d.

—— AN ELEMENTARY TREATISE ON LAPLACE'S, LAMÉ'S, AND BESSEL'S FUNCTIONS. Crown 8vo. 10s. 6d.

—— A TREATISE ON ANALYTICAL STATICS. Edited by J. D. EVERETT, M.A., F.R.S. 5th Edition. Crown 8vo. 10s. 6d.

TOM BROWN'S SCHOOL-DAYS. By AN OLD BOY.

Golden Treasury Edition. 18mo. 4s. 6d.
Illustrated Edition. Crown 8vo. 6s.
Uniform Edition. Crown 8vo. 3s. 6d.
People's Edition. 18mo. 2s.
People's Sixpenny Edition. With Illustrations. Medium 4to. 6d.—Also uniform with the Sixpenny Edition of Charles Kingsley's Novels. Medium 8vo. 6d.

TOM BROWN AT OXFORD. By the Author of "Tom Brown's School-days." Illustrated. Crown 8vo. 6s.
Uniform Edition. Crown 8vo. 3s. 6d.

TOURGÉNIEF.—VIRGIN SOIL. Translated by ASHTON W. DILKE. Crown 8vo. 6s.

TOZER (H. F.).—CLASSICAL GEOGRAPHY. 18mo. 1s.

TRAIL (H. D.).—STERNE. Crown 8vo. 1s. 6d.; sewed, 1s.

—— CENTRAL GOVERNMENT. Cr. 8vo. 3s. 6d.

—— WILLIAM III. Crown 8vo. 2s. 6d.

—— STRAFFORD. Portrait. Cr. 8vo. 2s. 6d.

—— COLERIDGE. Cr. 8vo. 1s. 6d.; sewed, 1s.

TRENCH (R. Chenevix).—HULSEAN LECTURES. 8vo. 7s. 6d.

TRENCH (Capt. F.).—THE RUSSO-INDIAN QUESTION. Crown 8vo. 7s. 6d.

TREVELYAN (Sir Geo. Otto).—CAWNPORE. Crown 8vo. 6s.

TRISTRAM (W. Outram).—COACHING DAYS AND COACHING WAYS. Illustrated by HERBERT RAILTON and HUGH THOMSON. Extra Crown 4to. 21s.

TROLLOPE (Anthony).—THACKERAY. Cr. 8vo. 1s. 6d.; sewed, 1s.

TRUMAN (Jos.).—AFTER-THOUGHTS: POEMS. Crown 8vo. 3s. 6d.

TULLOCH (Principal).—THE CHRIST OF THE GOSPELS AND THE CHRIST OF MODERN CRITICISM. Extra fcp. 8vo. 4s. 6d.

TURNER'S LIBER STUDIORUM. A Description and a Catalogue. By W. G. RAWLINSON. Medium 8vo. 12s. 6d.

TURNER (Charles Tennyson).—COLLECTED SONNETS, OLD AND NEW. Ex. fcp. 8vo. 7s. 6d.

TURNER (Rev. Geo.).—SAMOA, A HUNDRED YEARS AGO AND LONG BEFORE. Preface by E. B. TYLOR, F.R.S. Crown 8vo. 9s.

TURNER (H. H.).—A COLLECTION OF EXAMPLES ON HEAT AND ELECTRICITY. Cr. 8vo. 2s. 6d.

TYLOR (E. B.).—ANTHROPOLOGY. With Illustrations. Crown 8vo. 2s. 6d.

TYRWHITT (Rev. R. St. John).—OUR SKETCHING CLUB. 4th Ed. Cr. 8vo. 7s. 6d.

—— FREE FIELD. Lyrics, chiefly Descriptive. Globe 8vo. 3s. 6d.

—— BATTLE AND AFTER: Concerning Sergt. Thomas Atkins, Grenadier Guards; and other Verses. Globe 8vo. 3s. 6d.

UHLAND.—SELECT BALLADS. Edited by G. E. FASNACHT. 18mo. 1s.

UNDERHILL (H. G.).—EASY EXERCISES IN GREEK ACCIDENCE. Globe 8vo. 2s.

UPPINGHAM BY THE SEA. By J. H. S. Crown 8vo. 3s. 6d.

VAUGHAN (Very Rev. Charles J.).—NOTES FOR LECTURES ON CONFIRMATION. 14th Edition. Fcp. 8vo. 1s. 6d.

—— MEMORIALS OF HARROW SUNDAYS. 5th Edition. Crown 8vo. 10s. 6d.

—— LECTURES ON THE EPISTLE TO THE PHILIPPIANS. 4th Edition. Cr. 8vo. 7s. 6d.

VAUGHAN (Very Rev. C. J.).—LECTURES ON THE REVELATION OF ST. JOHN. 5th Edition. Crown 8vo. 10s. 6d.

—— EPIPHANY, LENT, AND EASTER. 3rd Edition. Crown 8vo. 10s. 6d.

—— HEROES OF FAITH. 2nd Ed. Cr. 8vo. 6s.

—— THE BOOK AND THE LIFE, AND OTHER SERMONS. 3rd Edition. Fcp. 8vo. 4s. 6d.

—— ST. PAUL'S EPISTLE TO THE ROMANS. The Greek Text with English Notes. 6th Edition. Crown 8vo. 7s. 6d.

—— TWELVE DISCOURSES ON SUBJECTS CONNECTED WITH THE LITURGY AND WORSHIP OF THE CHURCH OF ENGLAND. 4th Edition. Fcp. 8vo. 6s.

—— WORDS FROM THE GOSPELS. 3rd Edition. Fcp. 8vo. 4s. 6d.

—— THE EPISTLES OF ST. PAUL. For English Readers. Part I. containing the First Epistle to the Thessalonians. 2nd Ed. 8vo. 1s. 6d.

—— THE CHURCH OF THE FIRST DAYS. Series I. THE CHURCH OF JERUSALEM. 3rd Edition. 4s. 6d.—II. THE CHURCH OF THE GENTILES. 4s. 6d.—III. THE CHURCH OF THE WORLD. Fcp. 8vo. 4s. 6d.

—— LIFE'S WORK AND GOD'S DISCIPLINE. 3rd Edition. Extra fcp. 8vo. 2s. 6d.

—— THE WHOLESOME WORDS OF JESUS CHRIST. 2nd Edition. Fcp. 8vo. 3s. 6d.

—— FOES OF FAITH. 2nd Ed. Fcp. 8vo. 3s. 6d.

—— CHRIST SATISFYING THE INSTINCTS OF HUMANITY. 2nd Ed. Extra fcp. 8vo. 3s. 6d.

—— COUNSELS FOR YOUNG STUDENTS. Fcp. 8vo. 2s. 6d.

—— THE TWO GREAT TEMPTATIONS. 2nd Edition. Fcp. 8vo. 3s. 6d.

—— ADDRESSES FOR YOUNG CLERGYMEN. Extra fcp. 8vo. 4s. 6d.

—— "MY SON, GIVE ME THINE HEART." Extra fcp. 8vo. 5s.

—— REST AWHILE. Addresses to Toilers in the Ministry. Extra fcp. 8vo. 5s.

—— TEMPLE SERMONS. Crown 8vo. 10s. 6d.

—— AUTHORISED OR REVISED? Sermons on some of the Texts in which the Revised Version differs from the Authorised. Crown 8vo. 7s. 6d.

—— ST. PAUL'S EPISTLE TO THE PHILIPPIANS. With Translation, Paraphrase, and Notes for English Readers. Crown 8vo. 5s.

—— LESSONS OF THE CROSS AND PASSION. WORDS FROM THE CROSS. THE REIGN OF SIN. THE LORD'S PRAYER. Four Courses of Lent Lectures. Crown 8vo. 10s. 6d.

—— UNIVERSITY SERMONS, NEW AND OLD. Crown 8vo. 10s. 6d.

—— THE EPISTLE TO THE HEBREWS. With Notes. Crown 8vo.

VAUGHAN (D. J.).—THE PRESENT TRIAL OF FAITH. Crown 8vo. 9s.

VAUGHAN (E. T.).—SOME REASONS OF OUR CHRISTIAN HOPE. Hulsean Lectures for 1875. Crown 8vo. 6s. 6d.

VELEY (Marg.).—A GARDEN OF MEMORIES; MRS. AUSTIN; LIZZIE'S BARGAIN. Three Stories. 2 vols. Globe 8vo. 12s.

VENN (Rev. John).—ON SOME CHARACTERISTICS OF BELIEF, SCIENTIFIC AND RELIGIOUS. Hulsean Lectures, 1869. 8vo. 7s. 6d.

—— THE LOGIC OF CHANCE. 2nd Edition. Crown 8vo. 10s. 6d.

—— SYMBOLIC LOGIC. Crown 8vo. 10s. 6d.

—— THE PRINCIPLES OF EMPIRICAL OR INDUCTIVE LOGIC. 8vo. 18s.

VERNEY (Lady).—HOW THE PEASANT OWNER LIVES IN PARTS OF FRANCE, GERMANY, ITALY, AND RUSSIA. Cr. 8vo. 3s. 6d.

VERRALL (A. W.).—STUDIES, LITERARY AND HISTORICAL, IN THE ODES OF HORACE. 8vo. 8s. 6d.

VICTORIA UNIVERSITY CALENDAR, 1890. Crown 8vo. 1s.

VICTOR EMMANUEL II., FIRST KING OF ITALY. By G. S. GODKIN. 2nd Edition. Crown 8vo. 6s.

VIDA: STUDY OF A GIRL. By AMY DUNSMUIR. 3rd Edition. Crown 8vo. 6s.

VINCENT (Sir E.) and **DICKSON** (T. G.).—HANDBOOK TO MODERN GREEK. 3rd Ed. Crown 8vo. 6s.

VIRGIL.—THE WORKS OF VIRGIL RENDERED INTO ENGLISH PROSE. By JAS. LONSDALE, M.A., and S. LEE, M.A. Globe 8vo. 3s. 6d.

—— THE ÆNEID. Translated into English Prose by J. W. MACKAIL, M.A. Crown 8vo. 7s. 6d.

—— GEORGICS, I. Edited by T. E. PAGE, M.A. 18mo. 1s. 6d.

—— GEORGICS II. Edited by Rev. J. H. SKRINE, M.A. 18mo. 1s. 6d.

—— ÆNEID, I. Edited by A. S. WALPOLE, M.A. 18mo. 1s. 6d.

—— ÆNEID, II. Edit. by T. E. PAGE, M.A. 18mo. 1s. 6d.

—— ÆNEID, II. and III.: THE NARRATIVE OF ÆNEAS. Edit. by E. W. HOWSON, M.A. Fcp. 8vo. 3s.

—— ÆNEID, III. Edited by T. E. PAGE, M.A. 18mo. 1s. 6d.

—— ÆNEID, IV. Edited by Rev. H. M. STEPHENSON, M.A. 18mo. 1s. 6d.

—— ÆNEID, V.: THE FUNERAL GAMES. Ed. by Rev. A. CALVERT, M.A. 18mo. 1s. 6d.

—— ÆNEID, VI. Edit. by T. E. PAGE, M.A. 18mo. 1s. 6d.

—— ÆNEID, VII.: THE WRATH OF TURNUS. Ed. by Rev. A. CALVERT, M.A. 18mo. 1s. 6d.

—— ÆNEID, IX. Edited by Rev. H. M. STEPHENSON, M.A. 18mo. 1s. 6d.

—— SELECTIONS. Edited by E. S. SHUCKBURGH, M.A. 18mo. 1s. 6d.

VIRGIL. By Prof. NETTLESHIP, M.A. Fcp. 8vo. 1s. 6d.

VITA.—LINKS AND CLUES. By VITA (the Hon. Lady WELBY-GREGORY). 2nd Edition. Crown 8vo. 6s.

VOICES CRYING IN THE WILDERNESS. A New Novel. Cr. 8vo. 7s. 6d.

VOLTAIRE.—HISTOIRE DE CHARLES XII., ROI DE SUÈDE. Edited by G. EUGÈNE FASNACHT. 18mo. 3s. 6d.

VOLTAIRE. By John Morley. Gl. 8vo. 5s.

WALDSTEIN (C.).—Catalogue of Casts in the Museum of Classical Archæology, Cambridge. Crown 8vo. 1s. 6d.
Large Paper Edition. Small 4to. 5s.

WALKER (Prof. Francis A.).—The Wages Question. 8vo. 14s.

—— Money. 8vo. 16s.

—— Money in its Relation to Trade and Industry. Crown 8vo. 7s. 6d.

—— Political Economy. 2nd Ed. 8vo. 12s. 6d.

—— A Brief Text-Book of Political Economy. Crown 8vo. 6s. 6d.

—— Land and its Rent. Fcp. 8vo. 3s. 6d.

WALLACE (Alfred Russel).—The Malay Archipelago: The Land of the Orang Utang and the Bird of Paradise. Maps and Illustrations. 9th Ed. Cr. 8vo. 7s. 6d.

—— The Geographical Distribution of Animals. With Illustrations and Maps. 2 vols. Medium 8vo. 42s.

—— Island Life. With Illustrations and Maps. Demy 8vo. 18s.

—— Bad Times. An Essay on the present Depression of Trade. Crown 8vo. 2s. 6d.

—— Darwinism. An Exposition of the Theory of Natural Selection, with some of its Applications. Illustrated. 3rd Ed. Cr. 8vo. 9s.

WALLACE (Sir D. Mackenzie).—Egypt and the Egyptian Question. 8vo. 14s.

WALPOLE (Spencer).—Foreign Relations. Crown 8vo. 3s. 6d.

—— The Electorate and Legislature. Crown 8vo. 3s. 6d.

WALPOLE. By John Morley. Cr. 8vo. 2s. 6d.

WALTON and COTTON—LOWELL.—The Complete Angler; or, the Contemplative Man's Recreation of Izaak Walton and Thomas Cotton. With an Introduction by Jas. Russell Lowell. Illustrated. Extra crown 8vo. 2l. 12s. 6d. net.
Also an Edition on large paper, Proofs on Japanese paper. 3l. 13s. 6d. net.

WANDERING WILLIE. By the Author of "Conrad the Squirrel." Globe 8vo. 2s. 6d.

WARD (Prof. A. W.).—A History of English Dramatic Literature, to the Death of Queen Anne. 2 vols. 8vo. 32s.

—— Chaucer. Cr. 8vo. 1s. 6d.; sewed, 1s.

—— Dickens. Cr. 8vo. 1s. 6d.; sewed, 1s.

WARD (Prof. H. M.).—Timber and some of its Diseases. Illustrated. Cr. 8vo. 6s.

WARD (John).—Experiences of a Diplomatist. 8vo. 10s. 6d.

WARD (T. H.).—English Poets. Selections, with Critical Introductions by various Writers, and a General Introduction by Matthew Arnold. Edited by T. H. Ward, M.A. 4 vols. 2nd Ed. Crown 8vo. 7s. 6d. each.— Vol. I. Chaucer to Donne. — II. Ben Jonson to Dryden. — III. Addison to Blake.—IV. Wordsworth to Rossetti.

WARD (Mrs. T. Humphry).—Milly and Olly. With Illustrations by Mrs. Alma Tadema. Globe 8vo. 2s. 6d.

WARD (Mrs. T. H.).—Miss Bretherton. Crown 8vo. 3s. 6d.

—— The Journal Intime of Henri-Frédéric Amiel. Translated, with an Introduction and Notes. 2nd Ed. Cr. 8vo. 6s.

WARD (Samuel).—Lyrical Recreations. Fcp. 8vo. 6s.

WARD (Wilfrid).—William George Ward and the Oxford Movement. With Portrait. 8vo. 14s.

WARINGTON (G.). — The Week of Creation. Crown 8vo. 4s. 6d.

WARWICK, THE KING-MAKER. By C. W. Oman. Crown 8vo. 2s. 6d.

WATERTON (Charles).—Wanderings in South America, the North-West of the United States, and the Antilles. Edited by Rev. J. G. Wood. With 100 Illustrations. Crown 8vo. 6s.
People's Edition. With 100 Illustrations. Medium 4to. 6d.

WATSON.—A Record of Ellen Watson. Arranged and Edited by Anna Buckland. With Portrait. Crown 8vo. 6s.

WATSON (R. Spence).—A Visit to Wazan, the Sacred City of Morocco. 8vo. 10s. 6d.

WEBSTER (Augusta).—Daffodil and the Croäxaxicans. Crown 8vo. 6s.

WELBY-GREGORY (The Hon. Lady).— Links and Clues. 2nd Ed. Cr. 8vo. 6s.

WELCH (Wm.) and DUFFIELD (C. G.).— Latin Accidence and Exercises arranged for Beginners. 18mo. 1s. 6d.

WELLDON (Rev. J. E. C.).—The Spiritual Life, and other Sermons. Cr. 8vo. 6s.

WELLINGTON. By Geo. Hooper. With Portrait. Crown 8vo. 2s. 6d.

WESTBURY (Hugh).—Frederick Hazzleden. 3 vols. Crown 8vo. 31s. 6d.

WESTCOTT (Rev. Prof. B. F.)—A General Survey of the History of the Canon of the New Testament during the First Four Centuries. 6th Edition. Cr. 8vo. 10s. 6d.

—— Introduction to the Study of the Four Gospels. 7th Ed. Cr. 8vo. 10s. 6d.

—— The Gospel of the Resurrection. 6th Edition. Crown 8vo. 6s.

—— The Bible in the Church. 10th Edit. 18mo. 4s. 6d.

—— The Christian Life, Manifold and One. Crown 8vo. 2s. 6d.

—— On the Religious Office of the Universities. Sermons. Cr. 8vo. 4s. 6d.

—— The Revelation of the Risen Lord. 4th Edition. Crown 8vo. 6s.

—— The Historic Faith. 3rd Edition. Cr. 8vo. 6s.

—— The Epistles of St. John. The Greek Text, with Notes. 2nd Edition. 8vo. 12s. 6d.

—— The Revelation of the Father. Cr. 8vo. 6s.

—— Christus Consummator. 2nd Edition. Crown 8vo. 6s.

—— Some Thoughts from the Ordinal. Crown 8vo. 1s. 6d.

WESTCOTT (Rev. Prof.).—SOCIAL ASPECTS OF CHRISTIANITY. Crown 8vo. 6s.

—— GIFTS FOR MINISTRY. Addresses to Candidates for Ordination. Crown 8vo. 1s. 6d.

—— THE EPISTLE TO THE HEBREWS. The Greek Text, with Notes and Essays. 8vo. 14s.

—— THE VICTORY OF THE CROSS. Sermons preached during Holy Week, 1888, in Hereford Cathedral. Crown 8vo. 3s. 6d.

—— FROM STRENGTH TO STRENGTH. Three Sermons (In Memoriam J. B. D.) Cr. 8vo. 2s.

—— THOUGHTS ON REVELATION AND LIFE. Selections from the Writings of Canon WESTCOTT. Edited by Rev. S. PHILLIPS. Crown 8vo. 6s.

WESTCOTT (Rev. B. F.) and HORT (F. J. A.).—THE NEW TESTAMENT IN THE ORIGINAL GREEK. Revised Text. 2 vols. Crown 8vo. 10s. 6d. each.—Vol. I. Text.—Vol. II. The Introduction and Appendix.

—— THE NEW TESTAMENT IN THE ORIGINAL GREEK. An Edition for Schools. The Text revised by Professors WESTCOTT and HORT. 12mo, 4s. 6d.; 18mo, 5s. 6d.

WETHERELL (J.).—EXERCISES ON MORRIS' PRIMER OF ENGLISH GRAMMAR. 18mo. 1s.

WHEELER (J. Talboys).—A SHORT HISTORY OF INDIA. With Maps. Crown 8vo. 12s.

—— INDIA UNDER BRITISH RULE. 8vo. 12s. 6d.

—— COLLEGE HISTORY OF INDIA. Asiatic and European. Crown 8vo. 3s. 6d.

WHEN I WAS A LITTLE GIRL. By the Author of "St. Olave's." With Illustrations. Globe 8vo. 2s. 6d.

WHEN PAPA COMES HOME. By the Author of "When I was a Little Girl." With Illustrations. Globe 8vo. 4s. 6d.

WHEWELL.—DR. WILLIAM WHEWELL, late Master of Trinity College, Cambridge. An Account of his Writings, with Selections from his Literary and Scientific Correspondence. By I. TODHUNTER, M.A. 2 vols. 8vo. 25s.

WHITE (Gilbert).—NATURAL HISTORY AND ANTIQUITIES OF SELBORNE. Edited by FRANK BUCKLAND. With a Chapter on Antiquities by Lord SELBORNE. Cr. 8vo. 6s.

WHITE (John Williams).—A SERIES OF FIRST LESSONS IN GREEK. Adapted to Goodwin's Greek Grammar. Crown 8vo. 4s. 6d.

WHITE (Dr. W. Hale).—A TEXT-BOOK OF GENERAL THERAPEUTICS. Illustrated. Cr. 8vo. 8s. 6d.

WHITNEY (Prof. W. D.).—A COMPENDIOUS GERMAN GRAMMAR. Crown 8vo. 4s. 6d.

—— A GERMAN READER IN PROSE AND VERSE. With Notes and Vocabulary. Cr. 8vo. 5s.

—— A COMPENDIOUS GERMAN AND ENGLISH DICTIONARY. Crown 8vo. 7s. 6d.—German-English Part separately. 5s.

WHITTIER.—COMPLETE POETICAL WORKS OF JOHN GREENLEAF WHITTIER. With Portrait. 18mo. 4s. 6d.

WHITTIER.—THE COMPLETE WORKS OF JOHN GREENLEAF WHITTIER. 7 vols. Crown 8vo. 6s. each.—Vol. I. NARRATIVE AND LEGENDARY POEMS.—II. POEMS OF NATURE; POEMS SUBJECTIVE AND REMINISCENT; RELIGIOUS POEMS.—III. ANTI-SLAVERY POEMS; SONGS OF LABOUR AND REFORM.—IV. PERSONAL POEMS; OCCASIONAL POEMS; THE TENT ON THE BEACH; with the Poems of ELIZABETH H. WHITTIER, and an Appendix containing early and Uncollected Verses.—V. MARGARET SMITH'S JOURNAL; TALES AND SKETCHES. — VI. OLD PORTRAITS AND MODERN SKETCHES; PERSONAL SKETCHES AND TRIBUTES; HISTORICAL PAPERS.—VII. THE CONFLICT WITH SLAVERY, POLITICS AND REFORM: THE INNER LIFE, CRITICISM.

WICKHAM (Rev. E. C.)—WELLINGTON COLLEGE SERMONS. Crown 8vo. 6s.

WICKSTEED (Philip H.).—ALPHABET OF ECONOMIC SCIENCE.—I. ELEMENTS OF THE THEORY OF VALUE OR WORTH. Gl. 8vo. 2s. 6d.

WIEDERSHEIM—PARKER.—ELEMENTS OF THE COMPARATIVE ANATOMY OF VERTEBRATES. Adapted from the German of Prof. ROBERT WIEDERSHEIM, by Prof. W. NEWTON PARKER. Illustrated. Med. 8vo. 12s. 6d.

WILBRAHAM (Frances M.).—IN THE SERE AND YELLOW LEAF: THOUGHTS AND RECOLLECTIONS FOR OLD AND YOUNG. Globe 8vo. 3s. 6d.

WILKINS (Prof. A. S.).—THE LIGHT OF THE WORLD: AN ESSAY. 2nd Ed. Cr. 8vo. 3s. 6d.

—— ROMAN ANTIQUITIES. Illustr. 18mo. 1s.

—— ROMAN LITERATURE. 18mo. 1s.

WILKINSON (S.). — THE BRAIN OF AN ARMY. A Popular Account of the German General Staff. Crown 8vo. 2s. 6d.

WILLIAMS (Montagu).—LEAVES OF A LIFE. 2 vols. 8vo. 30s.

WILLIAMS (S. E.).—FORENSIC FACTS AND FALLACIES. Globe 8vo. 4s. 6d.

WILLOUGHBY (F.).—FAIRY GUARDIANS. Illustr. by TOWNLEY GREEN. Cr. 8vo. 5s.

WILLS (W. G.).—MELCHIOR: A POEM. Cr. 8vo. 9s.

WILSON (A. J.).—THE NATIONAL BUDGET; THE NATIONAL DEBT; RATES AND TAXES. Crown 8vo. 3s. 6d.

WILSON (Dr. George).—RELIGIO CHEMICI. Crown 8vo. 8s. 6d.

—— THE FIVE GATEWAYS OF KNOWLEDGE. 9th Edition. Extra fcp. 8vo. 2s. 6d.

WILSON.—MEMOIR OF PROF. GEORGE WILSON, M.D. By His Sister. With Portrait. 2nd Edition. Crown 8vo. 6s.

WILSON (Rev. Canon).—THE BIBLE STUDENT'S GUIDE. 2nd Edition. 4to. 25s.

WILSON (Sir Daniel, LL.D.).—PREHISTORIC ANNALS OF SCOTLAND. With Illustrations. 2 vols. Demy 8vo. 36s.

—— PREHISTORIC MAN: RESEARCHES INTO THE ORIGIN OF CIVILISATION IN THE OLD AND NEW WORLD. 3rd Edition. With Illustrations. 2 vols. Medium 8vo. 36s.

WILSON (Sir Daniel).—CHATTERTON: A BIOGRAPHICAL STUDY. Crown 8vo. 6s. 6d.

—— CALIBAN: A CRITIQUE ON SHAKESPEARE'S "TEMPEST" AND "A MIDSUMMER NIGHT'S DREAM." 8vo. 10s. 6d.

WILSON (Rev. J. M.).—SERMONS PREACHED IN CLIFTON COLLEGE CHAPEL, 1879—83. Crown 8vo. 6s.

—— ESSAYS AND ADDRESSES. Cr. 8vo. 4s. 6d.

—— SOME CONTRIBUTIONS TO THE RELIGIOUS THOUGHT OF OUR TIME. Crown 8vo. 6s.

—— ELEMENTARY GEOMETRY. Books I.—V. Containing the Subjects of Euclid's First Six Books, following the Syllabus of Geometry prepared by the Geometrical Association. Extra fcp. 8vo. 4s. 6d.

—— SOLID GEOMETRY AND CONIC SECTIONS. Extra fcp. 8vo. 3s. 6d.

WINKWORTH (Catherine). — CHRISTIAN SINGERS OF GERMANY. Crown 8vo. 4s. 6d.

WITHAM (Prof. J. M.).—STEAM ENGINE DESIGN. Illustrated. 8vo. 25s.

WOLSELEY (General Viscount).—THE SOLDIER'S POCKET-BOOK FOR FIELD SERVICE. 5th Edition. 16mo, roan. 5s.

—— FIELD POCKET-BOOK FOR THE AUXILIARY FORCES. 16mo. 1s. 6d.

WOLSTENHOLME (Joseph). — MATHEMATICAL PROBLEMS ON SUBJECTS INCLUDED IN THE FIRST AND SECOND DIVISION OF THE SCHEDULE OF SUBJECTS FOR THE CAMBRIDGE MATHEMATICAL TRIPOS EXAMINATION. 2nd Edition. 8vo. 18s.

—— EXAMPLES FOR PRACTICE IN THE USE OF SEVEN-FIGURE LOGARITHMS. 8vo. 5s.

WOOD (Andrew Goldie).—THE ISLES OF THE BLEST, AND OTHER POEMS. Globe 8vo. 5s.

WOOD (Rev. E. G.).—THE REGAL POWER OF THE CHURCH. 8vo. 4s. 6d.

WOODS (Miss M. A.).—A FIRST POETRY BOOK. Fcp. 8vo. 2s. 6d.

—— A SECOND POETRY BOOK. 2 Parts. Fcp. 8vo. 2s. 6d. each.

—— A THIRD POETRY BOOK. Fcp. 8vo. 4s. 6d.

WOOLNER (Thomas). — MY BEAUTIFUL LADY. 3rd Edition. Fcp. 8vo. 5s.

—— PYGMALION: A POEM. Cr. 8vo. 7s. 6d.

—— SILENUS: A POEM. Crown 8vo. 6s.

WOOLWICH MATHEMATICAL PAPERS. For Admission in the Royal Military Academy for the Years 1880—88. Edit. by E. J. BROOKSMITH, B.A. Cr. 8vo. 6s.

WORDS FROM THE POETS. With a Vignette and Frontispiece. 12th Ed. 18mo. 1s.

WORDSWORTH. By F. W. H. MYERS. Crown 8vo. 1s. 6d.; sewed, 1s.

—— SELECT POEMS. Edited by MATTHEW ARNOLD. 18mo. 4s. 6d.

Large Paper Edition. 8vo. 9s.

WORDSWORTH (William).—THE RECLUSE: A POEM. Fcp. 8vo. 2s. 6d.

—— THE COMPLETE POETICAL WORKS. Copyright Edition. With an Introduction by JOHN MORLEY, and Portrait. Cr. 8vo. 7s. 6d.

WORDSWORTHIANA: A SELECTION OF PAPERS READ TO THE WORDSWORTH SOCIETY. Ed. by W. KNIGHT. Cr. 8vo. 7s. 6d.

WORSHIP (THE) OF GOD, AND FELLOWSHIP AMONG MEN. By the late Prof. MAURICE and others. Fcp. 8vo. 3s. 6d.

WORTHEY (Mrs.).—THE NEW CONTINENT: A NOVEL. 2 vols. Globe 8vo. 12s.

WRIGHT (Rev. Arthur).—THE COMPOSITION OF THE FOUR GOSPELS. Crown 8vo. 5s.

WRIGHT (Miss Guthrie). — THE SCHOOL COOKERY-BOOK. 18mo. 1s.

WRIGHT (Rev. Josiah).—THE SEVEN KINGS OF ROME. Abridged from the First Book of Livy. 8th Edition. Fcp. 8vo. 3s. 6d.

—— FIRST LATIN STEPS. Crown 8vo. 3s.

—— ATTIC PRIMER. Crown 8vo. 2s. 6d.

—— A COMPLETE LATIN COURSE. Crown 8vo. 2s. 6d.

WRIGHT (Dr. Alder).—METALS AND THEIR CHIEF INDUSTRIAL APPLICATIONS. Extra fcp. 8vo. 3s. 6d.

WRIGHT (Lewis).—LIGHT. A Course of Experimental Optics, chiefly with the Lantern. With Illustrations and Coloured Plates. Crown 8vo. 7s. 6d.

WRIGHT (W. Aldis).—THE BIBLE WORD-BOOK. 2nd Edition. Crown 8vo. 7s. 6d.

WURTZ.—A HISTORY OF CHEMICAL THEORY. By AD. WURTZ. Translated by HENRY WATTS, F.R.S. Crown 8vo. 6s.

WYATT (Sir M. Digby).—FINE ARTS: A Sketch of its History, Theory, Practice, and Application to Industry. 8vo. 5s.

XENOPHON.—THE COMPLETE WORKS. Translated by H. G. DAKYNS, M.A. 4 vols. Crown 8vo.—Vol. I. "THE ANABASIS" AND BOOKS I. AND II. OF "THE HELLENICA." 10s. 6d.

—— ANABASIS. Book I. chaps. 1—8. For the Use of Beginners. Edited by E. A. WELLS, M.A. 18mo. 1s. 6d.

—— ANABASIS. Book I. With Notes and Vocabulary, by A. S. WALPOLE. 18mo. 1s. 6d.

—— ANABASIS. Book II. Edited by A. S. WALPOLE, M.A. 18mo. 1s. 6d.

—— ANABASIS. Books I.—IV. Edited, with Notes, by Professors W. W. GOODWIN and J. W. WHITE. Fcp. 8vo. 5s.

—— SELECTIONS FROM BOOK IV. OF THE ANABASIS. Edited by Rev. E. D. STONE, M.A. 18mo. 1s. 6d.

—— CYROPÆDIA. Books VII. and VIII. Edited by Prof. ALFRED GOODWIN, M.A. Fcp. 8vo. 5s.

—— HELLENICA. Books I. and II. Edited by H. HAILSTONE, M.A. With Map. Fcp. 8vo. 4s. 6d.

—— HIERO. Edited by Rev. H. A. HOLDEN, LL.D. Fcp. 8vo. 3s. 6d.

—— MEMORABILIA SOCRATIS. Edited by A. R. CLUER, B.A. Fcp. 8vo. 6s.

—— OECONOMICUS. Edited by Rev. H. A. HOLDEN, LL.D. Fcp. 8vo. 6s.

—— SELECTIONS FROM THE CYROPÆDIA. Edit. by Rev. A. H. COOKE. 18mo. 1s. 6d.

YONGE (Charlotte M.). — NOVELS AND TALES. Crown 8vo. 3s. 6d. each.

1. THE HEIR OF REDCLYFFE.
2. HEARTSEASE.
3. HOPES AND FEARS.
4. DYNEVOR TERRACE.
5. THE DAISY CHAIN.
6. THE TRIAL: MORE LINKS OF THE DAISY CHAIN.
7. PILLARS OF THE HOUSE. Vol. I.
8. PILLARS OF THE HOUSE. Vol. II.
9. THE YOUNG STEPMOTHER.
10. CLEVER WOMAN OF THE FAMILY.
11. THE THREE BRIDES.
12. MY YOUNG ALCIDES.
13. THE CAGED LION.
14. THE DOVE IN THE EAGLE'S NEST.
15. THE CHAPLET OF PEARLS.
16. LADY HESTER: AND THE DANVERS PAPERS.
17. MAGNUM BONUM.
18. LOVE AND LIFE.
19. UNKNOWN TO HISTORY.
20. STRAY PEARLS.
21. THE ARMOURER'S PRENTICES.
22. THE TWO SIDES OF THE SHIELD.
23. NUTTIE'S FATHER.
24. SCENES AND CHARACTERS.
25. CHANTRY HOUSE.
26. A MODERN TELEMACHUS.
27. BYE WORDS.
28. BEECHCROFT AT ROCKSTONE.

—— THE POPULATION OF AN OLD PEAR-TREE; OR, STORIES OF INSECT LIFE. From the French of E. VAN BRUYSSEL. Illustrated. Globe 8vo. 2s. 6d.

—— A REPUTED CHANGELING: OR, THREE SEVENTH YEARS TWO CENTURIES AGO. 2 vols. Crown 8vo. 12s.

—— THE PRINCE AND THE PAGE. Gl. 8vo. 4s. 6d.

—— A BOOK OF GOLDEN DEEDS. 18mo. 4s. 6d.
Cheap Edition. 18mo. 1s.
Globe Readings Edition. Globe 8vo. 2s.

—— P'S AND Q'S; OR, THE QUESTION OF PUTTING UPON. Illustrated. Gl. 8vo. 4s. 6d.

—— THE LANCES OF LYNWOOD. Illustrated. Globe 8vo. 2s. 6d.

—— LITTLE LUCY'S WONDERFUL GLOBE. Illustrated. Globe 8vo. 4s. 6d.

YONGE (Charlotte M.). — THE LITTLE DUKE. Illustrated. Globe 8vo. 2s. 6d.

—— A BOOK OF WORTHIES: GATHERED FROM THE OLD HISTORIES AND WRITTEN ANEW. 18mo. 4s. 6d.

—— CAMEOS FROM ENGLISH HISTORY. Extra fcp. 8vo. 5s. each.—Vol. I. FROM ROLLO TO EDWARD II.—Vol. II. THE WARS IN FRANCE.—Vol. III. THE WARS OF THE ROSES.—Vol. IV. REFORMATION TIMES.—Vol. V. ENGLAND AND SPAIN.— Vol. VI. FORTY YEARS OF STUART RULE (1603—1643).—Vol. VII. THE REBELLION AND RESTORATION (1642—78).

—— SCRIPTURE READINGS FOR SCHOOLS AND FAMILIES. Globe 8vo. 1s. 6d. each; also with Comments, 3s. 6d. each.—GENESIS TO DEUTERONOMY.—Second Series: JOSHUA TO SOLOMON.—Third Series: KINGS AND THE PROPHETS.—Fourth Series: THE GOSPEL TIMES.—Fifth Series: APOSTOLIC TIMES.

—— FRANCE. 18mo. 1s.

—— HISTORY OF FRANCE. Maps. 18mo. 3s. 6d.

—— THE LIFE OF JOHN COLERIDGE PATTESON. 2 vols. Crown 8vo. 12s.

—— THE PUPILS OF ST. JOHN. Illustrated. Crown 8vo. 6s.

—— PIONEERS AND FOUNDERS; OR, RECENT WORKERS IN THE MISSION FIELD. Crown 8vo. 6s.

—— THE STORY OF THE CHRISTIANS AND MOORS IN SPAIN. 18mo. 4s. 6d.

—— HISTORY OF CHRISTIAN NAMES. New Edition, revised. Crown 8vo. 7s. 6d.

—— THE HERB OF THE FIELD. A New Edition, revised. Crown 8vo. 5s.

—— THE VICTORIAN HALF-CENTURY. Crown 8vo. 1s. 6d.; sewed, 1s.

YOUNG (E. W.).—SIMPLE PRACTICAL METHODS OF CALCULATING STRAINS ON GIRDERS, ARCHES, AND TRUSSES. 8vo. 7s. 6d.

ZECHARIAH.—THE HEBREW STUDENT'S COMMENTARY ON ZECHARIAH HEBREW AND LXX. By W. H. LOWE, M.A. 8vo. 10s. 6d.

ZIEGLER.—A TEXT-BOOK OF PATHOLOGICAL ANATOMY AND PATHOGENESIS. By ERNST ZIEGLER. Translated and Edited for English Students by DONALD MACALISTER, M.A., M.D. With Illustrations. 8vo.—Part I. GENERAL PATHOLOGICAL ANATOMY. 2nd Edition. 12s. 6d.—Part II. SPECIAL PATHOLOGICAL ANATOMY. Sections I.—VIII. 2nd Edition. 12s. 6d. Sections IX.—XII. 8vo. 12s. 6d.